The American Literary Revolution
1783–1837

Documents in American Civilization Series

Documents in American Civilization Series

General Editors:
HENNIG COHEN AND JOHN WILLIAM WARD

Statement by the General Editors

The Anchor Series, "Documents in American Civilization," provides primary materials for the study of the history of the United States and for the understanding of
American culture. In the belief that neither history nor
culture can be properly studied without consideration of
a variety of sources, the editors have adopted the inter-
disciplinary approach in the selection of documents. In
our sense, a "document" is any idea, institution, or man-
made object that provides a clue to the way in which
subjective experience is organized at a specific moment
in time.

The purpose of the series is twofold: to show the per-
vasiveness of those themes which are central to particular
moments in history; and to underline the significance of
cultural documents in their total historical context—and
thus to illuminate problems or themes that characterize
American society.

HENNIG COHEN is Professor of English at the University
of Pennsylvania and editor of *American Quarterly*. He
is also editor of *Selected Poems of Herman Melville*
(Anchor Books, A375) and co-editor of *Folklore in
America*.

JOHN WILLIAM WARD is Professor of History and
American Studies at Amherst College. He is the author
of *Andrew Jackson: Symbol for an Age* and editor of *Society, Manners, and Politics in the United States* by
Michael Chevalier.

Robert E. Spiller was born in Philadelphia, Pennsylvania, on November 13, 1896 and received his A.B. and Ph.D. from the University of Pennsylvania where his father was Professor of Neurology and his uncle Professor of Philosophy. He also holds a Litt.D. from Thiel College and a Dr.phil.h.c. from the University of Kiel, Germany; and he is Honorary Fellow of the New York State Historical Association, Honorary Consultant in American Cultural History to the Library of Congress, and a Trustee of the American Scandinavian Foundation. He taught at Swarthmore College from 1921 to 1945, when he returned to the University of Pennsylvania where he is Felix E. Schelling Professor of English Literature and past Chairman of the American Civilization Department. He was an early Chairman of the American Literature Group of the Modern Language Association and was a First Vice-President of the Association; he was also a founder and past President of the American Studies Association and an editor of *American Literature* and of *American Quarterly*. He has taught American literature at various universities both here and abroad, including Duke, Michigan, Colorado, Harvard, Columbia, Oslo (Norway), and London (England). He is author of *The American in England during the First Half Century of Independence, Fenimore Cooper; Critic of His Times, The Cycle of American Literature*, and *The Third Dimension*, and an editor of *Literary History of the United States, The Roots of National Culture*, the writings of Cooper, Emerson, and Henry Adams, *Changing Patterns in American Civilization, American Perspectives, Social Control in a Free Society*, and *A Time of Harvest*; and he is associate editor of *Études Anglaises* and *Jahrbuch für Amerikastudien*.

The American Literary Revolution

1783–1837

Edited with a Preface and
Explanatory Notes by
Robert E. Spiller

Anchor Books
Doubleday & Company, Inc.
Garden City, New York
1967

The Anchor Books edition is the first publication
of *The American Literary Revolution, 1783–1837.*
A hardcover edition is available
from New York University Press.

Anchor Books edition: 1967

Library of Congress Catalog Card Number 67–12851

Preface

Prior to the American Revolution there was little thought given to the possibility that there might someday be an "American" literature as distinct from an "English" or "Western European" literary tradition. The colonies had become accustomed to thinking of themselves as but distant parts of the British Empire, and such literature as might come from them was almost exclusively written in the English language. It seemed obvious that American literary efforts were and would probably for some time continue to be somewhat inferior contributions to the substantial body of English literature.

To the literary historian, however, such a view ignores the immediate and relative aspects of human experience in favor of the hypothetical and absolute. To him, a work of literature must, to be worthy of the name, be the expression of the experience of somebody in a given place at a given time. The author must first comprehend his own life before he can, by some alchemy of the imagination, see above, behind, and beyond it and then relate his experience to the truths which men have sought in all times and all places. When a people are themselves emotionally and intellectually dependent, in whole or in part, on an alien cultural tradition, their literature will inevitably lack originality.

Such was the situation of the American colonies throughout the eighteenth century and even after political independence had been achieved. Because they were economically and intellectually more closely related to the mother country than to each other, their writings which attempted to deal with other than immediate and pressing issues were only sporadically American. A poem by Edward Taylor or an essay by Benjamin Franklin could be American and at the same time meet the criteria of the most exacting literary judgment, but there was no consistent body of literature in America until well into the nineteenth century because of the rawness and diversity of the American experience itself and the total lack of anything resembling a unified cultural tradition in the New World. Neither the conventions necessary to aesthetic expression nor the media of communication necessary to its growth had been developed.

With the successful outcome of the American Revolution and the existence of political independence as an actuality, it occurred quite logically to many Americans that the time had at last arrived when there could be a national literature and distinctively American forms and modes of the literary and other arts. No sooner said than done.

But there were disappointments and obstacles ahead.

It is the purpose of this volume to document from contemporary sources some of the ways in which the burst of revolutionary enthusiasm was carried over, in the years immediately following the peace of 1783, from the issue of political to that of literary independence and then to trace, by document rather than dictum, the course of its progress from that time until a genuinely American literature began to appear in the writings of Poe, Emerson, Thoreau, Hawthorne, and Melville. The earlier documents are chiefly prefaces to poems, plays, novels, or collections of essays which were conscious efforts to provide an American literature on immediate order, but as underlying issues became clearer and arguments became more deeply rooted in contemporary critical theory, the debate on the need for a national literature was taken up by the magazines in long reviews and articles and by the annual orations at Phi Beta Kappa and learned society meetings. Critical theory itself developed from the common sense philosophy which came to America chiefly in the writings of Lord Kames, through the more fluent rational-

ism of the Associationists of whom Archibald Alison had
a major influence, chiefly on the *North American* group,
and finally to the organicism of Coleridge which was felt
even before its full impact on Emerson and the Tran-
scendentalists.

Many of the documents in this volume are known at
least by title from discussions of literary nationalism
which are here listed in the bibliography. I reprinted a
few from original sources for the first time in 1933 in
The Roots of National Culture and others are even more
widely known, such as Bryant's essay on "American Poetry" and Emerson's on "The American Scholar." But
many of those which contribute most substantially to an
understanding of the temper and the issues of those times
are here first reproduced from their original pamphlet or
periodical appearances. Everyone knows Bryant's essay,
but few have consulted the atrocious poem by Solyman
Brown upon which it is based; Webster's views on an
American language will surprise no one, but they gain new
perspective when set in contrast to those of John Pickering. Emerson's Phi Beta Kappa oration gains new meaning
when set in the series which included those of William
Tudor, Edward Everett, and Francis Calley Gray. And
who knows much about the views of the other two Channings and their cousin R. H. Dana, Sr. on American literature? Or has read all of the masterfully comprehensive
review of American cultural achievement to that date by
Charles Jared Ingersoll, which inspired the best known
of the Channings to his now classic essay on "National
Literature"?

These are some of the incidental surprises which result
from a bringing of these documents together in one volume, but the principal surprise is that they tell a story
of their own. The generally accepted view that the expression of the need for a national literature in the years
following the Revolution gradually brought such a literature into being during the next half century still holds,
but the documents tell us that this was no steady and
consistent process. The chauvinistic closing years of the

eighteenth century were self-defeating and needed no
Fisher Ames or George Tucker to explain why, or Samuel
Miller's *Retrospect* to balance the ledger in the red. There
was too much in the American experience that was still
explosive and misunderstood for literature to find forms
and modes to give it expression. As the documents in
Part I of this collection reveal, the first decade of the
nineteenth century was a time of uncertainty about national existence itself.

The so-called War of 1812 may have been inconclusive
on the sea and in the world of politics, but in the development of a national cultural consciousness it was a
milestone. Before 1815, American authors were struggling
to constrict their violent experiences on a primitive continent into the literary forms and fashions of urban and
mercantile London; after 1815, they turned to the task
of trying to comprehend that experience in and for itself
and then to let it find its own forms of expression. The
problem of creating a national literature suddenly became
more vital, but it also became infinitely more complex.
American nationalism was reassured by mere survival in a
second war with Great Britain, but—even more important
—it found in the critical theory of the Scottish and British
rationalists, which was now available in the *Edinburgh*
(1802) and *Quarterly* (1809) *Reviews*, a working formula for the direct relating of new experience to its
literary expression. "When any object either of sublimity or beauty is presented to the mind, I believe every
man is conscious of a train of thought being immediately
awakened in his imagination analogous to the character
or expression of the original object," writes Archibald Alison (Document 29, p. 488), and he further relates
this basic tenet of Associationism with its nationalistic implications when he adds, "National associations have a
similar effect in increasing the emotions of sublimity and
beauty as they very obviously increase the number of images presented to the mind." (p. 494) The consequences
of this theory to the founding of the *North American
Review* in 1815, and therefore to the new literary nation-

alism, are documented in Part II of this collection, and the further unfolding of these ideas in Part III.

But to talk about literary nationalism and to do the actual work of providing a national literature were two very different tasks, and the new group of American writers were influenced in varying degrees by the development of an immediately useful literary theory. Part IV of this collection documents the actual attitudes toward their work of Irving, Cooper, Bryant, Longfellow, and others whose major writings began to appear in the 1820s and 1830s, and thus explains, at least in part, why the romantic movement finally found roots in America, as well as why its full flowering had to wait through years of trial and error until after 1835. The group of documents in Part V is more directly circumstantial: the first American copyright law, library lists of books ordered in England and later lists of books published in America, and finally excerpts (all too brief) from a few of the English literary theorists who were best known and therefore probably most influential in America.

I am indebted to the Rare Book Division of the Charles Patterson Van Pelt Library of the University of Pennsylvania, the Library Company of Philadelphia, the Free Library of Philadelphia, and the Library of the American Philosophical Society for helpful cooperation and for permission to Xerox rare volumes in their collections; but I am especially indebted to Neda M. Westlake and Edwin Wolf III for advice and assistance in locating and processing the selections finally included.

Texts are from the first or author-edited editions and are reproduced without substantive changes. The use of commas and a few other accidentals has been simplified, where it seemed desirable, for the modern reader.

R.E.S.

Wilmington, Vermont
July 1966

Contents

PART I

Aftermath of Independence
1783–1815

In the period between the Treaty of Paris (September 3, 1783), which determined the independence of the new nation, and the Treaty of Ghent (December 24, 1814), which seems to have confirmed independence as an accepted reality, Americans in general were intellectually and culturally on the defensive. The argument that political independence should bring with it autonomy of the mind and spirit, resulting in the rapid appearance of an indigenous culture, was enthusiastically seized upon, particularly by young intellectuals, but was immediately met by arguments that (1) a common language and a common cultural tradition made dependence on England for many years inevitable and even desirable, (2) the raw state of civilization in so unexplored and unexploited a land postponed indefinitely any hope for the amenities and cultivation of the Old World, and (3) the much-debated thesis, advanced by Buffon and early refuted by Jefferson, that the human race inevitably deteriorates in the Western Hemisphere. British and European travelers in the United States, eager to discourage emigration from their own countries and unhappy with the accommodations and habits of the Americans, as well as British critics of American writings in the revered London and Edinburgh reviews, did little to reassure American hopes and self-confidence.

Nevertheless, the Americans set to work to develop the instruments of literary culture (colleges, printing presses, book shops, reading rooms and literary societies, libraries, postal and other means of communication, protective copyright legislation, theatres, etc.) and to write, produce, and publish their own poems, plays, novels, and both familiar and formal essays on various aspects of American experience and American ideas. Some thought of "literature" merely as serious writing on any or all subjects of human concern (theology, law, medicine, morality, art, the physical and mechanical sciences, and *belles lettres* in the accepted eighteenth-century sense of the term); others limited their definition to the poetry, plays, novels, and lighter essays which were considered the evidences of a more cultivated and perhaps higher stage of civilization. But the majority of Americans during these years were fired with the desire for cultural accomplishment, aware of their handicaps and obstacles, and by 1800 pretty generally discouraged. The period of ten years or more just before the War of 1812 was psychologically a low point for American literary nationalism, a state of mind which the appearance of *The Columbiad* and *Salmagundi* did little to alleviate. American criticism, such as it was during these years, was pretty much dominated by the "common sense" philosophy of Lord Kames and Hugh Blair, with its emphasis on virtue, propriety, and universal standards of taste. The release into subjectivity came, within the Scottish school, with Archibald Alison's injection of the principles of Association psychology into aesthetic theory. But, although his *Essays* were published in 1790, they had little influence until they were belatedly reviewed by Francis Jeffrey in 1810. Basic statements, by themselves, of the views of Lord Kames, Archibald Alison, and Samuel Taylor Coleridge on the issue of Taste vs. Imagination are here offered as Document 29. The reader might wish to consult these now and then again later, after having considered the intervening documents.

DOCUMENT 1

Philip Freneau

It is fitting that this collection of opinions about the
prospects for an American literature should open with
the remark, "There are few writers of books in this new
world, and amongst these very few that deal in works
of imagination." The supposed writer of this essay is one
Mr. Robert Slender, who, in the eighteenth-century
fashion, was a recently expired and lamented *alter ego*
of the poet and political satirist, Philip Freneau (1752–
1832). As the facts about Mr. Slender are given in a
footnote of Freneau's fabrication, it will be unnecessary
here to provide them, but he speaks not only for his
contemporaries but unfortunately for the American imaginative writer of far too many years into the future.
The essay will be found in *The Miscellaneous Works of
Mr. Philip Freneau, containing his Essays and Additional Poems,* 1788. By this time, Freneau's reputation
as "the Poet of the Revolution" was firmly established,
but his acceptance by Jefferson as the fiery and partisan
editor of the *National Gazette,* and his recognition as the
pioneer poet of the American romantic movement were
still in the future. Mr. Slender's emphasis upon practi-
cality as a basic trait of the American character here
seems a mere humorous observation, but its serious import will become more apparent in the oration by
Charles J. Ingersoll (Document 15).

TEXT: from the first edition, Philadelphia, 1788.

Advice to Authors

BY THE LATE MR. ROBERT SLENDER.[1]

There are few writers of books in this new world, and amongst these very few that deal in works of imagination, and, I am sorry to say, fewer still that have any success attending their lucubrations. Perhaps, however, the world thinks justly on this subject. The productions of the most brilliant imagination are at best but mere beautiful flowers that may amuse us in a walk through a garden in a fine afternoon, but can by no means be expected to engage much of that time which God and nature designed to be spent in very different employments. In a country which two hundred years ago was peopled only by savages and where the government has ever, in effect, since the first establishment of the white men in these parts, been

[1] Many people, no doubt, will be anxious to know something of the history and character of the above named *Robert Slender*; and the Editor is really sorry it is not in his power to afford them the most ample information. Of two things, however, the reader may be assured, that he was a Pennsylvanian by birth, and a stocking and tape weaver by trade, and has now been dead something more than a year and an half; having been buried with very little ceremony by a few of his most intimate friends and neighbours.—Notwithstanding he was an author as well as a weaver of stockings and tape (both of which articles he manufactured on a curious loom of his own invention) we cannot say he ever possessed the least faculty or turn of mind for amassing the treasures of this world; so that when his executors came to examine his strong-box, little or nothing was discovered therein more than a bundle of manuscripts, penned in a very antiquated, obscure and perplexing hand; from which, however, we shall now and then present such extracts to the public in the course of this work, as shall appear to be best deserving of their notice. Indeed, had our old friend stuck closer to his loom for any length of time than he was wont to do, it is highly probable his box would have been stored with riches of a very different nature; but such as they are, gentle reader, they are wholly and sincerely at thy service.—Robert Slender was, in his person, a tall spare man with a meagre aspect, of a sociable disposition, fond of travelling from place to place, and was known to have made frequent visits to

no other than republican, it is really wonderful there should be any polite original authors at all in any line, especially when it is considered, that according to the common course of things, any particular nation or people must have arrived to, or rather passed, their meridian of opulence and refinement before they consider the professors of the fine arts in any other light than a nuisance to the community. This is evidently the case at present in our age and country; all you have to do then, my good friends, is to graft your authorship upon some other calling, or support drooping genius by the assistance of some mechanical employment, in the same manner as the helpless ivy takes hold of the vigorous oak and cleaves to it for support—I mean to say, in plain language, that you may make something by weaving garters, or mending old sails, when an Epic poem would be your utter destruction.

---

the several capitals of the American continent and islands while his brother weavers were more profitably employed at home at their looms. Writing and weaving seem to have been rather his amusements than his serious occupations; and one proof of his having been a man of sense is his not having depended upon authorship alone for a subsistence. In his temper he was extremely irascible; but I have often remarked that when he saw his writings treated with malevolence, contempt or neglect, he never became angry or outrageous; whereas, when his stockings or tape were calumniated, he was instantly changed into a monster of passion and revenge, breathing out nothing but menaces and curses against the enemies of his loom.

He was extremely fond of sunning himself in clear winter mornings, and has been known to sit three hours together on the south side of a hill in December or January, enjoying the salutary beams of the great and splendid luminary.—Reader, if these few particulars will at all gratify thee, our purpose is answered. In this miscellaneous collection of original papers we shall now and then present thee with an essay, a paragraph, a sentiment, or a poem of the late facetious *Robert Slender*; all of which, it is hoped, will be treated by the critics with more indulgence than the rest, since these effusions are to be considered as the works of a deceased author, who, it does not appear, ever intended his lucubrations, at least the greater part of them, for the eye of the public. The first piece of his with which we shall present thee is the above, containing his *Advice to Authors*, which, from several circumstances, we conclude was written in the latter part of his life.

But I see no reason that, because we are all striving to live by the same idle trade, we should suffer ourselves to be imbittered against each other, like a fraternity of rival mechanics in the same street. Authors (such I mean as are not possessed of fortunes) are at present considered as the dregs of the community: their situation and prospects are truly humiliating, and any other sett of men in a similar state of calamitous adversity would unite together for their mutual defence instead of worrying and lampooning each other for the amusement of the illiberal vulgar.—And I cannot do otherwise than freely declare that where the whole profits of a company amount to little or nothing at all, there ought not, in the nature of things, to be any quarrelling about shares and dividends.

As to those authors who have lately exported themselves from Britain and Ireland and boast that they have introduced the Muses among us since the conclusion of the late war, I really believe them to be a very good natured sett of gentlemen, nowithstanding they, in the course of the last winter, called me *poetaster* and *scribbler*, and some other names still more unsavoury. They are, however, excuseable in treating the American authors as inferiors; a political and a literary independence of their nation being two very different things—the first was accomplished in about seven years, the latter will not be completely effected, perhaps, in as many centuries. It is my opinion, nevertheless, that a duty ought to be laid upon all imported authors, the net proceeds of which should be appropriated to the benefit of real American writers, when become old and helpless and no longer able to wield the pen to advantage.

If a coach or a chariot constructed in Britain pays an impost of twenty pounds at the custom-house, why should not at least twice that sum be laid upon all imported authors who are able to do twice as much mischief with their rumbling pindaric odes and gorgeous apparatus of strophes, antistrophes and recitativos?—I, for my own part, am clearly of opinion that these gentlemen should be taxed; not that I would wish to nip their buds of beauty with the untimely frost of excise, but merely to teach them that our own natural manufactures ought to be primarily attended to and encouraged.

I will now, gentlemen, with your leave, lay down a few simple rules to which, in my opinion, every genuine author will make no difficulty to conform.

1. When you write a book for the public, have nothing to do with *Epistles dedicatory*. They were first invented by slaves, and have been continued by fools and sycophants. I would not give a farthing more for a book on account of its being patronized by all the noblemen or crowned heads in Christendom. If it does not possess intrinsic merit enough to protect itself and force its way through the world, their supposed protection will be of no avail: besides, by this ridiculous practice you degrade the *dignity authorial*, the honour of authorship, which ought evermore to be uppermost in your thoughts. The silly unthinking author addresses a great man in the stile of a servile dependent, whereas a real author, and a man of true genius, has upon all occasions a bold, disinterested and daring confidence in himself, and considers the common cant of adulation to the sons of fortune as the basest and most abominable of all prostitution.

2. Be particularly careful to avoid all connexion with doctors of law and divinity, masters of arts, professors of colleges, and in general all those that wear square black caps. A mere scholar and an original author are two animals as different from each other as a fresh and salt water sailor. There has been an old rooted enmity between them from the earliest ages, and which it is likely will forever continue. The scholar is not unlike that piddling orator, who, cold and inanimate, not roused into action by the impelling flame of inspiration, can only pronounce the oration he has learned by rote; the real author, on the contrary, is the nervous Demosthenes who, stored with an immensity of ideas awakened within him he knows not how, has them at command upon every occasion; and must therefore be disregarded as a madman or an enthusiast by the narrow and limited capacity as well as the natural self-sufficiency of the other.

3. It is risking a great deal to propose a subscription

for an original work. The world will be ready enough to anticipate your best endeavours; and that which has been long and anxiously expected, rarely or never comes up to their expectations at last.

4. If you are so poor that you are compelled to live in some miserable garret or cottage, do not repine, but give thanks to heaven that you are not forced to pass your life in a tub, as was the fate of Diogenes of old. Few authors in any country are rich, because a man must first be reduced to a state of penury before he will commence author. Being poor therefore in externals, take care, gentlemen, that you say or do nothing that may argue a poverty of spirit. Riches, we have often heard, are by no means the standard of the value of a man. This maxim the world allows to be true, and yet contradicts it every hour and minute in the year. Fortune most commonly bestows wealth and abundance upon fools and idiots; and men of the dullest natural parts are, notwithstanding, generally best calculated to acquire large estates and hoard up immense sums from small beginnings.

5. Never borrow money of any man, for if you should once be mean enough to fall into such a habit you will find yourselves unwelcome guests every where. If upon actual trial you are at length convinced you possess no abilities that will command the esteem, veneration or gratitude of mankind, apply yourselves without loss of time to some of the lower arts, since it is far more honourable to be a good bricklayer or a skilful weaver than an indifferent poet.—If you cannot at all exist without now and then gratifying your itch for scribbling, follow my example who can both weave stockings and write poems.— But, if you really possess that sprightliness of fancy and elevation of soul which alone constitute an author, do not on that account be troublesome to your friends. A little reflection will point out other means to extract money from the hands and pockets of your fellow citizens than by poorly borrowing what, perhaps, you will never be able to repay.

6. Never engage in any business as an inferior or un-

derstrapper. I cannot endure to see an author debase his profession so far as to submit to be second or third in any office or employment whatever. If fortune or the ill taste of the public compels you even to turn shallopman on the Delaware, let it be your first care to have the command of the boat. Beggary itself, with all its hideous apparatus of rags and misery, becomes at once respectable whenever it exhibits the least token of independence of spirit and a single spark of laudable ambition.

7. If you are in low circumstances, do not forget that there is such a thing in the world as a decent pride. They are only cowards and miscreants that poverty can render servile in their behaviour. Your haughtiness should always rise in proportion to the wretchedness and desperation of your circumstances. If you have only a single guinea in the world be complaisant and obliging to every one: if you are absolutely destitute of a shilling, immediately assume the air of a despot, pull off your hat to no one, let your discourse, in every company, turn upon the vanity of riches, the insignificancy of the great men of the earth, the revolution of empires, and the final consummation of all things.—By such means you will at least conceal a secret of some importance to yourself—that you have not a shilling in the world to pay for your last night's lodging.

8. Should you ever be prevailed upon to dedicate your book to any great man or woman, consider first whether the tenor and subject of it be such as may in some measure coincide with the age, temper, education, business and general conversation of the person whose patronage is requested. A friend of mine once committed a great error on this score. He wrote a bawdy poem, and dedicated it to the principal in the department of finance.

9. Never make a present of your works to great men. If they do not think them worth purchasing, trust me, they will never think them worth reading.

10. If fortune seems absolutely determined to starve you and you can by no means whatever make your works sell; to keep up as much as in you lies, the expiring dignity of authorship, do not take to drinking, gambling or bridge-

building* as some have done, thereby bringing the trade of authorship into disrepute; but retire to some uninhabited island or desert, and there, at your leisure, end your life with decency.

The above is all that has yet been found written by Robert Slender relative to authors and authorship—and further the copyist at this time sayeth not.

* [Tom Paine was a designer of bridges.]

DOCUMENT 2

Prefaces and Prologues

Perhaps the most obvious way for the new nation to acquire a national literature was for its authors to take Freneau's advice to spend only their spare time writing poems, plays, novels, and essays and to write about *American* experience. This was difficult because both writer and reader were familiar only with British models (or occasionally European), and the rigid literary conventions of the time made the adaptation of the new content to the old forms and traditions difficult to the point of impossibility. Nevertheless, groups of young men in the seacoast towns set about the task with enthusiasm, and the first quarter century of independence produced at least a sprinkling of poems and essays descriptive of American scenery, plays and novels about American history, society, and character, and familiar as well as formal essays on American problems and practices. As the book-lists in Part V show, the total of such experiments was slight in proportion to the great numbers of religious, political, and practical works which began to come from the American presses and to the competition of imported *belles lettres,* and most of these young men had lost courage and given up the battle by 1800; but the few Prefaces and Prologues which follow at least set the terms of the problem of literary nationalism if not its solution.

(a) *Joel Barlow*

Joel Barlow (1754–1812) was one of the "Connecti-cut Wits," a graduate of Yale, and a political sympa-thizer and friend of Tom Paine. Of American authors of the day, with the possible exceptions of Philip Fre-neau and Charles Brockden Brown, he was perhaps the most persistent in his determination to help create an *American* literature. A national literature, he argued, should have an epic celebrating its history and its he-roes, and the obvious place to begin was at the beginning with Columbus. But Columbus was a Genoese sailor in the employ of Spain and could not therefore symbolize a glorious American past. Barlow's solution was like those of Virgil and Milton before him, to substitute a dream of future glories for a history of past achieve-ments. This rejection of the past was to become a domi-nant theme in the national character, reflected with more philosophical depth in Emerson (Document 25) and persistent even today. *The Vision of Columbus*, 1787, was the first version of the epic which was later revised as *The Columbiad*, 1807. The portion of the "Introduction" here omitted is a brief and factual sum-mary of the biography of Columbus.

TEXT: from the Hartford printing of 1788.

The Vision of Columbus

INTRODUCTION

Every circumstance relating to the discovery and settle-ment of America is an interesting object of enquiry. Yet it is presumed, from the present state of literature in this country, that many persons who might be entertained with an American production of this kind are but slightly acquainted with the life and character of that great man whose extraordinary genius led him to the discovery of the continent, and whose singular sufferings ought to excite the indignation of the World.

The Spanish historians who treat of the discovery and settlement of South-America are very little known in the United States; and Doctor Robertson's history of that country* which, as is usual in the works of that judicious writer, contains all that is valuable on the subject is not yet reprinted in America and therefore cannot be supposed to be in the hands of American readers in general: and perhaps no other writer in the English language has given a sufficient account of the life of Columbus to enable them to understand many of the necessary allusions in the following Poem. . . .

The Author, at first, formed an idea of attempting a regular Epic Poem, on the discovery of America. But on examining the nature of that event, he found that the most brilliant subjects incident to such a plan would arise from the consequences of the discovery and must be represented in vision. Indeed, to have made it a patriotic Poem by extending the subject to the settlement and revolutions of North America and their probable effect upon the future progress of society at large would have protracted the vision to such a degree as to render it disproportionate to the rest of the work. To avoid an absurdity of this kind, which he supposed the critics would not pardon, he rejected the idea of a regular Epic form, and has confined his plan to the train of events which might be represented to the hero in vision. This form he considers as the best that the nature of the subject would admit, and the regularity of the parts will appear by observing that there is a single poetical design constantly kept in view, which is to gratify and sooth the desponding mind of the hero: It being the greatest pos-

* [History of America, by William Robertson (1721–93) 2 vols., 1777.]

sible reward of his services, and the only one that his situation would permit him to enjoy, to convince him that his labours had not been bestowed in vain, and that he was the author of such extensive happiness to the human race.

(b) *Timothy Dwight*

Although Timothy Dwight (1752–1817) echoes Barlow's promises of the future glories of America in the seventh and last section of his poem, *Greenfield Hill*, 1794, most of the poem is concerned with the domestic and pastoral virtues of Greenfield parish in Connecticut, where he was pastor of the Congregational Church for twelve years (1783–95). Dwight was also one of the Connecticut Wits, a student, tutor, and later President of Yale, and the writer of many weighty theological and patriotic poems, sermons, and tracts, as well as some lighter travel accounts and essays in the Addisonian vein. As he explains in his Introduction, he had thought of treating the American countryside and village life in a series of poems modeled on specific English counterparts by such poets as Goldsmith, Gray, and others, but the effort was too much and he relaxed into a less formal vein.

TEXT: from the first edition, New York, 1794.

Greenfield Hill

INTRODUCTION

In the Parish of Greenfield, in the Town of Fairfield in Connecticut, there is a pleasant and beautiful eminence called Greenfield Hill at the distance of three miles from Long-Island Sound. On this eminence there is a small but handsome Village, a Church, Academy, &c. all of them alluded to in the following Poem. From the highest part of the eminence the eye is presented with an extensive and delightful prospect of the surrounding Country and of the Sound. On this height the Writer is supposed to stand. The First object there offering itself to his view is the Landscape, which is accordingly made the governing subject of the First Part of the Poem. The flourishing and happy condition of the Inhabitants very naturally suggested itself next; and became of course the subject of the Second Part. The Town of Fairfield, lying in full view and, not long before the Poem was begun and in a great measure written out, burnt by a party of British Troops under the command of Governor Tryon, furnished the theme of the Third Part. A Field called the Pequod Swamp, in which most of the warriors of that nation who survived the invasion of their country by Capt. Mason were destroyed, lying about three miles from the eminence abovementioned and on the margin of the Sound, suggested not unnaturally the subject of the Fourth Part.

As the writer is the Minister of Greenfield, he cannot be supposed to be uninterested in the welfare of his Parishioners. To excite their attention to the truths and duties of Religion (an object in such a situation instinctively rising to his view,) is the design of the Fifth Part; and to promote in them just sentiments and useful conduct, for the present life, (an object closely connected with the preceding one) of the Sixth.

Many of the subjects mentioned in the Poem and suggested by the general state of this Country easily led a contemplative mind to look forward, and call up to view its probable situation at a distant approaching period. The solid foundations, which appear to be laid for the future greatness and prosperity of the American Republic, offered very pleasing views of this subject to a Poet; and of these the writer has, in the Seventh Part of the Work, endeavoured to avail himself.

To contribute to the innocent amusement of his countrymen and to their improvement in manners and in œconomical, political, and moral sentiments is the object which the writer wishes to accomplish. As he is firmly persuaded that his countrymen are furnished by Providence with as extensive and advantageous means of prosperity as the world has hitherto seen, so he thinks it the duty and the interest of every citizen to promote it by all the means in his power. Poetry appears to him to be one among the probable means of advancing this purpose. "Allow me to make the Songs of a nation," said a wise man, "and who will may make their Laws." Poetry may not, perhaps, produce greater effects in promoting the prosperity of mankind than philosophy;[1] but the effects which it produces are far from being small. Where truth requires little illustration and only needs to be set in a strong and affecting light, Poetry appears to be as advantageous an instrument of making useful impressions as can be easily conceived. It will be read by many persons who would scarcely look at a logical discussion; by most readers it will be more deeply felt and more lastingly remembered; and, to say the least, it will, in the present case, be an unusual and for that reason may be a forcible method of treating several subjects handled in this Poem.

When the writer began the work, he had no design of publishing it, aiming merely to amuse his own mind, and to gain a temporary relief from the pressure of melancholy. Hence it was dropped at an early period when other avocations or amusements presented themselves. The greater part of it was written seven years ago. Additions have been made to it at different periods from that time to the present—This will account for the dates of several things mentioned in it which would otherwise seem to be improperly connected.

Originally the writer designed to imitate, in the several parts, the manner of as many British Poets; but finding himself too much occupied, when he projected the publication, to pursue that design, he relinquished it. The little appearance of such a design still remaining was the result of distant and general recollection. Much of that nature he has rejected, and all he would have rejected, had not even that rejection demanded more time than he could

[1] See Lowth's Lectures on Heb. Po. [Lowth, Robert: *Lectures on the Sacred Poetry of the Hebrews*, delivered in 1741 and published in Latin in 1753.]

afford for such a purpose. These facts will, he hopes, apologize to the reader for the mixed manner which he may, at times, observe in the performance.

Greenfield, June 13th, 1794.

(c) *Royall Tyler*

The concern of Royall Tyler (1757–1826) with the corrupting influence of foreign manners on the simple and honest American character is even better treated in his comedy *The Contrast* (Document 2c), than in his novel, *The Algerine Captive,* 1797, where he attempts to explore the possibilities of American involvement with the Barbary Pirates of North Africa, a running adventure for many years of American privateersmen of the infant American Navy. Tyler's picaresque hero of seven years' captivity in Algiers bears little resemblance to the Vermont lawyer-author who joined with Joseph Dennie in the writing of light verse and prose under the pseudonym of the firm of Colon and Spondee, or who later dashed off an American comedy after a visit to New York during which he saw Sheridan's *School for Scandal,* and who generally followed Freneau's advice of letting his literary gifts, which were lively and productive, cling like a vine to the vigorous oak of his military and legal careers. The Preface to his novel is one of the earliest attacks on the importation of British *belles lettres* as a deterrent to native originality as well as an early attempt to use the recent American past as a source for a romance of adventure.

TEXT: from the first edition, Walpole, New Hampshire, 1797.

The Algerine Captive

PREFACE

One of the first observations the author of the following sheets made, upon his return to his native country after an absence of seven years, was the extreme avidity with which books of mere amusement were purchased and perused by all ranks of his countrymen. When he left New England, books of Biography, Travels, Novels, and modern Romances were confined to our sea ports; or, if known in the country, were read only in the families of Clergymen, Physicians, and Lawyers; while certain funeral discourses, the last words and dying speeches of Bryan Shaheen, and Levi Ames, and some dreary somebody's Day of Doom, formed the most diverting part of the farmer's library. On his return from captivity, he found a surprising alteration in the public taste. In our inland towns of consequence, social libraries had been instituted, composed of books designed to amuse rather than to instruct, and country booksellers, fostering the new born taste of the people, had filled the whole land with modern Travels and Novels almost as incredible. The diffusion of a taste for any species of writing through all ranks, in so short a time, would appear impracticable to a European. The peasant of Europe must first be taught to read before he can acquire a taste in letters. In New England, the work is half completed. In no other country are there so many people, in proportion to its numbers, who can read and write; and therefore, no sooner was a taste for amusing literature diffused than all orders of country life with one accord forsook the sober sermons and Practical Pieties of their fathers for the gay stories and splendid impieties of the Traveller and the Novelist. The worthy farmer no longer fatigued himself with Bunyan's Pilgrim up the "hill of difficulty" or through the "slough of despond," but quaffed wine with Brydone in the hermitage of Vesuvius or sported with Bruce on the fairy land of Abysinia*; while Dolly, the dairy maid, and Jonathan, the hired man, threw aside the ballad of the cruel stepmother, over which they had so often wept in concert, and now amused themselves into so agreeable a terrour with the haunted houses and

* [James Bruce (1730–94), Scottish traveler who visited Goudar, the capital of Abyssinia, in 1770; and probably Corneille le Bryn (1652–?), Dutch painter and traveler who visited Naples in 1677.]

hobgobblins of Mrs. Ratcliffe that they were both afraid to sleep alone.

While this love of literature, however frivolous, is pleasing to the man of letters, there are two things to be deplored. The first is that, while so many books are vended, they are not of our own manufacture. If our wives and daughters will wear gauze and ribbands, it is a pity they are not wrought in our own looms. The second misfortune is that Novels being the picture of the times, the New England reader is insensibly taught to admire the levity and often the vices of the parent country. While the fancy is enchanted, the heart is corrupted. The farmer's daughter, while she pities the misfortune of some modern heroine, is exposed to the attacks of vice from which her ignorance would have formed her surest shield. If the English Novel does not inculcate vice, it at least impresses on the young mind an erroneous idea of the world in which she is to live. It paints the manners, customs, and habits of a strange country; excites a fondness for false splendour; and renders the homespun habits of her own country disgusting.

There are two things wanted, said a friend to the author: that we write our own books of amusement, and that they exhibit our own manners. Why then do you not write the history of your own life? The first part of it, if not highly interesting, would at least display a portrait of New England manners, hitherto unattempted. Your captivity among the Algerines, with some notices of the manners of that ferocious race, so dreaded by commercial powers and so little known in our country, would be interesting; and I see no advantage the Novel writer can have over you unless your readers should be of the sentiment of the young lady mentioned by Addison in his Spectator, who, he informs us, borrowed Plutarch's lives, and, after reading the first volume with infinite delight supposing it to be a Novel, threw aside the others with disgust because a man of letters had inadvertently told her the work was founded on FACT.

(d) *Charles Brockden Brown*

Charles Brockden Brown (1771–1810) by his burst of creative energy in the two years 1798–1800 came near to establishing himself as the first professional American novelist, but he then became discouraged and turned to magazine editing for livelihood. As he correctly points out, however, in his Preface to *Edgar Huntly*, 1799, he not only substitutes for the usual "puerile superstition" and "Gothic Castles" of the English Gothic novel the incidents and perils of the western wilderness, but he recognizes that "new springs of action" and other daily American experiences must be essentially different from those of Europe and "peculiar to ourselves." Even though he makes very little of the issue of nationalism as such and explores rather the subjective regions of morbid psychology and pseudo-science, he implicitly draws the distinction which Poe later developed between superficial nationalism and genuine originality (Document 24) and thus helped to prepare the way for the "black" romance which has only recently become recognized as a characteristic American literary genre.

TEXT: from the first edition, Philadelphia, 1799.

Edgar Huntly, or, Memoirs of a Sleep-walker

TO THE PUBLIC

The flattering reception that has been given by the public to Arthur Mervyn has prompted the writer to solicit a continuance of the same favour, and to offer to the world a new performance.

America has opened new views to the naturalist and politician, but has seldome furnished themes to the moral painter. That new springs of action and new motives to curiosity should operate; that the field of investigation opened to us by our own country should differ essentially from those which exist in Europe, may be readily conceived. The sources of amusement to the fancy and instruction to the heart that are peculiar to ourselves are equally numerous and inexhaustible. It is the purpose of this work to profit by some of these sources; to exhibit a series of adventures growing out of the condition of our country, and connected with one of the most common and most wonderful diseases or affections of the human frame.

One merit the writer may at least claim; that of calling forth the passions and engaging the sympathy of the reader by means hitherto unemployed by preceding authors. Puerile superstition and exploded manners, Gothic castles and chimeras, are the materials usually employed for this end. The incidents of Indian hostility, and the perils of the western wilderness, are far more suitable; and for a native of America to overlook these would admit of no apology. These, therefore, are in part the ingredients of this tale, and these he has been ambitious of depicting in vivid and faithful colours. The success of his efforts must be estimated by the liberal and candid reader.

C. B. B.

(e) *Royall Tyler*

When *The Contrast* by Royall Tyler was produced by Thomas Wignell, the English actor, at the John Street Theatre in New York City on April 16, 1787, it made dramatic and literary history as well as the reputation of its author because it was the first American play on an American theme to be professionally produced in the United States. In the Advertisement to the Philadelphia edition, dated January 1, 1790 (here quoted in full), its relationship to literary nationalism is clearly recognized and unequivocally stated, for Tyler had accurately copied the spirit and style of the English comedies of Sheridan and Goldsmith, then so popular on both British and American stage, and created the stage Yankee by adding to them the theme of the simple honesty of the democratic native American, a theme which echoes Jefferson's *Notes on The State of Virginia* (1784). This is the most successful attempt up to this time to use a popular British literary form almost without change to give expression to a distinctively American patriotic idea.

TEXT: from the first edition, Philadelphia, 1790.

The Contrast

ADVERTISEMENT

The Subscribers (to whom the Editor thankfully professes his obligations) may reasonably expect an apology for the delay which has attended the appearance of THE CONTRAST; but, as the true cause cannot be declared without leading to a discussion which the Editor wishes to avoid, he hopes that the care and expence which have been bestowed upon this work will be accepted, without further scrutiny, as an atonement for his seeming negligence.

In justice to the Author, however, it may be proper to observe that this Comedy has many claims to the public indulgence independent of its intrinsic merits: It is the first essay of American genius in a difficult species of composition; it was written by one who never critically studied the rules of the drama and, indeed, had seen but few of the exhibitions of the stage; it was undertaken and finished in the course of three weeks; and the profits of one night's performance were appropriated to the benefit of the sufferers by the fire at *Boston*.

These considerations will therefore it is hoped supply in the closet the advantages that are derived from representation, and dispose the reader to join in the applause which has been bestowed on this Comedy by numerous and judicious audiences in the Theatres of *Philadelphia*, *New-York*, and *Maryland*.

PROLOGUE

Written by a YOUNG GENTLEMAN *of New-York, and Spoken by* MR. WIGNELL

Exult each patriot heart!—this night is shewn
A piece, which we may fairly call our own;
Where the proud titles of "My Lord! Your Grace!"
To humble Mr and plain Sir give place.
Our Author pictures not from foreign climes
The fashions, or the follies of the times;
But has confin'd the subject of his work
To the gay scenes—the circles of New-York.
On native themes his Muse displays her pow'rs;
If ours the faults, the virtues too are ours.
Why should our thoughts to distant countries roam,
When each refinement may be found at home?
Who travels now to ape the rich or great,
To deck an equipage and roll in state;
To court the graces, or to dance with ease,
Or by hypocrisy to strive to please?

Our free-born ancestors such arts despis'd;
Genuine sincerity alone they priz'd;
Their minds, with honest emulation fir'd,
To solid good—not ornament—aspir'd;
Or, if ambition rous'd a bolder flame,
Stern virtue throve, where indolence was shame.

But modern youths, with imitative sense,
Deem taste in dress the proof of excellence;
And spurn the meanness of your homespun arts,
Since homespun habits would obscure their parts;
Whilst all, which aims at splendour and parade,
Must come from Europe, and be ready made.
Strange! we should thus our native worth disclaim,
And check the progress of our rising fame.
Yet one, whilst imitation bears the sway,
Aspires to nobler heights, and points the way,
Be rous'd, my friends! his bold example view;
Let your own Bards be proud to copy you!
Should rigid critics reprobate our play,
At least the patriotic heart will say,
"Glorious our fall, since in a noble cause.
"The bold attempt alone demands applause."
Still may the wisdom of the Comic Muse
Exalt your merits, or your faults accuse.
But think not, 'tis her aim to be severe;—
We all are mortals, and as mortals err.
If candour pleases, we are truly blest;
Vice trembles, when compell'd to stand confess'd.
Let not light Censure on your faults, offend.
Which aims not to expose them, but amend.
Thus does our Author to your candour trust;
Conscious, the free are generous, as just.

(f) William Dunlap

After the success of *The Contrast* other American dramatists were encouraged to experiment with American themes, not only in social comedy but in historical tragedy as well. James Nelson Barker (1784–1858) experimented with themes of domestic comedy, the Indians, and New England history, while William Dunlap (1766–1839), painter, playwright, producer, and translator, ventured a tragedy based on a recent historical event fraught with political implications, the story of Major André. That he realized the difficulties and the significance of his experiment is revealed in his Preface and Prologue to the play.

TEXT: from the first edition, New York, 1798.

André

PREFACE

More than nine years ago the Author made choice of the death of Major André as the subject of a Tragedy, and part of what is now offered to the public was written at that time. Many circumstances discouraged him from finishing his Play, and among them must be reckoned a prevailing opinion that recent events are unfit subjects for tragedy. These discouragements have at length all given way to his desire of bringing a story on the Stage so eminently fitted, in his opinion, to excite interest in the breasts of an American audience.

In exhibiting a stage representation of a real transaction, the particulars of which are fresh in the minds of many of the audience, an author has this peculiar difficulty to struggle with, that those who know the events expect to see them *all* recorded; and any deviation from what they remember to be fact, appears to them as a fault in the poet; they are disappointed, their expectations are not fulfilled, and the writer is more or less condemned, not considering the difference between the poet and the historian, or not knowing that what is intended to be exhibited is a free poetical picture, not an exact historical portrait.

Still further difficulties has the Tragedy of André to surmount, difficulties independent of its own demerits, in its way to public favor. The subject necessarily involves political questions; but the Author presumes that he owes no apology to any one for having shewn himself an American. The friends of Major André (and it appears that all who knew him were his friends) will look with a jealous eye on the Poem, whose principal incident is the sad catastrophe which his misconduct, in submitting to be an instrument in a transaction of treachery and deceit, justly brought upon him: but these friends have no cause of offence; the Author has adorned the poetical character of André with every virtue; he has made him his Hero; to do which, he was under the necessity of making him condemn his own conduct, in the one dreadfully unfortunate action of his life. To shew the effects which Major André's excellent qualities had upon the minds of men, the Author has drawn a generous and amiable youth, so blinded by his love for the accomplished Briton, as to consider his country, and the great commander of her armies, as in the commission of such horrid injustice, that he, in the anguish of his soul, disclaims the service. In this it appears, since the first representation, that the Author has gone near to offend the veterans of the American army who were present on the first night, and who not knowing the sequel of the action, felt much disposed to condemn him: but surely they must remember the diversity of opinion which agitated the minds of men at that time, on the question of the propriety of putting André to death; and when they add the circumstances of André's having saved the life of this youth, and gained his ardent friendship, they will be inclined to mingle with their disapprobation, a sentiment of pity, and excuse, perhaps commend, the Poet, who has represented the action without sanctioning it by his approbation. . . .

The Poem is now submitted to the ordeal of closet examination, with the Author's respectful assurance to every reader, that as it is not his interest, so it has not been his intention to offend any; but, on the contrary, to impress, through the medium of a pleasing stage exhibition, the sublime lessons of Truth and Justice upon the minds of his countrymen.

W. DUNLAP.

New-York, April 4th, 1798.

PROLOGUE

Spoken by Mr. Martin.

A Native Bard, a native scene displays,
And claims your candour for his daring lays:
Daring, so soon, in mimic scenes to shew,
What each remembers as a real woe.
Who has forgot when gallant André died?
A name by Fate to Sorrow's self allied.
Who has forgot, when o'er the untimely bier,
Contending armies paus'd, to drop a tear.

Our Poet builds upon a fact to-night;
Yet claims, in building, every Poet's right:
To choose, embellish, lop, or add, or blend,
Fiction with truth, as best may suit his end;
Which, he avows, is pleasure to impart,
And move the passions but to mend the heart.

O, may no party-spirit blast his views,
Or turn to ill the meanings of the Muse:
She sings of wrongs long past, Men as they were,
To instruct, without reproach, the Men that are;
Then judge the Story by the genius shown,
And praise, or damn it, for its worth alone.

(g) *Charles Brockden Brown*

Some of the reasons why the thin stream of native literary production became a trickle after 1800 and then all but dried up may be found in this apologetic Preface by Charles Brockden Brown to the first bound volume of his quarterly review. Two years of publishing his journal as a *Monthly Magazine, and American Review* had taught him that the hope of contributions from his fellow members of the Friendly Club and others was vain and the effort to fill the pages himself could not be forever sustained. The decision to publish only quarterly and to use more informational and borrowed material had likewise failed to solve the problem. There was as yet an insufficient public to support a genuinely literary journal; and the reasons Brown gives are the usual ones: Americans are too busy with practical matters to give attention to original and creative work in either science or literature, and London is too near to permit competition from an American center of the arts. The first period of national literary effort was drawing to a disappointing close.

TEXT: from the first edition, 1802.

The American Review and Literary Journal
for the Year 1801

PREFACE

The people of the United States are, perhaps, more distinguished than those of Europe as a people of business; and by an universal attention to the active and lucrative pursuits of life. This habit has grown out of the necessities of their situation, while engaged in the settlement of a new country, in the means of self-preservation, in defending their possessions, in removing the obstacles and embarrassments arising from their colonial condition, and in forming and establishing independent systems of government. When, now that our population is increased, our national independence secured, and our governments established, and we are relieved from the necessities of colonists and emigrants, there is reason to expect more attention to polite literature and science.

Nothing, it is thought, will tend more to excite this attention and to render the pursuits of knowledge more compatible with those of business than those periodical publications which impart information in small portions; by which, men engaged in active occupations may gradually acquire a degree of intellectual cultivation and improvement without any infringement of the time allotted to their customary and necessary concerns.

Much has been said about the claims which the natives of America may urge to the praise of genius and learning. Some European critics hold our pretensions in contempt; and many among ourselves seem inclined to degrade our countrymen below the common level. Their judgment has been formed from very imperfect evidence, and very narrow views, though it must be admitted that we have not contributed our share to the great fund of knowledge and science, which is continually receiving such vast accessions from every part of Europe.

Genius in composition, like genius in every other art, must be aided by culture, nourished by patronage, and supplied with leisure and materials. The genius of the poet, orator, and historian cannot be exercised with vigour and effect without suitable encouragement, any more than that of the artist and mechanic. Neither the one or the other is beyond the sphere of social affections and domestic duties and wants; neither can be expected to produce works of ingenuity and labour without such a recompense as the natural ambition of man and the necessities of his nature and situation demand.

No one is so absurd as to suppose that the natives of

America are unfitted by any radical defect of understanding for vieing with the artizans of Europe in all those useful and elegant fabrics which are daily purchased by us. Similar and suitable circumstances would show Americans equally qualified to excel in arts and literature as the natives of the other continent. But a people much engaged in the labours of agriculture, in a country rude and untouched by the hand of refinement, cannot, with any tolerable facility or success, carry on, at the same time, the operations of imagination and indulge in the speculations of Raphael, Newton, or Pope.

The causes, indeed, why the intellectual soil of America is so comparatively sterile are obvious. We do not cultivate it; nor, while we can resort to foreign fields, from whence all our wants are so easily and readily supplied, and which have been cultivated for ages, do we find sufficient inducement to labour in our own. We are united by language, manners, and taste, by the bonds of peace and commercial intercourse, with an enlightened nation, the centre of whose arts and population may be considered as much *our* centre, as much the fountain whence *we* draw light and knowledge through books, as that of the inhabitants of Wales and Cumberland. In relation to the British capital as the centre of English literature, arts, and science, the situation of *New* and *Old-York* may be regarded as the same. It is only the gradual influence of time, that, by increasing our numbers and furnishing a ready market for the works of domestic hands and heads, will at length generate and continue a race of artists and authors, purely indigenous, and who may vie with those of Europe.

This period is, probably, at no great distance; and no means seem better calculated to hasten so desirable an event than those literary repositories in which every original contribution is received and the hints and discoveries of observation and ingenuity are preserved, and which contain a critical examination of the books which our country happens to produce. It is from the want of a clear and comprehensive survey of our literary products that we are, in a great measure, to ascribe the censures of foreign critics who are yet in ignorance of us and our affairs.

The plan of a REVIEW, so *new* in America, has had many prejudices to encounter and many obstacles to surmount. It was thought that American writers would not *bear* criticism: that, as this was a *young* country, its authors must be treated with peculiar indulgence, and be encouraged by praise rather than intimidated by censure. This objection originates from a very imperfect and partial conception of the nature and end of criticism; and which experience has proved to be without foundation. It is applicable rather to the supposed incapacity of the critic, than to the business of criticism itself. If the critic have formed to himself an ideal standard of excellence of the most elevated kind, or is enslaved by the authority of any individual example, there is danger lest the disappointment of unreasonable expectations should prompt him to pronounce a severe and inequitable judgment. But if possessed of liberality and candour and a just view of the end of writing, as well as a sense of the imperfection of all human skill and capacity, he cannot fail to satisfy the public by the justice of his decision, and to benefit, if not please, the author himself by the exposition of the defects, as well as the merits of his performance.

How far those who have executed the department of criticism are qualified for the undertaking, the public have it in their power to decide. Their purpose is not so much to exhibit their own opinions as the spirit and manner of the authors themselves. To boast of an exemption from prejudice or bias of every kind would evince their ignorance and presumption. Their prejudices, they would fain believe, are of a salutary kind and favourable to the true interest and happiness of mankind. Though not indifferent in the great questions of politics, which are so often discussed and which at present agitate the world, they hope to be above the influence of that *party-spirit* which engenders so many unworthy and selfish passions, and whose views are limited by personal, local and temporary considerations.

It is not probable that any individual can be found who, with the requisite ability and inclination, has leisure and perseverance enough successfully to conduct a work of this kind. Depending, then, as it must do, on persons of various pursuits, and different political sentiments, drawn together by their common attachment to letters and a desire to promote the literature and science of their country, it is not surprising that occasional differences of opinion should appear in the course of their labours. Sincere as may be the endeavour of each to speak on political topics with impartiality and justice, it is more than probable that what he may say will partake of the predominant hue of his own particular creed. But whatever bias may at times appear, on the one side or the other, it is hoped nothing will be discerned that indicates the narrow and mean spirit of little minds, intent on petty distinctions rather than general principles, on names rather than things. They who look for the ordinary effusions of party-politics must turn from the pages of this Review, to those numerous diurnal gazettes which are the appropriate vehicles of invective and sarcasm, of anger and contempt, and in which the keen encounter of hostile pens is expected and enjoyed. Nothing, it is believed, will be found in this work which has any tendency to impair that fair form of government so wisely established, or to disturb those opinions which are essentially necessary to its just operation and lasting support. *Morality* and *Religion*, the pillars which uphold the fabrics of society and government, we feel it our duty, on this and on every other occasion, to strengthen and maintain to the best of our ability. And we may offer this volume as a proof of the force of the sentiments here expressed.

In the VIEW presented to the public, though no promise was given, yet it was confidently hoped that *original essays on moral, literary and scientific subjects; and biographical memoirs and anecdotes of remarkable and eminent persons, particularly in America,* would have formed a portion of this volume. We are free to acknowledge that any expectations which may have been excited of this part of our plan, which was thrown in provisionally, will be, at this time, disappointed. This deficiency may, perhaps, be regarded as, in some degree, compensated by the fulness of the Review. But on this subject, as on every other, we rely on the indulgence of the public, rather than on any supposed merits of our own. No part, however, of our original design will be lost sight of, though to fulfil it demands the aid of the intelligent and communicative in every part of the United States, whose contributions will always be thankfully received.

We have been cautious of making brilliant promises, aware how often they fail of performance. We trust that the public will not have less reason in future than they have hitherto had to be satisfied with our exertions.

New-York, January, 1802.

DOCUMENT 3

Samuel Miller

The Rev. Samuel Miller (1769–1850) was Pastor of
a Presbyterian Church in New York City at the time of
writing *A Brief Retrospect of the Eighteenth Century;
containing a Sketch of the Revolutions and Improvements in Science, Arts, and Literature during that
Period.* This backward glance grew out of a pastoral discourse delivered on the first day of the new century and
was expanded with the aid of his friends and published
in 1803. A member, with his brother Dr. Edward
Miller, of the circle to which Charles Brockden Brown
looked for support in his literary undertakings, Miller,
in his *Retrospect,* provides all the needed evidence for
their failure. The passages here selected as bearing most
directly on the problem of literary nationalism give as
thorough a survey as we have of the state of learning
and culture in the United States in general and in the
individual regions at this time, and offer some reasons
why the level is not as high as one might wish; but they
also, by their emphasis on theological, classical, scientific, and mechanical achievements, give indirect evidence of why *belles lettres* and the fine arts of literature and painting did not prosper. A comparison of this
document with the summary and analysis of James Fenimore Cooper a quarter of a century later (Document
23) reveals a shift of emphasis not only in the offered
explanations and solutions, but in the focus of the problem itself.

TEXT: from the first edition, New York, 2 vols., 1803 (II,
pp. 384–89 and 394–410).

FROM A *Brief Retrospect of the Eighteenth Century*

The establishment of the Federal Government, in 1789, may be considered as the last grand epocha in the progress of knowledge in America. From this period public tranquillity and confidence began to rest on a foundation more solid than before; wealth flowed in on every side; the extension of our intercourse with Europe, the great seat of civilization, refinement and literature, rendered us every day more familiar with trans-atlantic productions and improvements; and a sense of national dignity and independence becoming gradually more strong and general, all conspired to furnish the means and to excite an ambition for enriching our own country with the treasures of knowledge.

From this time till the end of the century, literary institutions of various kinds were multiplied with astonishing rapidity in the United States. Besides Colleges, Academies, and subordinate Schools, Scientific Associations were formed; Libraries began to be established in the most remote parts of the country; Printing Presses and Bookstores appeared in great numbers where they were never before known; Newspapers became numerous to a degree beyond all precedent; and the rewards of literary labour, though still too small, were considerably augmented. The establishment of the *Historical Society of Massachusetts*, in 1791; of the *Medical Schools* of New-Hampshire and Kentucky, in 1798; of the *Connecticut Academy of Arts and Sciences*, in 1799; and of the numerous *Medical* and *Agricultural Societies* in almost every part of the United States, within a few years past, deserve particular notice and form interesting items in the annals of our literary progress.

At the beginning of the century there were *two* Colleges in the American Colonies. At the close of it there were *twenty-five*, from which it may be estimated that *four hundred* students are annually sent forth with academic honours. At the beginning of the century the number of Academies was small, and even these were on a comparatively narrow plan and were ill attended by students; but at the close of it, the number of these institutions had become so great in almost every State in the Union, especially in the Eastern and Middle States, that it would be difficult to form a tolerably correct estimate of their number. At the commencement of the century there were but *two* public *Libraries* in the American Colonies: these belonged to Harvard College and to the Province of South-Carolina, and were very small.[1] Since that period the number has increased to *many hundreds* and is every year becoming still greater.[2] Private Libraries have also become numerous and extensive in a still more remarkable degree.

At the commencement of the period under review, there were but *three* or *four Printers* in the American Colonies, and these carried on their business upon a very small scale and in a very coarse, inelegant manner. But at present the number of Printers in the United States may be considered as near *three hundred*, and many of these perform their work with a neatness and elegance which are rarely exceeded in Europe. At that time the printing an original American work, even a small pamphlet, was a rare occurrence, and seriously weighed, as an important undertaking; while the reprinting of foreign works was seldom attempted. But now at least *one hundred* American works, some of which are large and respectable, annually issue from our presses; and the re-publication of foreign books is carried on in almost every part of our country, and particularly in the capital towns, with a degree of enterprize

[1] In the seventeenth century, some of the Congregational Churches in Massachusetts began to form *Church Libraries*. These were considerably numerous and useful and some of them remain till the present day. The use of these Libraries, however, was chiefly confined to the particular congregations whose property they were.

[2] The number of incorporated *Libraries* in Massachusetts is said to be about *one hundred*. The number in the other Eastern States is not known, but institutions of this kind are far more numerous in New-England than in any other part of our country.

and to an extent which would not disgrace some of the most cultivated parts of the European world.

Before the revolutionary war the *Booksellers* in the American Colonies were few and carried on their business on a contracted plan. Since that time their number has increased more than *fifty fold*, and the extent of their annual sales, perhaps, in a still greater proportion.[3] Thirty years ago, he who undertook to dispose of a moderately large edition, even of a Spelling-book, considered himself as engaging in a hazardous enterprize. But in 1790, a single bookseller thought himself warranted in attempting an American edition of the *Encyclopædia Britannica*, in eighteen quarto volumes, and completely succeeded in making it a profitable undertaking.[4] And since the last-mentioned year, a number of works extending to many volumes have been carried through American presses, with great ease and readiness.

The first edition of the *Bible* ever printed in America was that by the Rev. John Eliot, the celebrated *Apostle* of the Indians, in the language of the *Naticks*. This monument of pious labour was first printed at Cambridge, in Massachusetts, in 1664, and a second edition at the same place sixteen years afterwards. From this period till near the close of the revolutionary war, at so low an ebb was the book-trade in our country, that we hear of no attempt to print an edition of the Bible on this side of the Atlantic. About the year 1781, Mr. Robert Aitken, of Philadelphia, undertook to present the American public with a duo-

[3] In 1802, the German plan of disposing of books by means of *Literary Fairs* was adopted in the United States. The first Book-fair was held in New-York; and it is proposed, in future, to hold them statedly in that city. It is believed that Mr. Mathew Carey, a well informed and enterprizing bookseller of Philadelphia, was one of the first who suggested the propriety and utility of the undertaking, which has so far happily succeeded and bids fair to be highly useful, both to the book-trade and to the cause of literature.

[4] The person here alluded to is Mr. Thomas Dobson, of Philadelphia, an intelligent and respectable bookseller, who has probably contributed as much as any individual in his line to the promotion of American literature.

decimo edition of the Sacred Scriptures. This laudable
undertaking was executed, but with great difficulty arising
from the peculiar situation of the country at that time.[5]
But within the last eighteen or twenty years, undertakings
of this kind have become so numerous and so familiar,
that the importation of Bibles for the supply of the American market, though not entirely, has in a great measure
ceased. The first *quarto* edition of the Bible printed in
the United States was in the year 1791, by Mr. Isaac Col-
lins, then residing at Trenton, in New-Jersey. In a few
months afterwards, another quarto edition was published
by Mr. Isaiah Thomas, of Worcester, in Massachusetts;
who, in the same year, laid before the public the first *folio*
edition of the Holy Scriptures that was printed in the
United States. Since that time several folio editions of the
Bible and a number of quarto editions have been printed
in our country and begin to be considered by our printers
and booksellers as small and easy undertakings.

Those kinds of literary productions which have been
most common and most successful in the United States
are *theological* and *political* works and those intended for
the use of *schools*. For the *first* we are indebted to that
seriousness and taste for religious inquiry which prevails
in New-England, and in a considerable though less degree
in the Middle and Southern States. The almost universal
taste for the *second* class of books we owe to the nature
of our government, which is eminently calculated to foster, to bring forward, and to display political talents, and
to excite the attention of every class of citizens to political
inquiries. And the general encouragement given to productions of the last-mentioned kind arises from that disposition to attend to the education of children which has
long characterized the Eastern States and which, during

[5] Immediately after the publication of this edition of the Bible,
peace took place, when it was soon found that Bibles could be
imported from Great-Britain cheaper than it was possible to print
them here. Mr. Aitken, therefore, not obtaining a ready sale for
his edition, which had been carried on with great difficulty, was
nearly ruined by the undertaking.

the last ten years of the century under review, rapidly extended itself through every part of the Union.

The *School establishments* of New-England, especially in the States of Massachusetts and Connecticut,[6] though they took their rise in the seventeenth century, yet underwent such modifications and received so many improvements in the eighteenth that it would be improper to pass them without notice in this retrospect.[7] These establishments have been carried to such a degree of perfection, that in New-England, and particularly in the two States above-mentioned, scarcely an individual can be found, of either sex, who has not been instructed in reading, writing and arithmetic and who does not habitually read more or less in newspapers and a few of the best books on religion and morality. Attempts have been made in some of the Middle and Southern States to adopt similar plans of general education, but though much has been done in several of these States towards rendering the elements of English literature a boon within the reach of all classes in the community, yet the habits of the people not being so favourable to the diffusion of knowledge and their characters and manners being less homogeneous, they have made less progress towards maturing and perfecting their school establishments than the Eastern States. . . .

In the *Mechanic Arts*, so far as respects the ingenuity of individuals, and the important service rendered by numerous inventions and improvements, America yields to no nation under heaven. Perhaps, considering the amount of our population, and the peculiar circumstances of our

[6] The *School* system of Connecticut is generally considered the most perfect in the United States. The parish Schools in that State amount to at least *twelve hundred*, containing, on an average, *forty Scholars* each, or *forty-eight thousand* in the whole. Next to that of Connecticut in point of excellence we may place the School system of Massachusetts. The number of Schools in that State is not known to the Author. He presumes, however, that it cannot be less than in Connecticut.

[7] The Author takes pleasure in acknowledging his obligation to Noah Webster, jun. Esquire, for some valuable information respecting the literature of Connecticut during the eighteenth century; and especially for a more satisfactory account of the School establishments in that State than he had before received.

people, we have furnished even a greater number of these inventions and improvements than our just proportion. On this subject, as it would be difficult to enter into details without exceeding all convenient limits, so there can be no doubt that a number of instances, abundantly sufficient to support the assertion here made, will readily occur to every reader. The *Quadrant*, by Godfrey; the *Orrery*, by Rittenhouse; the Machinery for manufacturing *Cards*, by Whittemore; and that for manufacturing *Firearms*, by Whitney, form but a very small number of the large list that might be presented.

Of talents in the *Fine Arts*, America has been less productive. But we have satisfactory evidence that this arises not so much from the want of native genius as from the want of cultivation and encouragement of the genius we possess. The names of West, Trumbull, Copley, and Stuart are more than sufficient to rescue their country from any imputations of deficiency on this head.

When we pass on to *Theology*, the noblest and most important of all sciences, it will be found that on this subject America may claim high distinction. To omit many names of less note, the theological writings of President Edwards, and of the Rev. Dr. Hopkins, have excited much attention in the religious world. The former, in particular, deserves, perhaps, to be considered as one of the greatest divines that ever lived. Besides many Tracts of high reputation, on detached points of theology, and which have been well received, not only in America but also in Europe, a number of volumes of *Sermons* have been produced by our countrymen, which show that the eloquence of the pulpit is by no means neglected. The first volume of Sermons ever published in America that had any just claim to correctness and elegance of style was printed in Boston in the year 1727 by Ebenezer Pemberton, pastor of a Church in that town. Since that time, the collections of Sermons by President Davies,[8] Dr. Lathrop, Dr. Seabury,

8 Rev. Samuel Davies was born in the County of Newcastle, in the State of Delaware, November 3, 1724. He received the greater part of his academic and theological education under the care of the Rev. Mr. Samuel Blair, of Fog's Manor, in Pennsylvania, and

President Smith, Dr. Linn, Dr. Strong, Dr. Clarke, Dr. Emmons and several others of different kinds and degrees of merit, have received much public approbation.[9]

In the *Philosophy of the Human Mind*, the eighteenth century did not produce a greater effort of genius than the *Treatise on the Will*, by President Edwards. And perhaps it may be asserted that within the last thirty years a fondness for metaphysical subtleties and refined speculations has remarkably characterized the theological publications, particularly in the Eastern States of America.

In *Classic Literature*, the United States have given birth to little that can be deemed remarkable. The first translation of a classic author ever made and published in America was by James Logan, several times before mentioned, who, in 1744, published a version of Cicero's treatise *De Senectute* with explanatory notes. Since that time several works of a similar kind have been executed in the United States. Among many others who might be mentioned as distinguished for their classic learning and taste, it would be improper to omit the name of Charles

---

was licensed to preach the gospel by the Presbytery of Newcastle about the year 1745. Soon after this event, he travelled into Virginia where he settled in the ministry in Hanover County and remained there in an extensive sphere of usefulness and highly respected for a number of years. In 1753, he was chosen by the Synod of New-York, at the solicitation of the Trustees of New-Jersey College, to accompany the Rev. Gilbert Tennent on a mission to Great-Britain and Ireland to solicit benefactions for said College. In 1759, he was elected to succeed Mr. Edwards in the Presidency of that institution. In this station he remained but eighteen months, being removed by death in January, 1761, in the thirty-seventh year of his age. The genius, taste, learning, and eminent piety of President Davies have been so much celebrated that it is unnecessary to dwell on them here. His *Sermons*, in three volumes, were first published in 1765. Their uncommon merit is well known. They have undergone a number of impressions.

[9] Besides the more formal volumes of Sermons above mentioned, it would be easy to select smaller collections of discourses on particular subjects, which do honour to the genius, learning, and taste of their respective authors, and the single Sermons of merit are much more numerous; but it is obviously impossible to indulge such minute details, consistently with the requisite brevity.

Thomson, Esq.[10] late Secretary of the American Congress.
The erudition and skill of this gentleman, especially in
Greek literature, do honour to our country. He has com-
pleted a translation of the *Septuagint* version of the Old
Testament Scriptures and of the Original of the New
Testament, which the friends of Biblical literature in
America hope soon to see published and which, in the
opinion of good judges, will be a valuable acquisition to
sacred criticism.

Of *Oriental Literature*, the votaries in America have
been few, and of the fruits of their erudition little has
been laid before the public. With regard, indeed, both to
Classic and Oriental literature, our country has rather lost
than gained ground within the last hundred years. For
though a greater number of persons now gain a smattering
of classic literature than at the beginning of the century;
yet of those who pay attention to this study, much fewer
are deeply and thoroughly instructed. And with respect
to Oriental learning, those who have any tolerable acquaintance with it in the United States are rare indeed.
To the names of those Americans mentioned in former
parts of this work, who were distinguished by their knowledge of the Hebrew language, that of the Rev. Dr. Stiles,
President of Yale College, may be added. At the time of
his death, he probably left no superior among his countrymen in this branch of literature.[11]

[10] This gentleman received the rudiments of his education at
the Academy of Dr. Francis Allison, before mentioned, where he
was associated in study with Dr. Ewing, Governor M'Kean, and
a number of other Americans of literary distinction.

[11] Ezra Stiles, D. D. and LL. D. was born at North-Haven, in
Connecticut, December 10, 1727. He was educated at Yale College, where he received the degree of A. B. in the year 1746. He
was ordained to the work of the Gospel ministry, and installed
Pastor of a Church at Newport, Rhode-Island, in 1755; and was
chosen President of the College at which he had received his education in 1777; in which important office he continued till his
death, in 1795. Dr. Stiles was one of the most learned men that
our country ever produced. He had a great amount of general
knowledge, but he was particularly attached to Oriental literature.
Besides an acquaintance with the Hebrew language more than
commonly extensive and profound, very few on this side of the

It has been asserted, and probably with truth, that in *Political science* and in *Parliamentary eloquence*, the United States will bear a very honourable comparison with any nation. Besides the eminent political writers mentioned in a former page, the names of Adams, Hamilton, Madison, Jay, and several other native citizens, are known and celebrated in Europe. In addition to these, many Counsellors and Juridical characters might be enumerated, who not only hold a high station among ourselves, but who would also be considered as ornaments of the bar and the bench in the most enlightened countries of Europe.

The *Historians* of America were enumerated in a former chapter, and some references made to their respective merits. None of them, indeed, can boast of having attained that elaborate polish and that exquisite felicity of manner which distinguish the first class of English historians. But the most of them are respectable writers and several have acquitted themselves in a manner which does credit to their taste in composition as well as to their fidelity in collecting and communicating information.[12]

The respectable *Poets* of America are not numerous. The most conspicuous of these were noticed in a preceding division of this work. It is not necessary here to repeat their names, or to attempt a comparative estimate of their merits. Their number is gradually increasing;[13] and when

Atlantic ever made so great progress in the knowledge of the Arabic, Chaldaic, Syriac, and Samaritan dialects; and on the Persic and Coptic he had bestowed some attention. He corresponded with learned *Rabbis* in the Hebrew language, and revived the study of it in the College over which he presided. For upwards of thirty years he held a distinguished place among the active friends and promoters of literature in the United States.

[12] Histories of different American States have been promised by several writers. The public, particularly, look forward with high expectation to the appearance of *The History of North-Carolina*, which has been for some time prepared by Dr. Hugh Williamson, whose talents and learning are a pledge that it will prove an interesting and instructive work.

[13] Since the close of the eighteenth century, another writer has appeared, who, if we may judge by his first production, is destined to hold a high place in the catalogue of native Poets of America. This writer is the Rev. John B. Linn, D. D. of Phila-

that leisure and encouragement shall be afforded to men of genius in this country which are enjoyed in many parts of Europe, we may expect to produce Poets who shall vie with the most celebrated of the old world.

But in no respect does the literary enterprize of America appear more conspicuous than in the rapid increase of the number and circulation of *Newspapers* within the last thirty years. The ratio and amount of this increase were stated in another place. In this respect we go beyond every other nation. It were well if these vehicles of information had improved as much in purity, intelligence, and instructiveness, as in other respects; but the blindest partiality for American literature must perceive and lament the sad reverse!

It may not be improper to attempt in a few sentences a comparative estimate of the extent to which different branches of knowledge are cultivated in different parts of the United States.

That amount of knowledge which is usually acquired at common schools, viz. reading, writing, and arithmetic, is more generally diffused among all classes of the people in New-England, and particularly in Massachusetts and Connecticut, than in any other portion of our country and indeed than in any other part of the globe. This may be ascribed to the superior excellence of their School establishments, to the number, piety, and diligence of the Clergy, to the regular organization of their towns and parishes, to the honourable point of light in which the instructors of youth are considered,[14] and to the general

---

delphia, whose *Powers of Genius*, a didactic and descriptive Poem, published in 1801, displays imagination, taste, and reading. This Poem was so favourably received, that a second edition was called for in less than a year, into which the Author has introduced large and valuable improvements.

[14] This circumstance has a most benign influence in New-England. In the Middle, but more especially in the Southern States, the employment of a *Schoolmaster* is considered by many as rather degrading and has sometimes been used as a ground of reproach. The consequence is that too many of the instructors of youth in these States are ignorant and vicious adventurers; those who are well qualified rather shunning an office to which so little

spirit of activity and enterprize which must be admitted to enter into the national character of New-England.

It may also be observed, as another circumstance of discrimination, that in the Eastern States a larger portion of the youth pass through a regular collegiate course of education, than in any other part of our country. In New-England, the mass of the people are more generally taught to respect literature and to make exertions for conferring this advantage on their children. In that part of the Union also the expense attending an Academic course is rather less than in most of the other American Seminaries. These two circumstances have a natural tendency to fill their Colleges with a greater number of Students than are to be found elsewhere.

The *Classic Literature* of the United States, as was before remarked, is almost every where superficial. It is believed, however, that the learned languages, and especially the Greek language, are rather less studied in the Eastern than in the Middle and Southern States. It is true, many more individuals attend to this branch of learning in the former than in the latter, but they read fewer books and devote a less portion of time to the object.[15] For this fact, many reasons might be assigned, but it is not necessary to mention more than two. The one is that, owing to the superior wealth enjoyed by a number of individuals in the Middle and Southern States, it was more common, during a great part of the eighteenth century, to send young men to Europe for their education from those States than from New-England. The youth

---

respect is attached. In the New-England States it is otherwise. Some of their greatest Divines and Statesmen were Schoolmasters in early life. The employment is considered and treated as an honourable one. The consequence is that the common parish schools are generally under the care of well informed and virtuous men.

[15] The Author is aware that in tracing the literary history of New-England, the names of some classical Scholars of great eminence are found. He means, however, only to speak of the degree of attention *generally* paid to Classic literature by those who go through a collegiate course in the Eastern States, and especially within the last twenty or thirty years.

thus educated might be expected, of course, to bring back with them to their native country a larger portion of classic literature than could be easily acquired in American seminaries. Another reason is that, while almost all the instructors of youth in New-England and especially the higher classes of them, during the last hundred years, have been natives, a large portion of the Superintendents of Academies and of the Presidents and Professors of Colleges in the Middle and Southern parts of our country, during the same period, were Europeans and many of them eminently accomplished in classic literature. If, therefore, the knowledge in this branch of learning, acquired in the best seminaries of Europe, were usually more accurate and profound than could ordinarily be obtained from our native citizens, it must follow of course that those who derived their classical learning from the former of these sources were, in general, more thoroughly instructed themselves and consequently more capable of instructing others than those who had access only to the latter.

In the study of *Oriental Literature*, it is believed that New-England has generally excelled the Middle and Southern States. Certain it is that we hear of more eminent Orientalists in the former than in the latter, if we except a few foreigners occasionally residing among us. This we may ascribe to the great Oriental learning of several of those distinguished divines who came with the first settlers to New-England or who soon afterwards followed them thither. The influence of these men has continued, in a degree, to the present day. To this circumstance it may be added, that the University of Cambridge, in Massachusetts, is the only seminary of learning in the United States in which a Professorship for instruction in the Oriental languages has been steadily maintained through the whole of the eighteenth century.

In the cultivation of *Mathematics* and *Natural Philosophy*, it is difficult to say to what part of our country the preference ought to be given. Probably an impartial judge, taking the whole history of the country together, would give the palm, in this respect, to Pennsylvania and Massachusetts.

The Sciences of *Chemistry*, *Natural History*, and *Medicine*, have long been, and continue to be, more successfully cultivated in the Middle and Southern than in the Eastern States. The same reasons apply in this case that were suggested with respect to Classic literature. Comparatively few young men have been sent at any period from the Eastern States to European seminaries to complete their medical education. Besides this consideration, foreigners, even of literary and scientific character, have received less encouragement to settle in those States than in most other parts of the Union. On the other hand, from the Middle and Southern States a number of young men have been, every year, sent to the Medical Schools of Europe, who not only attended the ordinary courses of instruction in *Medicine*, strictly so called, but also the Lectures delivered on *Chemistry* and *Natural History*, as important auxiliary branches of Philosophy. It is further to be observed, that several learned and enterprizing foreigners who visited and resided for some time in New-York, Pennsylvania, Virginia, and South-Carolina devoted much of their time and attention to Natural History,[16] excited some of the native citizens in their respective neighbourhoods to engage in this study,[17] and thus introduced that taste for inquiries of this nature which has ever since existed, in a greater or less degree, in some individuals in those States.

New-England has given birth to the greatest number

[16] There is a particular reference here to Catesby, Garden, and Walter, who resided in South-Carolina; to Mitchell, who spent a number of years in Virginia; to Professor Kalm, who devoted several years to travelling in the Middle States; to Schoepf and Wangenheim, who came to America with the German troops, during the Revolutionary war; to whom may be added, Dr. Colden and Dr. Muhlenberg, whose talents and zeal in the study of Botany have been before repeatedly mentioned.

[17] It was probably owing to the conversation and influence of these, or of some other foreigners visiting the country, that Clayton, Starke, Cary, and Greenway, of Virginia; and the Bartrams, Marshall, and others, of Pennsylvania, were so much devoted to botanical pursuits.

and the most eminent of the native *Theological* writers of America. And there is no doubt that by far the larger portion of the *Sermons* printed in the United States, whether in volumes or single discourses, is produced in that part of our country. It may also be asserted that almost all the valuable disquisitions on the *Philosophy of the human mind* which have been published on this side of the Atlantic were written in New-England.

In the literature and science of *Politics*, it is not easy to say which part of our country is most entitled to credit. If we pronounce in favour of those States which have produced the greatest number of eminent political writers, we must give the first honours to Massachusetts, New-York, Pennsylvania, and Virginia. But there is no subject more generally studied in every State in the Union than Political science, none on which our literary men so frequently write, and, of course, none which so constantly calls forth the exertion of talents.

Of *Historical* composition, the Eastern States have produced their full proportion, and rather more. Of respectable *Poets*, they have given birth to a greater number than any other proportional division of the Union. And in *Belles Lettres* generally, there is, without doubt, more cultivation in New-England than in any other part of our country, if we except the larger cities in the Middle and Southern States.

With respect to the *Mechanic Arts*, New-England has furnished her full proportion of those inventions and improvements which do honour to American genius. And with regard to the *Fine Arts, three* out of *four* of our greatest native *Painters* were born in that division of the country.

It must, however, after all be acknowledged that what is called a *liberal education* in the United States is, in common, less accurate and complete; the erudition of our native citizens, with some exceptions, less extensive and profound; and the works published by American Authors, in general, less learned, instructive, and elegant[18] than

---

[18] It is not meant to be denied that a few of the works published in America are as profound and instructive as any on simi-

are found in Great-Britain and some of the more enlightened nations on the Eastern continent. These facts, it is apprehended, arise not from any deficiency of talents in our country, nor from any inaptitude in its soil or atmosphere to promote the growth of genius, but from one or another and, in some cases, from a combination of the following causes.

1. *Defective plans and means of instruction in our Seminaries of learning.* The great majority of our Colleges have very inadequate funds. The consequence is that in most of them the Professors are few in number and have assigned to them too large a field of instruction. Hence they can convey but very superficial knowledge of the various branches which it is made their duty to teach, and if well qualified themselves, which is far from being always the case, find it impossible to do justice to the pupils. In some instances also, the Trustees or Governors of American Colleges, either from their own ignorance or in compliance with popular prejudice, have so contracted the time requisite for completing a course of instruction as to render it necessary wholly to dispense with or lightly to hurry over some of the most important branches of knowledge. Accordingly in some of these institutions, Mathematical Science is unpopular and the acquisition of as little as possible especially of the higher branches of it enjoined on the student. In others, Classic literature, and especially the Greek language,[19] is in low estimation and not more studied than is indispensibly necessary to obtaining a *diploma.* If well bred scholars ever issue from such Seminaries, they must be formed by a degree of private and individual application rarely to be met with in youth.

2. *Want of Leisure.* The comparatively equal distribu-

---

lar subjects published elsewhere. It is simply intended to give a *general* character of American publications, liable to such exceptions as the mind of the well-informed reader will readily supply.

[19] In some American Colleges, we are told that no more knowledge of Greek is required in those who graduate *Bachelor of Arts* than that which may be derived from the Grammar and the Greek Testament.

tion of property in America, while it produces the most benign political and moral effects, is by no means friendly to great acquisitions in literature and science. In such a state of Society, there can be few persons of leisure. It is necessary that almost all should be engaged in some active pursuit. Accordingly in the United States, the greater number of those who pass through a course of what is called liberal education in the hurried manner which has been mentioned engage, immediately after leaving College, in the study or business to which they propose to devote themselves. Having run over the preliminary steps of instruction in this business, probably in a manner no less hurried and superficial than their academic studies, they instantly commence its practical pursuit, and are, perhaps, during the remainder of life consigned to a daily toil for support, which precludes them from reading and especially from gaining much knowledge out of their particular profession. Such is the career of ninety-nine out of an hundred of those in our country who belong to the learned professions. When the alternative either lies or is supposed to lie between erudition and poverty or comfortable affluence and moderate learning, it is not difficult to conjecture which side will be chosen; nor is it surprizing that, in such a state of things, there should be less profound erudition, less elegant accomplishment in literature, than where a considerable number enjoy all the advantages of exemption from laborious duties, and all the accommodations of opulent leisure.

To this circumstance may be ascribed the superficial and unpolished character of many of our native publications. All that their authors, in many cases, want, to render them more replete with instruction, more attractive in manner and, of course, more worthy of public approbation, is *leisure*. But, able only to redeem a few hasty hours for literary pursuits from the employments which give them bread, they must necessarily, if they publish at all, send forth productions from time to time bearing all the marks of haste and immature reflection.

3. *Want of encouragement to learning.* Men cannot be expected to labour without the hope of some adequate

reward. Genius must be nourished by patronage as well as strengthened by culture. Where substantial emoluments may be derived from literary exertion, there, and there alone, will it be frequently undertaken to any considerable extent. Hence in those countries where genius and learning are best rewarded, there they are ever found to be most cultivated. In the United States, the rewards of literature are small and uncertain. The people cannot afford to remunerate eminent talents or great acquirements. Booksellers, the great patrons of learning in modern times, are in America too poor to foster and reward the efforts of genius. There are no rich *Fellowships* in our Universities to excite the ambition of students; no large ecclesiastical benefices to animate the exertions of literary divines.[20] Academic chairs are usually connected with such small salaries that they present little temptation to the scholar; and, finally, the State offers very inconsiderable motives for the acquisition of knowledge and the exertion of talents. Its rewards are small and its favour capricious. Can it be wondered, then, that those who have some acquaintance with books and hold important stations are more anxious to secure pecuniary advantages and to place themselves in a situation independent of popular favour than to make advances in literature, or to do honour to their country by the display of intellectual pre-eminence?

Besides, the spirit of our people is *commercial*. It has been said, and perhaps with some justice, that the *love of gain* peculiarly characterizes the inhabitants of the United States. The tendency of this spirit to discourage literature is obvious. In such a state of Society, men will not only be apt to bend their whole attention to the acquirement of property and neglect the cultivation of

[20] The Author would by no means be understood to express an opinion, that such immoderately lucrative places, either in Church or in State, are, on the whole, useful, or desirable. He is persuaded that they are much more productive of mischief than of advantage. But that they often excite literary ambition, and afford, in many instances, convenient and useful leisure to literary characters, will scarcely be questioned by those who have paid any attention to the subject.

their minds as an affair of secondary moment, but letters and science will seldom be found in high estimation; the amount of wealth will be the principal test of influence; the learned will experience but little reward either of honour or emolument; and, of course, superficial education will be the prevailing character.

Nor is it of less importance here to recollect that the nature of our connection with Great-Britain has operated and continues to operate unfavourably to the progress of American literature. Long accustomed to a state of colonial dependence on that enlightened and cultivated Nation, we have also been accustomed to derive from her the supplies for our literary wants. And still connected with her by the ties of language, manners, taste, and commercial intercourse, her literature, science and arts may be considered as ours. Being able, therefore, with so much ease to reap the fruits of her fields, we have not sufficient inducement to cultivate our own. And even when an excellent production of the American soil is offered to the public, it is generally undervalued and neglected. A large portion of our citizens seem to entertain the idea that nothing worthy of patronage can be produced on this side of the Atlantic. Instead of being prompted to a more liberal encouragement of genius because it is American, their prejudices, on this account, are rather excited against it.[21]

4. *Want of Books.* In the capital cities of Europe, the votary of literature is surrounded with immense Libraries to which he may easily obtain access, and even in many of the smaller towns, books on any subject and to almost

[21] The writer in the *Monthly Magazine*, whose strictures on American literature were before mentioned, represents the inhabitants of the United States as having strong prejudices in favour of their own productions, and ridicules them for preferring American publications to all others. In this, as well as in most of his assertions, he discovers profound ignorance of the subject. The fact is directly the reverse. Americans are too apt to join with ignorant or fastidious foreigners in undervaluing and decrying our domestic literature; and this circumstance is one of the numerous obstacles which have operated to discourage literary exertions on this side of the Atlantic and to impede our literary progress.

any number may be easily obtained. It is otherwise in America. Here the student, in addition to all the other obstacles which lie in his way, has often to spend as much time and thought to obtain a particular book as the reading it ten times would cost. Our public Libraries are few and, compared with those of Europe, small. Nor is this defect supplied by large private collections; these are also rare. And to render the evil still more grievous, the number of literary and enterprizing booksellers is yet smaller. It is only within two or three years that we have begun to receive, with any kind of regularity or promptitude, the best British works as they issue from the press.

Such are some of the causes which have hitherto impeded the progress of American Literature. Their influence, however, is gradually declining and the literary prospects of our country are brightening every day. Letters and science are becoming more important in the public estimation. The number of learned men is becoming rapidly greater. The plans and means of instruction in our Seminaries of learning, though by no means improving in all respects, are, in some, receiving constant melioration. The emulation of founding and sustaining a national character in science and learning begins to be more generally felt, and, from time to time, will doubtless be augmented. A larger proportion of the growing wealth of our country will hereafter be devoted to the improvements of knowledge, and especially to the furtherance of all the means by which scientific discoveries are brought within popular reach and rendered subservient to practical utility. American publications are every day growing more numerous and rising in respectability of character. Public and private Libraries are becoming more numerous and extensive. The taste in composition among our writers is making very sensible progress in correctness and refinement. American authors of merit meet with more liberal encouragement; and when the time shall arrive that we can give to our votaries of literature the same leisure and the same stimulants to exertion with which they are favoured in Europe, it may be confidently predicted that letters will flourish as much in America as in any part of the world, and that we shall be able to make some return to our trans-atlantic brethren for the rich stores of useful knowledge which they have been pouring upon us for nearly two centuries.

DOCUMENT 4

Noah Webster

The arguments for and against a national *American* language paralleled those on literature, but had fewer voices on both sides. One of the most persistent, logical, and effective advocates for the standardization of a native language distinct from the English of England and free of the vagaries of local American dialectal differences, was Noah Webster (1758–1843). In 1789 when, at Franklin's suggestion, he attempted to put his principles into systematic form in a series of *Dissertations on the English Language, with Notes, Historical and Critical,* his famous speller had already been widely adopted and he had been forced into politics to attempt to protect his literary rights. His theory, which at this stage included radical suggestions for spelling reform, can best be described as a kind of organic Federalism: "organic" because he believed that language is determined by usage rather than by grammatical rules; "Federalist" because he believed that the nation as a whole rather than the local community should evolve the accepted standard usage. Further study caused him to modify but not to change his theories (Document 18), and others like John Pickering later entered the lists (Document 11). The relevance of this debate on linguistic nationalism to the problem of literary nationalism is of course subsidiary, but language is an essential part of the foundations of all literary argument; only a few documents on this aspect of the problem are therefore included in this collection, but these few are basic in that they present the essence of the debate. The passage here quoted is the first part of Dissertation I.

TEXT: from the first edition, Boston, 1789.

Dissertations on the English Language, etc.

DISSERTATION I. INTRODUCTION

A regular study of language has in all civilized countries formed a part of a liberal education. The Greeks, Romans, Italians and French successively improved their native tongues, taught them in Academies at home, and rendered them entertaining and useful to the foreign student.

The English tongue, tho later in its progress towards perfection, has attained to a considerable degree of purity, strength and elegance, and been employed by an active and scientific nation to record almost all the events and discoveries of ancient and modern times.

This language is the inheritance which the Americans have received from their British parents. To cultivate and adorn it is a task reserved for men who shall understand the connection between language and logic and form an adequate idea of the influence which a uniformity of speech may have on national attachments.

It will be readily admitted that the pleasures of reading and conversing, the advantage of accuracy in business, the necessity of clearness and precision in communicating ideas, require us to be able to speak and write our own tongue with ease and correctness. But there are more important reasons why the language of this country should be reduced to such fixed principles as may give its pronunciation and construction all the certainty and uniformity which any living tongue is capable of receiving.

The United States were settled by emigrants from different parts of Europe. But their descendants mostly speak the same tongue; and the intercourse among the learned of the different States, which the revolution has begun and an American Court will perpetuate, must gradually destroy the differences of dialect which our ancestors brought from their native countries. This approximation of dialects will be certain; but without the operation of other causes than an intercourse at Court, it will be slow and partial. The body of the people, governed by habit, will still retain their respective peculiarities of speaking and for want of schools and proper books, fall into many inaccuracies which, incorporating with the language of the state where they live, may imperceptibly corrupt the national language. Nothing but the establishment of schools and some uniformity in the use of books can annihilate differences in speaking and preserve the purity of the American tongue. A sameness of pronunciation is of considerable consequence in a political view for provincial accents are disagreeable to strangers and sometimes have an unhappy effect upon the social affections. All men have local attachments which lead them to believe their own practice to be the least exceptionable. Pride and prejudice incline men to treat the practice of their neighbors with some degree of contempt. Thus small differences in pronunciation at first excite ridicule—a habit of laughing at the singularities of strangers is followed by disrespect—and without respect friendship is a name and social intercourse a mere ceremony.

These remarks hold equally true with respect to individuals, to small societies and to large communities. Small causes, such as a nick-name or a vulgar tone in speaking, have actually created a dissocial spirit between the inhabitants of the different states, which is often discoverable in private business and public deliberations. Our political harmony is therefore concerned in a uniformity of language.

As an independent nation, our honor requires us to have a system of our own in language as well as government. Great Britain, whose children we are and whose language we speak, should no longer be *our* standard; for the taste of her writers is already corrupted and her language on the decline. But if it were not so, she is at too great a distance to be our model and to instruct us in the principles of our own tongue.

It must be considered further that the English is the common root or stock from which our national language will be derived. All others will gradually waste away and within a century and a half, North America will be peopled with a hundred millions of men, *all speaking the same language*. Place this idea in comparison with the present and possible future bounds of the language in Europe—consider the Eastern Continent as inhabited by nations whose knowlege and intercourse are embarrassed by differences of language; then anticipate the period when the people of one quarter of the world will be able to associate and converse together like children of the same family.[1] Compare this prospect, which is not visionary, with the state of the English language in Europe, almost confined to an Island and to a few millions of people; then let reason and reputation decide how far America should be dependent on a transatlantic nation for her standard and improvements in language.

Let me add that whatever predilection the Americans may have for their native European tongues, and particularly the British descendants for the English, yet several circumstances render a future separation of the American tongue from the English necessary and unavoidable. The vicinity of the European nations, with the uninterrupted communication in peace and the changes of dominion in war, are gradually assimilating their respective languages. The English with others is suffering continual alterations. America, placed at a distance from those nations, will feel, in a much less degree, the influence of the assimilating causes; at the same time, numerous local causes, such as a new country, new associations of people, new combinations of ideas in arts and science, and some intercourse with tribes wholly unknown in Europe, will introduce new words into the American tongue. These causes will produce, in a course of time, a language in North America as different from the future language of England, as the modern Dutch, Danish and Swedish are from the German or from one another: Like remote branches of a tree

[1] Even supposing that a number of republics, kingdoms or empires, should within a century arise and divide this vast territory; still the subjects of all will speak the same language, and the consequence of this uniformity will be an intimacy of social intercourse hitherto unknown, and a boundless diffusion of knowlege.

springing from the same stock, or rays of light shot from the same center and diverging from each other in proportion to their distance from the point of separation.

Whether the inhabitants of America can be brought to a perfect uniformity in the pronunciation of words, it is not easy to predict; but it is certain that no attempt of the kind has been made, and an experiment, begun and pursued on the right principles, is the only way to decide the question. Schools in Great Britain have gone far towards demolishing local dialects—commerce has also had its influence—and in America these causes, operating more generally, must have a proportional effect.

In many parts of America, people at present attempt to copy the English phrases and pronunciation—an attempt that is favored by their habits, their prepossessions and the intercourse between the two countries. This attempt has, within the period of a few years, produced a multitude of changes in these particulars, especially among the leading classes of people. These changes make a difference between the language of the higher and common ranks, and indeed between the *same* ranks in *different* states, as the rage for copying the English does not prevail equally in every part of North America.

But besides the reasons already assigned to prove this imitation absurd, there is a difficulty attending it, which will defeat the end proposed by its advocates; which is, that the English themselves have no standard of pronunciation, nor can they ever have one on the plan they propose. The Authors who have attempted to give us a standard make the practice of the court and stage in London the sole criterion of propriety in speaking. An attempt to establish a standard on this foundation is both *unjust* and *idle*. It is unjust because it is abridging the nation of its rights; the *general practice* of a nation is the rule of propriety, and this practice should at least be consulted in so important a matter as that of making laws for speaking. While all men are upon a footing and no singularities are accounted vulgar or ridiculous, every man enjoys perfect liberty. But when a particular set of men in exalted stations undertake to say, "we are the standards

of propriety and elegance, and if all men do not conform
to our practice, they shall be accounted vulgar and ignorant," they take a very great liberty with the rules of
the language and the rights of civility.

But an attempt to fix a standard on the practice of any
particular class of people is highly absurd; as a friend of
mine once observed, it is like fixing a light house on a
floating island. It is an attempt to *fix* that which is in
itself *variable*; at least it must be variable so long as it
is supposed that a local practice has no standard but a
local practice; that is, no standard but *itself*. While this
doctrine is believed, it will be impossible for a nation to
follow as fast as the standard changes—for if the gentlemen
at court constitute a standard, they are above it themselves, and their practice must shift with their passions
and their whims.

But this is not all. If the practice of a few men in the
capital is to be the standard, a knowlege of this must be
communicated to the whole nation. Who shall do this? An
able compiler perhaps attempts to give this practice in a
dictionary; but it is probable that the pronunciation, even
at court or on the stage, is not uniform. The compiler
therefore must follow his particular friends and patrons;
in which case he is sure to be opposed and the authority
of his standard called in question; or he must give two
pronunciations as the standard, which leaves the student
in the same uncertainty as it found him. Both these events
have actually taken place in England with respect to the
most approved standards, and of course no one is universally followed.

Besides, if language must vary, like fashions, at the
caprice of a court, we must have our standard dictionaries
republished, with the fashionable pronunciation, at least
once in five years; otherwise a gentleman in the country
will become intolerably vulgar by not being in a situation
to adopt the fashion of the day. The *new* editions of them
will supersede the *old*, and we shall have our pronunciation to re-learn, with the polite alterations, which are
generally corruptions.

Such are the consequences of attempting to make a

local practice the *standard* of language in a *nation*. The attempt must keep the language in perpetual fluctuation, and the learner in uncertainty.

If a standard therefore cannot be fixed on local and variable custom, on what shall it be fixed? If the most eminent speakers are not to direct our practice, where shall we look for a guide? The answer is extremely easy; the *rules of the language itself* and the *general practice of the nation* constitute propriety in speaking. If we examine the structure of any language, we shall find a certain principle of analogy running through the whole. We shall find in English that similar combinations of letters have usually the same pronunciation, and that words, having the same terminating syllable, generally have the accent at the same distance from that termination. These principles of analogy were not the result of design—they must have been the effect of accident or that tendency which all men feel towards uniformity.[2] But the principles, when established, are productive of great convenience, and become an authority superior to the arbitrary decisions of any man or class of men. There is one exception only to this remark: When a deviation from analogy has become the universal practice of a nation, it then takes place of all rules and becomes the standard of propriety.

The two points therefore which I conceive to be the basis of a standard in speaking are these; *universal undisputed practice*, and the *principle of analogy*. *Universal*

---

[2] This disposition is taken notice of by Dr. Blair, Lect. 8. Where he observes, "that tho the formation of abstract or general conceptions is supposed to be a difficult operation of the mind, yet such conceptions must have entered into the first formation of languages"—"this invention of abstract terms requires no great exertion of metaphysical capacity"—"Men are *naturally* inclined to call all those objects which resemble each other by one common name—We may daily observe this practised by children, in their first attempts towards acquiring language."

I cannot, with this great critic, call the process by which *similar* objects acquire the *same* name, an act of *abstraction*, or the name an *abstract term*. Logical distinctions may lead us astray. There is in the mind an *instinctive disposition*, or *principle of association*, which will account for all common names and the analogies in language.

practice is generally, perhaps always, a rule of propriety; and in disputed points, where people differ in opinion and practice, *analogy* should always decide the controversy.

These are authorities to which all men will submit—they are superior to the opinions and caprices of the great and to the negligence and ignorance of the multitude. The authority of individuals is always liable to be called in question—but the unanimous consent of a nation, and a fixed principle interwoven with the very construction of a language, coeval and coextensive with it, are like the common laws of a land or the immutable rules of morality, the propriety of which every man, however refractory, is forced to acknowlege and to which most men will readily submit. Fashion is usually the child of caprice and the being of a day; principles of propriety are founded in the very nature of things and remain unmoved and unchanged amidst all the fluctuations of human affairs and the revolutions of time.

It must be confessed that languages are changing, from age to age, in proportion to improvements in science. Words, as Horace observes, are like leaves of trees; the old ones are dropping off and new ones growing. These changes are the necessary consequence of changes in customs, the introduction of new arts, and new ideas in the sciences. Still the body of a language and its general rules remain for ages the same and the new words usually conform to these rules; otherwise they stand as exceptions which are not to overthrow the principle of analogy already established.

But when a language has arrived at a certain stage of improvement, it must be stationary or become retrograde; for improvements in science either cease or become slow and too inconsiderable to affect materially the tone of a language. This stage of improvement is the period when a nation abounds with writers of the first class, both for abilities and taste. This period in England commenced with the age of Queen Elizabeth and ended with the reign of George II. It would have been fortunate for the language had the stile of writing and the pronunciation of words been fixed as they stood in the reign of Queen Ann and her successor. Few improvements have been made since that time, but innumerable corruptions in pronunciation have been introduced by Garrick, and in stile by Johnson, Gibbon and their imitators.[3]

The great Sidney wrote in a pure stile, yet the best models of purity and elegance are the works of Sir Wil-

[3] The progress of corruption in language is described with precision, and philosophical reasons assigned with great judgement, by that celebrated French writer, Condillac, in his Origin of Human Knowledge. Part 2.

"It is nearly the same here as in physics, where motion, the source of life, becomes the principle of destruction. When a language abounds with original writers in every kind, the more a person is endowed with abilities, the more difficult he thinks it will be to surpass them. A mere equality would not satisfy his ambition; like them he wants the pre-eminence. He therefore tries a new road. But as every stile analagous to the character of the language and to his own, has been already used by preceding writers, he has nothing left but to deviate from analogy. Thus in order to be an original, he is obliged to contribute to the ruin of a language, which, a century sooner, he would have helped to improve.

"Tho such writers may be criticized, their superior abilities must still command success. The ease there is in copying their defects, soon persuades men of indifferent capacities, that they shall acquire the same degree of reputation. Then begins the reign of strained and subtle conceits, of affected antitheses, of specious paradoxes, of frivolous and far-fetched expressions, of new-fangled words, and in short, of the jargon of persons, whose understandings have been debauched by bad metaphysics. The public applauds; foolish and ridiculous writings, the beings of a day, are surprisingly multiplied; a vicious taste infects the arts and sciences, which is followed by a visible decrease of men of abilities."

One would think that Condillac had designed here to give a description of the present taste of the English writers and a state of their literature.

The foregoing sentiments seem to have been borrowed from Velleius Paterculus. Hist. Rom. L. 1. Cap. 17.

The same passage is copied by Sig. Carlo Denina, Professor of Eloquence and Belles Lettres in the University of Turin, in his "Revolutions of Literature," page 47; and if I mistake not, the sentiments are adopted by Lord Kames, in his Sketches of the History of Man.

Similar reasons may be assigned for the prevalence of an affected and vitious pronunciation.

liam Temple, Dr. Middleton, Lord Bolingbroke, Mr. Addison and Dean Swift. But a little inferior to these are the writings of Mr. Pope, Sir Richard Steele, Dr. Arbuthnot, with some of their cotemporaries. Sir William Blackstone has given the law stile all the elegance and precision of which it is capable. Dr. Price and Dr. Priestley write with purity and Sir William Jones seems to have copied the ease, simplicity and elegance of Middleton and Addison.

But how few of the modern writers have pursued the same manner of writing? Johnson's stile is a mixture of Latin and English; an intolerable composition of Latinity, affected smoothness, scholastic accuracy and roundness of periods. The benefits derived from his morality and his erudition will hardly counterbalance the mischief done by his manner of writing. The names of a Robertson, a Hume, a Home and a Blair almost silence criticism, but I must repeat what a very learned Scotch gentleman once acknowleged to me, "that the Scotch writers are not models of the pure English stile." Their stile is generally stiff, sometimes very awkward, and not always correct.[4] Robertson labors his stile and sometimes introduces a word merely for the sake of rounding a period. Hume has borrowed French idioms without number; in other respects he has given an excellent model of historical stile. Lord Kames' manner is stiff; and Dr Blair, whose stile is less exceptionable in these particulars, has however introduced into his writings several foreign idioms and ungrammatical phrases. The Scotch writers now stand almost the first for erudition, but perhaps no man can write a foreign language with genuin purity.

Gibbon's harmony of prose is calculated to delight our ears, but it is difficult to comprehend his meaning and

---

[4] Dr. Witherspoon is an exception. His stile is easy, simple and elegant. I consider Dr. Franklin and Dr. Witherspoon as the two best writers in America. The words they use and their arrangement appear to flow spontaneously from their manner of thinking. The vast superiority of their stiles over those of Gibbon and Gillies is owing to this circumstance, that the two American writers have bestowed their labor upon *ideas* and the English historians upon *words*.

the chain of his ideas, as fast as we naturally read, and almost impossible to recollect them at any subsequent period. Perspicuity, the first requisite in stile, is sometimes sacrificed to melody, the mind of a reader is constantly dazzled by a glare of ornament or charmed from the subject by the music of the language. As he is one of the *first*, it is hoped he may be the *last*, to attempt the gratification of our *ears* at the expense of our *understanding*.

Such however is the taste of the age; simplicity of stile is neglected for ornament, and sense is sacrificed to sound.[5]

Altho stile, or the choice of words and manner of arranging them, may be necessarily liable to change, yet it does not follow that pronunciation and orthography cannot be rendered in a great measure permanent. An orthography in which there would be a perfect correspondence between the spelling and pronunciation would go very far towards effecting this desireable object. The Creek language suffered little or no change in these particulars, for about a thousand years, and the Roman was in a great degree fixed for several centuries.

Rapid changes of language proceed from violent causes, but these causes cannot be supposed to exist in North America. It is contrary to all rational calculation that the United States will ever be conquered by any one na-

[5] The same taste prevailed in Rome under the Emperors, when genius was prostituted to the mean purposes of flattery. "It must be acknowleged indeed, that after the dissolution of the Roman republic, this art began to be perverted by being too much admired. Men grew excessively fond of the numerous stile, and readily sacrificed the strength and energy of their discourse to the harmony of their language. Pliny the younger often complains of this contemptible affectation: And Quintilian speaks of certain prose writers in his time, who boasted that their compositions were so strictly numerous, that their hearers might even beat time to their measures. And it should seem that even in Tully's time, this matter was carried to excess; since even then the orators dealt so much in numbers, that it was made a question, wherein they differed from the Poets."—Mason's Essay on the Power and Harmony of Prosaic Numbers. Introduction, page 4.

This was an abuse of the art. Melody should be studied, but not principally.

tion speaking a different language from that of the country. Removed from the danger of corruption by conquest, our language can change only with the slow operation of the causes before-mentioned and the progress of arts and sciences, unless the folly of imitating our parent country should continue to govern us and lead us into endless innovation. This folly however will lose its influence gradually as our particular habits of respect for that country shall wear away, and our *amor patriæ* acquires strength and inspire us with a suitable respect for our own national character.

We have therefore the fairest opportunity of establishing a national language and of giving it uniformity and perspicuity in North America that ever presented itself to mankind. Now is the time to begin the plan. The minds of the Americans are roused by the events of a revolution; the necessity of organizing the political body and of forming constitutions of government that shall secure freedom and property has called all the faculties of the mind into exertion; and the danger of losing the benefits of independence has disposed every man to embrace any scheme that shall tend, in its future operation, to reconcile the people of America to each other and weaken the prejudices which oppose a cordial union.

My design, in these dissertations, is critically to investigate the rules of pronunciation in our language; to examin the past and present practice of the English, both in the pronunciation of words and construction of sentences; to exhibit the principal differences between the practice in England and America and the differences in the several parts of America with a view to reconcile them on the principles of *universal practice* and *analogy*. I have no system of my own to offer; my sole design is to explain what I suppose to be authorities, superior to all private opinions, and to examin local dialects by those authorities.

Most writers upon this subject have split upon one rock: They lay down certain rules, arbitrary perhaps or drawn from the principles of other languages, and then condemn all English phrases which do not coincide with those rules. They seem not to consider that grammar is formed on language and not language on grammar. Instead of examining to find what the English language *is*, they endeavor to show what it *ought to be* according to their rules. It is for this reason that some of the criticisms of the most celebrated philologers are so far from being just that they tend to overthrow the rules and corrupt the true idiom of the English tongue. Several examples of this will appear in the course of these Dissertations.

To learn the English language in its purity, it is necessary to examin and compare the best authors from Chaucer to the present time. In executing the following work, the most approved compilations have been consulted and the opinions of the learned authors considered as respectable, not as decisive, authorities. The language itself has been examined with great industry with a view to discover and defend its principles on the best grounds, *analogies in structure*, and *immemorial usage*. I have had recourse to the works of authors who wrote prior to Chaucer and have even borrowed some light upon this subject from the early ages of Gothic ignorance. Believing, with the author of "Diversions of Purley," that the peculiar structure of our language is Saxon and that its principles can be discovered only in its Teutonic original, it has been my business, as far as the materials in my possession would permit, to compare the English with the other branches of the same stock, particularly the German and the Danish. These researches have thrown light upon the meaning and construction of particular phrases and enabled me to vindicate some expressions in the language which are often used but generally condemned by grammarians.

My knowlege of the practice of speaking in different parts of America is derived from personal observation. My knowlege of the past and present state of the language in England, is taken from the writers who have treated expressly of the subject.[6] The authorities necessary to prove particular points will be quoted as occasion shall require.

The talk of examining words cannot be agreeable to a

[6] Wallis, Johnson, Kenrick, Sheridan, with a multitude of inferior compilers.

writer nor can his criticisms be very entertaining to the
reader. Yet this task I have imposed upon myself, for I
believe it the only method to correct common mistakes.
A general rule may be sufficient for a classical scholar,
who makes it his business to apply the rule to all cases:
But most readers must have their particular errors laid
before their eyes, or they will not discover them.

To offer to correct the mistakes of others is also a
hazardous task and commonly exposes a man to abuse and
ill will. To avoid this I can only say that my motives for
the undertaking were not local nor personal; my enquiries
are for truth, and my criticisms, it is hoped, will be
marked with candor.

DOCUMENT 5

Fisher Ames

Fisher Ames (1758–1808) was more famous in his day for his eloquence and mastery of rhetoric than for his staunch Hamiltonian Federalism as representative from Massachusetts to the first United States Congress. Most of the "Works" which were collected by his friends and published the year after his death are political speeches, but as an amateur classical scholar, he was concerned with the cultural aspects of life in his place and time. In the essay here quoted, he draws some ominous parallels between the civilizations of Greece and Rome and those of modern nations, particularly the American. Ames, in this essay, is notable as one of the earliest to seek in other than superficial factors the causes for the failure of the new nation at once to produce a literature. The argument that equalitarianism and commercialism, as basic elements in the structure of American life, are in themselves destructive of the human spirit, and that therefore America cannot hope to develop a life of the mind and the arts, will be heard again many times but perhaps not with the same passionate eloquence and gloomy despair.

TEXT: from *The Works of Fisher Ames*, Compiled by a Number of His Friends, Boston, 1809, pp. 458–72.

American Literature

Few speculative subjects have exercised the passions more or the judgment less than the inquiry, what rank our country is to maintain in the world for genius and literary attainments. Whether in point of intellect we are equal to Europeans or only a race of degenerate creoles; whether our artists and authors have already performed much and promise every thing; whether the muses, like the nightingales, are too delicate to cross the salt water, or sicken and mope without song if they do, are themes upon which we Americans are privileged to be eloquent and loud. It might, indeed, occur to our discretion that, as the only admissible proof of literary excellence is the measure of its effects, our national claims ought to be abandoned as worthless the moment they are found to need asserting.

Nevertheless, by a proper spirit and constancy in praising ourselves, it seems to be supposed, the doubtful title of our vanity may be quieted in the same manner as it was once believed the currency of the continental paper could, by a universal agreement, be established at par with specie. Yet, such was the unpatriotick perverseness of our citizens, they preferred the gold and silver for no better reason than because the paper bills were not so good. And now it may happen that, from spite or envy, from want of attention or the want of our sort of information, foreigners will dispute the claims of our pre-eminence in genius and literature, notwithstanding the great convenience and satisfaction we should find in their acquiescence.

In this unmanageable temper or indocile ignorance of Europe, we may be under the harsh necessity of submitting our pretensions to a scrutiny; and, as the world will judge of the matter with none of our partiality, it may be discreet to anticipate that judgment, and to explore the grounds upon which, it is probable, the aforesaid world will frame it. And after all we should suffer more pain than loss, if we should in the event be stripped of all that does not belong to us; and, especially, if by a better knowledge of ourselves we should gain that modesty which is the first evidence and, perhaps, the last of a real improvement. For no man is less likely to increase his knowledge than the coxcomb who fancies he has already *learned out*. An excessive national vanity, as it is the sign of mediocrity if not of barbarism, is one of the greatest impediments to knowledge.

It will be useless and impertinent to say a greater proportion of our citizens have had instruction in schools than can be found in any European state. It may be true that neither France nor England can boast of so large a portion of their population who can read and write and who are versed in the profitable mystery of the rule of three. This is not the footing upon which the inquiry is to proceed. The question is not, what proportion are stone blind, or how many can see when the sun shines; but what geniuses have arisen among us like the sun and stars to shed life and splendour on our hemisphere.

This state of the case is no sooner made than all the firefly tribe of our authors perceive their little lamps go out of themselves, like the flame of a candle when lowered into the mephitick vapour of a well. Excepting the writers of two able works on our politicks, we have no authors. To enter the lists in single combat against Hector, the Greeks did not offer the lots to the nameless rabble of their soldiery; all eyes were turned upon Agamemnon and Ajax, upon Diomed and Ulysses. Shall we match Joel Barlow against Homer or Hesiod? Can Thomas Paine contend against Plato? Or could Findley's history of his own insurrection vie with Sallust's narrative of Catiline's? There is no scarcity of spelling-book-makers, and authors of twelve cent pamphlets; and we have a distinguished few, a sort of literary nobility, whose works have grown to the dignity and size of an octavo volume. We have many writers who have read and who have the sense to understand what others have written. But a right perception of the genius of others is not genius; it is a sort of business talent and will not be wanting where there is much occasion for its exercise. Nobody will pretend that the Americans are a stupid race; nobody will deny that we justly boast of many able men and exceedingly useful publications. But has our country produced one great original work of genius? If we tread the sides of Parnassus, we do not climb its heights: we even creep in our path, by the light that European genius has thrown upon it. Is there one luminary in our firmament that shines with unborrowed rays? Do we reflect how many constellations blend their beams in the history of Greece, which will appear bright to the end of time, like the path of the zodiack, bespangled with stars.

If, then, we judge of the genius of our nation by the success with which American authors have displayed it, our country has certainly hitherto no pretensions to literary fame. The world will naturally enough pronounce its opinion that what we have not performed we are incapable of performing.

It is not intended to proceed in stripping our country's honours off till every lover of it shall turn with disgust from the contemplation of its nakedness. Our honours have not faded—they have not been worn. Genius, no doubt, exists in our country, but it exists, like the unbodied soul on the stream of Lethe, unconscious of its powers till the causes to excite and the occasions to display it shall happen to concur.

What were those causes, that have for ever consecrated the name of Greece? We are sometimes answered, she owes her fame to the republican liberty of her states. But Homer, and Hesiod, to say nothing of Linus, Orpheus, Musæus, and many others, wrote while kings governed those states. Anacreon and Simonides flourished in the court of Pisistratus, who had overthrown the democracy of Athens. Nor, we may add in corroboration, did Roman genius flourish till the republick fell. France and England are monarchies and they have excelled all modern nations by their works of genius. Hence we have a right to conclude, the form of government has not a decisive and certainly not an exclusive influence on the literary eminence of a people.

If climate produces genius, how happens it that the great men who reflected such honour on their country appeared only in the period of a few hundred years before the death of Alexander? The melons and figs of Greece are still as fine as ever; but where are the Pindars?

In affairs that concern morals, we consider the approbation of a man's own conscience as more precious than all human rewards. But, in the province of the imagination, the applause of others is of all excitements the strongest. This excitement is the cause; excellence, the effect. When every thing concurs, and in Greece every thing did concur, to augment its power, a nation wakes at once from the sleep of ages. It would seem as if some Minerva, some present divinity, inhabited her own temple in Athens and by flashing light and working miracles had conferred on a single people, and almost on a single age of that people, powers that are denied to other men and other times. The admiration of posterity is excited and overstrained by an effulgence of glory as much beyond our comprehension as our emulation. The Greeks seem to us a race of giants, Titans, the rivals, yet the favourites of their gods. We think their apprehension was quicker, their native taste more refined, their prose poetry, their poetry musick, their musick enchantment. We imagine they had more expression in their faces, more grace in their movements, more sweetness in the tones of conversation than the moderns. Their fabulous deities are supposed to have left their heaven to breathe the fragrance of their groves and to enjoy the beauty of their landscapes. The monuments of heroes must have excited to heroism; and the fountains, which the muses had chosen for their purity, imparted inspiration.

It is, indeed, almost impossible to contemplate the bright ages of Greece without indulging the propensity to enthusiasm.

We are ready to suspect the delusion of our feelings and to ascribe its fame to accident, or to causes which have spent their force. Genius, we imagine, is for ever condemned to inaction by having exhausted its power as well as the subjects upon which it has displayed itself. Another Homer or Virgil could only copy the Iliad and Æneid; and can the second poets, from cinders and ashes, light such a fire as still glows in the writings of the first. Genius, it will be said, like a conflagration on the mountains, consumes its fuel in its flame. Not so—It is a spark of elemental fire that is unquenchable, the contemporary of this creation, and destined with the human soul to survive it. As well might the stars of heaven be said to expend their substance by their lustre. It is to the intellectual world what the electrick fluid is to nature, diffused every where, yet almost every where hidden, capable by its own mysterious laws of action and by the very breath of applause, that like the unseen wind excites it, of producing effects that appear to transcend all power except that of some supernatural agent riding in the whirlwind. In an hour of calm we suddenly hear its voice and are moved with the general agitation. It smites, astonishes, and confounds, and seems to kindle half the firmament.

It may be true, that some departments in literature are so filled by the ancients, that there is no room for modern excellence to occupy. Homer wrote soon after the heroick ages, and the fertility of the soil seemed in some measure to arise from its freshness: it had never borne a crop. Another Iliad would not be undertaken by a true genius, nor equally interest this age, if he executed it. But it will not be correct to say, the field is reduced to barrenness from having been over-cropped. Men have still imagination and passions, and they can be excited. The same causes that made Greece famous, would, if they existed here, quicken the clods of our vallies, and make our Bœotia sprout and blossom like their Attica.

In analyzing genius and considering how it acts, it will be proper to inquire how it is acted upon. It feels the power it exerts, and its emotions are contagious because they are fervid and sincere. A single man may sit alone and meditate till he fancies he is under no influence but that of reason. Even in this opinion, however, he will allow too little for prejudice and imagination; and still more must be allowed when he goes abroad and acts in the world. But masses and societies of men are governed by their passions.

The passion that acts the strongest, when it acts at all, is fear; for, in its excess, it silences all reasoning and all other passions. But that which acts with the greatest force, because it acts with the greatest constancy, is the desire of consideration. There are very few men who are greatly deceived with respect to their own measure of sense and abilities, or who are much dissatisfied on that account; but we scarcely see any who are quite at ease about the estimate that other people make of them. Hence it is that the great business of mankind is to fortify or create claims to general regard. Wealth procures respect and more wealth would procure more respect. The man who, like Midas, turns all he touches into gold, who is oppressed and almost buried in its superfluity, who lives to get, instead of getting to live, and at length belongs to his own estate and is its greatest incumbrance, still toils and contrives to accumulate wealth, not because he is deceived in regard to his wants, but because he knows and feels that one of his wants, which is insatiable, is that respect which follows its possession. After engrossing all that the seas and mountains conceal, he would be still unsatisfied, and with some good reason, for of the treasures of esteem who can ever have enough? Who would mar or renounce one half his reputation in the world?

At different times, the opinions of men in the same country will vary with regard to the objects of prime consideration, and in different countries there will ever be a great difference; but that which is the first object of regard will be the chief object of pursuit. Men will be most excited to excel in that department which offers to excellence the highest reward in the respect and admiration of mankind. It was this strongest of all excitements that stimulated the literary ages of Greece.

In the heroick times, it is evident, violence and injustice prevailed. The state of society was far from tranquil or safe. Indeed, the traditional fame of the heroes and demigods is founded on the gratitude that was due for their protection against tyrants and robbers. Thucydides tells us that companies of travellers were often asked whether they were thieves. Greece was divided into a great number of states, all turbulent, all martial, always filled with emulation and often with tumult and blood. The laws of war were far more rigorous than they are at present. Each state, and each citizen in the state, contended for all that is dear to man. If victors, they despoiled their enemies of every thing; the property was booty, and the people were made slaves. Such was the condition of the Helots and Messenians under the yoke of Sparta. There was every thing, then, both of terrour and ignominy to rouse the contending states to make every effort to avoid subjugation.

The fate of Platæa, a city that was besieged and taken by the Spartans and whose citizens were massacred in cold blood, affords a terrible illustration of this remark. The celebrated siege of Troy is an instance more generally known and no less to the purpose. With what ardent love and enthusiasm the Trojans viewed their Hector and the Greeks their Ajax and Achilles, is scarcely to be conceived. It cannot be doubted that to excel in arms was the first of all claims to the popular admiration.

Nor can it escape observation that in times of extreme danger the internal union of a state would be most perfect. In these days we can have no idea of the ardour of ancient patriotism. A society of no great extent was knit together like one family by the ties of love, emulation, and enthusiasm. Fear, the strongest of all passions, operated in the strongest of all ways. Hence we find that the first traditions of all nations concern the champions who defended them in war.

This universal state of turbulence and danger, while it would check the progress of the accurate sciences, would greatly extend the dominion of the imagination. It would be deemed of more importance to rouse or command the feelings of men than to augment or correct their knowledge.

In this period it might be supposed, that eloquence displayed its power; but this was not the case. Views of refined policy and calculations of remote consequences were not adapted to the taste or capacity of rude warriours who did not reason at all or only reasoned from their passions. The business was not to convince, but to animate; and this was accomplished by poetry. It was enough to inspire the poet's enthusiasm to know beforehand that his nation would partake it.

Accordingly, the bard was considered as the interpreter and favourite of the gods. His strains were received with equal rapture and reverence as the effusions of an immediate inspiration. They were made the vehicles of their traditions to diffuse and perpetuate the knowledge of memorable events and illustrious men.

We grossly mistake the matter if we suppose that poetry was received of old with as much apathy as it is at the present day. Books are now easy of access and literary curiosity suffers oftener from repletion than from hunger. National events slip from the memory to our records; they miss the heart, though they are sure to reach posterity.

It was not thus the Grecian chiefs listened to Phemius or Demodocus, the bards mentioned by Homer. It was not thus that Homer's immortal verse was received by his countrymen. The thrones of Priam and Agamemnon were both long ago subverted; their kingdoms and those of their conquerors have long since disappeared and left no wreck nor memorial behind; but the glory of Homer has outlived his country and its language, and will remain unshaken like Teneriffe or Atlas, the ancestor of history and the companion of time to the end of his course. O! had he in his lifetime enjoyed, though in imagination, but a glimpse of his own glory, would it not have swelled his bosom with fresh enthusiasm and quickened all his powers? What will not ambition do for a crown? and what crown can vie with Homer's.

Though the art of alphabetick writing was known in the East in the time of the Trojan war, it is no where mentioned by Homer who is so exact and full in describing all the arts he knew. If his poems were in writing, the copies were few; and the knowledge of them was diffused, not by reading, but by the rhapsodists who made it a profession to recite his verses.

Poetry, of consequence, enjoyed in that age, in respect to the vivacity of its impressions and the significance of the applauses it received, as great advantages as have ever since belonged to the theatre. Instead of a cold perusal in a closet, or a still colder confinement, unread, in a bookseller's shop, the poet saw with delight his work become the instructer of the wise, the companion of the brave and the great. Alexander locked up the Iliad in the precious cabinet of Darius, as a treasure of more value than the spoils of the king of Persia.

But though Homer contributed so much and so early to fix the language, to refine the taste, and inflame the imagination of the Greeks, his work, by its very excellence, seems to have quenched the emulation of succeeding poets to attempt the epick. It was not till long after his age, and by very slow degrees, that Æschylus, Sophocles, and Euripides carried the tragick art to its perfection.

For many hundred years there seems to have been no other literary taste, and, indeed, no other literature than poetry. When there was so much to excite and reward genius, as no rival to Homer appeared, it is a clear proof that nature did not produce one. We look back on the history of Greece and the names of illustrious geniuses thicken on the page like the stars that seem to sparkle in clusters in the sky. But if with Homer's own spirit we could walk the milky-way, we should find that regions of unmeasured space divide the bright luminaries that seem to be so near. It is no reproach to the genius of America if it does not produce ordinarily such men as were deemed the prodigies of the ancient world. Nature has provided for the propagation of men—giants are rare; and it is forbidden by her laws that there should be races of them.

If the genius of men could have stretched to the giant's size, there was every thing in Greece to nourish its growth and invigorate its force. After the time of Homer, the Olympick and other games were established. All Greece, assembled by its deputies, beheld the contests of wit and valour and saw statues and crowns adjudged to the victors who contended for the glory of their native cities as well as for their own. To us it may seem that a handful of laurel leaves was a despicable prize. But what were the agonies, what the raptures of the contending parties we may read but we cannot conceive. That reward which writers are now little excited to merit because it is doubtful and distant, "the estate which wits inherit after death," was in Greece a present possession. That publick so terrible by its censure, so much more terrible by its neglect, was then assembled in person and the happy genius who was crowned victor was ready to expire with the transports of his joy.

There is reason to believe that poetry was more culti-vated in those early ages than it ever has been since. The great celebrity of the only two epick poems of antiquity was owing to the peculiar circumstances of the ages in which Homer and Virgil lived; and without the concur-rence of those circumstances their reputation would have been confined to the closets of scholars, without reaching the hearts and kindling the fervid enthusiasm of the multi-tude. Homer wrote of war to heroes and their followers, to men who felt the military passion stronger than the love of life; Virgil, with art at least equal to his genius, addressed his poem to Romans who loved their country with sentiment, with passion, with fanaticism. It is scarcely possible that a modern epick poet should find a subject that would take such hold of the heart, for no such subject worthy of poetry exists. Commerce has supplanted war as the passion of the multitude; and the arts have divided and contracted the objects of pursuit. Societies are no longer under the power of single passions that once flashed enthusiasm through them all at once like electric-ity. Now the propensities of mankind balance and neu-tralize each other and, of course, narrow the range in which poetry used to move. Its coruscations are confined, like the northern light, to the polar circle of trade and poli-ticks, or, like a transitory meteor, blaze in a pamphlet or magazine.

The time seems to be near, and, perhaps, is already arrived, when poetry, at least poetry of transcendent merit, will be considered among the lost arts. It is a long time since England has produced a first rate poet. If America has not to boast at all what our parent country boasts no longer, it will not be thought a proof of the deficiency of our genius.

It is a proof that the ancient literature was wholly occu-pied by poetry, that we are without the works, and, in-deed, without the names of any other very ancient authors except poets. Herodotus is called the father of history; and he lived and wrote between four and five hundred years after Homer. Thucydides, it is said, on hearing the ap-plauses bestowed at the publick games on the recital of

the work of Herodotus, though he was then a boy, shed
tears of emulation. He afterwards excelled his rival in that
species of writing.

Excellent, however, as these Grecian histories will ever
be esteemed, it is somewhat remarkable that political science never received much acquisition in the Grecian democracies. If Sparta should be vouched as an exception
to this remark, it may be replied, Sparta was not a democracy. Lest that, however, should pass for an evasion
of the point, it may be further answered, the constitution
of Lycurgus seems to have been adapted to Sparta rather
as a camp than a society of citizens. His whole system is
rather a body of discipline than of laws, whose sole object
it was, not to refine manners or extend knowledge, but to
provide for the security of the *camp*. The citizens with
whom any portion of political power was entrusted were
a military cast or class; and the rigour of Lycurgus's *rules
and articles* was calculated and intended to make them
superiour to all other soldiers. The same strictness that
for so long a time preserved the Spartan government se-
cures the subordination and tranquillity of modern armies.
Sparta was, of course, no proper field for the cultivation
of the science of politicks. Nor can we believe that the
turbulent democracies of the neighbouring states favoured
the growth of that kind of knowledge, since we are certain
it never did thrive in Greece. How could it be that the
assemblies of the people, convened to hear flattery or to
lavish the publick treasures for plays and shews to amuse
the populace, should be any more qualified than inclined
to listen to political disquisitions, and especially to the
wisdom and necessity of devising and putting in operation
systematical checks on their own power which was threatened with ruin by its licentiousness and excess, and which
soon actually overthrew it? It may appear bold, but truth
and history seem to warrant the assertion that political
science will never become accurate in popular states; for
in *them* the most salutary truths must be too offensive
for currency or influence.

It may be properly added, and in perfect consistency
with the theory before assumed, that fear is the strongest

of all passions, that in democracies writers will be more afraid *of* the people than afraid *for* them. The principles indispensable to liberty are not therefore to be discovered, or, if discovered, not to be propagated and established in such a state of things. But where the chief magistrate holds the sword and is the object of reverence if not of popular fear, the direction of prejudice and feeling will be changed. Supposing the citizens to have privileges and to be possessed of influence, or, in other words, of some power in the state, they will naturally wish so to use the power they have as to be secure against the abuse of that which their chief possesses; and this universal propensity of the publick wishes will excite and reward the genius that discovers the way in which this may be done. If we know any thing of the true theory of liberty, we owe it to the wisdom or, perhaps more correctly, to the experience of those nations whose publick sentiment was employed to check rather than to guide the government.

It is, then little to be expected that American writers will add much to the common stock of political information.

It might have been sooner remarked that the dramatick art has not afforded any opportunities for native writers. It is but lately that we have had theatres in our cities; and till our cities become large like London and Paris, the progress of taste will be slow and the rewards of excellence unworthy of the competitions of genius.

Nor will it be charged as a mark of our stupidity that we have produced nothing in history. Our own is not yet worthy of a Livy, and to write that of any foreign nation where could an American author collect his materials and authorities? Few persons reflect that all our universities would not suffice to supply them for such a work as Gibbon's.

The reasons why we yet boast nothing in the abstruse sciences are of a different and more various nature. Much, perhaps all, that has been discovered in these is known to some of our literati. It does not appear that Europe is now making any advances. But to make a wider diffusion of these sciences and to enlarge their circle would require the learned leisure which a numerous class enjoy in Europe, but which cannot be enjoyed in America. If wealth is accumulated by commerce, it is again dissipated among heirs. Its transitory nature, no doubt, favours the progress of luxury more than the advancement of letters. It has among us no uses to found families, to sustain rank, to purchase power, or to pension genius. The objects on which it must be employed are all temporary and have more concern with mere appetite or ostentation than with taste or talents. Our citizens have not been accustomed to look on rank or titles, on birth or office as capable of the least rivalship with wealth, mere wealth, in pretensions to respect. Of course the single passion that engrosses us, the only avenue to consideration and importance in our society, is the accumulation of property: our inclinations cling to gold, and are bedded in it as deeply as that precious ore in the mine. Covered as our genius is in this mineral crust, is it strange that it does not sparkle? Pressed down to earth, and with the weight of mountains on our heads, is it surprising that no sons of ether yet have spread their broad wings to the sky, like Jove's own eagle, to gaze undazzled at the sun or to perch on the top of Olympus and partake the banquet of the gods.

At present the nature of our government inclines all men to seek popularity as the object next in point of value to wealth; but the acquisition of learning and the display of genius are not the ways to obtain it. Intellectual superiority is so far from conciliating confidence that it is the very spirit of a democracy, as in France, to proscribe the aristocracy of talents. To be the favourite of an ignorant multitude a man must descend to their level; he must desire what they desire and detest all that they do not approve; he must yield to their prejudices and substitute them for principles. Instead of enlightening their errours, he must adopt them; he must furnish the sophistry that will propagate and defend them.

Surely we are not to look for genius among demagogues: the man who can descend so low has seldom very far to descend. As experience evinces that popularity, in other words consideration and power, is to be procured by the meanest of mankind, the meanest in spirit and under-standing, and in the worst of ways, it is obvious that at present the excitement to genius is next to nothing. If we had a Pindar, he would be ashamed to celebrate our chief and would be disgraced if he did. But if he did not, his genius would not obtain his election for a selectman in a democratick town. It is party that bestows emolument, power, and consideration; and it is not excellence in the sciences that obtains the suffrages of party.

But the condition of the United States is changing. Luxury is sure to introduce want; and the great inequalities between the very rich and the very poor will be more conspicuous and comprehend a more formidable host of the latter. The rabble of great cities is the standing army of ambition. Money will become its instrument and vice its agent. Every step, and we have taken many, towards a more complete, unmixed democracy is an advance towards destruction: it is treading where the ground is treacherous and excavated for an explosion. Liberty has never yet lasted long in a democracy; nor has it ever ended in any thing better than despotism. With the change of our govern-ment, our manners and sentiments will change. As soon as our emperour has destroyed his rivals and established order in his army, he will desire to see splendour in his court and to occupy his subjects with the cultivation of the sciences.

If this catastrophe of our publick liberty should be mi-raculously delayed or prevented, still we shall change. With the augmentation of wealth there will be an increase of the numbers who may choose a literary leisure. Literary curiosity will become one of the new appetites of the na-tion; and as luxury advances, no appetite will be denied. After some ages we shall have many poor and a few rich, many grossly ignorant, a considerable number learned, and a few eminently learned. Nature, never prodigal of her gifts, will produce some men of genius who will be ad-mired and imitated.

DOCUMENT 6

George Tucker

In Virginia as well as Massachusetts before 1815, there were gentlemen scholars who were dismayed by the slow progress of their countrymen toward cultural and literary independence. George Tucker (1775–1861), a native of Bermuda, emigrated as a young man to Virginia and settled in Richmond where he participated in various literary associations and activities. His "Thoughts of a Hermit" essays were written in 1813 and published in the Philadelphia *Port Folio*. Some of his essays were collected in 1822 and issued as by "A Citizen of Virginia." In the one here quoted, he defines literature as including all forms of writing, and his explanations of the differences between peoples as due to "moral" rather than "physical" causes, and of the lack of American achievement up to that time as the mere result of the slowness of an inevitable upward progress, do much to refute the theory that man deteriorates in the Western Hemisphere. But he implicitly acknowledges American cultural inferiority by thus trying to explain it.

TEXT: from *Essays on Various Subjects of Taste, Morals, and National Policy*, by a citizen of Virginia. Georgetown, D.C., 1822, pp. 41–66.

On American Literature

The inferiority of the United States to most of the countries in Europe in literary productions is a fact too manifest to be disputed. In Great Britain and Ireland, containing about eighteen millions of people, there are between five hundred and a thousand new books annually published; whilst here, with more than one-third of that population, the number of new publications in a year can scarcely be reckoned at twenty. Although on a comparison with other European countries the difference may be considerably less, it is still with few exceptions very great.

Is this difference owing to the inferiority of our natural genius, as some have alleged, or to causes that are temporary and accidental? Does so very scanty a product indicate poverty in the soil, or merely its negligent and unskilful culture?

These questions, so humiliating to our pride, and so derogatory to our literary character, have been differently answered on the different sides of the Atlantic—the Europeans, and among them names of high authority, maintaining that we are an inferior work of nature; whilst the Americans claim an equal place in the scale of rational being. But surely it is due to ourselves and to truth to give this controversy a full and fair discussion; and either expose the false pretentions of our adversaries or honestly surrender our own.

It will scarcely be denied that if we examine the individuals of the two continents with a view to compare their senses and their bodily powers, no difference can be observed. The former are possessed in as great perfection here as in Europe: they are as acute, as delicate, as lasting and as capable of intense action. We perceive also the same vigour of body, the same strength, the same agility. Perhaps, from the greater difficulty of procuring subsistence in Europe and the greater liability to confinement and restraint in sedentary occupations, these qualities are enjoyed in a superior degree by the Americans. The same remark may be applied to the symmetry of their forms and features. Now, if we suppose, with some philosophers, that the operations of the mind are but the workings of matter in its most subtle form, it would not be irrational to infer, that where, on a comparison of different subjects, the grosser parts of the material man appeared to be the same or, if different, superior, there would be the same relative equality or superiority in those finer parts which constitute the mind. Judging by this rule, we must believe that our intellects are at least as flexible, as alert, and as susceptible of vigorous and continued action as those of Europeans.

But it will be said that all this is mere hypothesis and that minds, as well as bodies, can be best compared by comparing their respective productions. These, it must be admitted, do afford the most certain criterion, and if the difference is shown to exist and cannot be accounted for from the particular circumstances of our present situation, then we must confess that the alleged inferiority of genius will have the best proof of which the subject is susceptible and one which ought to prevail against the beforementioned hypothesis. But if, on the other hand, all the inferiority in literature that is proved can be satisfactorily explained by resorting to moral causes alone, then indeed may we, the natives of the New World, with propriety insist on the argument from analogy and confidently ask our haughty adversaries for some further proof that nature who has been so bountiful to us in the formation of our bodies should have acted a niggardly part in the structure of our minds. If none can be given, the question ought to be considered as settled and they who should still profess to doubt would have as little claim to philosophy as to liberality.

One of the most obvious causes of the present humble state of our literature is the small number of persons among us whose minds have been disciplined by academical instruction. There are about ten or twelve colleges in the United States which profess to teach the dead languages and the principles of science. The whole number of students in our seminaries of the first class seldom exceeds five or six hundred, whereas in Great Britain and Ireland, at the two English universities, the four in Scotland, and the one in Dublin, according to the accounts of recent travellers, the number of students can be little, if at all, short of ten thousand. Here then, we perceive that the United Kingdom contains nearly twenty times the number of persons whose minds have had that training which experience shows to be, if not indispensable, at least the most favourable to the formation of an author.

Nor are the superior advantages enjoyed by their students inconsiderable. The same narrowness of private income which limits the benefits of a college education to a small portion of the community with us also abridges the term of their studies. Few of our young men spend more than two or three years at college whilst in Europe they often remain six or seven years at the university. When there too, they have the benefit of libraries and museums and all the apparatus which can impart knowledge through the senses; which costly appendages the slender funds of our institutions do not permit. There must also be a great inferiority on the part of our professors. The same attainments, the same course of preparation and study which would qualify a man to be a college professor fit him for becoming a lawyer, physician, statesman, or divine. But the small number of persons in this country thus qualified is not more than sufficient to fill the learned professions, and these will generally be preferred to professorships because they are more lucrative, they give more influence in society, and their duties are less irksome. Our professors, accordingly, seldom possess the highest order of talents; and we are fain to put up with such as we can get. Many of them are foreigners who would in vain seek similar employment in the countries from whence they came. In Europe, however, the large redundancy of men of learning and science, which remains after supplying an adequate number of practitioners of law and physic, of statesmen and divines, makes it easy to procure able professors in every department of literature, more especially as they are, by the gradual accumulation of public and private bounty, most liberally rewarded.

The reason assigned why we are so imperfectly supplied with academical teachers suggests another important consideration in our defence. Inasmuch as the great body of cultivated intellect in the community is engrossed by the liberal professions, there is no such thing among us as a separate class of authors. It is from the *redundancy* of educated men that this class is naturally formed. When learning and science have aided in protecting the health of the community, in defending and distributing its property, in superintending its morals and religion, in framing and administering its laws, when they have discharged these active duties, then and not before they find leisure to amuse and instruct through the medium of books. With us, these important duties absorb all the improved talents of the country, of course there are none among us, as in Europe, who practice writing as a trade and but few who can find leisure to write or even to qualify themselves for writing.

Perhaps, however, it will be said that the circumstances I have mentioned merely account for our inferiority in classical and scientific learning, but that the powers of creative genius might still display themselves and that in works of imagination our inferiority is, to the full, as great as in works of learning and science.

To this we answer that all those who within the last century have distinguished themselves in Europe as poets or as authors of works of imagination have been indebted to the universities for their education. There is indeed, at this time, little room for original genius to exert itself in poetry without deriving great assistance from reading and from science since the whole stock of natural images have been long ago occupied and appropriated by preceding writers. Those who now seek reputation as poets may yet, indeed, acquire the praise of elegant correctness; they may avoid those blemishes and defects into which the rude taste of their predecessors have betrayed them; they may, moreover, convey a great deal of instruction and good sense in very musical lines. But all this requires and implies a course of severe and patient study. Poetry of this sort is the child of art rather than of natural genius; and this art, and the labour and leisure necessary to mature it, our busy occupations will not permit us to bestow.

In fact, nearly all those who have obtained distinction in Great Britain as writers of poetry or in any of the departments of polite literature have been authors by profession. They have followed writing as a business, sometimes to purchase a name, but often, most often, to earn a livelihood. The connexion between poets and poverty has grown into a proverb and it will generally be found that their poverty has made them poets rather than that their poetry has made them poor. This most powerful stimulus does not yet exist among us; and it is happy for us in every respect, but in that of our literary reputation, that it will not exist for ages.

Yet in those lighter effusions which are produced on a sudden and require a single effort of thought, such as sonnets, epigrams, and the like, as much originality and vigour of mind is perceived as in similar productions from the other side of the Atlantic; or if a difference is perceptible, it is to be ascribed to the inferior taste which less disciplined minds may be expected to have.

If the best modern poetry, then, is invariably the effect of diligence and labour and a singleness of pursuit, there seems to be no reason for discriminating between our poetical productions and those of learning and science in making a comparison between the writers on the opposite sides of the Atlantic; more especially, as the less the labour and art required in any particular species of poetry, the less is our inferiority; and in those smaller productions, which are elicited at a single heat of the mind and which owe most to genius and least to art, little or no difference can be perceived.

It is, indeed, only by laborious study and long continued exercise that genius is matured and literary excellence is attained. This truth is strongly exemplified in the case of Dr. Johnson, the most conspicuous personage among the writers of his day. If we compare his earlier with his later productions, we shall perceive the extent of his improvement as well as the gradual steps by which it advanced; take, for example, his first attempts at biography, published in the Gentleman's Magazine and compare them with "the Lives of the Poets." We can scarcely persuade ourselves they have proceeded from the same pen. Like dowlas and cambric, they are both indeed of the same useful materials but most widely different in the texture.

We have also a native example of the improvement effected by exercise in Marshall's life of Washington. Perhaps there is no book in which there is a greater difference in the different parts. Whilst the first volumes very gen-

erally disappointed expectation, the last has never yet
received the praise to which it is fairly entitled. Though
it is manifestly a defence of that political party to which
Mr. Marshall belongs, and was probably so intended by
him, yet he has called to his aid a great deal of good sense,
much ingenious argument, and no ordinary knowledge of
human nature. His style too is all the while acquiring
elegance and improving still more in life and spirit. The
subject of the first volumes is without doubt less fitted
to display the higher powers of an author, but where it
could not be embellished, it might have been abridged.
Livy had no better materials for the first books of his history, and yet how entertaining is every part of his immortal
work!

In considering "the Life of Washington" as a specimen
of literary talents in America, a caution must be used
which is also applicable to almost all our native productions: we must regard not so much what the writer is, as
what, from the intrinsic evidence of the work itself, it
appears he might have been. The fact is that with the
advantage of merely a private and but an ordinary education, he had passed the best years of his life industriously
engaged in the duties of a profession which, however it
may have improved his powers of discrimination and logical deduction, had left him little leisure to acquire that
various knowledge which are indispensable to the accomplished historian and that refined polish of style which the
delicacy of modern taste requires in every writer. Those
great masters of historical sagacity and chaste elegance,
the Greek and Roman historians, were turned over day
and night and studied for twenty years before Hume, or
Robertson, or Gibbon ventured upon their respective histories; but probably those fine models were not known by
our American annalist except through the medium of
translations and many of them not even in this less perfect
and less impressive form. To make the comparison fair, as
it regards this subject, we should ask how they would have
written under his disadvantages, or how he would have
written had he enjoyed the benefits of their study and
education. But the writers themselves have furnished us

with some *data* for answering these questions. They have occasionally tried their powers in clearing up some important fact involved in doubt and obscurity, and have endeavoured, by the mere force of analogical reasoning, to demonstrate the truth of some one of the conflicting opinions. Let any of these attempts be compared with the similar attempts of Mr. Marshall, as with his argument in the case of Jonathan Robbins,[1] and in precision, discrimination, orderly arrangement—in short, in every part of that rare faculty of connecting a long series of undisputed propositions in a chain by which the mind is unresistingly conducted to the most recondite and seemingly inaccessible truths, he will be found as superior to them as they are to him in the general character of historians.

We have also a striking example of what native genius, improved by ardent study, can do, in the instance of the late John Thompson, of Virginia, who, at an age when men are chiefly engaged in acquiring ideas, rather than endeavoring to impart them, attained a pure and copious eloquence of style and a facility of prose composition to which no English writer, not even Chatterton, affords a parallel. The "letters of Curtius" have indeed little to recommend them but the beauty of diction, but it is surely no mean praise to do that well of which all are ambitious and which no other has ever accomplished, without the advantages of longer study and experience.

Another reason why there are few original publications among us may be found in our former colonial dependence, and in the identity of our language and manners with those of Great Britain. When we were humble colonies of that nation, it was natural that we should look up to it with sentiments of reverence and admiration. Power never fails to impart an additional lustre on all which it possesses. The wit and talents of princes have often received unmerited praise, not only from their parasites, but also from those who have been unconsciously dazzled by the illusive splendour of rank. The high ideas which the American colonists entertained of every thing English were

[1] Delivered in the House of Representatives in the year 1800.

diligently cherished, as well by the policy of the regal government as by the national vanity of the English merchants and adventurers who migrated hither. Opinions thus firmly settled could not be easily changed. Though this habitual veneration for the English name is very much diminished, it is far from being extinguished. We still continue to adopt their fashions in dress, their customs and manners, and follow them through all their capricious changes. Public taste in that country, being thus allowed to control the public taste in this in so many particulars of ordinary occurrence, cannot fail to influence our opinions on the more important subjects of politics, religion, morals, and literature.

Thus accustomed to require on every thing the stamp of English approbation before we give it a general currency, our indigenous productions are received with distrust and have to fight their way through the prejudice against what is homebred before they can hold the place they are entitled to occupy. Besides, the great number of new English productions which are imported and which gratify the thirst for novelty in every branch of literature, prove formidable rivals to the native writer. The number of the readers and, consequently, of the purchasers of his book is diminished in the same degree that the foreign importation supplies the demand. Nor can he contend with them for the public favour upon equal terms since the new works which are imported have already passed through their course of probation before a public whose decisions we are accustomed to consider as infallible. These unpropitious circumstances must operate to check the efforts of native genius, so far as they withhold its just quantum of profit and praise, and must be particularly discouraging to those who have once essayed the public favour in the character of authors. Whilst, therefore, they lessen the number of indigenous productions, they have also a tendency to take away that improvement of individuals which exercise alone can give.

Nor do we yet possess that favourable theatre for introducing the young author to the world which a large city affords. The reputation which a work of merit here creates is not sounded and reverberated by a thousand echoes in the author's ears. It is doomed faintly to murmur in the cold and cautious praises of a few half-doubting judges. To the mass of the people it is unknown. But there is nothing like the clamorous applause of a nation, whether it be enjoyed or anticipated, to cheer the author in his labours and to encourage him to bolder and more felicitous exertions. From the deep-rooted connexion between sensibility and genius, the *laudum immensa cupido*, that boundless thirst of praise which is so generally the parent of every public excellence is at least as likely to be felt by the writing class as any other.

Most of the English authors by profession are to be found in London; and wheresoever educated, it is there that they are cherished and matured. It is curious to read a piece of Edmund Burke's early correspondence with a Mr. Smith with whom he had been intimate in Ireland. Judging by the long letter from this gentleman to Burke, who had then lately arrived in England, he appears to be the superior man of the two, yet after a lapse of some years, Burke, who happened to be placed in a spot favourable to the development of his powers, reached the highest point of celebrity whilst his friend, remaining in obscurity behind, made no advances in reputation and would never have been heard of but for the friendship which connected him with his more fortunate countrymen. Can it be supposed that Johnson and Garrick would have exhibited their unrivalled talents for instructing and delighting mankind if they had remained at Litchfield? Reasoning on probabilities, it seems much more likely that they owed their subsequent eminence, in a great degree, to the favourable circumstances in which we know they were placed than that two men, born and bred in the same small town and leaving it on the same day, with similar hopes and views, should in natural endowments so far outstrip their contemporaries. Possibly, the day they set out from their native city for London, they left some equals behind them. Indeed, the hope of praise or of gain and the spirit of rivalship, which are obviously no where so likely to be produced as in a wealthy and populous city, have always been found necessary to excite genius to great exertion. But without exertion, the most ardent and persevering exertion, how, in this age of multifarious knowledge and fastidious refinement, can literary excellence be attained?

In support of the reasons that have been assigned for the acknowledged inferiority of our literature, it fortunately happens that there are forms of exhibiting the powers of intellect in which the circumstances of the American and European are not dissimilar: cases in which either previous study is not of the same importance, or nearly the same diligent labour is bestowed by both. In these, if our wishes do not mislead us, we think we shall not suffer by a comparison.

In the application of mechanical principles to the abridgment of labour and for the advancement of human comfort, no people are supposed to have shown a readier, or more fruitful invention than the Anglo-americans. The inventor of the instrument usually called Hadley's quadrant was a Pennsylvanian by the name of Godfrey. The machine for making cotton cards, the saw gin, the improved machinery in flour mills, the application of steam to inland navigation, and the almost countless multitude of inventions and contrivances to be seen at the patent office in Washington evince singular acuteness and activity of intellect. The ruder mechanical employments being as familiar to us as to Europeans, if they had struck out to us fewer or inferior schemes of improvement, there might have been some reason for imputing to us duller intellects, but when we herein display a more fertile and more successful invention, we may claim without meriting the imputation of vanity the praise of possessing some powers of the mind in a higher degree than Europeans. The fact is that our faculties are stimulated in this direction by the high bounty with which success in saving labour is always here rewarded; from whence we may infer that learning and science will similarly flourish when they shall be similarly encouraged. In speaking of inventive genius, it would be unpardonable not to mention Dr. Franklin, whose discovery of the identity of lightning and the electric fluid, if we consider its immediate utility—the light it has thrown upon more than one branch of physics—and that it was the pure result of philosophical sagacity, is not to be equalled in modern times.

In the elegant art of painting, though it has been so little cultivated in our country, we have excelled in a wonderful degree. Indeed, it would seem as if nearly all those who have sought excellence in this pursuit have attained it. Copley, West, Trumbull, and Stuart, are almost the only American painters we know,[2] and they are all eminent. Two of them are probably not surpassed, in their respective branches of historical and portrait painting by any of their cotemporaries. Nor should it be forgotten that it was in Europe that these artists received both the instruction and the patronage which were necessary to mature their natural endowments and which their own country was unable to afford them. This fact furnishes us with additional evidence that we shall experience no want of native genius when the circumstances of our situation shall be calculated to call it into action.

In the exercise of the highest legislative functions; that is, in the structure of their political constitutions and forms of government, the Americans are believed to have improved upon every model with which either ancient or modern history furnished them, prudently adopting that which was suited to their situation, and boldly rejecting that which was not, changing nothing for the sake of change, yet occasionally venturing on new experiments when innovation promised substantial benefit. Surely, if any human concern requires consummate wisdom, it is the construction of a form of government, especially of a free government. To make a correct estimate of the good it is practicable to attain and the evils that may be avoided —to measure the influence of human passions and interests in their endless combinations and variety—to frame rules for the regulation of these passions and interests, indulg-

[2] With these we may now name Allston, Leslie, Vanderlyn, and some younger aspirants after fame in this elegant art. If Sully is not added to these, it is because, though brought up in this country, he is a native of England.

ing some, and controlling others—and lastly, to guard and
protect the work against decay from time or violence, both
from within and without, requires, in a pre-eminent degree, comprehension of mind, foresight, judgment, and
invention. Although it may be said that the most important of these political fabrics, the federal constitution,
has not yet been sufficiently tested by time to prove its
permanence, yet it has already lasted long enough to falsify
the predictions of its enemies. It has so far given encouragement and protection to the most rapid course of prosperity that history records. If it has been so successful in
advancing the happiness of the nation, the first and wor-
thiest object for which it was framed, let us hope that it
will prove no less successful in its next object, the making
that happiness permanent. The series of essays, entitled
"The Federalist," though the production of haste and intended for the purpose of influencing and enlightening
the public mind at a particular crisis, are supposed to
contain as much political wisdom as any other work extant, and whilst the writers demonstrate our claims to
superior legislative sagacity, they further vindicate our
intellectual character by the profound and cogent reasoning they themselves have displayed. The principal author
of the Federalist, Alexander Hamilton, was, indeed, not a
native of the United States, yet as he was born on one of
the Islands of the New World, he is fairly adduced as a
specimen of American genius.

In the administration of the government, thus wisely
framed, our countrymen seem to show no less ability than
the transatlantic politicians. They may be compared in the
different characters of ministers, negotiators, and writers
of state papers.

If we consult the zealots of the different political parties which divide our country, and always must divide it
whilst it preserves its freedom, each will aver, nay, and
labour to prove, that the acts of the administration he has
opposed were one continued series of error and folly. But
when it is considered that the two parties are diametri-
cally opposite in some fundamental principles and objects
and, consequently, that the opponents of every adminis-

tration will censure its measures because these are well calculated to advance the policy they condemn, it follows that the obloquy and reproaches of one party, no less than the warm encomiums of the other, often bear testimony to the *ability* which has guided the helm of state. The destinies of nations, however, are so much influenced by circumstances that can neither be controlled nor foreseen, and the character of the chief minister of a nation depends upon so many qualities that are not intellectual, upon the virtues of temper, disposition, and manners, that not much can be inferred from a comparison on this head.

As to our diplomatists, it is here that the American character has shone forth with unremitting lustre. In the discussion of national controversies, the parties profess to address themselves to the understanding of the world in the application of acknowledged principles of right and wrong, and in few cases will it be denied by those who are equally indifferent to either party that we have manifested a decided superiority over our adversaries, not merely in the justice of our cause, but in the ability with which it has been supported. In proof of this position may be mentioned the correspondence between Mr. Jefferson and Mr. Hammond, in 1792; between Mr. Jefferson and Mr. Genet in 1793; the embassy to France, in 1798; together with the several correspondences of Mr. King, Mr. [William] Pinkney, Mr. Monroe, Mr. Madison, and some of their successors.

On the subject of our state papers, not comprehended under the head of diplomatic correspondence, it may be observed that the speeches and messages of our presidents and state governors, and our other public addresses, may well compare with similar productions in Europe. But if we take the various reports made by Mr. Hamilton when secretary of the treasury and by Mr. Jefferson when secretary of state, together with the occasional reports of committees in congress on important subjects, I know nothing corresponding to these papers in England, whose institutions most resemble our own, which discovers as much profound research or as ingenious and solid reasoning.

With regard to the talent of public speaking, although

the same circumstances which occasion a smaller number
of literary men among us must have their effect upon the
number and even character of our orators, yet from the
genial influence of our republican government, we are
probably not inferior to Great Britain in this noble art. It
is even believed that our house of representatives, with
less than one-third the number of members selected from
not half the population, furnishes more good speakers
than the British house of commons. As a popular orator,
generally, and in sarcastic and vituperative eloquence more
especially, Mr. ********* is not to be equalled and has
probably never been surpassed in extemporary speaking
in the whole British dominions. If as much ability is not
displayed from the pulpit,[3] it is because this species of
eloquence is not as well rewarded in the United States as
in Great Britain and because the greater number of our
preachers are self-taught and illiterate. At the bar, however, we are little inferior either in eloquence or learning.
In all the larger states, the most eminent pleaders would
not suffer by a comparison with the barristers and ser-
jeants of Westminster Hall, for promptitude and ingenuity, for accurate discrimination, and clear orderly deduction. If we do not often see the same rich exuberance of
diction, the same felicity of allusion, the same variety and
extent of embellishment which have contributed to the
celebrity of Erskine or Curran, it is because our lawyers
have not the same opportunity of acquiring these valuable
auxiliaries. They have generally begun with a smaller stock
of the materials for ornament, and have proceeded on
with less leisure for acquiring them. Yet even in these
oratorical decorations, we have some advocates who shine
with conspicuous merit.[4]

[3] Such an improvement has taken place within the last ten
years in this department of public speaking, that probably our
pulpit orators are not now inferior to those of any other country.
[4] Among these it would not *now* be invidious to particularize
William Pinkney, whose recent death has left so lamented a void
in the Senate and the Bar of his country. This gentleman, though
great in all the qualifications of a public speaker except in manner, was most distinguished for the beauty and brilliancy of his
diction. Naturally gifted with an easy and copious flow of lan-

In the science of medicine, our rapid advancement furnishes us with a further argument that our inferiority in other branches of knowledge is to be ascribed to accident and will cease with its temporary cause. A medical school at Philadelphia was at first resorted to by those who could not afford the greater expense of European instruction. This encouragement soon occasioned an active emulation in the professors with each other and with other similar institutions. Their efforts have at length produced their natural reward, both of profit and reputation and the institution is now esteemed, little, if at all, inferior to the celebrated University of Edinburgh. Most of the professors are authors and their works seem to have equal merit with European productions on the same subjects. In several of the other states, the faculty can boast of names which have obtained respect on both sides the Atlantic. It is to be expected that a correspondent encouragement in other departments of literature will be attended with correspondent success.

If we consult the pages of history, we shall find abundant evidence to show that the state of literature in every country depends upon moral causes alone, however difficult it may be to trace their operation in every particular instance. The same region which at one time blazed with the light of genius is at another enveloped in the darkest ignorance. What evidence does Athens now give that it was once peopled by poets, orators, and philosophers? Its political circumstances, indeed, are changed, most

---

guage, he had with unwearied assiduity devoted a whole life to perfecting it, until at length his words were so well selected and so happily put together that he could impart to the commonest thoughts an air of novelty and dignity, and to the most elaborate, the semblance of ease and nature. This species of excellence, however, approaches so near the confines of affectation, as to make him an unsafe model for the youthful votary of eloquence. It is greatly to be regretted that Mr. Pinkney's speeches on the Missouri question had not been reported, and that there is now no vestige of them except in the memory of those who heard them, as they would probably afford the best specimen of the force and compass of his mind, as well as the unrivalled felicity of his language.

wofully changed, but the natural remain the same. Rome, too, formerly so distinguished for talents in every species of polite literature, now exhibits no proof of genius except by the cultivation of the fine arts. If they have survived that chilling influence which has blighted every nobler production of intellect, it is because tyranny and superstition have never ceased to cherish them with extraordinary munificence. But she can no longer produce a Virgil, a Tacitus, or a Cicero. The literary glories of Egypt and of Persia have in like manner passed away, leaving scarcely a visible trace of their former existence. But, on the other hand, whilst the ancient mistress of the world has descended from her proud pre-eminence, in letters as well as arms, the posterity of those whom she once justly despised as barbarians, have, by their noble struggles, reached the same high pinnacles of glory. France and England, indeed, which were among the most rude and unlettered of the Roman colonies, have carried every branch of human science and all the useful arts of life to a higher point of improvement than was ever before known.

In the above striking examples, the literature of each nation has kept an equal pace with its civilization and general prosperity. In other instances, however, no such connexion is to be perceived. Yet where the causes of the declension or advancement of letters are so minute as to escape observation, they are evidently not natural and permanent, but accidental and temporary. Thus, until within little more than the last fifty years, Scotland had scarcely a poet or a dramatic writer to balance against Chaucer, Spenser, Shakspeare, Johnson, Cowley, Milton, Dryden, Pope, and twenty others produced in England, except Allan Ramsay, a name that would hardly have risen to notice if it had belonged to the other part of the Island. Yet since that time, Scotland has produced its full quota of literary genius. In a very dignified species of composition, history, it is indeed unrivalled, and at the present day, the names of Campbell and Scott stand higher on the list of poets than any of their cotemporaries in England.[5] Ireland, too, containing nearly half as many inhabitants as England, has not produced a single poet except Parnell and Goldsmith, before the amorous effusions of *Anacreon* Moore; for the witty rhymes of Swift, who has also been claimed by England, scarcely deserve the name of poetry. Can Ireland be supposed incapable of giving birth to eminent and original genius? The names of Goldsmith, Berkeley, Sheridan, Burke, Curran, and without doubt, we may add Swift, are a conclusive answer to this question.

If then, it appears that the intellectual character of the same nation at different times is widely different, and that the change is sometimes from high to low as with Athens and Rome, and sometimes from low to high as with England and France, that there is often a striking difference between different parts of the same nation at the same period as with England and Scotland, and that this difference is not permanent, we must be compelled to acknowledge, however the causes of this irregularity may elude our researches, that these causes are moral and not physical—that genius is not the exclusive gift of any country, but that its seeds are scattered by nature, with her wonted profusion over every region of the earth and readily take root in every climate and soil; yet, unless they meet with a more cherishing culture than can fall to the lot of many, the stinted plants, producing neither flowers nor fruit, live and die as useless and unnoticed as the weeds which grow around them.

[5] When this sentence was penned, the star of Lord Byron had just begun to appear above the horizon.

PART II

The Challenge of Nationalism
1815–1820

Historians seem to agree that there was a sharp rise in the spirit of nationalism in the United States after the second war with Great Britain in 1812–14. Even though the actual terms of the peace treaty "left every thing much as it had been before the war began," says George Dangerfield, it actually "meant that in the future Britain would cease to regard the United States as a colony which paid its own expenses, and that she would look upon American expansion with a favorable eye, so long as it provided an enlargement of British industrial opportunity."[1] In an even larger sense, it meant the end of the Napoleonic era during which the American continent had been one of Europe's outlying battlefields, and the beginning of an era in which the United States was in a position to realize its "manifest destiny" as a wholly independent political power.

The founding of the *North American Review* in 1815, the first American literary journal to be wholly original in content, may or may not have been one of the by-products of these events. Certainly the early issues, which carried the sub-title "Miscellaneous Journal" and appeared bi-monthly, revealed no sharp break with its predecessors; but its first editor, William Tudor, succeeded where Charles Brockden Brown had failed in rallying to his aid a strong group of cooperating contributors in the former members of the Anthology Club, the sponsors of the *Monthly Anthology* (1803–1811). Although there were many vigorous if usually short-lived literary magazines in Philadelphia, New York, Baltimore, and other towns during this period, the discussion of the problem of literary and cultural national-

[1] [*The Awakening of American Nationalism*, 1815–1828, by George Dangerfield. New York: Harper & Row, 1965, p. 2.]

ism in their pages, where it occurred, did not probe
much beneath the level of the earlier debate.[2]

The *North American* group had, however, developed
among themselves a far deeper and more searching understanding of the issues involved, and for five years
they conducted a debate in its pages which can only be
appreciated by bringing their best essays together. As
Harry Hayden Clark has pointed out, the reputation
for political and literary reaction which the *Review*
earned and ultimately deserved does not apply to these
early years when Tudor, the Channings, Gray, Phillips,
Palfrey, John Knapp, and Edward Everett were cham-
pioning the new romantic poetry and novel, and were
vigorously arguing for a national literature.[3]

The secret of the unanimity and firmness of the intellectual and aesthetic grounds upon which this group
of critics based their opinions, and even their differences, lay in their familiarity with the best current
Scottish, English, and even, indirectly, German critical
thought. Robert E. Streeter has identified the Scottish
rationalist, Archibald Alison, author of *Essays on the
Nature and Principles of Taste* (1790), and the Association psychology upon which his critical principles
were based, as the primary influence in the critical
thinking of the American group.[4] Although Mme. de
Staël's work on literature and social institutions had
been published in Boston in 1813, it was too soon for
the impact of her *De l'Allemagne* or of Coleridge's critical theories to be felt, but Association psychology was
widely known and supplied a sufficient rationale for the
relationship between author, material, and reader to provide the debate on literary nationalism with the theoretical discipline it had lacked.

[2] [*The Quest for Nationality,* by Benjamin T. Spencer. Syracuse, 1957, pp. 74–75.]
[3] ["Literary Criticism in the *North American Review,* 1815–
1835," *Transactions of the Wisconsin Academy of Sciences, Arts
and Letters,* Madison, Wisconsin, 1940, pp. 299–315. See also
The Origins of American Critical Thought, 1810–1835, by William Charvat. Philadelphia: University of Pennsylvania Press,
1936.]
[4] ["Association Psychology and Literary Nationalism in the
North American Review, 1815–1825," by Robert E. Streeter.
American Literature, XVII (November 1945), 243–54.]

It would be easy to put too much emphasis on the doctrinaire aspects of this influence, for the American critics did not always fully understand the philosophical concepts with which they were working, but the essential principle of Associationism—that thought is composed of elements drawn from immediate experience —provided a new justification for denying the neo-classical emphasis on forms, standards, and imitation, and substituting an emphasis on the immediate materials of experience and on the active process of shaping them into artistic expression. The arguments, therefore, that Americans should stop imitating British and European literary models, should seek to understand their own scenery, history, and social experience, and should put into writing what they actually saw, heard, and felt now had something more than a patriotic justification. On these principles, this first group of *North American* reviewers were in substantial agreement. Where they were likely to disagree was in the timing of the process: some condemned previous American writers as incompetents and laggards and urged the immediate realization of the potentials of a national literature; others preached patience and a constant discrimination between what was really good or bad in the American literary product while continuing to read and enjoy foreign current writings and classics. Walter Channing is perhaps the most vehement of the first group and R. H. Dana, Sr., the most cautious of the second; but on basic principles they agreed and each contributed his share to the laying of native foundations for the literature to come.

DOCUMENT 7

Walter Channing

The opening shot in the new battle of wits was fired by Walter Channing (1786–1876), physician brother of William Ellery and Edward Tyrell Channing (both of whom were soon to make important contributions to the unfolding debate) and father of Emerson's poet-friend, William Ellery Channing, the younger. Walter Channing was born in Newport, Rhode Island, and after studying at Harvard and at the University of Pennsylvania Medical School settled in Boston as a practicing obstetrician and contributor to medical and literary journals. His "Essay on American Language and Literature" appeared in the September 1815 issue of the *North American Review* and was followed by a second installment of his argument, "Reflections on the Literary Delinquency of America" in November. The two essays are here reprinted as two parts of the same document.

The fresh and fiery tone of Channing's statement comes as something of a shock after the apologies and excuses and abortive experiments which preceded it. Not only does he issue a vigorous call to cultural nationalism, but he also deplores the "melancholy record" of American literary effort to date and supplies the elements of a philosophical approach to the problem in the proposition that literature is the expression of experience in forms which that experience itself creates by arousing associations in the mind. About the future possibilities of achievement in literature and science he has no doubt if once Americans can be awakened to an appreciation of the unique and distinctive nature of life on the new continent. Other writers in the *North American* took it from there.

TEXT: from the *North American Review*, I (September 1815), 307–14, and II (November 1815), 33–43.

Essay on American Language and Literature

"So multiplied are the connexions existing between nation and nation in modern times, that intellectual originality may justly be regarded as one of the greatest phenomena in nature."

Lond. Quart. Review, Oct. 1814.

The remark which stands at the head of this article comes with peculiar force from the work which contains it. It has, with the writer of the following pages, unqualified belief. He has only regretted that the authors of that work have not always written under the influence of so liberal a sentiment. They might have found in its truth some good reasons for the barrenness of American Literature.

National literature seems to be the product, the legitimate product, of a national language. Literary peculiarities and even literary originality being, the one little more than peculiarities of language, the other the result of that uncontrolled exercise of mind which a slavery to a common tongue almost necessarily prevents. If then we are now asked, why is this country deficient in literature? I would answer, in the first place, because it possesses the same language with a nation totally unlike it in almost every relation; and in the second, delights more in the acquisition of foreign literature than in a laborious independent exertion of its own intellectual powers.

Unhappily, so enslaving are these influences that it is hardly to be hoped that we shall ever make our language conform to our situation, our intellectual vigour and originality. But is it true that a nation of real spirit and character will for ever consent to copy, even though it does not get rid of the language it inherited? would not what we have already accomplished in literature be thought well for a young people if we wrote in our *own* tongue? Is it not the fact that when we write we are regarded as Englishmen, and are required to do as well as if we lived in England?—With these inquiries we have at present no concern; our object is rather the causes why we have done no more.

The remotest germs of literature are the native peculiarities of the country in which it is to spring. These are diversified beyond all estimation by the climate and the various other circumstances which produce them.—Next to these are the social institutions, into which the various tribes of intellectual beings resolve themselves for certain specifick objects. Then follow the relations which issue from these, which constitute the moral, religious, and political states, together with all the other various objects of history. All the circumstances now mentioned as the elements of literature are essentially peculiar to every nation. And we accordingly find states, even bordering on each other, and the subjects at times of the same government, exhibiting striking peculiarities in their literary character. It will not refute this remark to point to a celebrated modern poet of Scotland and ask how he has done so much with a language similar to that, nay the same with that, of a sister kingdom. Mr. Scott has given us a mere translation of his national dialect and has most happily rendered native beauties of idiom, and even national peculiarities, by another language. But his works do not form the smallest part of the Scotch literature. We look for that in the verses of Allan Ramsay and in the far sweeter ones of Robert Burns. These authors are essentially original. They not only give us manners, which are but practical, intellectual operations, but give them to us in the language that was made for them and which only can give them their true form and pressure.

It will be easy to shew the importance of a peculiar language to the rise and progress of literature in a country. In the first place, every nation has a strong attachment to its language. This enters into the sum total of its patriotism. Its language is valued because it is the vehicle of the intellectual state of a country to all others. It is cultivated that the character it may be the means of establishing may be exalted. Above all other reasons it is loved because it is peculiar, gives a peculiar national character, and preserves the intellectual labours of man. Unfortunately for this country, language in itself can never have these attractions and this importance. The language in which we speak and write is the vernacular tongue of a nation which thinks it corrupted on every other lip but its own;—of a nation, which has limited its perfection by pronouncing it already perfect;—of a nation whose natural, political, religious, and literary relations and peculiarities are totally unlike our own.

The whole external character of our country is totally unlike that of England. Our descriptions, of course, which must, if we ever have a poetry, be made in the language of another country, can never be distinctive. They can never possess the peculiar claims which those of native individuality teem with; which are more beautiful to a foreigner because he is willing in reading them to heighten the beauties of an obscure passage by lending it the aid of his own imagination. How tame will his language sound who would describe Niagara in language fitted for the falls at London bridge,[1] or attempt the majesty of the Mississippi in that which was made for the Thames? It is not meant to be even hinted that the English language is incapable of all that language can do; but that peculiarities of country, especially the great distinctive characteristick ones, and manners likewise, can be perfectly rendered only by the language which they themselves have given use to. I mean a peculiar language.

If there be nothing peculiar in the language of a country, if it be strictly the same with that of a nation very distant from it, to say the least;—if it be a country, or rather *nation of ease*,[2] if I may so say, a receptacle in the first place of men who had in view by emigration any thing but a literary speculation, their descendants will have nothing less at heart than the cultivation of their

---

[1] These are specified because they are the only falls the author recollects to have seen in *England*.

[2] This allusion may not be perfectly familiar to every reader in this country. In Great Britain, as the parishes increase, so that the original parish church will not contain all the parishioners, new chapels are erected, connected with the original parish church, and these are called *Chapels of ease*.

language, and other nations will hardly look to them for literary originality.—The peculiarities of character of his ancestors will more or less tincture the descendant, and if they depended on others for their language, he will be very willing to look to the same source for his literature. If he should presume to write, however, and endeavour to convey the sentiments and emotions which peculiar circumstances have given birth to in his heart, if he should attempt the still harder task of description, how incapable would foreigners to his country and his home be, to judge of the truth of his feelings or descriptions; and though in his own countrymen the language might excite kindred feelings, to his transatlantick brethren, how little would there be in his labours to admire, but the *American language, and the American literature?*

In matters of science, and especially in those of the fine arts, the new country may even excel the old. By the pursuit of the first, they improve their physical condition, and original genius may find in the labours of his own pencil, a language which all nations understand and which none has been daring enough to monopolize as the peculiar vehicle of its own genius. In science, and more especially in the fine arts, America has done its part for the world. If I loved their excellence in these pursuits half as much as Englishmen, or rather English reviewers despise our literary attainments, I would pay a passing compliment to the venerable President of the Academy, and hunt for a sentence of eulogy for the memory of Dr. Franklin.

In nothing perhaps can we so little pride ourselves on account of our ancestry as for its entails on our literature. And in the Babel of the revolution, which gave us a different moral and political existence, it is for our literature most heartily to be lamented that we had not found a confusion of tongues. We might to this day have wanted a grammar and a dictionary; but our descendants would have made for themselves a literature. Any man at all conversant with other languages besides his own is perpetually sensible how much the foreign literature depends upon its language. We even read most familiar thoughts

as if they were new. New words, to us, give the old sentiment a new form and spirit. And, I have little doubt, few
have read the pleasures of memory, as contained in the
Italian of Maffei in his Merope, without pronouncing it
original, though he had read the same things before, as
well, perhaps, better sung by another poet.

The importance of a national language to the rise and
progress of the literature of a country can be argued from
all we know of every nation which has pretended to originality. All will be found to have attached so much consequence to their own language as to have despised most
heartily, or carelessly regarded, all others but their own.
Thus the French, in their best days, slighted the Augustan
age of England, and even now regard her best literary
productions with but slight admiration. It is also of great
importance for a nation to possess and cherish peculiarities. These result from situation, from mind, or rather
from the circumstances which most powerfully affect the
mind. The institutions of government, &c. in the first instance borrow their peculiarities from the character of the
people; and from the government these are transferred
to the people, a peculiarity of feeling is thus found at last
to result from the government and other various institutions of the country. Unfortunately for this country, there
is no national character, unless its absence constitute one:
all acknowledge the wisdom which framed its constitution,
but how few have been willing to permit its influence over
their characters? Their biases have all been foreign. How
unlike is this to what exists in other countries? The smaller
as well as the largest states of Europe have regarded all
others with a jealousy which has bound them immovably
to their national peculiarities. Hence all that we know of
them is original. Hence their literary eminence. Now if the
Germans had caught the foppery of France and the language of England; if they had ever adopted the government of the one, and the mode of religion of the other,
we should not have been dazzled with the splendid obscurity of their metaphysicks, much less overwhelmed with
the power of their drama or enchanted with their senti-
mentality. The German government and the German es-

tablished faith gave rise to remarkable character, and their language could alone embody it. The genuine patriotism which the political institutions of this country might have produced, and even with the aid of the English language, might have lent its aid to the rise of literature among us, has been lost in a servile dependence on foreign politicians for political creeds, and the liberality with which nature has ornamented our native scenery has been unnoticed in a love for the mere descriptions of foreign poetry. That we are not destitute of the materials for the poet may be gained from what Mr. Campbell has done with them. His Gertrude only affords us the mournful reflection of regret that a foreigner can do as much with all that is peculiar now left us as one of our own countrymen, and that he has done more than we have any good reason to expect from them.

There is something peculiarly opposed to literary originality in the colonial existence which was unfortunately so long the condition of America. This is mentioned incidentally under the head of the importance of a peculiar language to national literature. This circumstance precluded the possibility of our possessing such a language. All that can be expected from such a colony, made up of all sorts of materials, speaking not only the dialects of the original language, but the different languages of the three different nations from which it sprung, is to preserve a purity in one of them. It must first choose one, then guard it from even the least corruption to which it would be remarkably liable. It must be for ever jealous to prevent and put down that adaptation of new terms for new objects, and especially for the new ideas, that different scenes and new relations might give rise to. It must wait for all improvements from abroad, acquire a literary tone from the mother country, and like the civil jurisprudence of India, should it be as original in literature as that may be in crime, it must wait for a decision on its merits or demerits from the higher authorities of London. Farther, as a colony, it would never be supposed capable of altering or improving its literature any more than its political or religious systems. When did England look to the West-

Indies for any thing but its sugars, or to Canada for any thing but its furs?

If it should happen that a mind of superiour capability should find its birth in such a country, the very character of such a mind would drive it from home. It might not find time in its greater operations of thought to preserve the perfection of its language, and it would dread the contamination of an ill educated and strictly economical association. Such minds were phenomena in the American colonies, and the possibility of this occurrence was never admitted: hence the agents of government, and the leaders at the bar, &c. like the institutions themselves, were all transatlantick. The growth of prejudice was the natural production of the country, and in due time this flourished into revolution and independence.

Farther, so far are we from possessing a literature, that men of some considerable poetical merit, men who have cultivated their talents, have shrunk from American publication and sought in another region for the patrons of genius. This country has a literature notwithstanding all that has been said in this paper to the contrary. But it is not the least indebted for it to the labour of its colonies. I now refer to the oral literature of its aborigines.

In their original language we have names of places and things which are but feebly rendered by our own, I should say by the English. Their words of description are either derived from incidents, and of which they are famed to convey most exact ideas, or are so formed as to convey their signification in their sounds; and although so ridiculous in the English dress as to be a new cause for English satire and merriment, are in themselves the very language for poetry, for they are made only for expression, and their objects are the very element for poetry.

The language of the Indian is no less peculiar than his manners. With him as with all other beings, language is but the expression of manner. It was made to express his emotions during his observance of nature, and these emotions were taught him at a school in which the master was nature and a most unsophisticated heart the scholar. Hence it is as bold as his own unshackled conceptions, and as rapid as his own step. It is now as rich as the soil on which he was nurtured, and ornamented with every blossom that blows in his path. It is now elevated and soaring, for his image is the eagle, and now precipitous and hoarse as the cataract among whose mists he is descanting. In the oral literature of the Indian, even when rendered in a language enfeebled by excessive cultivation, every one has found genuine originality. Its beauties are most of them to be traced to its peculiarities. We are delighted with what appears its haughty independence, although we feel conscious at the same time it has never been submitted by its authors to the test of comparison. They have not advanced far enough in the diplomacy of letters to hazard a competition with neighbouring tribes. They are most perfectly contented with their language, and if it may be so called, their literary condition. That this remark is correct I will hazard the following anecdote. A Lancastrian school was established in one of the English provinces in this country, whose benevolent object it was to improve the intellectual condition of the neighbouring Indians. One Indian submitted for a few hours to the task of being taught writing. His rude efforts were applauded and he was asked if he would return to the school the next day. His answer is remarkable and highly characteristick. 'How much will you pay me for coming?' This anecdote is not introduced with a view to show that the Indian was fearful of the debilitating effects of an English education on his *national literature*, but to shew with what perfect contentment he reposed in the knowledge of that which was peculiarly his own. The length to which this discussion has already extended compels the writer to bring it to a close; and this without entering more fully than has already been done, on what was considered the second cause of the barrenness of American literature, viz. the dependence of Americans on English literature, and their consequent negligence of the exertion of their own intellectual powers.

Reflections on the Literary Delinquency of America

The title of this paper contains a serious charge. It charges Americans with delinquency in that to which every other civilized nation chiefly owes its character. It implies that this country wants literary distinction; that we have not entered the service of literature; that we want the results of intellectual labour; that were we to cease from a distinct national existence the great events of our history would stand alone on the blank of our national character, unsupported by their causes, unsanctioned by their effects; that the whole elements of our literature, were they collected into one mass, would amount merely to accidental efforts of a very few adventurous individuals; our history would be found little more than state topography; our politicks ephemeral effusions of party zeal, and our poetry without a character. An appeal might be made from this melancholy record to our philosophy and science and the labours of Franklin and Rittenhouse claimed as the heralds of our literary character. But it is hardly to be expected that the phenomena of the age should confer national character. They are accidents of intellect. They are claimed for science and literature in general, not yielded to one nation to give it a character. These extraordinary men very rarely appear in any country, and their having once appeared is not an assurance that their like will be looked upon again.

Neither is the gift they make us in their works often like the Prophet's mantle. So careless are the beings among whom they appear about the fate of their venerable intellectual remains that at times the only perfect collections of their works are made by foreigners; as if the country in which they may chance to have been born were fearful of the imputation of vanity and selfishness, by making itself the herald of their fame. Thus England boasts the first and best editions of the works of our own Franklin. But Franklin's address was 'the world.'

Yielding therefore the reputation which may be challenged on account of the remarkable individuals who may have appeared among us to the claims of the literary world at large, let us examine our pretensions to that reputation which rests on the broader basis of common occurrence, or to that character for letters which a majority of our publications gives rise to, and if it be a reputation with which we cannot be very much delighted, let us search for the causes of our literary deficiencies.

If it be with states as with individuals, we should look for our reputation from others, rather than from ourselves: and who of us is ignorant of our reputation abroad? The information we have gained on this subject and which may be acquired from an hour's reading of any foreign works of criticism in which our books are noticed has indeed but little to flatter our national pride. Our larger works, if reprinted in Europe, are soon lost in the ocean into which they are thrown. A more disastrous fate, however, commonly awaits them. They are submitted to the common test of literary tyranny, criticism, the very bed of Procrustes, and I have scarcely heard of a volume's being of the standard dimensions.

It is not worth while to inquire for the fate of our smaller, lighter works. We do not feel jealous of the reputation their authors flattered themselves they might be instrumental in producing. Knowing then what is thought of us abroad, and perhaps still willing to act as individuals, in like cases, whose self-complacency is generally in a direct ratio to the bad opinions of others, we may seek for some consolation in what we think of ourselves. But how little is there to delight us even from this source? Who is there among us who has dared to write a book that has received from our literary republick one smile to reward his literary labours? How few works have survived the question of our own criticism? How little has our literature gained from the success of this fortunate number! Who now, we may ask here, in this winter and famine of reputation at home and abroad, will venture to give his days and his nights to the labours of the mind that he may do something towards the literature of his country? Who that has talent among us is wanting in that honest pride and dignified selfishness which must deter a man from trusting his intellectual labours to criticks destitute of independence and to a publick too liberal and *patriotick* to allow of the excellence of domestick manufacture? The individual who is bold enough to make the attempt and feels for our literary interests what every body among us does for our commercial reputation –the man who strives to rouse the pride of the nation into action will encounter hardly less difficulty, or perform a smaller task, than he who gave us a new political existence.—He will not have merely to reform, but to create. He will encounter that most fatal principle to all individual exertion, a deep rooted jealousy of each other. He will meet the sarcastick regards of men who have burdened their minds with the good and bad of literature of Europe, and be confounded with the astonishment of others who, before his declaration to the contrary, had really thought us the most learned as well as the 'greatest' people under heaven.

From the common-place of opinion among us it is easily discovered that we enjoy but a feeble literary character any where. The candidates for literary distinction among us, or those that may be, are therefore destined to a high distinction. But let us inquire, who are to award it? Men who have themselves done much and are zealous that more may be done? Men who are weary of the weight of literary responsibility and are willing and desirous, to find not only successors but assistants in their labours? No—it is rather to come from men who have done nothing but have gained a real susceptibility of successful mental exertion in laborious study, or a fancied one in a fastidious taste. Men who can understand more than they can achieve; men too who are more successful in detecting deformity than in perceiving beauty. From men, in short, who are too indolent to be great and who will not be very anxious to yield what they have wanted resolution to make their own. If what has been now said be true, let us inquire why we have done so little for literature; and ask whether our prospects are more promising than our retrospections are melancholy.

Our literary delinquency may principally be resolved

into our dependence on English literature. We have been so perfectly satisfied with it that we have not yet made an attempt towards a literature of our own. In the pre-eminent excellence of this foreign literature we have lost sight of or neglected our own susceptibility of intellectual labour. So easy is it for us to read English books that we have hardly thought it worth while to write any for ourselves. Perhaps if it had been as difficult to command these inexhaustible literary resources as we should find it to command those of the Germans, we might have gone seriously to work and entered vigorously on the noble, dignified employment of our minds. Apologists for our literary delinquency, however, reply that we were colonies of Great Britain and virtually as much Englishmen as the inhabitants of any county in England. That place signifies nothing; at least, that the pious Antonine said so; that the mind is the same every where; that it lends its own influences to the circumstances in which it is placed and admits those of things and beings around it, just as far as it pleases and no farther. That a peculiarity of language is of no consequence to a literature; that the language of the mind is its own vigorous, overpowering operations; that these last only require language to be clothed with, not to be known by. We are told that the different modes of using language, viz. its various styles, are distinctive of those who invent or adopt them; that Milton will never be confounded with Shakespeare because they used a common language, and that when Americans write books, their works will at once be distinguished from those of England. In fine, we are told, that we are destined to the highest literary reputation.

Now, all this may be very true in theory, but what is the fact? Did our venerable fathers, when they deserted their own country, bring with them a thread of that literary tissue, so varied, so rich, and so beautiful, which had been the result of the dignified and delightful labour of England through so many ages of its history? Have we, their descendants, united our industry to theirs? And can we now look back and find that our labours have been continuous in their extent and as respectable in character

as those of Great Britain? If we cannot, it ill becomes us
to seek an apology in our colonial dependence, as some
have done, for we were descended from a literary nation.
We cannot trace our delinquency to our new form of government and lose our mental imbecility in the necessary
entails of a republican form, for we were once known by
the name and condition of subjects. Colonies, however, we
confess may not be the favourites of the muses. Rome became literary when she ceased to be republican. But we
have not always wanted a crown, nor have we always been
colonies. It is said that the mind acknowledges no distinction of place. Why have we made it appear so dependant?
We have not wanted books. We have not been left alone
to erect a fabrick of letters. We have been absolutely beset
with circumstances infinitely diversified and infinitely new.
Foreigners, however, have almost invariably discovered
their novelty and literary character. In natural science how
much might we not have done? Distinguished naturalists
of France and Sweden, however, were among the first who
traversed our forests and gathered the sweetest and rarest
flowers that blossom there; and we owe to Scotland an
American Ornithology. It is admitted that when we write,
our books may be distinguished from those of English
writers. Not, however, that difference of style alone will
ever designate the literature of a nation; but because our
writers can never keep entirely clear of one species of literary treason, viz. the coinage of new terms. These therefore may distinguish our writers. No one however will contend that these will ever challenge a genuine literary
reputation.

The truth is, we have wanted literary enterprise and
been sadly deficient in genuine intellectual courage. Circumstances beyond a doubt existed to prevent our fathers
from leaving us a literature. It was hard for them to print,
even if they wrote. They were perhaps too dependant on
the rough and toilsome circumstances in which they were
cast, to lay the foundation of a literature. Perhaps they
did enough in founding an empire. They also came here
well versed in the learning of their own country, for such
was England, though no longer their home; and if they

depended on what their brethren in England did for literature, they had claims which an American can never have. In founding colleges for us perhaps they dreamt they were laying the corner stone of literature.

The literary dependence to which we have been long reconciled has become so much a part of our character that the individual who ventures to talk about surmounting it is thought the wildest of schemers. He is assailed on every hand with the *cui bono?* that most fatal of questions to any plan which is not cast in the mould of domestick economicks, or which would tend to allure a society from the dull contemplation of its physical wants and the cheapest means of supplying them. Literary reputation! what is its worth? what *need* have we of a literature?

> "Oh reason not the need:—
> Allow not nature more than nature needs,
> Man's life is cheap as beasts':"

Again we are told the literary market is full. Our importations cannot be consumed. There is no demand for American literature. There is not a stall for its literary wares, in the whole market of letters. Shall then the natural productions of our soil find a kind reception every where? Shall their luxuriance not only satisfy ourselves, but go to supply the wants of distant nations, and by their exchange give us the varied products of every climate; and are we willing in literary commerce, the noblest traffick, to depend on the productions of all other nations, without dreaming even of labouring for them ourselves? We seem to relish the literary productions of other countries and descant with freedom and taste on the results of their literary labours.—We have books of criticism occasionally among us, and in these 'Gazette' our authors at home when they appear among us, and through them get a sort of introduction into the bureaus of foreign literature.

It might be well to dwell for a moment on these works which make up so much of our literature. But it is melancholy to dwell long even on this subject. Our recollections carry us into a sad region of ephemeral ruins whose vestiges are so faint that we hardly believe the tales of their having ever been. To trace their various authors would be a task unprofitable and fruitless indeed. Almost every number, or new year, of our longest lived journals has boasted a new author. The best written of them all have soon found repose either in the reputation they have gained their former authors or have dragged out a miserable existence in the hands of their successors. Their labours of criticism, however, it must be confessed, have had all the effect they were intended to have. Our literature has faded before their smiles as surely as before their censures. As certainly perhaps would it have died without either. Many of the best works we have written slumber with the worst. Each successive generation of individuals among us, or most of them, smile at the failure of their cotemporaries, shrink from the task of tracing our literary history by examining what has already been done, despair of doing better and willingly yield the energies of their own minds to the mere perusal of the dignified effects which have followed from the intellectual activity of others. So listless have we been that we have not done enough to supply the waste of time, much less to yield a superflux to preserve our literary character.

Some men have traced our deficiencies in letters to our want of the profession or trade of authorship and of that degree of wealth which would afford it patronage and support. Our predecessors or those who lived in the earliest periods of our history might have been excused for resorting to such a subterfuge. For theirs were the times when the *physique* stood in greater jeopardy than the *morale*. We live in times however which put this argument to perfect silence. Authorship is no longer a trade. At least the literary reputation of a country no longer depends on the fitful and uncertain exertions of genius in rags, nor the still more hazardous condition of patronal charity. The Muses, in our days, have flown the garret, at least in England, and now figure in the parlours of the nobility; and even a banker of Liverpool has amassed for us the literary wealth of Italy.

It must be confessed, however, we are destitute of many of the elements of literature. Thus we want a remote antiquity. In tracing our history, therefore, we are not tracing the developement of human society, the most interesting pursuit which is offered the mind for it is intrinsically the developement of the mind itself. In the want of a history of the kind just indicated, we want a vast variety of topicks of the very first interest in literature. We are destitute, for instance, of the materials for exercising the highest range of dramatick talent, viz. the historical. To be sure we have not always slumbered in national peace and we have had many distinguished heroes among us and one we are ever proud to name stands at their head. But with all our respect and love for this hero, we fear we could hardly brook to have his name among the *Dramatis personæ*. In the most elevated walk of the muses, the Epick, we cannot hope much distinction, and this for the same reason which appears so fatal to the American theatre. We live in the same age; we are too well acquainted with what has been, and is, among us, to trust them to the imagination. It would be an 'old story' to our criticks, for the events transpired yesterday, and some of our oldest heroes are not yet dead. Another fact is, we are all acquainted with them, or feel so. We have therefore no curiosity to excite for we have no information to give.

Notwithstanding the kind of apology thus furnished for much of our literary delinquency, we cannot but lament that we have been so deficient when we reflect how much has been done in the same time and under perhaps as unfavourable circumstances in England. What if the historians of an earlier period have exhausted the materials of historical originality and interest? What if Milton has inimitably written and Shakespeare exhausted the passions? What if Newton and Bacon and Boyle were the best scholars in the academy of nature? What if neighbouring and rival nations have entered with pride and talent and antiquity and wealth the lists against her? Has England ceased from her dignified labours of intellect? Has England done less than other nations? No. Every year has yielded something to the literary character of England. The mind never seems at rest there. It is now active for science and we can hardly keep pace with the scientifick discoveries that are made. Notwithstanding the inexhaustible treasures of poetry in England, almost every year adds something which is destined to live. The mind of the nation seems to have suffered no exhaustion by all that has been done. Where new topicks have seemed wanting from the immense intellectual labour already bestowed and an individual has appeared possessing extraordinary mental vigour, we find him venturing on fields long trodden before and returning with a harvest we could never have anticipated.

Is there not something besides our youthfulness on which we may charge our literary delinquency? Is it because so much has been done by others, that we withhold our assistance from the commonwealth of letters? Is it because we are a commercial people, and the mind of the nation thus necessarily diverted from the pursuits of literature? Is it because we are poor and feel that our utmost charity will hardly support the paupers of the state, much less supply the poverty of literature? Let an affirmative answer be given to each of these questions and is there one of them which will not apply as truly to England as to America? Nay, is it not matter of greater wonder that considering all things we have not done more for literature than England, viz. in science, have been more original?

Notwithstanding the literary delinquency of America, still we have done something. Perhaps it would not be fair to place the period of our national existence among the dark ages of letters. But our best writers have been unfortunate in the vehicles they have chosen as depositories of their intellectual productions. These depositories have been chiefly newspapers and pamphlets of various kinds. Now there is something ephemeral and temporary in the very nature of these publications. Hence their contents are not safe. A man who writes in them does not think of writing for immortality. His mental labour of course soon is over and almost of course badly done. If it turn out that his communication pleases, it excites but a momentary emotion of pleasure, and his successor into the columns fills his place as perfectly and almost as successfully

as the types which were devoted to their several compositions. The literature, farther, of newspapers and pamphlets is almost always controversial literature; and in controversy we are always more interested for the champions
of party than for their writings. Controversy, it must be
confessed however, among us has done as much for literature as controversy has among other nations. It has gratified the passions, the prejudices, the whims of the parties
concerned, and when the flame is extinguished, the pamphlets which did so much to support it repose in their
own ashes.

Another and very powerful objection might be offered
to the vehicles chosen for our literature. They are very
short. Their limits allow but a very narrow view of any
subject. The writers in them are confined almost to a single topick of their subject and when they begin to write,
they must reduce their minds as well as their thoughts
within the limits prescribed either by themselves, their
partizans, their printer, or their bookseller. Now, there is
a great deal in all this which has a bad tendency in relation
to literature. A bold and vigorous mind might not be
willing to submit to such circumscription and of course
we should lose the results of its labours; and, beyond all
doubt, many a bold and vigorous mind among us has by
this submission exhausted itself in ephemeral labours for
these short lived works.

If we have been successful in detecting some of the
causes of our literary delinquency, it may be expected that
some means for correcting this national fault should be
suggested. It is a trite but true saying, however, that it is
easier to discover the causes of evils than to find their
remedies. And some have argued that it is but a stinted
charity which is only successful in doing the first. It may
require an apology too that we have ventured on the discussion of our literary deficiencies at all. But we are all
partakers in this sin, and all and each of us, of course,
have some reason and right to inquire into its nature and
extent. It may be that we may be solicitous for amend-
ment in ourselves, or if we find that hopeless, that we may
become instrumental in some degree towards that of

others. If it be not arrogant, we would ask what are the means which appear to promise to do most to remedy our literary delinquency? Would they not principally, nay at the present moment wholly, consist in the vigorous exertion of our own minds? And what are some of the topicks on which they may be exerted? Would not the complete history of the United States of America be a subject worthy of writing? We do not mean a work of a day or of a volume, but a work which should embrace our political history in its widest extent;—which should contain a discussion of all that is peculiar in our civil polity,—which should investigate and decide the effects of our religious toleration, which, except in America, has never been perfect in any part of Christendom,—which should give the history of our literary labours in all their varieties and degrees—and which, above all, should give the moralist and philosopher our genuine national character? Would not a collection of all that has been done for poetry among us which is worthy the name be an honourable labour for a vigorous mind? It might embrace the biography of our poets,—It might contain the real state of this department of literature among us, and if it were found deficient, trace the causes of its deficiency, and show the remedy.—But we will leave this ungrateful office of tacit reproof, and only lament that for literature, the pride of a nation,—an earnest of its immortality,—this country has done no more.

Document 8

William Tudor

William Tudor (1779–1830), Boston merchant, former member of the Anthology Club, and founding editor of the *North American Review*, takes up the argument of Dr. Channing without questioning his premises, but in a calmer mood and at a slower pace. His essay was delivered without specific title as the annual address to the Phi Beta Kappa Society at Cambridge and was one of the series (Documents 9, 16, and 19) which culminated in Emerson's more famous address of 1837. It was published in the same issue of the *North American* which contained Dr. Walter Channing's second essay. His final footnote lists the works he consulted (probably in the newly founded Boston Athenaeum which he had also helped to establish) in collecting his material on American nature, aborigines, and history which he believed to be untouched sources of inspiration and nourishment for the American literature yet to come. Although his sources were different, his general approach to the problem of poetry was that which James Fenimore Cooper adopted in his experiments with fiction which began a half dozen or more years later. Did Cooper read this essay after the failure of *Precaution?*

TEXT: from the *North American Review*, II (November 1815), 13–32.

An Address Delivered to the Phi Beta Kappa Society

. . . . It has been said that one reason why we have not produced more good poems was owing to the want of subjects and though

> The poet's eye in a fine phrensy rolling,
> Glances from Heaven to earth, from earth to Heaven,

and makes the universe his domain, yet that the appropriate themes of other countries had been exhausted by their own poets and that none existed in ours. Thinking this opinion to be unfounded, the attempt to prove the latter part of it to be so may furnish a theme for this discourse during the few moments that I can presume to solicit your attention.

The early history of illustrious nations has been the source of the great master pieces of poetry: the fabulous ages of Greece are the foundation of the Iliad and Odyssey, and the same period gave Virgil his hero for the Æneid. Many modern epicks have taken the heroes of the earlier periods and revolutions of modern times. The American Revolution may some centuries hence become a fit and fruitful subject for an heroick poem; when ages will have consecrated its principles and all remembrance of party feuds and passions shall have been obliterated—when the inferiour actors and events will have been levelled by time, and a few memorable actions and immortal names shall remain the only monuments to engage and concentrate the admiration of a remote posterity.

From the close of the 16th to the middle of the 18th century many most interesting events took place on this continent and circumstances have concurred with time in casting a shade of obscurity resembling that of antiquity over the transactions of that period; while, by the great revolutions which have since happened, the connexion between those days and our own is interrupted, and they are so disconnected with the present era that no passionate feeling is blended with their consideration; they are now exclusively the domain of history and poetry. All the communities then standing have passed away or exist under new relations. The remarkable Confederacy of Indian tribes under the name of the five nations is extinct. The foundations of the French Empire in America have been torn up, the possessions that were once French are now held by the British, and the English colonies have become an independent nation. All these changes have insulated this portion of history and divested it of the irritation attendant on recent political affairs.

The region in which these occurrences took place abounds with grand and beautiful scenery, possessing some peculiar features. The numerous waterfalls, the enchanting beauty of Lake George and its pellucid flood, of Lake Champlain, and the lesser lakes, afford many objects of the most picturesque character; while the inland seas from Superiour to Ontario, and that astounding cataract whose roar would hardly be increased by the united murmurs of all the cascades of Europe, are calculated to inspire vast and sublime conceptions. The effects too of our climate composed of a Siberian winter and an Italian summer furnish peculiar and new objects for description. The circumstances of remote regions are here blended, and strikingly opposite appearances witnessed in the same spot, at different seasons of the year—In our winters, we have the sun at the same altitude as in Italy, shining on an unlimited surface of snow which can only be found in the higher latitudes of Europe where the sun in the winter rises little above the horizon. The dazzling brilliance of a winter's day, and a moon-light night when the utmost splendour of the sky is reflected from a surface of spotless white attended with the most excessive cold, is peculiar to the northern part of the United States. What too can surpass the celestial purity and transparency of the atmosphere in a fine autumnal day when our vision and our thoughts seem carried 'to the third heaven;' the gorgeous magnificence of their close, when the sun sinks from our view surrounded with varied masses of clouds, fringed with gold and purple, and reflecting in evanescent tints all the hues of the rainbow.[1]

[1] There is no climate in the world that presents more remarkable contrasts than that of the middle and northern parts of the United States. Boston, for instance, is in the same latitude with Rome, the cold in winter is occasionally as intense and the snow as deep as at Stockholm and St. Petersburg; but the sun hardly gleams on them in the winter months, while here his rays are shed from the same altitude as in Italy, and interrupts during the day that severity of cold, induced by the prevalence of the winds in

A most remarkable feature in the landscape at this same season, and which those who see it for the first time must behold with astonishment, is the singular appearance of the woods; where all the hues of the most lively flowers, the vivid colours of tulips, are given to the trees of the

the western quarter, coming to us over a continent of such vast extent covered with dense forests which shadow the earth and prevent the sun from warming and drying its surface. Our climate affords some of the worst and some of the finest weather that can be felt in any part of the world. The spring generally is the most capricious and disagreeable, the autumn the mellowest and most serene. Persons who are in the habit of remarking the appearance of the atmosphere cannot fail of admiring the extreme beauty of the sky at most seasons of the year. To witness the same effects, it is necessary in Europe to get into the same latitudes. The climate of England, modified by an insular situation, and the wide spread cultivation of its surface is peculiarly temperate, but constantly vapoury and humid. France and Germany, colder and warmer than England, are still more temperate than the United States; it is necessary to cross the Alps to find the same bright and beautiful atmosphere that surrounds us. In England it is seldom that any distant object can be seen distinctly, and there is always such a degree of haziness in the air that even neighbouring objects are never so clearly defined as they are under a purer sky; the artists of the Continent commonly reproach the artists of England with carrying this imitation of nature in their own country into their representations of the scenery of others, and in their engravings (the remark was made particularly in criticising that magnificent work, Stuart's Antiquities of Athens,) giving the misty, indistinct outline which they were accustomed to and which is not without its beauties but which was entirely foreign to the appearance of objects in Greece. This same effect of great distinctness, which is common to the south of Europe, may very often be seen here, especially in the summer. Any person may judge of this in a clear day by regarding elevated buildings, looking from the sun and observing with what sharpness and distinctness their edges and angles are marked and how bold the relief and distant the sky recedes. The most careless eye can hardly fail to be struck with the beauty of an evening sky, after sunset, and the appearance of the western horizon when the darkness has encroached on the eastern. On a summer or autumnal evening, when there are no clouds, as the twilight is advancing, the purity, transparency, brilliancy and harmonious subsiding and blending of the warmer tints from where the sun has set, to the fine *chiaro oscuro* of the opposite point, where the shadows of night are approaching, will afford a few minutes of delightful contemplation to the lover of nature. In contending for this forest, and nature appears in a moment of capricious gayety to have attired the groves in the gaudiest and most fantastick livery. Nothing comparable to this effect can be seen in any part of Europe.[2]

---

splendour of our atmosphere which has sometimes been denied it I am well aware of all its disadvantages and would gladly take a little less brilliance and a little more comfort; but, as we are fully sensible, and are habitually repining at its inconveniences, it is well to know what compensation may be derived from its beauties. To the poet and the artist it is replete with picturesque effect.

[2] This singular and beautiful appearance of the forests is peculiar to this country. It arises partly from the greater variety of trees and perhaps from the early occurrence of frosts when the leaves are still vigorous and filled with juices and which may be decomposed by the cold so as to produce these vivid colours; when they might merely fade and be partially changed if their fall was not produced prematurely. The forests in Europe in their autumnal dress have many shades of brown and yellow intermixed, but there is nothing equal to the effect produced here. To select two of our forest trees for instance, the white walnut and the maple, these trees attaining the height of forty feet and upwards and the whole foliage of the former of the brightest yellow and the latter the deepest scarlet. No artist has hitherto ventured to give this appearance in its full effect. There are many features in our forest scenery that are highly beautiful from their variety and strong contrasts. Europeans who have a knowledge and love of botany always admire them. Most of our trees and plants have been transplanted into the nurseries of Europe, and are much in request for all their ornamental plantations. It is not only the aspect of our forests, but the general aspect of our country, which have both been too much neglected by the American poets, who have written their descriptions more from the study of the classick poets of ancient and modern Europe than from meditating on the scenes familiar to them.—A painter who only makes pictures from copying the ideas and style of the great masters, without animating his manner by a study of nature, may produce correct but always cold and dry performances. Descriptive poetry, which borrows the fashion of other countries, however classick its allusions, will be languid and spiritless, it will possess no raciness and can never be rendered interesting. The general physiognomy of the United States is different from that of every country in Europe, its buildings, its cultivation, its natural and artificial objects have many peculiar features. There is no species of cultivation in Europe, not even the vine, except when cultivated on espaliers or pendant between trees, which is seldom seen, that can compare with a field of Indian corn, next to the sugar cane the richest in appearance of all plants. The care and labour which

Many other beauties of inanimate nature might be enumerated, and these just mentioned are only cited as being in a degree peculiar. These extensive and variegated forests afford shelter to a variety of animals, beautiful in form and curious in their habits, such among others, are the beaver and the deer; and to birds of most exquisite plumage. The graceful shape and various species of some of the diminutive quadrupeds, the very abundance of some of these animals, and of certain kinds of birds, which almost darken the air in their flight, serve to enrich and animate the scenery. Prominent among objects of this class, is the king of birds, Jove's own imperial Eagle, the sacred emblem of our country: 'Formed by nature for braving the severest cold, feeding equally on the produce of the sea and of the land, possessing powers of flight capable of outstripping even the tempests themselves; unawed by any but man; and from the etherial heights to which he soars, looking abroad at one glance to an immeasurable expanse of forests, fields, lakes and ocean deep below him, he appears indifferent to the little localities of change of seasons; as in a few minutes he can pass from summer to winter, from the lower to the higher regions of the atmosphere, the abode of eternal cold, and from thence descend at will to the torrid and arctick zones of the earth.'[3] In the same territories are found those enormous bones of animals now extinct that have generated so many fables among the savages and speculations among philosophers; and those extensive fortifications so buried in obscurity that even tradition is silent respecting them;—objects which lead to that musing on former times most propitious to poetry.

---

is bestowed on this grain in the Eastern States, the neatness and beauty of its appearance, form a strong contrast with the too careless and neglected appearance of other fields. This is the most splendid of all the gifts of Ceres, and it is difficult to say whether it is most pleasing to the eye in its growing state or at the period of harvest, when the ripened, luxuriant ears are discovered through their faded covering. It would extend this note too far to notice all the objects that may be cited as peculiar in some degree to our scenery.

[3] Wilson's Ornithology.

Such are some of the subordinate subjects that would be fruitful of allusion and fertile in description to the poet. The human actors on this theatre are still more striking and their history replete with interest and romantick adventure. The English and French were founding extensive empires here and their contiguous possessions produced a century of conflicts which terminated at last in the exclusive power of the former. European affairs were more than once affected by the disputes of these two nations in the regions of Canada, and the decision of the most important contests on the Old Continent has been produced by the issue of operations in the remote wilds of North America. The period also was one of great interest in European annals; France and England were rivals in glory, both in arts and arms.

Between these powers were interposed the Aborigines, who became the allies of these nations and the most efficient part of their force. Before speaking more particularly of them, it will be necessary to deprecate the prejudices naturally entertained on the subject from what we now see. The degenerate, miserable remains of the Indian nations which have dwindled into insignificance and lingered among us as the tide of civilization has flowed, mere floating deformities on its surface, poor, squalid and enervated with intoxicating liquors, should no more be taken for the representatives of their ancestors who first met the Europeans on the edge of their boundless forests, severe and untamed as the regions they tenanted, than the Greek slaves who now tremble at the frown of a petty Turkish tyrant can be considered the likeness of their immortal progenitors, of those immoveable bands, before whom at Platœa, Thermopylæ and Marathon, the whole Persian empire broke and subsided like the waves of the sea against the rocks they defended. To form an idea of what they once were, to see them in the energy and originality of their primitive condition, we must now journey a thousand miles. They possessed so many traits in common with some of the nations of antiquity that they perhaps exhibit the counterpart of what the Greeks were in the heroick ages, and particularly the Spartans during the vigour of their institutions. Their origin has been the source of many theories and conjectures, few of which are more reasonable than the suggestion of Spenser in his Fairy Queen that they are the descendants of the man whom Prometheus animated by stealing fire from Heaven. Whether this race of men could like the Greeks have gradually acquired civilization, or whether they are a distinct species incapable of being tamed, may be uncertain: sudden civilization at least has been shewn to be impossible; they diminish and waste before its progress like snow before the vernal influence. The sublime allegorical painting of Guido,[4] in which Apollo encircled by the hours is chasing night and her shadows over the surface of the globe might almost represent the extinction of our savage precursors before the dawn of science and cultivation. The history of these people then is not less interesting since in a short period they will exist no where else, and even in the next century the Indian warriour and hunter will perhaps only be found on the shores of the Pacifick ocean.

The virtues and vices of the original inhabitants of America have been generally exaggerated by their enemies or admirers. It would be as foolish to vindicate the one as to deny the other; both grew out of their condition: the influence of civilized society destroyed the former and nourished the latter. Their virtues were hospitality, reverence to age, unalterable constancy in friendship, and undaunted fortitude in every species of enterprise and suffering. They lived in a state of proud savage equality and had no esteem for any merit except that which was derived from superiority in the arts of hunting, war, and eloquence. These were their general characteristicks, but the difference between Indian was almost as great as among European nations, and the inferiority of some to others was quite as remarkable as that which exists between civilized people.

Among those who were distinguished, few are more eminent than the confederated tribes which were first known to us under the name of the Five Nations. These

[4] In the Rospigliosi Palace at Rome.

nations resided originally in the district where now stands
Montreal. The Algonquins lived more in the interiour.
The former were peaceable in their habits and subsisted
by cultivating the earth; the latter were warlike and depended on hunting; the two nations were friendly and
exchanged their corn and venison. At a certain period,
when game was scarce, the Algonquins requested the Five
Nations to send them some of their young men to assist
in the increased toil of procuring food. These becoming
very expert huntsmen, were murdered by the Algonquin
employers out of jealousy and apprehension. When complaint was made of this treacherous cruelty, they only
blamed the murderers and made some slight presents to
the injured people, fearless of the resentment of a nation
who subsisted by the effeminate employment, as they esteemed it, of agriculture. The Five Nations determined on
revenge, which being discovered by the Algonquins, they
resolved to reduce them to absolute obedience by force.
In pursuing this scheme, they chased them from their
place of living and obliged them to seek shelter in the
region between the Hudson and Lakes Erie and Ontario.
The Confederacy, goaded by the injustice of their enemies
to relinquish their peaceable employments, gradually acquired a knowledge of war and courage to face them; and,
though the latter aided by the French had the great advantage of the previous use of fire arms, the Five Nations
eventually triumphed and, with the exception of a small
number that were driven to the vicinity of Quebec, finally
extinguished the Algonquins, one of the most warlike,
numerous and politick tribes of North America. Having
once acquired the habits and knowledge of war, they extended their dominion with restless ambition till they had
either formed alliances with, or reduced to submission,
most of the nations between the St. Lawrence, the sea
coast, and the Ohio. The Dutch formed a treaty with them
in 1609. The English made their first treaty of alliance
with them in 1664, which was continued from time to
time and never violated. They had also particular treaties
with Massachusetts, New-York, Pennsylvania, Maryland
and Virginia.

From this slight sketch of their history, it may be imagined that these nations must have held an important part in all the contests between the French and English. Indeed, the affairs of the former were more than once brought to the very brink of destruction by them. At a very critical moment, the English withdrew from the contest by the most positive orders of the Sovereign, which were artfully obtained by the French Ministry, from the bigoted subservience of the Stuarts to the Court of Rome, while, under pretence of religion, the Jesuit Missionaries were promoting the designs of France in that vast scheme of Colossal aggrandizement which, with one foot at New Orleans and the other at Quebec, would have bestrode the Empire of North America.

The actions of these people in war had a strong character of wildness and romance; their preparations for it and celebrations of triumph were highly picturesque. The solemn councils of their Sachems, the war-dance which preceded their expeditions, like the Pyrrhick Dance of antiquity, was full of terrifick expression. Many of their achievements were performed by a few or sometimes only one or two individuals. These were savage in their character and not admitted now in the practice of war among civilized nations and yet such actions may be rendered highly interesting in poetry. What was the nocturnal excursion of Diomed and Ulysses in the 10th book of the Iliad, in which they slew Rhesus, king of the Thracians, with many of his officers in their sleep, and brought away his beautiful horses? what was the enterprise of Nisus and Euryalus in the 9th book of the Æneid, in which they murdered so many in their sleep, and in which Euryalus, by taking from one of them his splendid helmet and belt was afterwards discovered by the moon gleaming on its polished surface, and the death of both occasioned by this spoil? These episodes are two of the finest in those immortal Epicks, yet it is only to the genius of Homer and Virgil that they are indebted for more than may be found in several Indian adventures.

Many of their friendships were as strong as that of the two followers of Æneas; their affection generally for those of their own nation was of the most powerful kind; a proof of this may be found in the speech of a Sachem of the Mohawks to an officer who was hurrying them to undertake an expedition, just after they had returned from holding a Council at Albany, where they had lost by sickness some of their finest young men: 'You seem,' said he 'to think that we are brutes, that we have no sense of the loss of our dearest relations, and some of them the bravest men we had in our nation; you must allow us time to bewail our misfortunes'—They were guilty of ferocious cruelty towards their enemies. Alas! cruelty is not peculiar to savages. They condemned to torture the foes who would have tortured them.—How many Christian nations are free from the reproach at every period of their history of having tortured their own subjects for mere matters of opinion? In war they laid waste the dwellings and cornfields of their enemies and murdered the defenceless.—Is there nothing in the conduct of nations pretending to the highest civilization that will, under this head, interfere with their exclusive claim to barbarism?

That they were not merely hunters and warriours, but sagacious in the management of affairs and capable of deep laid schemes of policy, there are many historical anecdotes to prove. One must suffice on this occasion. The most accomplished statesman of the Italian school could hardly surpass the following perfidious and subtle policy of an Indian Chieftain. In the year 1687, Adario, a very distinguished Sachem of the Hurons, finding that his nation had become suspected by the French on account of the intercourse they had held with the English, determined to recover their good graces by some signal action against the Five Nations, their common foe. For this purpose he left Michilimackinack with an hundred men and called on his way at the fort of Cadaraqui for intelligence. The French, after many attempts, had just succeeded in obtaining from a part of the Five Nations that they would send Ambassadours to Montreal to form a treaty of peace. The French commander informed the Huron Chief of this state of affairs, that the deputies were then on their way, and begged him to return home and attempt no enterprise that might interrupt these favourable prospects.

Surprised at this intelligence, the wily savage was under the greatest concern for his nation, least they should be sacrificed to the French interests if the latter could make peace with the Confederacy. Dissembling his feelings, he left the fort, not to return home as the Commander supposed, but to proceed to a spot where he knew the Ambassadours must pass, to await them. After a short time they made their appearance, guarded by forty young warriours. They were surprised, and all their guards either killed or made prisoners. When these latter were all secured, Adario told them that he had been informed by the Governour of Canada that fifty of their warriours were to pass that way about this period and that he had formed this ambush to intercept them. The deputies, astonished at this perfidy of the French, related the purpose of their journey to Adario; on hearing which he affected the utmost fury and rage at the atrocity which the French government had caused him to commit and swore he would be revenged. Then looking steadfastly on the prisoners, one of whom was Decanesora, a famous Chief of the Oneidas, he said, go, my brethren, I loose your bonds and send you home again, though our nations be at war; I shall never rest easy till the Five Nations have taken their revenge of the French for this treachery.

The Deputies were persuaded by his conduct and told him that he and his nation might make peace with them when they pleased. Adario, who had lost but one man in the affair, took one of theirs as usual to supply his place; then giving them a supply of arms and ammunition, dismissed them. These Chiefs were from the Oneida and Onondagua tribes which had received the Jesuit Missionaries, were the best disposed towards the French, and now returned home most deeply incensed.

One circumstance remained to complete the effect; Adario, on his return, gave up his prisoner to the French officer commanding, who being ignorant of these circumstances, to nourish the hatred between the Five Nations and the Hurons, ordered him to be shot. The Huron Chief called an Indian of the former people to witness this execution of his countryman and the cruelty of the French from which even he was not able to save his own prisoner, and then bid him make his escape and relate what he had seen. The fugitive arrived at the very time when the French had sent to disown Adario in the action he had committed; but this additional circumstance exasperated them so highly that they would listen to no representations. Their thoughts were all bent on revenge. A short time after they made a descent on the island of Montreal, took all the Forts in their way, destroyed, with indiscriminate havock, men, women and children, and reduced the French power in Canada to the very verge of ruin.

As the government of these people was a republick, the practice of eloquence was of the highest importance, since the art of persuasion was a principal source of influence and power. None of the Indian Nations carried the science of speaking to greater perfection, of which there are many proofs on record. The general characteristicks of their style are well known. We have received their speeches under every disadvantage, since they come to us through the medium of ignorant interpreters who were incapable of transfusing the spirit and ornament of one language into the idiom of another when they thoroughly understood neither. The solemnity of their councils, the dignity and animation of their manner, their style of address, 'Sachems and Warriours,' were all suited to command attention and respect. Colden thus describes one of their orators: 'Decanesora had for many years the greatest reputation among the Five Nations for speaking and was generally employed as their speaker in their negotiations with both French and English: he was grown old when I saw him and heard him speak, he had great fluency and a graceful elocution, that would have pleased in any part of the world. His person was tall and well made, and his features to my thinking resembled much the busto's of Cicero.'[5]

[5] There were many metaphors which were transmitted down among the Indians by the women whose business it was to retain and repeat them from one generation to another. The following

The speeches given by Homer to the characters in the Iliad and Odyssey, form some of the finest passages in those poems. The speeches of these Indians only want similar embellishment to excite admiration. A few frag-

---

remarks on the language and oratory of the Five Nations are taken from Colden's history.

'The people of the Five Nations are much given to speech-making, ever the natural consequence of a perfect Republican government; where no single person has a power to compel, the arts of persuasion alone must prevail. As their best speakers distinguish themselves in their public councils and treaties with other nations, and thereby gain the esteem and applause of their countrymen, (the only superiority which any one of them has over the others) it is probable they apply themselves to this art by some kind of study and exercise in a great measure. It is impossible for me to judge how far they excel, as I am ignorant of their language; but the speakers whom I have heard had all a great fluency of words and much more grace in their manner than any man could expect among a people entirely ignorant of all the liberal arts and sciences.

'I am informed that they are very nice in the turn of their expressions, and that few of themselves are so far masters of their language as never to offend the ears of their *Indian* auditory by an unpolite expression. They have, it seems, a certain *urbanitas* or *atticism* in their language, of which the common ears are ever sensible, though only their great speakers attain to it. They are so much given to speech-making that their common compliments to any person they respect at meeting and parting are made in harangues.

'They have some kind of elegance in varying and compounding their words, to which not many of themselves attain, and this principally distinguishes their best speakers. I have endeavoured to get some account of this, as a thing that might be acceptable to the curious; but, as I have not met with any one person who understands their language and also knows any thing of grammar or of the learned languages, I have not been able to attain the least satisfaction. Their present minister tells me that their verbs are varied, but in a manner so different from the *Greek* or *Latin* that he cannot discover by what rule it was done and even suspects that every verb has a peculiar mode. They have but few radical words, but they compound their words without end; by this their language becomes sufficiently copious and leaves room for a good deal of art to please a delicate ear. Sometimes one word among them includes an entire definition of the thing; for examples they call *wine, Oneharadesehoengtseragherie,* as much as to say, *a liquor made of the juice of the grape.* The words expressing things lately come to their knowledge are all compounds;

ments of one may serve as a specimen. It was delivered under the following circumstances. James the second, at the solicitation of the French Court, having given orders to the Colonies not to interfere, the French were determined to bring the Five Nations to their own terms. For this purpose the governor of Canada proceeded with a strong force in 1684 to Lake Ontario. The Indian Chiefs had meanwhile been persuaded by the Jesuits to send a deputation to meet him having been promised that they should be cordially received and kindly treated. The French army however became so much weakened by sickness, so many of the soldiers had died, that all the formidable preparations were rendered useless and their Commander was unable to prosecute his designs by force. This situation of the French was well understood by the Indians. When they met, after many ceremonies the conference was opened with due form, the parties being drawn up in a circle of which the French officers formed one half and the Savages the other. The Governor delivered a most arrogant, menacing speech, to impress them with fear of the tremendous power of France. Garangula, the Indian speaker on this occasion, was much surprised at the difference of its tone from what he had been led to expect by the Jesuits and immediately returned an answer of which the following are extracts. The Indians called the Governor of Canada, Onondio; it was their custom to give a surname as a mark of honour to the Governor of each of the Provinces, which was never changed.

'ONONDIO

'I honor you, and the warriors that are with me all likewise honor you. Your interpreter has finished your speech, I now begin mine. My words hasten to reach your ears, pray listen to them.

---

they have no labeals in their language, nor can they perfectly pronounce a word wherein there is a labeal; and when one endeavours to teach them to pronounce words, they tell one, they think it ridiculous that they must shut their lips to speak. Their language abounds with gutturals and strong aspirations; these make it very sonorous and bold; and their speeches abound with metaphors, after the manner of the Eastern nations, as will best appear by the speeches that I have copied.'

'Onondio, you must have believed when you left Quebec that the sun had burnt up all the Forests which render our country inaccessible to the French, or that the Lakes had overflowed their banks and surrounded our Castles so that it was impossible for us to get out of them. Yes, Onondio, you must surely have dreamt this, and curiosity to see so great a wonder has brought you so far. Now you are undeceived, since I and the warriors here present are come to assure you that the Senekas, Cayugas, Onondagas, Oneidas and Mohawks are yet alive. I thank you, in their name, for bringing back into their country that Calumet which your predecessor received from their hands. I congratulate you for your good fortune in having left under ground that murdering hatchet which has been so often dyed with the blood of the French. Listen, Onondio, I am not asleep, I have my eyes open, and that sun which enlightens me discovers to me a great Captain at the head of a Company of soldiers who speaks as if he were dreaming. He says that he only came to the Lake to smoke on the great Calumet with the Onondagas. But Garangula asserts that he sees the contrary, that it was to have destroyed them if sickness had not weakened the arms of the French.

'I see Onondio raving in a camp of sick men whose lives the great Spirit has saved by inflicting this sickness on them. Hear, Onondio, our women had taken their clubs, our children and old men had carried their bows and arrows into the heart of your camp if our warriors had not disarmed them and kept them back when your messenger Oquesse came to our castles. Enough, I say no more on this subject.

'We may go where we please, and carry with us whom we please, and buy and sell what we please. If your allies be your slaves, use them as such, command them to receive no other but your people. This belt confirms my words.

'What I say is the voice of all the five nations; hear what they answer, open your ears to what they speak: The Senakas, Cayugas, Onondagas, Oneidas and Mohawks say, that when they buried the hatchet at Cadaracqui, in the presence of your predecessor, in the centre of the Fort, they planted the tree of peace in the same place to be there carefully preserved, that in place of being a retreat for soldiers, it might become a rendezvous for merchants; that in place of arms and ammunitions of war, beavers and merchandize should only enter there.

'Hearken Onondio, take care for the future, that so great a number of soldiers as appear there do not choak the Tree of Peace planted in so small a fort. It would be a great misfortune if after it had so easily taken root, you should stop its growth and prevent its covering your country and ours with its branches. I assure you in the name of the Five Nations that our warriors shall dance to the Calumet of peace under its leaves, and shall remain quiet on their matts, and shall never dig up the hatchet, till their brethren Onondio, or Corlaer, shall either jointly or separately endeavour to attack the country which the Great Spirit has given to our ancestors. This belt confirms my words, and this other the authority given to me by the Five Nations.'—Then addressing himself to the French Interpreter, he said—'Take courage, Oquesse, you have spirit, speak, explain my words, omit nothing, tell all that your brethren and friends say to Onondio, your Governor, by the mouth of Garangula, who loves you and desires you to accept this present of beaver and take part with him in his feast to which he invites you. This present of beaver is sent to Onondio on the part of the Five Nations.'

This speech may be compared with the celebrated message of the Scythians to Alexander in Quintius Curtius, and it affords materials which, if they were drest in the style of the great Roman Historians, would vie with any that they have transmitted to us; indeed, its figurative language, pungent sarcasm, and lofty tone can hardly be surpassed.

Perilous and romantick adventures,[6] figurative and elo-

---

[6] The early history of our country furnishes many characters, adventures and incidents of the strongest interest. Prominent among the former is Capt. John Smith whose common and familiar name is the only thing pertaining to his history which is not elevated and heroick. His life is now very rare and the book com-

quent harangues, strong contrasts and important interests, are as frequent in this portion of history as the theatre on which these actions were performed is abundant in grand and beautiful scenery. There are many inferiour circum-

---

mands a high price, but a very able abstract of it may be found in Dr. Belknap's American Biography. And there is hardly a marvellous tale on the shelves of any circulating library that can surpass the real adventures of this extraordinary man. From his very infancy to his death, which happened in the middle period of life, his whole career is a series of daring and romantick achievements in many different parts of the world. His reputation appears without stain, and he is a genuine hero of romance, being equally distinguished for the gallantry of love and war. He gave to the northern Cape of Massachusetts bay the name of a Turkish lady who interested herself in his fate, when a prisoner of the Turks; but *Cape Tragabizanda*, afterwards got the name of Cape Ann, which it will no doubt retain, though the other out of regard to Smith might be used in poetry. His name is best known in this country, from his encounters with the father of Pocahontas and the devoted affection of that interesting Indian princess towards him. The character of Standish among the Plymouth colonists; of the Sachem of Mount Hope, and the wars which ended in his destruction: the singular and heroick character of Madame de la Tour of whom some account may be found in Hubbard's history recently published by the Historical Society from an ancient Ms.: the religious fanaticism and intrigues of Mrs. Hutchinson and her supporter in Sir Henry Vane, which caused as much trouble and commotion in the colony of Massachusetts as the Mystical doctrines of Madame Guyon occasioned in Paris and to the Court of Louis 14th. These and many others are interesting materials. The incident mentioned by President Stiles is very striking, of Dixwell one of the regicides suddenly emerging from his concealment, and by his presence animating an infant settlement when suddenly assailed from the Indians to repel the savages, and then returning unnoticed to his retreat; which made many of the people who knew nothing of his concealment regard him as a mysterious being, a good angel sent for their deliverance. If remarkable characters and actions are to be found in our history, the scenes where they lived or occurred must be interesting from association of ideas. There are many such, though they have been too much neglected. We have all felt the interest excited by Scott for the scenery he describes in the Lady of the Lake. Its natural beauty is doubtless great—yet, give a bard of equal genius, the spot described in the last volume of the Historical collections as the one chosen by Gosnold in his first voyage—on one of the Elizabeth Islands there is a small lake in which there is a rocky islet where is still to be seen the foundations of the first dwelling stances that might contribute appropriate materials for poetry. The armorial bearings of the Indians, their Hieroglyphick writings, and some of their superstitions may be made subservient to poetical effect. For instance, there is in Lake Champlain a high rock against which the waves dash with vehemence and the spray is thrown to a great height. The Savages believed that an ancient Indian resided under this rock, who had power over the winds; to propitiate him they always threw over a pipe, or made some other oblation in passing. A man of distinction among the early Dutch inhabitants of New York, by the name of Corlaer, who was held in such high veneration by the Indians that they treated with him as the Governor of that Province and ever after called the Governor by his name, while on his way to visit the Governor of Canada, ridiculed this Indian Eolus. He was drowned directly afterwards by the upsetting of his canoe, which the Indians always attributed to his disrespect for the old man who had

---

erected on these shores by Europeans. The remarkable security of this situation, its natural beauty, the interest attending this attempt to colonize a country which has since played such an important part in the world, make this secluded spot more interesting than the Highland Lake; the time will come when this spot will be visited with as much interest, as the traveller at Rome goes to the Fountain of Egeria.

It would be encroaching too far to dwell longer on these topicks. No prejudice is more common, none more unfounded, none will more certainly be hereafter destroyed, than the one which supposes the early history of our country to be deficient in interest. To a person totally unacquainted with it, the mere mention of the leading circumstances on which it is founded would prove on very slight reflection that it was indeed impossible it should be so. Even saints and miracles may be incorporated in it if such be the taste of the poet. In the 'Lettres edifiantes' published at Paris in 1807, there are the letters of Father Charlevoix and the other Jesuits in Canada relating all the minute circumstances of the deaths of some holy Indian Virgins, who died in the odour of sanctity, and at whose tombs miracles were performed duly attested and sworn to by divers honourable men. Those who wish to investigate this department, may consult, Smith's Life, Belknap's Biography, Hubbard's history, Colden's history of the Five Nations, La Hontan's Travels, and the histories of Virginia and Massachusetts. Charlevoix Nouvelle France. Lafitau's Mœurs des Sauvages, Adair's American Indians.

the control of the winds. This at least is not more extravagant than Homer's account of the present made by the monarch of Eolia to Ulysses of an assortment of winds secured in bags which being untied by his sailors, a tempest was created that drove them on the coast of the Lestrigons.

There is an ingenious device of Epick poetry that might be here used with great effect. This is the prophetick narration, a prophecy after the facts have occurred. Such is the celebrated Ode of Gray, in which the last of the Bards predicts the misfortunes of Edward's posterity; such are the adventures of Ulysses in the 11th book of the Odyssey, and of Æneas in the 6th book of the Æneid, in which those heroes are told among the shades the future fortunes of their race. The poet might introduce the expedient as his fancy suggested. It may be supposed that a French and English Officer and an American Colonist should accompany an Indian Sachem deputed by his tribe to consult some Indian sorcerer or divinity; the scene may be in one of those islands of Lake Superiour which some of their traditions represent as the abode of the blest, on shores perhaps untrodden by the foot of man, lone, distant and obscure as those Cimmerian climes in which lay the opening to Tartarus. In seeking for a knowledge of destiny, what wonderful events would be unfolded.

The prescient expounder of fate would declare to the Chieftain of the Five Nations, the alliances, contests, triumphs and utter extinction of his race; that they should disappear with the animals they hunted and the forests that sheltered both—they should vanish before the spirit of civilization, like the mist of the Lakes before the morning sun, and leave no trace of their existence, but in the records of the white men. To the Englishman he would foretell the civil war, the death of Charles on the scaffold, the fanatical austerity of the times, the usurpation of Cromwell, and, at his decease, the restoration of Royalty and the licentious gayety that ensued—the final expulsion of the Stuarts and extinction of that family—the lustre of arts and arms during the reign of Anne; with the subsequent increasing splendour and grandeur of his nation till their empire should extend over both the Indies. To the American Colonist would be foretold the American Revolution, the fame of its heroes and statesmen—he would announce to him the first of these, the man who should be first in war, first in peace, and first in the hearts of his countrymen; the successful issue of the glorious contest for Independence would be predicted and he would be shewn the future greatness, happiness and glory of his country. To the Frenchman he would narrate the conquests, the splendour of the arts and of literature, the bigotry, disasters and miseries of the reign of Louis 14th—the profligacy and corruption of the regency, the loss of their possessions on this continent, and in the last conflict the death of the victorious and the vanquished Generals under the walls of Quebec. The constant increase of luxury and refinement to the era of the Revolution. In revealing that Revolution, he would describe the contagious enthusiasm of hope which would intoxicate all nations at its dawn; the crimes, the horrours and wonderful events that would accompany its progress; and the foul, gloomy despotism that would attend its close.—The King, his family, and his nobles perishing on the scaffold, or withering in exile; religion prohibited, its altars profaned, its ministers proscribed.—France covered with the dust of her ruined palaces and drenched with the blood of her citizens. He would foretell the rapid rise, energetick progress, and portentous grandeur of the great usurper; his ambition, wars, and victories; the ravages committed, the remote regions invaded, the kingdoms overthrown, while

at his heels
Lash'd in like hounds, should famine, sword and fire,
Crouch for employment,

he would predict at the hour of deepest gloom, the reaction of publick feeling, the overwhelming wave of retributive conquest pursuing him back from every country of Europe to his own capital, his abdication, the return of the—but no, plain prose and sober reason are confounded by these events, they must be left to the madness of verse, and the inspiration of the poet.

This is a cursory sketch of some of the scenes and ev
that would be fruitful in poetry. When we recollect w.
delightful performances have been composed by one mo
ern poet out of the obscure quarrels of Border Banditt
in barbarous ages, how another in thoughts that breathe
and words that burn has immortalized the pirates of the
Archipelago, much may surely be expected from this
region when it shall be explored with the torch of imagination. The materials are rude, yet talent only is wanting
to mould and animate them. The same block of marble
which in the hands of an artisan might only have formed
a step for the meanest feet to trample on, under the
touch of genius unfolded the Belvidere Apollo, glowing
with divine beauty and immortal youth, the destroyer of
the Python, the companion of the Muses, the majestick
God of Eloquence and Poetry.

DOCUMENT 9

Edward Tyrell Channing

The youngest of the Channing brothers, Edward Tyrell Channing (1790–1856), was the only one whose primary professional concern was with literature. As Boylston Professor of Rhetoric and Oratory at Harvard from 1819 to 1851 he was undoubtedly a major influence in shaping the mind and writing of Emerson, Thoreau, and many of their contemporaries. His emphasis, therefore, in this remarkable essay, upon the sanctity of original genius, the possible tyranny of too much study of the classics, and the need for a national literature which is the direct expression of experience, may help to explain the difference between the reliance of Ames and Dana on classical models and that of Thoreau and Emerson on direct inspiration of nature.

TEXT: from the *North American Review*, III (July 1816), 202–9.

On Models in Literature

"Yet still uppermost,
Nature was at his heart, as if he felt,
Though yet he knew not how, a wasting power
In all things, which from her sweet influence,
Might tend to wean him."
WORDSWORTH.

When I lay down the reviews or go home from a party of fashionable criticks, I pity the whole race of authors. If they would be the favourites of the age they live in, they must stand in awe of its opinions and taste, however various or chilling. They are surrounded by tribunals and

judges in almost every class; and all put in their claims
to special deference and respect. The frivolous and gay,
one would think, had no concern with the depths of the
heart, nor even with the landscape, any farther than the
tints that overlay it. Still they are readers and judges. They
lay up a little poetry or wit for conversation's sake, or at
least to gild their affectation—and therefore they must be
consulted.—Then again, we have exact scholars who require a sustained faultlessness and elegance in every thing.
They are shocked with blemishes or occasional dulness and
judge a man by failures that are merely accidental and
which do not indicate in the least the original cast or
defects of his mind. They never look at gleams or regions
of clear azure in a sleepy sky. They laugh at foolish simplicity till they cannot discern the real which is very often
in the neighbourhood.—There is too, a great middling
crowd of readers whose vocabulary of criticism extends
little further than to *"unnatural, out-of-life,"* &c.; and
words of this sort they are sure to level against every man
who ventures upon the marvellous, wild, and unreal. These
are the practical men who judge every thing by what they
call common sense. They laugh at the folly of encouraging
men in the indolent luxuries and unprofitable excesses of
imagination and feeling when we were sent here to work,
to be useful, to conquer the vices, and bring home the
wanderings of the mind.—Other readers, however, are so
fastidious and ethereal that they cannot bear to see a Poet
in the streets or workshops.

And shall authors then never be allowed to lose sight of
the motley race who are to judge them? A heavy day it
will be for poetry when society is made the school of
genius instead of solitude. You might as well take a man
from the quiet, unconfined seclusion in which he has lived
and rioted from infancy, and fit up a cell for him in the
inquisition, in some large city, where the tread of the
tormentor is heard above and the laughter of the world
without the walls.

We may differ in our tastes as much as we please. It is
a way to encourage all sorts of mind and bring to light
every thing fitted for poetry. But we must get out of

the bad habit of dictating to great minds and striving to bring them up in our own way. Genius is not willing to be interfered with and told how to work, where to travel, and what to admire. And yet there are men who go so far as to hold up models for imitation and standards of taste for writers of every age and country, let their minds be ever so lofty and original. We shall say a little of this interference, for it appears to be the most mischievous of all.

It may be well for minds of a common cast to read and obey. They may profitably give themselves up all their lives, to the superiour intellects about them. They are not made nor wanted for authors, and they only leave a gap in the busier parts of society when they venture to be such. It is the great men of a country who are to make and support its literature. And to tell such men that they must give their days and nights to any models, ancient or modern, is to destroy the whole worth and character of genius. It is to make men look at creation and society through another man's eyes and communicate all that their hearts labour with by the help of a remembered manner they learnt in the schools. It is to educate different men by one rule and force all minds to one taste and pursuit. It comes in the way of nature and reduces all her irregularities, crooks, and violence, her endless change, into straightness, smoothness, and harmony. It is to make the difference of country, of habits, and institutions wholly ineffectual as to literature, and to bring the native of the mountains and plains, of the inland and coast, to a lifeless similarity of taste.

Where is a mind thus trained to get its food and excitement? It is irksome and exhausting to walk in the dusty track of an earlier traveller, especially when the whole world in "morning freshness" lies open to the observing, intrepid, and ardent. Their refreshment is in toils and adventures of their own seeking. Their imaginations are filled with bright forms of unattained excellence, kindling enthusiasm and hope for a man to dream about when he grows tired of what others have done and burns to make more perfect what he attempts himself. Such men owe their power over the reader chiefly to something all their own in their notice of things, their manner, feelings, partialities, and taste. There is a savour of genius and individuality in all they say. They write from the heart, and we know them every where. They sit alone and work by themselves, leaving friends unconsulted, enemies neglected, and doing nothing merely because it has been pointed out. They speak with freedom and infant fearlessness as if they were alone in the world and had all to themselves. They are never dried up by the fear that nature is failing but feel that something is left for them every where.

The imitator, the man who gets his stock of thought and sentiment of beauty from books, is cautious, constrained, and modelled throughout. Every thing, even to his enthusiasm, seems disciplined and artificial. He will have no sins of overgrowth to repent of. He seems under a careful process of emaciation to keep in the fashion of grace and slenderness. His business is to select and trim where others, with the prodigality of invention, have thrown heaps and masses. He burnishes old jewels or sets them anew and submits cheerfully to other labours about as generous and nourishing to a hungry mind. When he is among the great, either of the living or dead, he does not feel himself in society. He does not come within the touch of greatness. There is no friendly action of other minds on his own—no level on which they can meet and be happy and useful together. He goes as a worshipper, to wonder and obey, not as an equal, to question, value, and surpass. Is this the way to make writers of whom a nation is to be proud or who shall be happy from themselves? The reader will tell you that works fashioned by models, or infected with books, are but old stories, the more tedious for the finish and elegance which is intended to make up for freedom and originality. They have no carelessness nor waste thought about them—no indication that the mind was the lighter and happier for throwing off its constant growth. The writer has the stiff, genteel way of a man who is trying to entertain strangers and is afraid of committing himself, and so prepares himself for the occasion. There is none of that gracious, fearless familiarity which one feels with those of his own home, whom he has seen every hour and whose characters have rather grown upon him than been studied.

If the borrowers and imitators are only encouraged, the swarm will go on thickening. There is enough now in the stores of poetry, heaped up by others, to serve them for ages. They need not once look out of doors to see things for themselves. There are rules for versification, laws of taste, books of practical criticism, and approved standards of language, to make one go right and safely. And surely it is very easy for men (except those who have the indignant freedom of genius,) to write with such helps. Besides, it looks hard now-a-days to be original when so many have already gone over the land of poetry and soiled and made common all that lay on the surface or in secret. Alas, when the world grows rich, heirs will be indolent; and we should not wonder at it. The habit of living on other minds naturally creates a spirit of self indulgence, and at last of weak timidity. Instead of being kindled into effort by what others have done, the heart sinks into cowardly admiration. It is content to relish what it dares not rival. It sets much by a refined, artificial taste, and thinks it enough to be exquisite in criticism and eloquent in praise. You will see idolaters leaning upon the broken columns of ancient Temples or in ecstacies before pictures and statues. The student sits at his window with a book before him, but he never looks out upon the fields. Knowledge must now be drawn from libraries and collections. The difficulties of acquiring which were once encountered are now done away, and with them the wholesome and invigorating labour. We need not confound ourselves any longer in the wastes and thickets which our fathers so eagerly plunged into. We have masters and schools at our very doors, to teach us every thing and to reduce every thing to system and simplicity. Here then is the very mischief of learning—the way to turn great men into confectioners and second-hand caterers. Their minds are surfeited with what other men have said, and toiled hard and all alone, to come at. No wonder that they grow sickly, acquiescing, and unproductive.

Let us just look at one or two ways in which freedom and originality of mind are assailed or endangered. The first is by inculcating an excessive fondness for the ancient classicks and asserting their supremacy in literature. By some means or other the ancients have exerted an enormous influence among literary men, and in nations too that have had hardly any thing of real congeniality with them. And many a lover of his own home, of the domestick fame and character of his country, has in his fits of vexation been tempted to wish that the Barbarians had either done their work more faithfully among the fair fabricks of Greece and Rome or else left those illustrious nations to live and provoke the rest of the world to independent greatness, instead of being their school or nurse. As it now is, the old nations survive in a sort of mixed state of grandeur and desolation. We grow tender among ruins and fragments. We love to soften down the errours and grossness of the fallen and to extol and venerate the remains of their greatness without making a very scrupulous estimate of its real worth. The grave-yard is common ground where the living from every land may come together. There is no rancour nor heart-burning there. We can all give praise with generous complacency when no pretensions are set up. The Romans worshipped Greece after they had conquered her.

Besides, the earliest nations in letters have a sort of patriarchal claim to the reverence of those who come after. Nothing remains of them but their finished and best works. We have no records of their early attempts and failures—nothing to inspire pity, to lessen admiration, or to encourage us when we fail. They seem to have started up at once, as if by an "over-night creation," into elegance and beauty, full of the ease, delight, and earnestness of men who draw directly from nature. They are set off from the earlier world and connected with every after age by appearing to be the very beginners of literature. They become the lights and helps of other nations who are slower and later in attention to the mind. And even when their

followers have surpassed their guides, and become quite
equal to looking about and making a fortune for themselves, it is still hard to throw off the veneration and
deference which all have felt and which gives them something common in their taste, pride, and obligations.

The boy at school (in the best but most complying
hours of his life) is set to work upon the ancient classicks.
He hears and reads of the god-like people who began and
finished the world's literature. This is taken in with his
rudiments, and along with it, indifference towards his own
language which he acquired as unconsciously as he grew,
and thinks too familiar for study or respect, while every
thing ancient is brought home to him in solemnity and
wonders and fastens itself upon him more closely than his
prayers.

The effect of this is, in many cases, to make what is
foreign, artificial, and uncongenial, the foundation of a
man's literary habits, ambition, and prejudices. It is hardly
possible that a man, thus trained and dependent, should
not lose self respect and come to think every thing vulgar
at home.

But it ought to be remembered that the question is not
upon the merits of the ancients, or any models whatever.
Men will always settle this matter for themselves according to their own taste and feelings. What we contend for
is that the literature of a country is just as domestick and
individual as its character or political institutions. Its
charm is its nativeness. It is made for home, to be the
luxury of those who have the feeling and love of home
and whose characters and taste have been formed there.
No matter for rudeness, or want of systems and schools.
It is enough that all is our own and just such as we were
made to have and relish. A country then must be the
former and finisher of its own genius. It has, or should
have, nothing to do with strangers. They are not expected
to feel the beauty of your old poetical language, depending as it does on early and tender associations; connecting
the softer and ruder ages of the country, and inspiring an
inward and inexplicable joy, like a tale of childhood. The
stranger perhaps is only alarmed or disgusted by the

hoarse and wild musick of your forests or sea-shore, by the frantick superstition of your fathers, or the lovely fairy scenes that lie far back in the mists of your fable. He cannot feel your pride in the splendid barbarism of your country when the mind was in health and free and the foundations of your character and greatness laid for ever. All these things are for the native. They help to give a character to his country and her literature, and he loves them too well to be concerned at the world's admiration or contempt.

So long then as a country is proud of itself, it will repel every encroachment upon its native literature. Improvements will offer themselves under a thousand forms. Intimacy with other nations, especially if they are polished and the leaders of fashion, will tempt men to imitate them in every thing. But a nation should keep itself at home and value the things of its own household. It will have but feeble claims to excellence and distinction when it stoops to put on foreign ornament and manner, and to adopt from other nations, images, allusions, and a metaphorical language which are perfectly unmeaning and sickly out of their own birth-place. The most polished will be the dreariest ages of its literature. Its writers will be afraid to speak the language that God has given them till they have mingled the rough torrent with the allaying streams of a softer region. A strange idiom will be introduced into style. And the whole literature of a country will be mere gaudy patchwork, borrowed from every region that has any beauty to lend.

It may be well too just to hint that it is not foreign models alone which are to be feared. We must also be shy of ourselves. For men of real genius and independence will sometimes introduce dangerous novelties, and make errours and corruptions popular and contagious, however short-lived they may prove. And besides this, there is good reason to fear that every country, as it falls into luxury and refinement, will be doomed to have an Augustan age, a classical era of its own, when fine writers will determine what shall be correct taste, pure language, and legitimate poetry. A domestick master may not be as alarming as a foreigner, and long before a man has ceased to study and love the early literature of his country, he may expect to hear that the old language is barbarous and obsolete and rejected by all chaste authors who wish to keep the national literature uniform and pure. As to all this, a man must judge for himself. And one would think that if there must be models, a writer would do well to go as near to the original as possible, even to the very fathers of poetry. If there is luxury for him in such society, and if his books can find readers, in spite of the old cast about them, let him turn to the rougher and more intrepid ages of his country, before men troubled themselves about elegance or plan and wrote right on as they felt, even though they were uttering a thought for the first time, feeling probably very little concern whether a softer age laughed at or worshipped them—whether they were to be ranked among the classicks or barbarians of poetry, whether theirs was to be called an Augustan era, or merely the plain old English days of Elizabeth.

DOCUMENT 10

Francis Calley Gray

Francis Calley Gray (1790–1856) was invited to deliver the annual Phi Beta Kappa oration in Cambridge in August 1816, the year following that of William Tudor. A Boston lawyer of private means who spent his life in public affairs and literary pursuits, he speaks to the problem of literary nationalism from a less assured base of conviction than do some others of the *North American* group, who published his oration. Although Gray retains his respect for English culture and raises some doubts about the possibility of achieving a native culture to match it in the very near future, he at least accepts the desirability of striving in that direction. A long aside on history in general and on the cruelty of the early settlers toward the Indians has here been omitted.

TEXT: from the *North American Review*, III (September 1816), 289–305.

An Address Pronounced before the Society of Phi Beta Kappa

Men of letters have always been reproached with ignorance of the world. I do not mean ignorance of the forms of society but of the interests and characters of their fellow creatures. This reproach is generally merited. The gratification of the desires by which most of them are impelled does not demand any very profound knowledge of human nature.

But while crowds frequent the paths of literature in pursuit of pleasure, wealth or applause, it is the object of the philosophy which forms our bond of union to improve our own characters and that of the society in which we live. The attainment of this object requires an intimate acquaintance with the wants, the feelings, and the capacities of those whom we wish to improve. Personal observation is the most obvious means of acquiring this knowledge: but observation is confined to a narrow circle, narrower even than the influence of our actions, for their consequences descend upon generation after generation; it regards but a small territory and a single age. All within its view are early warped in the same direction, disguised by the same manners and customs, disfigured by the prejudices, which are stamped and branded upon them by the same education and the same examples.

It is impossible to discriminate how much of this motley being is his own work and how much that of his maker, how far he has improved or corrupted his natural character, without examining him in every diversity of climate and education, and government, and distinguishing those faculties and feelings which remain every where the same from those which vary with his situation.

To accomplish this by observation alone would require a life of ages. We must have recourse to the experience of others to assist us in the task. Not to that of travellers; for the most faithful of their narratives sketches only the dress, the habits and manners of the people whom it describes, but cannot acquaint us with the schemes of their ambition, their intrigues, their rivalries, or their moral revolutions. The only adequate resource is History which developes, not only the projects, and labours, and fortunes of a single generation, but their long train of causes and effects through successive ages, and displays the consequences on distant nations of events whose effects seemed to our narrow experience to terminate in the little circle where they were performed and with the lives of those who performed them. . . .

To gratify this generous ambition, it is necessary to be familiar with the annals of our country, to learn by what means this unexampled improvement has been effected, in what manner the same means may be applied to our own age, what changes in them are required by the difference of our situation, and how those changes may be produced; that the principles and institutions of our ancestors may be strengthened and extended, and the manners which we inherit from them, deprived of their rudeness, without losing any thing of their purity. Its tendency to promote these objects recommends our history to the attention of every citizen and gives it the strongest claim on yours. For the influence of men of letters on the institutions, the customs, and the manners of their country, though less ostentatious, is not less powerful than that of the government. By instructing the understanding and elevating the feelings, learning prevents the crimes which the law punishes, it regulates the motives of our conduct, it purifies the sources of life and controls those finer sensibilities of our nature which are too subtle and too sacred to be touched by the rude hand of legislation; it is the guardian of the publick manners, and what are laws without them?

Nor is this all. Men of letters are also the guardians of the publick instruction. It is their care to promote the diffusion of knowledge, to extend the boundaries of science, and increase the treasures of literature.

Nay more, they are the founders of their country's fame, they only can render her illustrious by celebrating the achievements of her heroes; they display the encouragement and distribute the rewards of merit.

Do you think that the jurist traces the principles of justice through the mazes of form and precedent to settle the boundaries of a cornfield? that the soldier sheds his blood for his paltry pittance? that the sleepless anxiety of the statesman is compensated by the bows and the flattery of courtiers; or the midnight labours of the orator by the momentary plaudits of the crowd? No; they toil for immortality, and the hand of learning only can give them their reward.

In order to fulfil these obligations imposed on them by their country, men of letters must be perfectly acquainted with its history: and there is a previous duty, which demands this knowledge no less imperiously, the selection by each individual of the particular department of learning to which his studies shall be directed. In making this selection, he ought to consider not only his own abilities and taste but the situation and the wants of the society in which he lives. The neglect of this duty has occasioned all that waste of learned labour, that toilsome trifling, so much ridiculed and deplored.

It is impossible to recur to the history of our literature without remarking that since the settlement of America, while the ancient states of Europe have produced generation after generation of illustrious writers, we cannot boast one worthy of immortality, though we acknowledge no deficiency in any other species of merit. Our fleets and armies have witnessed many a gallant deed. The popular assembly, the senate, and the hall of justice, have been charmed by the eloquence, and enlightened by the wisdom of men who deserve our admiration and gratitude. Our country has produced many whose labours will improve the condition of posterity but none whose writings will be models for its imitation; many, whose names are worthy of being recorded, but where are they who should record them?[1]

[1] "Our poets and historians, our criticks and orators, the men of whom posterity are to stand in awe, and by whom to be instructed, are yet to appear among us. The men of letters who are to direct our taste, mould our genius, and inspire our emulation, the men, in fact, whose writings are to be the depositories of our national greatness, have not yet shown themselves to the world."

Mr. Buckminster's Oration before the φ. в. к. 1809.

In a note, Mr. Buckminster approves, without excepting them, the works of Minot, Belknap, and Dr. Holmes. I regret that a man whose approbation was an honour did not add other names to those here enumerated; there are others worthy of this distinction.

The passage above cited, and some others in Mr. Buckminster's oration, have excited against him the reproach of being indifferent to the honour of his country. But the best of countries has its imperfections. And the criticism which descends to particulars, pointing out each merit and each failing and giving the reasons of its judgment is a proof of attachment, not of indifference; its praise is more useful and more honourable than the unmeaning plaudits of that blind affection which admires every thing without distinction; it knows not what nor why. He who most readily discerns the defects of the picture is generally most enthusiastick in admiring its beauties.

It is no idle speculation to investigate the causes of this deficiency, to ascertain from the history of our country what obstacles have hitherto opposed its progress in literature, and to inquire by what means they may be evaded or surmounted hereafter.

A slight examination of some of these obstacles, will best illustrate the importance of this study to all men of letters and may tend to brighten the hopes and strengthen the resolution of those who are just quitting the guidance of their literary parent to become the directors of their own studies. Indeed, my friends, you need every encouragement to perseverance. Many of us have, like you, made literature the ornament of youth, but how few grasp it as the jewel of their lives as their friend, their companion, their guide, their refuge, their consolation, and their hope. The thousand occupations which, in our country, court the hand of enterprise and promise earlier and richer rewards, have tempted them all away from the toilsome pursuit of science. For however tranquil and easy and indolent the life of a scholar may appear untried, it is indeed painful and laborious and discouraging; like the mountain whose side at a distance seems to form a regular and gentle acclivity, such as an active foot might easily ascend: but when we make the attempt, then come the woody mazes, the slippery path, the steep ascent, the sudden precipice, and above all, the hours of toil which add nothing perceptible to our progress. And you who tread the path of science have also competitors to contend with whose eagerness allows you no time for repose, to refresh you after the labour that is past or invigorate you for the next,

> "For honour travels in a straight so narrow,
> Where but one walks abreast.
> And emulation hath a thousand sons,
> That one by one pursue. If you give way,
> Or hedge aside from the direct forthright,
> Like to an entered tide, they all rush by,
> And leave you hindmost."

The difficulties and disgusts of learning are not indeed peculiar to our country, but their effects have been peculiarly unfortunate here because they are not counteracted by still stronger motives. Among us it is so easy and so common to succeed in undertakings commenced even at a late period of life that a new employment may always be entered on with a rational expectation of success; and this facility induces many to abandon the pursuit of learning at the first moment of weariness, impatience or disappointment. Men of letters in all other countries have the same obstacles before them, but in other countries, despair is planted behind: every avenue to distinction is so crowded, that after devoting the first years of manhood to one pursuit, it is too late to begin upon another. In other countries, therefore, these obstacles are only subjects of complaint and incentives to exertion. The necessity of surmounting them supplies the means. The means by which you may surmount them must be sought in your own minds, in that resolute pride which never shrinks from what it has once undertaken; or still better, in the steadiness of principle.

Thus the very prosperity of our country has strengthened the obstacles which oppose the cultivation of letters. Its political situation also, though often varying, has in all its changes been unfavourable to the interests of science. On its first settlement, the immediate care of our ancestors was to obtain the means of comfortable subsistence. Before this could be effected, war with the Indian tribes began and continued without an interval of security for nearly a century. Not like the wars of our age, contests between armies and mere subjects of speculation to the rest of the community to whom their progress is communicated only by celebrations of victory or apologies for defeat; but war by surprise, war of extermination, war on the defenceless in which peace itself was only a stratagem. During this period, every man was obliged to hang his arms at his fireside, every cottage was the scene of a skirmish, the tomahawk hung over every head, and blood was shed on every threshold. In such a state of society, it is no wonder that little time was devoted to the cultivation of letters. The din of arms stifles the voice of the muses, as well as that of the laws.

But as the population of the country increased and the Indians were driven to a greater distance from our principal settlements, something like security was felt in our towns, and learning advanced almost as rapidly as the employments of commercial industry or the arts of civilization till the revolutionary war. During that war, whose history is too familiar to you all to need a comment, every thing was neglected, every thing was forgotten but the cause of liberty. After peace was concluded, the attention of the people was directed to another enterprise more difficult, more important, and more glorious even than the acquisition of independence. I mean the establishment of government.

On the adoption of the constitution, it was natural and right that all eyes should watch the result of this delicate and momentous experiment, that the first struggles of established authority, with opposition, should excite a trembling interest in every friend of his country; and particularly in those, whose genius had framed, whose eloquence had recommended, and whose authority had established this new form of government and thus rendered them responsible for its success. But it is not natural that their descendants should inherit their fears, that those who saw nothing of the difficulty of framing our constitution but have witnessed only its success should tremble for its safety in spite of experience and think it the duty of every individual to devote his life to the contrivance of new means for its support. Men establish governments not to find employment in administering them, but in order that every citizen knowing the ability and the duty of the community to protect him may pursue with confidence and security his own path to happiness; and the government which inspires this confidence and affords this security is one of the greatest of blessings. But, if the end must be sacrificed to the means, if the pursuit of happiness and excellence must be abandoned for ever to preserve a particular form of government, if our constitution is so frail that every eye must be fixed in restless anxiety on the tottering fabrick and every hand be always raised for its support, let it fall, it is not worth supporting. May we not hope better things of our political institutions? They have resisted adversity, and what is much more, they have survived twenty years of unexampled prosperity; may we not then, now believe that they are well adapted to the character and situation of the people and therefore calculated to endure? may we not at length be persuaded that the foundations of the temple are deeply laid, its superstructure firmly established, and that it is now time to decorate it with the labours of the muses, and kindle the flame of science on its altar?

This persuasion is already prevalent, the popular assembly is no longer considered the only theatre for talents, the noiseless labours of the scholar are respected. The political situation of our country now opposes no considerable obstructions to the progress of literature, though he who is ambitious of immediate distinction may still be tempted to enter a career where applause is early and surely obtained by every one who deigns to court it.

Our language presents another obstacle to the celebrity of our writers. The excellence of modern authors is estimated by comparing their productions with other works written in the same language, most of their readers being masters of one language only. This comparison is just in Europe where those who write in the same language generally reside in the same country and possess the same advantages. But our language, our literature, our taste are English, and we determine the merit of our literary productions by comparing them with those of men who enjoy better means and stronger motives for the cultivation of letters than America affords.

Their vast capital and wealthy institutions assemble crowds whose lives are devoted to learning and whose rivalries and friendships alike promote the interests of science.

Their libraries, containing the best works of every age and nation and on every subject, not only supply the student with the means of acquiring knowledge, but by informing him what others have written, prevent the useless labour of seeking what has long since been discovered and explaining what is already known.

Their system of education is far more complete than ours. They are conducted by the most eminent of their predecessors through a long and laborious course of study till they have attained an equality with their masters and have become acquainted with every discovery previously made in the department of science to which their studies are directed, so that all the knowledge, afterwards acquired by their unassisted exertions, is an addition to the stock of human learning.

But how is it with us? I should blush to uncover the nakedness of my country if it were not that her wants must be generally known and felt before they will be supplied.

Our libraries are small, and not always well selected, wanting many of those works to whose excellence ages have born witness, and abounding with magazines and journals too well adapted to the taste of many who frequent them, mere students of reviews, readers of extracts, who give only their praise to the wise and the great, while their time is devoted to triflers.[2]

We have excellent institutions for the instruction of youth, but none for the accomplishment of men. We are just led to the portal of the labyrinth of learning and left to find our own way through its mazes; happy, if after many an errour, our wanderings do not terminate in despair. I would not undervalue our seminaries of education. They are well calculated to diffuse a little learning through every class of the community, admirably adapted to the situation and wants of the people; and we could not exchange them for those of any other country without suffering by the experiment. But we must add to them es-

[2] It is not asserted that the funds of our *principal* Libraries are injudiciously applied. The chief source of our regret is the insufficiency of their funds, in consequence of which many of them owe a large portion of their contents to donations of books from individuals, a mode of forming a library which precludes the possibility of systematical selection.

This sentence has no reference to the reading room of the Atheneum, an establishment of a different nature, and which increases instead of diminishing the funds appropriated to the Library.

tablishments like those of Europe before we can expect the glory of being a literary nation.

This must be the labour of more than one generation; but every effort to improve our libraries or to extend our literary institutions is an important service to learning and to the publick.

But is it hence to be inferred that our generation can serve the cause of letters only by improving the means of educating their posterity, by preparing the way to fame for others without the hope of attaining it themselves. By no means. If you shrink from a competition with the scholars of Europe, there are still some departments of science, where no Transatlantick competitor can easily cross your path, such for instance is Natural History. To eminence in this study, the patronage and the rewards of Europe are offered, the education requisite for its commencement is easily acquired even in our country, and the means of pursuing it are in our hands, are all around us, are under our feet, "and the dull swain treads on them daily with his clouted shoon." They are all the productions of nature, every insect, every plant, every pebble. Living in a vast and fertile country, almost the only civilized portion of the earth, which has not been explored by the zeal of the Naturalist,[3] we possess advantages for the cultivation of this science, superiour to those of any other people. Yet even in this what have we done? Nothing—comparatively nothing.

Scotland has given us an Ornithology, and for most of our knowledge of American Botany we are indebted to natives of Sweden, France, and Germany.[4]

Since then we are as deficient in this branch of knowledge as in every other, notwithstanding the superiour advantages which we possess for acquiring it, *some* may con-

---

[3] ———"sylvas saltusque sequamur,
    Intactos."

[4] The publications of our countrymen on the Natural History of America are not to be compared in magnitude or importance with the works of Europeans on the same subject. But I seem to see a far brighter star rising in New-England.
    "Credimus! an qui amant ipsi sibi somnia fingunt?"

clude that it is not the want of means, or motives, or education, which has prevented our progress in the other sciences. According to the true rule of philosophy, they may seek one simple cause commensurate with the effect, one which will account equally for our inferiority in every department of letters, and may think that they find it in the political situation of our country which every day opposes fewer obstacles to the progress of learning, or in the temptation to pursue more lucrative occupations which it requires only firmness to resist.

Animated by this belief, they may regard without discouragement the failure of the few efforts for literary eminence hitherto made in America, and the superior advantages possessed by the inhabitants of Europe, and may resolve to seek celebrity in those higher departments of literature where illustrious men of all ages have laid the foundations of their fame; to consider as their rivals the learned of other countries engaged in the same pursuits and not only the living but the dead.

If there be any such among you, who are confident that all defects of education may be supplied by industry, who ask no means but the talents which God has given them, no motive but their hopes and their ambition, who considering every conflict as a prelude to victory and anticipating in every obstacle a monument of success, delight to struggle with the strongest rivals and to tread the steepest ascent to distinction, to you I would not breathe a whisper of discouragement. In such attempts it is glorious even to fail, and success will confer renown upon yourselves and blessings on mankind.

But there are few who can indulge such hopes as these; few in any nation of those "superiour spirits, who are born for something more and better than just to breathe the common air, and walk about this globe," and fulfil the obligations of private life, and be forgotten; whose perogative and whose duty it is to raise some monument for the instruction of other generations, to enlighten their age and country, "and shed new lustre on the name of man."

But our duties should not be neglected, because they are of an humbler class. Though not many of us can hope to write their names on the annals of a nation, to be distinguished by the honours which they receive from their country or still more nobly by the services which they render her; yet each may add at least, a nameless stone to the pyramid of her glory, may contribute something to the instruction of his fellow-citizens and something to the stability of the government. The humblest among us has a little circle round him whom his warning checks, his example guides, and his approbation animates, by enlightening whose understandings and elevating whose sentiments, he may give material, if not illustrious support to institutions which are founded solely on the principles and feelings of the people; for under such institutions and among such a people, private virtue is the first of publick duties and an honourable life the noblest service that we can render to our country.

DOCUMENT 11

John Pickering

While the contributors to the *North American* were debating the problem of an American literature, John Pickering (1777–1846), a Boston lawyer and student of many languages (Classic, Romance, Turkish, Arabic, Chinese) contributed to the American Academy of Arts and Sciences a "Vocabulary; or, a collection of various words and phrases, which have been supposed to be peculiar to this country" and prefaced it with a "Memoir on the Present State of the English Language in the United States of America." Rejecting Webster's thesis that there was an American language in the making (Document 4), he solemnly warned that American variations of standard English should be regarded as corruptions, and then attempted to point out the proper way of dealing with the problem. The "Vocabulary" itself is too long to be reprinted here, and a selection would be arbitrary and not representative.

TEXT: from *Memoirs of the Academy of Arts and Sciences*, III, pt. 2 (1816), pp. 439–51.

Memoir on the Present State of the English Language in the United States of America

The preservation of the English language in its purity throughout the United States is an object deserving the attention of every American who is a friend to the literature and science of his country. It is in a particular manner entitled to the consideration of the Academy; for, though subjects which are usually ranked under the head of the physical sciences were doubtless chiefly in view with the founders of the Academy, yet as our language is to be

the instrument of communicating to the world the speculations and discoveries of our countrymen in science and
literature, it seems also necessarily "to fall within the design of the institution"; because, unless that language is
well settled and can be read with ease and satisfaction by
all to whom it is addressed, our authors will write and
publish certainly under many disadvantages though perhaps not altogether in vain.

It is true, indeed, that our countrymen may speak and
write in a dialect of English which will be generally understood in the United States; but if they are ambitious of
having their works read by Englishmen as well as Americans, they must write in a language that Englishmen can
read with facility and pleasure. And if for sometime to
come it should not be the lot of many Americans to publish any thing which shall be read out of their own country, yet all who have the least tincture of learning will
continue to feel an ardent desire to acquaint themselves
with the works of English authors. Let us then for a moment imagine the time to have arrived when Americans
shall be no longer able to understand the works of Milton,
Pope, Swift, Addison, and the other English authors, justly
styled classic, without the aid of a translation into a language that is to be called at some future day the American
tongue! By such a change, it is true, our loss would not be
so great in works purely scientific, as in those which are
usually termed works of taste; for the obvious reason that
the design of the former is merely to communicate information without regard to elegance of language or the
force and beauty of the sentiments. But the excellencies
of works of taste cannot be felt even in the best translations; a truth which, without resorting to the example of
the matchless ancients, will be acknowledged by every man
who is acquainted with the admirable works in the various
living languages.

Nor is this the only view in which a radical change of
language would be a loss to us. To say nothing of the
facilities afforded by a common language in the ordinary
intercourse of business between the people of the two
countries, it should not be forgotten that our religion and

our laws are studied in the language of the nation from which we are descended; and with the loss of the language we should finally suffer the loss of those peculiar advantages which we now derive from the investigations of the jurists and divines of that country.

But it is often asked among us, do not the people of America now speak and write the English language with purity? A brief consideration of the subject will furnish a satisfactory answer to this question; it will also enable us to correct the erroneous opinions entertained by some Americans on this point and at the same time to defend our countrymen against the charge made by some English writers, of a design to effect a radical change in the language.

As the inquiry before us is a simple question of fact, it is to be determined, like every other question of that nature, by proper evidence. What evidence then have we that the English language is not spoken and written in America with the same degree of purity that is to be found in the writers and orators of England?

In the first place, although it is agreed that there is greater uniformity of dialect throughout the United States (in consequence of the frequent removals of people from one part of our country to another) than is to be found throughout England, yet none of our countrymen, not even those who are the most zealous in supporting what they imagine to be the honour of the American character, will contend that we have not in some instances departed from the standard of the language. We have formed some entirely new words, and to some old ones that are still used in England we have affixed new significations; while others that have long since become obsolete in England are still retained in common use with us. For example: it is admitted by all that the verb *to advocate*, the adjective *lengthy*, and a few others are of American origin; and, that the adjective *clever* and some other words of English origin have been generally used by us in a sense different from their present signification in England. If then, in connexion with these acknowledgments of our own countrymen, we allow any weight to the opinions of Englishmen (who must surely be competent judges in this case) it cannot be denied that we have in many instances deviated from the standard of the language, as spoken and written in England at the present day. By this, however, I do not mean that so great a deviation has taken place as to have rendered any considerable part of our language unintelligible to Englishmen; but merely that so many corruptions have crept into our English as to have become the subject of much animadversion and regret with the learned of Great Britain. And as we are hardly aware of the opinion entertained by them of the extent of these corruptions, it may be useful if it should not be very flattering to our pride to hear their remarks on this subject in their own words. We shall find that these corruptions are censured, not by a few contemptible critics but, so far as the fact is to be ascertained from English publications, by all the scholars of that country who take any interest in American literature. In proof of this I request the attention of the Academy to the following extracts from several of the British Reviews, some of which are the most distinguished of the present day and all of which together may be considered as expressing the general opinion of the literary men of Great Britain. That all the remarks are just, to the extent in which they will naturally be understood, few of our countrymen will be willing to admit.

The *British Critic*, for February 1810, in a review of the Rev. Mr. Bancroft's Life of Washington, says—"In the style we observe, with regret rather than with astonishment, the introduction of several *new* words, or *old* words in a new sense; a deviation from the rules of the English language, which, if it continues to be practised by good writers in America, will introduce confusion into the medium of intercourse, and render it a subject of regret that the people of that continent should not have an entirely separate language as well as government of their own. Instances occur at almost every page; without pains in selecting, the following may be taken as specimens," &c. The Reviewers then mention several words which are all inserted in the Vocabulary annexed to this memoir.

The same Reviewers (in April 1808) in their account of

Chief Justice Marshall's Life of Washington, have the following remarks:—"In the writings of Americans we have often discovered deviations from the purity of the English idiom, which we have been more disposed to censure than to wonder at. The common speech of the United States has departed very considerably from the standard adopted in England, and in this case it is not to be expected that writers, however cautious, will maintain a strict purity. Mr. Marshall deviates occasionally, but not grossly," &c.

The *Critical Review* (for September 1809) in remarks upon *Travels through France, by Col. Pinckney,* says of the author's style—"He falls into occasional inaccuracies . . . . . but the instances are rare, and by no means so striking as we have frequent occasions of remarking in most American writers."

The same Reviewers (in July 1807) in speaking of Marshall's Life of Washington, have the following, among other remarks on the style of that work—that "it abounds with many of those idioms which prevail on the other side of the Atlantic."

The *Annual Review,* for 1808, in speaking of the same work, after pointing out several instances of false English (in respect to many of which, however, the Reviewers have been misled by the incorrectness of the English edition of that work, as will be seen in the following Vocabulary,) has the following observations; which, if they had been made in a manner somewhat different, would probably have been more favourably received by those for whose benefit they seem to be intended:—"We have been more particular in noticing these faults in Mr. Marshall's language because we are not at all certain that the Americans do not consider them as beauties; and because we wish, if possible, to stem that torrent of barbarous phraseology, with which the American writers threaten to destroy the purity of the English language."

The *Monthly Reviewers,* in their account of a little work, entitled *A Political Sketch of America,* cite, with approbation, the following passage—"The national language should be sedulously cultivated; and this is to be accomplished by means of schools. This circumstance de-

mands particular attention, for the language of conversation is becoming incorrect; and even in America authors are to be found who make use of new or obsolete words which no good writer in this country would employ."
Monthly Rev. May 1808.

The *Edinburgh Review* for October 1804 (which is the last I shall cite) has the following general observations on this subject:—

"If the men of birth and education in that other England which they are building up in the West will not diligently study the great authors who purified and fixed the language of our common forefathers, we must soon lose the only badge that is still worn of our consanguinity."

The same Reviewers, in their remarks on Marshall's and Ramsay's Lives of Washington, say—

"In these volumes we have found a great many words and phrases which English criticism refuses to acknowledge. America has thrown off the yoke of the British nation, but she would do well for some time to take the laws of composition from the Addisons, the Swifts and the Robertsons of her ancient sovereign. . . . . These remarks, however, are not dictated by any paltry feelings of jealousy or pride. We glory in the diffusion of our language over a new world where we hope it is yet destined to collect new triumphs; and in the brilliant perspective of American greatness, we see only pleasing images of associated prosperity and glory of the land in which we live."

Such is the strong language of the British literati on this subject. And shall we at once, without examination, ascribe it wholly to prejudice? Should we not by such a hasty decision expose ourselves to the like imputation? On the contrary, should not the opinions of such writers stimulate us to inquiry that we may ascertain whether their animadversions are well founded or not? We see the same critics censure the Scotticisms of their northern brethren, the peculiarities of the Irish and the provincial corruptions of their own English writers. We cannot therefore be so wanting in liberality as to think that, when deciding upon the literary claims of Americans, they are governed wholly by prejudice or jealousy. A suspicion of this sort should be the less readily entertained as we acknowledge that they sometimes do justice to our countrymen. The writings of Dr. Franklin, for example, have received their unqualified praise; and a few other American authors have been liberally commended by them. The opinions of these critics too are supported by those of some distinguished men in our own country. Dr. Franklin censures, without reserve, "the popular errors several of our own states are continually falling into," with respect to "expressions and pronunciation." Dr. Witherspoon who, by having been educated in Great Britain and by his subsequent long residence in the United States, was peculiarly well qualified judge on this subject, remarks:—"I shall also admit, though with some hesitation, that gentlemen and scholars in Great Britain speak as much with the vulgar in common chit chat as persons of the same class do in America; but there is a remarkable difference in their public and solemn discourses. I have heard in this country in the senate, at the bar, and from the pulpit, and see daily in dissertations from the press, errors in grammar, improprieties and vulgarisms, which hardly any person of the same class in point of rank and literature would have fallen into in Great Britain."

With these opinions of such distinguished writers before us, shall we entertain the illiberal jealousy that justice is intentionally withheld from us by our English brethren? Let us rather imitate the example of the learned and modest Campbell who, though he had devoted a great part of a long life to the study of the English language, yet thought it no disgrace to make an apology for his style in the following terms: "Sensible," says he, "of the disadvantages, in point of style, which my northern situation lays me under, I have availed myself of every opportunity of better information in regard to all those terms and phrases in the version, [of the Gospels] of which I was doubtful. I feel myself under particular obligations on this account to one gentleman, my valuable friend and colleague Dr. Beattie who, though similarly situated with myself, has with greater success studied the genius and idiom of our language; and of whom it is no more than justice to add that the acknowledged purity of his own diction is the least of his qualifications as an author. But if, notwithstanding all the care I have taken, I shall be found, in many places, to need the indulgence of the English reader, it will not much surprise me. . . . . The apology which Irenæus, Bishop of Lyons in Gaul in the second century, makes for his language in a book he published in defence of religion, appears to me so candid, so modest, so sensible, at the same time so apposite to my own case, that I cannot avoid transcribing and adopting it:—'Non autem exquires a nobis, qui apud Celtas commoramur, et in barbarum sermonem plerumque avocamur, orationis artem quam non didicimus, neque vim conscriptoris quam non affectavimus, neque ornamentum verborum, neque suadelam quam nescimus'. . . ."[1]

Upon an impartial consideration of the subject then, it seems impossible to resist the conclusion that although the language of the United States has perhaps changed less than might have been expected, when we consider how many years have elapsed since our ancestors brought it from England, yet it has in so many instances departed from the English standard that our scholars should lose no time in endeavouring to restore it to its purity and to prevent future corruption.

This, it is obvious, is to be effected, in the first place, by carefully noting every unauthorised word and phrase; or (as Dr. Franklin many years ago recommended, in his letter to Mr. Webster on this subject[2]) by "setting a discountenancing mark" upon such of them, as are not rendered indispensably necessary by the peculiar circumstances of our country; and, even if we should continue to have a partiality for some of those expressions, and should choose to retain them, it will always be useful to know them. By knowing exactly what peculiar words are in use with us, we should, among other advantages, have it in our power to expose the calumnies of some prejudiced and ignorant writers who have frequently laid to the charge

[1] Campbell's Four Gospels, preface, p. 28.
[2] See the word *Improve* in the *Vocabulary* [not here included].

of our countrymen in general the affected words and phrases of a few conceited individuals;—words and phrases which are justly the subject of as much ridicule in America as they are in Great Britain. As a general rule also we should undoubtedly avoid all those words which are noticed by English authors of reputation as expressions with which they are unacquainted; for although we might produce some English authority for such words, yet the very circumstance of their being thus noticed by well educated Englishmen is a proof that they are not used at this day in England and, of course, ought not to be used elsewhere by those who would speak correct English.

With a view to this important object I have taken some pains to make a collection of words and phrases which I offer to the Academy, not as a perfect list of our real or supposed peculiarities of language but merely as the beginning of a work which can be completed only by long and accurate observation, especially of intelligent Americans who shall have an opportunity of residing in England and of well educated Englishmen who may resort to this country. It has long been the wish of our scholars to see a work of that sort; but, though several words have been occasionally noticed by Dr. Witherspoon, Dr. Franklin, and some others, yet nobody seems to have been willing to undertake the laborious task of making a general collection of them. Seeing no prospect of such a work and observing, with no small degree of solicitude, the corruptions which are gradually insinuating themselves into our language, I have taken the liberty to ask the attention of the Academy to this subject by laying before them the following Vocabulary: a performance which I am sensible is not so worthy of their notice as more time and ability might have rendered it.

In making this Vocabulary I have resorted to all the sources of information in my power and have, under each word, given some of the authorities for and against the use of it. I have also subjoined to some of the words the criticisms of Dr. Franklin, Dr. Witherspoon, and other writers at large, in order that the reader may avail himself of their instructive observations without the trouble of searching for them through the numerous volumes of their works; and in all cases where any word had been noticed by English or American writers, which I had also myself observed, (particularly during my residence in England, where my attention was first drawn to this subject) I have chosen to give it upon their authority rather than my own. Many words will be found in the list which are not in fact of American origin, or peculiar to Americans; but it appeared to me that it would be useful to insert all words the legitimacy of which had been questioned, in order that their claim to a place in the English language might be discussed and settled. Several of the words have been obtained from British Reviews of American publications; and I may here remark how much it is to be regretted that the reviewers have not pointed out all the instances that have come under their notice of our deviations from the English standard. This would be doing an essential service to the cause of literature and be the most effectual means of accomplishing what those scholars appear to have so much at heart—the preservation of the English language in its purity wherever it is spoken.

It has been asserted that we have discovered a much stronger propensity than the English to add new words to the language; and the little animadversion which, till within a few years, such new-coined words have met with among us, seems to support that opinion. With us, every writer takes the liberty to contaminate the language with the barbarous terms of his own tasteless invention; but in England, new words are seldom hazarded even by authors of the highest rank. The passion for these ridiculous novelties among us, however, has for some time past been declining. Our greatest danger now is that we shall continue to use antiquated words which were brought to this country by our forefathers nearly two centuries ago—(some of which too were at that day provincial words in England) and that we shall affix a new signification to words which are still used in that country in their original sense. Words of these descriptions having long been a part of the language, we are not led to examine critically the authority on which their different significations rest; but those that are entirely new, like strangers on their first appearance, immediately attract our attention and induce us to inquire into their pretensions to the rank they claim.

But it is not enough for us to note single words; our idiom, it would seem, is in some degree changed and is in danger of still greater corruptions.[3] At the same time, therefore, that we are "setting a discountenancing mark" upon unauthorised words, we should assiduously study the language of the best authors, especially Dryden, Swift, and Addison, to the last of whom, Dr. Blair, in his Lectures on Rhetoric, justly applies Quintilian's well-known remark upon Cicero—that "to be highly pleased with his manner of writing is the criterion of a good taste in English style—Ille se profecisse sciat cui Cicero valde placebit;" and of whom Dr. Johnson emphatically says—"whoever would attain a good English style, familiar but not coarse, and elegant but not ostentatious, must give his days and nights to Addison." Dr. Franklin, who informs us in his *Life*, that it was one of the greatest objects of his ambition to write English well, formed his style upon that of Addison; and Franklin is one of the very few American writers whose style has satisfied the English critics. This is the discipline to which the most distinguished scholars of Great Britain have submitted and without which neither they nor the scholars of our own country can acquire and preserve a pure English style. It is related of Mr. Fox, that when speaking of his intended History of England, he said, he would "admit no word into his book for which he had not the authority of Dryden." This determination may perhaps seem at first view to have been dictated by too fastidious a taste or an undue partiality for a favourite author; but unquestionably, a rule of this sort, adopted in the course of our education, (extending, however, to two or three of the best authors,)

---

[3] That a radical change in the language of a people so remote from the source of it as we are from England, is not a chimerical supposition will be apparent from the alterations that have taken place among the nations of Europe; of which no instance, perhaps, is more striking than the change and final separation of the languages of Spain and Portugal, notwithstanding the vicinity and frequent intercourse of the people of those two countries.

would be the most effectual method of acquiring a good English style. And surely if Fox found no necessity for any other words than Dryden had used, those authors have little excuse who take the liberty not only of using all the words they can find in the whole body of English authors, ancient and modern, but also of making new terms of their own at pleasure. Who shall have a right to complain of scarcity, where that distinguished orator found abundance? Such standard authors, therefore, should be made the foundation of our English; but as our language like all others is constantly though slowly changing, we should also, in order to perfect our style as we advance to mature age, study those authors of our own time who have made the older writers their models. Every word in the writings of Addison is not now in general use in England; and many words have been adopted since his time and are now sanctioned by all the best writers of that country. Such writers, therefore, as well as their illustrious masters, ought to be diligently read; for we should always remember, that in language, as in the fine arts, we can only attain to excellence by incessant study of the best models.

DOCUMENT 12

Solyman Brown

Meanwhile a maverick appeared in New Haven in the person and book of Solyman Brown (1790–1876), rhymster, teacher, clergyman, and ultimately practicing dentist, who could turn out pentameters on any of these subjects endlessly. *An Essay on American Poetry, with several miscellaneous pieces on a variety of subjects* was published there in 1818, and a copy came to the *North American* where it was turned over to the young William Cullen Bryant for review. The selection here is the Preface and two pages of the verse, which stimulated Bryant to his pioneering review of American accomplishment to that date in the art of poetry.

TEXT: from the first edition, New Haven, 1818, pp. 5–15 and 24–25.

An Essay on American Poetry

PREFACE

The proudest freedom to which a nation can aspire, not excepting even political independence, is found in complete emancipation from literary thraldom. Few nations, however, have arrived at this commanding eminence. Greece once possessed it and she was the glory and wonder of the world. Her arms were then victorious over every foe. The arts that polish life and distinguish cultivated man from the unlettered savage elevated her sons to the height of human greatness; and every improvement was exactly commensurate with her scientific monopoly. She perfectly understood what advantages she gained from her intellectual superiority and that every nation from which she could exclude Learning and the Arts was, of course, her slave.

In this magisterial career she retained for a long time the monarchy of the world. The nations submitted to her command with the same deference with which they bowed to the immortal geniuses that sparkled in her literary galaxy. They could scarcely doubt that she who had nourished and reared to manhood a Xenophon, a Demosthenes, and a Homer, was the mother and mistress of the human race and had an indisputable right to arbitrate the destinies of man.

But we soon behold as her vigilance is declining, a neighbouring nation, fired by her example and with a masterly effort, leaping into mental rivalry. Rome struggled for the palm. Her Maro was carefully reared in the nursery of Augustus as a literary champion to encounter the Grecian Bard; while her Tully, by the thunders of the Roman forum, was shaking the statue of Demosthenes from its golden pedestal. So successful were the assailants in this intellectual conflict that the capitol of the scientific and of the political world was immediately transferred to the banks of the Tyber.

The Learning, the Arts, and the Arms of Rome were now on their march to perfection and the glory of Greece was consequently fading in the splendors of the new and rising luminary. Rome was for a long time the arbitress of the world; nor did the powers of this vast empire decline till Bigotry shook her sceptre over the throne of the Cæsars and Wit and Genius retired to the cells of Superstition.

During the dark ages of the world there was too little science for either literary eminence or literary ambition. An eminence in ignorance, fanatacism, and vice, was the only superiority. From this intellectual and moral insensibility France was the first to awake; but the prize was contested, and England eventually obtained the ascendancy. Her course has indeed been luminous and the splendor of her achievements has excited the wonder of the world. Her attainments have been as universal if not as distinguished as those of Greece and Rome. In the group of English worthies a counterpart is presented of all the varieties of Genius which adorned the Grecian or the Augustan age. Poetry, epic, pastoral, and lyric, with all its minor diversities; Philosophy, natural and moral; Architecture, Statuary, and Painting, together with the useful arts of life, have all been cultivated with encouraging success and to the immortal honour of the British name.

But although it would be folly to assail the literary fame of England, purchased by Shakespeare, Dryden, Spencer, Milton, Locke, Newton, Pope, Addison, Young, and Cowper, it is not to be concealed that she has long understood her own interests too well not to assume a dictatorial aspect towards other nations utterly inconsistent with their welfare. It is thus she has subjugated Scotland and Ireland and used all her efforts to smother, in its cradle, the rising genius of both these countries. It has ever been the policy and practice of England to decry Scotch and Irish intellect and affect a sovereign contempt for all that are born on the Forth or the Liffey. As these countries have now coalesced under the crown of England, it has become less her interest to urge hostilities in those directions. America is therefore the principal object of her literary persecution. It was seen that the United States threatened to become the rival of the mother country. Already had the Eagle of Columbia, stooping from his inaccessible Ærie, plucked the brightest gem from the British diadem and bore it away for ever beyond the reach of recovery. That such a nation would one day contest the palm of priority with the fellow countrymen even of Shakespeare, Swift, and Locke, was no unreasonable presumption. It would be inconsistent with the design of a Preface to enter minutely into all the artifices incessantly employed for half a century to maintain the ideal superiority of British over American Genius. We were at first represented as cannibals, feasting only on the tortures of suffering humanity and deriving our habits and religion from the savage that prowls in the desert. When this charm was dissolved and the English populace began to love as brethren the fellow patriots of Washington, we were immediately exhibited as a race of intellectual pigmies; bunglers in Art and pedants in Science.

It was no difficult task for an English pamphleteer to demonstrate beyond the fear of confutation that the human mind was unable to sustain a voyage across the Atlantic; that a giant on the Thames was a dwarf on the Hudson; in short, that all who landed on the shores of the New World found themselves only the skeletons of man, deprived at once of animal instinct and of a rational soul.

The manifest design of the English ministry, at whose instigation these absurdities were palmed upon the vulgar, was to aid the national revenue by the exportation of English books for the use of the people of the United States; to fill these publications with slanders on the scientific character of Americans; to suppress the growing spirit of emigration in England, and to excite in the minds of the people of this country a prejudice against the literary works of their compatriots.—By a little observation we may learn the fatal success of this scheme. No inconsiderable portion of the schools in this country are now supplied with elementary books of English edition. Even American authors are reprinted there and the profits of the sales in the United States are converted to the support of the British government. These facts must produce unavoidable conviction of the propriety of the preceding remarks.

And it is perfectly easy to trace these effects to their causes and show their tendency to undermine the structure of our National Independence. One of the greatest institutions established to produce the effects here spoken of and under the eye of the British ministry is that of their numerous Reviews. These unmasked batteries, erected on the Forth and the Thames,[1] are in the republic of letters what the English navy is upon the ocean—the terror of mankind. The two grand designs of these periodical publications are to extol the literary productions of England and ridicule those of every other country. These Reviews are sedulously circulated in the United States for which

[1] The *Edinburgh* and *Quarterly* (London) *Reviews.*

they seem principally designed. The respect which the American people are accustomed to pay their mother country has engendered an incredible credulity to all the assertions, how groundless and preposterous soever, which issue from the English Press. Thus the design of England is exactly accomplished; and the contempt which they only affect to possess for American genius is actually instilled into many of the inhabitants of this republic. It seems to be sufficient to immortalize any work that it has once been published in England though it may have been a jest in its own country and become a voluntary exile to America to avoid the sneers of its countrymen. What wonder if such cringing obsequiousness render the name of an American a byword across the ocean? And what could more effectually prove that we form our opinions from the scribbles of an English Pamphleteer and surrender our judgments to the dogmatical asseverations of a swaggering Reviewer?

A second cause of the evils of which America so justly complains is the importation of books into the United States, often at reduced prices, to prevent improvement in the arts of Printing and Binding and thus annihilate that profession which in all countries and ages has given the first impulse to latent genius.

On the article of books more than on most exports it has ever been the policy of England to make pecuniary sacrifices when necessary to the destruction of American Manufactures. This artifice strikes at the soul of intellectual improvement as well as of advancements in the Arts. On the respectability of Booksellers and Printers much of the literary glory of any country depends. They have it in their power to encourage the timid but worthy adventurer in the race of Fame; and in all ages since the art of printing was invented, they have been the first patrons of those men who, from obscurity have risen by their talents to a mental nobility, which royal blood or royal favour could never impart. As the Freedom of the Press has been uniformly when not perverted the bulwark of independence, so any infringement on its native rights in a land of freedom is a national evil. It matters not whether that infringement arise from force at home or from secret and artful fraud in a foreign power.

But it requires no spirit of prophecy to predict the consequences if the influx of foreign books, maps, and charts, is so great and the prices so much reduced as to render the manufacture of those articles rather a detriment than a benefit to the artisan—that in the first place, it will drive the printer from his work-shop; and secondly, render it the interest of the bookseller to encourage the use of imported books which he has bought at reduced prices and on which he makes a greater profit than on those manufactured in his own country. Little sagacity is necessary to discover the success of this scheme in checking the advancement of American Literature. We find our presses to a degree inactive, native genius without patrons and the shelves of the bookseller bending beneath a weight of imported volumes. These are evils which every true friend to his country will deprecate and which, it is hoped, patriotism will ere long remove.

A third source of the evils under consideration is found in the determined resolution of men of letters in the parent country not to give the smallest credit to American productions, how meritorious soever. The patriotism of the English in this respect is without a parallel. From the prince to the beggar the same spirit is manifest through all grades of community. It pervades the writings of the learned and the conversation of the illiterate. It grows with the growth of every son of Britain and journeys with him to the remotest nations. Even the renegade from the justice of his country who seeks an asylum in America from the avenger of blood and who intends to make this country his future home is fraught with the same spirit. It affords a fit topic for the exhibition of national pride; and we often meet with those who are unable to distinguish the brilliant beauties of Rasselas from the dull monotony of Pilgrim's Progress venting unmeaning reproach at the names of Edwards and Dwight, whose intellectual greatness would not suffer them to desire a conquest in the struggle for literary glory over thousands of the deified witlings of England.

Another artifice employed by the British ministry to reproach America and exalt their own nation is that of sending through the United States hireling emissaries, to compose on their way, what they denominate "Travels." These fabrications they palm upon the vulgar as real history and sanction the whole by a solemn act of licensed perjury. They contain just what the addle brains of these prostituted knaves happen to conceive; and if this should be found a libel on the American character, it is sure of the approbation of the employers.

Such are some of the causes which have contributed to suppress the spirit of literary enterprize in this republic and to throw a shade over those geniuses that have burst the incumbent darkness. That they will ever be removed until the spirit of independence shall teach the inhabitants of these States that true liberty is incompatible with literary bondage is not to be expected. We may learn the effects of emancipation upon other countries. We have seen the dungeon of mental slavery crumbled before the strong arm of Roman and British patriotism and the chains of the oppressor melted in the fire of Genius. The example of these nations, contending for victory, is bright and alluring; and the triumph of intellect, when thus vigorously exerted, affords a consolatory hope that the land of the exile will assume ere long its appropriate place among the nations of the earth.

ESSAY

. . . Has Europe, then, an undisputed claim
To light her Genius at the Muse's flame;
To deck her brow with Fame's immortal wreath,
And all the perfumes of Parnassus' breathe?
Say, trans-atlantic Wits, a critic throng,
Who live by maiming prose and mangling song,
Do Wealth and Fame and Genius favour more,
Atlantic's Eastern, than her Western shore?
Believe who will—one principle is clear,
If *there* 'tis policy—'tis treason *here*:

One dares to boast; the other fears to chide;
'Tis here servility; there, lordly pride.

Whatever foreign critics may advance,
Irish or Scotch, in England or in France,
I heed it not;—we look not there for candour:
But, shall Americans retail their slander?
Shall Nature's Freemen bow to Nature's Slaves,
And watch the beck of prostituted knaves?
Our presses change to execrable sewers,
To catch the loathsome filth of Scotch Reviewers?
Where sleeps the pride that spurn'd a foreign yoke,
And lordly England's iron-sceptre broke?
Oh! wake to life, avenging spirit! wake,
And her assuming critic sceptre break;
Dash from her lip th' inebriating bowl,
And rescue Genius from her curst control!
Beneath the baleful influence of her reign,
The hopes of Genius and of Wit are vain:
No matter how exalted be the verse,
It dies beneath a snarling critic's curse:
However sweet the song, or sound the sense,
It is not British, and has no defence.
An Humphreys or a Dwight may charm the skies—
Those strains die soonest, which the highest rise.
'Tis with the critic's as with Nature's laws,
The tallest spire the livid lightning draws.

'Tis Country then, not Merit, wins the prize,
And Prejudice, not Truth, the meed supplies. . . .

DOCUMENT 13

William Cullen Bryant

With his review of Solyman Brown's *Essay*, in July 1818, William Cullen Bryant (1794–1878) turned the attention of the *North American* critics from exhortation and theory to the less exciting job of taking inventory of American literary achievement. He had just the year before published *Thanatopsis*, but he had hardly, at the age of twenty-four, attained the critical stature to assume the authority and judgment which this review reveals. Nevertheless, most of his opinions, with the exception perhaps of those on Freneau and Clifton, have stood the test of time. A youth spent in study and contemplation had made him already familiar with both the poetry and the poetic theory of his English and Scottish contemporaries, and he spoke from a knowledge of eighteenth-century neo-classical theory and practice and of the early romantic view of poetry as a "suggestive" art. His debt to Alison and Burke for the theory of Association was almost as great as that to Wordsworth and the earlier poets of nature. His *Lectures on Poetry*, delivered in New York in 1825, are the first attempt by an American to develop a systematic poetic theory.

TEXT: from the *North American Review*, VII (July 1818), 198–211.

Essay on American Poetry

Of the poetry of the United States different opinions have been entertained, and prejudice on the one side and partiality on the other have equally prevented a just and rational estimate of its merits. Abroad, our literature has fallen under unmerited contumely from those who were but slenderly acquainted with the subject on which they professed to decide; and at home, it must be confessed that the swaggering and pompous pretensions of many have done not a little to provoke and excuse the ridicule of foreigners. Either of these extremes exerts an injurious influence on the cause of letters in our country. To encourage exertion and embolden merit to come forward, it is necessary that they should be acknowledged and rewarded—few will have the confidence to solicit what has been withheld from claims as strong as theirs or the courage to tread a path which presents no prospect but the melancholy wrecks of those who have gone before them. National gratitude—national pride—every high and generous feeling that attaches us to the land of our birth or that exalts our characters as individuals, ask of us that we should foster the infant literature of our country, and that genius and industry, employing their efforts to hasten its perfection, should receive from our hands that celebrity which reflects as much honour on the nation which confers it as on those to whom it is extended. On the other hand, it is not necessary for these purposes—it is even detrimental to bestow on mediocrity the praise due to excellence, and still more so is the attempt to persuade ourselves and others into an admiration of the faults of favourite writers. We make but a contemptible figure in the eyes of the world and set ourselves up as objects of pity to our posterity when we affect to rank the poets of our own country with those mighty masters of song who have flourished in Greece, Italy and Britain. Such extravagant admiration may spring from a praise-worthy and patriotic motive, but it seems to us that it defeats its own object of encouraging our literature by seducing those who would aspire to the favour of the public into an imitation of imperfect models, and leading them to rely too much on the partiality of their countrymen to overlook their deficiencies. Were our rewards to be bestowed only on what is intrinsically meritorious, merit alone would have any apology for appearing before the public. The poetical adventurer should be taught that it is only the productions of genius, taste, and diligence that can find favour at the bar of criticism—that his writings are not to be applauded merely because they are written by an American, and are not decidedly bad; and that he must produce some more satisfactory evidence of his claim to celebrity than an extract from the parish register. To show him what we expect of him, it is as necessary to point out the faults of his predecessors as to commend their excellencies. He must be taught as well what to avoid as what to imitate. This is the only way of diffusing and preserving a pure taste, both among those who read and those who write and, in our opinion, the only way of affording merit a proper and effectual encouragement.

It must however be allowed that the poetry of the United States, though it has not reached that perfection to which some other countries have carried theirs, is yet even better than we could have been expected to produce, considering that our nation has scarcely seen two centuries since the first of its founders erected their cabins on its soil, that our literary institutions are yet in their infancy, and that our citizens are just beginning to find leisure to attend to intellectual refinement and indulge in intellectual luxury, and the means of rewarding intellectual excellence. For the first century after the settlement of this country, the few quaint and unskilful specimens of poetry which yet remain to us are looked upon merely as objects of curiosity, are preserved only in the cabinet of the antiquary, and give little pleasure if read without reference to the age and people which produced them. A purer taste began after this period to prevail—the poems of the Rev. John Adams, written in the early part of the eighteenth century, which have been considered as no bad specimen of the poetry of his time, are tolerably free from the faults of the generation that preceded him and show the dawnings of an ambition of correctness and elegance. The poetical writings of Joseph Green, Esq. who wrote about the middle of the same century, have been admired for their humour and the playful ease of their composition.

But, previous to the contest which terminated in the independence of the United States, we can hardly be said to have had any national poetry. Literary ambition was not then frequent amongst us—there was little motive for it and few rewards. We were contented with considering ourselves as participating in the literary fame of that nation of which we were a part and of which many of us were natives and aspired to no separate distinction. And indeed we might well lay an equal claim with those who remained on the British soil to whatever glory the genius and learning as well as the virtue and bravery of other times reflected on the British name. These were qualities which ennobled our common ancestors; and though their graves were not with us and we were at a distance from the scenes and haunts which were hallowed by their deeds, their studies, and their contemplations, yet we brought with us and preserved all the more valuable gifts which they left to their posterity and to mankind—their illumination—their piety—their spirit of liberty—reverence for their memory and example and all the proud tokens of a generous descent.

Yet here was no theatre for the display of literary talent —the worshippers of fame could find no altars erected to that divinity in America, and he who would live by his pen must seek patronage in the parent country. Some men of taste and learning amongst us might occasionally amuse their leisure with poetical trifles, but a country struggling with the difficulties of colonization and possessing no superfluous wealth wanted any other class of men rather than poets. Accordingly we find the specimens of American poetry before this period mostly desultory and occasional—rare and delicate exotics, cultivated only by the curious.

On our becoming an independent empire, a different spirit began to manifest itself and the general ambition to distinguish ourselves as a nation was not without its effect on our literature. It seems to us that it is from this time only that we can be said to have poets of our own, and from this period it is that we must date the origin of American poetry. About this time flourished Francis Hopkinson whose humorous ballad entitled the Battle of the Kegs is in most of our memories and some of whose attempts, though deficient in vigour, are not inelegant. The

keen and forcible invectives of Dr. Church, which are still
recollected by his contemporaries, received an additional
edge and sharpness from the exasperated feelings of the
times. A writer in verse of inferiour note was Philip Freneau whose pen seems to have been chiefly employed on
political subjects and whose occasional productions, distinguished by a coarse strength of sarcasm and abounding
with allusions to passing events, which is perhaps their
greatest merit, attracted in their time considerable notice
and in the year 1786 were collected into a volume. But
the influence of that principle which awoke and animated
the exertions of all who participated in the political enthusiasm of that time was still more strongly exemplified
in the Connecticut poets—Trumbull, Dwight, Barlow,
Humphreys and Hopkins—who began to write about this
period. In all the productions of these authors there is a
pervading spirit of *nationality* and patriotism—a desire to
reflect credit on the country to which they belonged, which
seems, as much as individual ambition, to have prompted
their efforts and which at times gives a certain glow and
interest to their manner.

McFingal, the most popular of the writings of the former of these poets, first appeared in the year 1782. This
pleasant satire on the adherents of Britain in those times
may be pronounced a tolerably successful imitation of the
great work of Butler—though, like every other imitation
of that author, it wants that varied and inexhaustible
fertility of allusion which made all subjects of thought—
the lightest and most abstruse parts of learning—every
thing in the physical and moral world—in art or nature,
the playthings of his wit. The work of Trumbull cannot
be much praised for the purity of its diction. Yet perhaps
great scrupulousness in this particular was not consistent
with the plan of the author and to give the scenes of his
poem their full effect it might have been thought necessary to adopt the familiar dialect of the country and the
times. We think his Progress of Dulness a more pleasing
poem as more finished and more perfect in its kind and
though written in the same manner, more free from the
constraint and servility of imitation. The graver poems of

Trumbull contain some vigorous and animated declamation.

Of Dr. Dwight we would speak with all the respect due to talents, to learning, to piety, and a long life of virtuous usefulness—but we must be excused from feeling any high admiration of his poetry. It seems to us modelled upon a manner altogether too artificial and mechanical. There is something strained, violent, and out of nature in all his attempts. His Conquest of Canaan will not secure immortality to its author. In this work the author has been considered by some as by no means happy in the choice of his fable—however this may be, he has certainly failed to avail himself of the advantages it offered him—his epic wants the creations and colourings of an inventive and poetical fancy—the charm, which, in the hands of genius, communicates an interest to the simplest incidents and something of the illusion of reality to the most improbable fictions. The versification is remarkable for its unbroken monotony. Yet it contains splendid passages which, separated from the body of the work, might be admired, but a few pages pall both on the ear and the imagination. It has been urged in its favor that the writer was young— the poetry of his maturer years does not however seem to possess greater beauties or fewer faults. The late Mr. Dennie at one time exerted his ingenuity to render this poem popular with his countrymen; in the year 1800 he published in the Farmer's Museum, a paper printed at Walpole; of which he was the editor, a series of observations and criticisms on the Conquest of Canaan, after the manner of Addison in those numbers of the Spectator which made Milton a favourite with the English people. But this attempt did not meet with success—the work would not sell and loads of copies yet cumber the shelves of our booksellers. In the other poems of Dr. Dwight, which are generally obnoxious to the same criticisms, he sometimes endeavours to descend to a more familiar style and entertains his reader with laborious attempts at wit, and here he is still unsuccessful. Parts of his Greenfield Hill, and that most unfortunate of his productions, the

Triumph of Infidelity, will confirm the truth of this remark.

Barlow when he began to write was a poet of no inconsiderable promise. His Hasty Pudding, one of his earliest productions, is a good specimen of mock-heroic poetry, and his Vision of Columbus at the time of its first appearance attracted much attention and was hailed as an earnest of better things. It is no small praise to say that when appointed by the General Assembly of Churches in Connecticut to revise Watts' Version of the Psalms and to versify such as were omitted in that work, he performed the task in a manner which made a near approach to the simplicity and ease of that poet who, according to Dr. Johnson, 'has done better than any body else what nobody has done well.' In his maturer years, Barlow became ambitious of distinguishing himself and doing honour to his country by some more splendid and important exertion of his talents and, for this purpose, projected a national epic in which was sung the Discovery of America, the successful struggle of the states in the defence of their liberties, and the exalted prospects which were opening before them. It is to be regretted that a design so honourable and so generously conceived should have failed. In 1807 appeared the Columbiad, which was his poem of the Vision of Columbus, much enlarged, and with such variations as the feelings and reflections of his riper age and judgment led him to make. The Columbiad is not, in our opinion, so pleasing a poem, in its present form, as in that in which it was originally written. The plan of the work is utterly destitute of interest and that which was at first sufficiently wearisome has become doubly so by being drawn out to its present length. Nor are the additions of much value on account of the taste in which they are composed. Barlow in his later poetry attempted to invigorate his style, but instead of drawing strength and salubrity from the pure wells of ancient English, he corrupted and debased it with foreign infusions. The imposing but unchaste glitter which distinguished the manner of Darwin and his imitators appears likewise to have taken strong hold on his fancy, and he has not scrupled to bestow on his poem much of this meretricious decoration. But notwithstanding the bad taste in which his principal work is composed—notwithstanding he cannot be said to write with much pathos or many of the native felicities of fancy, there is yet enough in the poetry of Mr. Barlow to prove that, had he fixed his eye on purer models, he might have excelled, not indeed in epic or narrative poetry nor in the delineation of passion and feeling, but in that calm, lofty, sustained style which suits best with topics of morality and philosophy and for which the vigour and spirit of his natural manner, whenever he permits it to appear, shew him to have been well qualified.

Humphreys was a poet of humbler pretensions. His writings, which were first collected in 1790, are composed in a better taste than those of the two last, and if he has less genius, he has likewise fewer faults. Some of his lighter pieces are sufficiently pretty. He is most happy when he aims at nothing beyond an elegant mediocrity and to do him justice this is generally the extent of his ambition. On the whole, he may be considered as sustaining a respectable rank among the poets of our country.

A writer of a different cast from those we have mentioned and distinguished by a singular boldness of imagination, as well as great humour, was Dr. Samuel Hopkins, who, in 1786, and the year following, in conjunction with Trumbull, Barlow, and Humphreys, and other wits of that time, wrote the Anarchiad, a satire on a plan similar to that of the Rolliad, which appeared in the New Haven Gazette of those years and of which the mildest parts are attributed to him. He was likewise author of the Speech of Hesper, and some smaller poems which have been praised for their wit. There is a coarseness and want of polish in his style; and his imagination, daring and original but unrestrained by a correct judgment, often wanders into absurdities and extravagances. Still, if he had all the madness, he must be allowed to have possessed some of the inspiration of poetry.

One material error of taste pervades the graver productions of these authors, into which it should seem they were led by copying certain of the poets of England who flourished near the period in which they began to write. It was their highest ambition to attain a certain lofty, measured, declamatory manner—an artificial elevation of style from which it is impossible to rise or descend without abruptness and violence, and which allows just as much play and freedom to the faculties of the writer as a pair of stilts allows the body. The imagination is confined to one trodden circle, doomed to the chains of a perpetual mannerism, and condemned to tinkle the same eternal tune with its fetters. Their versification, though not equally exceptionable in all, is formed upon the same stately model of balanced and wearisome regularity. Another fault which arises naturally enough out of the peculiar style which we have imputed to these poets is the want of pathos and feeling in their writings—the heart is rarely addressed and never with much power or success. Amidst this coldness of manner, sameness of imagery and monotony of versification, the reader lays down his book dazzled and fatigued.

In 1800 appeared the poems of William Clifton who fell at the age of twenty seven a victim to that scourge of our climate which ceases not to waste when other diseases are sated—the pulmonary consumption. There is none of our American poetry on which we dwell with more pleasure, mingled indeed with regret at the untimely fate of the writer, than these charming remains. Amidst many of the immature effusions of his greener years and unfinished productions which were never meant to meet the eye of the world, there are to be found specimens of poetry not only more delicate, classical and polished, but more varied in imagery and possessing more of that flexibility of style of the want of which in others we have complained, and more faithful to nature and the feelings, than it has often been our lot to meet with in the works of our native poets. In his later and more finished productions, his diction is refined to an unusual degree of purity, and through this lucid medium the creations of his elegant fancy appear with nothing to obscure their loveliness.

Several respectable additions have been made to the mass of American poetry by Mr. Alsop. His monody on the death of Washington was admired at the time of its appearance. The public is likewise indebted to him for a version of the poem of Silius Italicus on the Punic war and another of the Second Canto of Berni's Orlando Inamorato. Often elegant, but occasionally relapsing into feebleness and languor, his poetry is that of a man of correct and cultivated taste but of no very fervid genius, nor bending the faculties of his mind with much intensity to the work in which he was engaged.

The posthumous works of St. John Honeywood, Esq. were published in the year 1801. These modest remains, the imperfect but vigorous productions of no common mind, have not been noticed as they deserved. They contain many polished and nervous lines.

We should not expect to be easily pardoned were we to pass by the writings of a poet who enjoyed, during his life time so extensive a popularity as the late Mr. Paine. The first glow of admiration which the splendid errors of his manner excited in the public is now over and we can calmly estimate his merits and defects. He must be allowed to have possessed an active and fertile fancy. Even in the misty obscurity which often shrouds his conceptions not only from the understanding of the reader but, it should seem, from that of the writer himself, there sometimes break out glimpses of greatness and majesty. Yet with a force and exuberance of imagination which, if soberly directed, might have gained him the praise of magnificence, he is perpetually wandering in search of conceits and extravagances. He is ambitious of the epigrammatic style and often bewilders himself with attempts to express pointedly what he does not conceive clearly. More instances of the false sublime might perhaps be selected from the writings of this poet than from those of any other of equal talents who lived in the same period. The brilliancy of Paine's poetry is like the brilliancy of frost-work—cold and fantastic. Who can point out the passage in his works in which he speaks to the heart in its own language? He was a fine but misguided genius.

With respect to the prevailing style of poetry at the present day in our country, we apprehend that it will be found, in too many instances, tinged with a sickly and affected imitation of the peculiar manner of some of the late popular poets of England. We speak not of a disposition to emulate whatever is beautiful and excellent in their writings,—still less would we be understood as intending to censure that sort of imitation which, exploring all the treasures of English poetry, culls from all a diction that shall form a natural and becoming dress for the conceptions of the writer,—this is a course of preparation which every one ought to go through before he appears before the public—but we desire to set a mark on that servile habit of copying which adopts the vocabulary of some favourite author and apes the fashion of his sentences and cramps and forces the ideas into a shape which they would not naturally have taken and of which the only recommendation is, not that it is most elegant or most striking, but that it bears some resemblance to the manner of him who is proposed as a model. This way of writing has an air of poverty and meanness—it seems to indicate a paucity of reading as well as perversion of taste —it might almost lead us to suspect that the writer had but one or two examples of poetical composition in his hands and was afraid of expressing himself except according to some formula which they might contain—and it ever has been, and ever will be, the resort of those who are sensible that their works need some factitious recommendation to give them even a temporary popularity.

We have now given a brief summary of what we conceived to be the characteristic merits and defects of our most celebrated American poets. Some names of which we are not at present aware, equally deserving of notice with those whom we have mentioned, may have been omitted —some we have passed over because we would not willingly disturb their passage to that oblivion towards which, to the honour of our country, they are hastening—and some elegant productions of later date we have not commented on because we were unwilling to tire our readers with a discussion which they may think already exhausted.

On the whole there seems to be more good taste among those who read than those who write poetry in our country. With respect to the poets whom we have enumerated, and whose merits we have discussed, we think the judgment pronounced on their works by the public will be found, generally speaking, just. They hold that station in our literature to which they are entitled and could hardly be admired more than they are without danger to the taste of the nation. We know of no instance in which great poetical merit has come forward and finding its claims unallowed, been obliged to retire to the shade from which it emerged. Whenever splendid talents of this description shall appear, we believe that there will be found a disposition to encourage and reward them. The fondness for literature is fast increasing in our country—and if this were not the case, the patrons of literature have multiplied, of course, and will continue to multiply with the mere growth of our population. The popular English works of the day are reprinted in our country—they are dispersed all over the union—they are to be found in every body's hands—they are made the subject of every body's conversation. What should hinder our native works, if equal in merit, from meeting an equally favourable reception?

We suppose that Mr. Brown would not think himself greatly obliged to us were we to say nothing of the book whose title we have placed at the head of this article. He has come before the public, it seems, with the laudable purpose of rescuing the poetical reputation of his countrymen from the calumnies of foreigners, not only by a zealous defence of their poetry, but by the examples which he gives the world of his own. In a strange sort of preface to the volume, after saying a great deal about Greece and Rome, he accuses the British ministry of having endeavoured to detract from the literary character of the people of the United States for the purpose of discouraging the emigration of the subjects of that kingdom to this country. We cannot afford any extracts from this curious production, but pass on to that part of the volume which is in verse. The principal poem in the collection is the Essay on American Poetry in which, after beginning, as in his preface, with something about Greece and Rome, he takes up the gauntlet against the Reviewers of Great Britain—the Scotch Reviewers in particular, against whom he inveighs with peculiar bitterness. Why all this gall towards the Scotch Reviewers we cannot imagine, especially if he alludes, as is probable, to the writers of the Edinburgh Review, whose opinions concerning our nation we have ever considered as more liberal than those of most of their brethren and who must be allowed by all who have read the article in that work on the subject of Peace with America, written not long before the close of the late war —a composition, which we might defy any American to read, without a glow of national exultation—to have done ample justice to all the honourable and generous traits of our character. The author proceeds to introduce the Genius of Columbia, a personage who has so often appeared in our poetry—not to speak of innumerable patriotic songs and the like, where she is employed as a convenient piece of standing pageantry—that we must confess her company has, with us, grown a little stale. The following lines however, on this common subject, in no very difficult style of composition, nor putting the author to the perplexity of much thought or invention, we think the best in the volume.

'High on a sapphire throne, in royal state,
The guardian Genius of Columbia sat;
Suspended arms adorn the spacious Hall;
The star-decked banner floats along the wall;
The tombs of sleeping worthies rise around,
And silence treads the consecrated ground.
Across the harp her graceful arms she flings,
And all her "flying fingers kiss the strings."
Of heroes, long she sung, in battle slain,
While ravished mortals listened to her strain;
She told the deeds their warrior-hands had done,
Their toils encountered and their laurels won.'

Into the mouth of this Genius he puts a profuse panegyric on the poets of America—in particular on his three favourites, Dwight, Barlow, and Paine, who, in the opinion of Mr. Brown, are destined to shine forth in all the splendour of immortality, when the mists of malice and prejudice shall have passed away. The work concludes with

an address to the nine Muses, whom, to shew his familiarity with ancient learning, he summons before him one
by one, calls each of them by name, tells her what are her
proper attributes and province, and what he expects her
to do. In the following line he lets us still farther into the
secret of the extent of his classical attainments.

'And sportive *Thalia!* Mirth's facetious queen.'

Till we read the work of Mr. Brown, we had supposed,
that in the word Thalia, the accent should be placed on
the second syllable. But what will be said to such a star-
tling outrage on all quantity and pronunciation as the
following.

'Thou, *Terpsichore*, the mazy dance shalt lead.'

To the Essay on American Poetry succeeds a variety of
miscellaneous poems to which is prefixed the following
singular advertisement.

> 'In the following *fugitives*, it has been the express design
> of the author to cultivate variety. He has introduced between
> forty and fifty different kinds of measure—not only to re-
> lieve the reader but also to exemplify the most approved
> diversities of English metre. Several species of verse have been
> necessarily omitted lest the volume should exceed its in-
> tended size.'

So that we may now add to our other literary boasts that
we have American poetry of every kind of metre! We have
sentimental poetry too, and moral poetry, and descriptive
poetry, and patriotic poetry—all the offspring of the prolific
genius of Mr. Brown, as we are told in the title page. At
first we thought this rather an extraordinary division of
poetry into its different kinds, but in the writings of Mr.
Brown they are easily distinguishable from one another.
The reader shall have a taste of each. For a specimen of
his sentimental poetry—

> 'If Valentine Day
> Should not vanquish the charmer,
> The love-kindling May,
> Will surely disarm her.

This Damon found,
And Cynthia too, who felt the wound.

Of music, now, no more let Poets tell,
Since Love can wield a more effective dart—
    Though that possess a magic spell
    This wins a Maiden's heart.'

Of his moral poetry the reader must content himself with the following sample.

'Britannia shall know,
That Columbia's foe
Shall e'er in the slumbers of Death be laid low.'

The instances which we intend to present the reader of his talents at description are taken from his Essay on American Poetry.

'Where meets the orient sun a lovelier scene
Than in Columbia's fields of vernal green?
And where does Cynthia spread her midnight vision
O'er lands so like the fabled fields Elysian?'

And again,

'Pile Alps on Appenines and o'er the whole,
Let Atlas rise to fright the astonished soul;
When Chimborazo looks through tempests down,
The mole hill crumbles at his Gothic frown.

IIis patriotic poetry the reader may see exemplified in the following lines.

'And while the world shall stand,
    Or oceans lave the shore,
    Or naval thunders roar,
Macdonough's splendid victory
To Englishmen shall teach, though never taught before,
    That strange as it may be,
While others conquered them by land,
    He vanquished them *at sea!'*

To these precious effusions are appended a few notes which contain a great deal of such interesting information as the following. 'This immense body of fresh water, (Lake Superior,) the largest in the world, is 1600 miles in circumference,' &c. 'Chimborazo, the highest elevation of land on the globe, is nearly under the equator in South America,' &c. 'Whether the Mammoth, whose bones were found on the banks of the Ohio and its branches, were the Leviathan of Scripture or not, he is the largest animal of whom we have any account,' &c. &c. &c. The patriotic song by Dr. Dwight beginning with

Columbia, Columbia, to glory arise!

and Paine's Adams and Liberty, are inserted among the notes to the work not, we presume, for the sake of the present age, for these very popular poems have been printed a hundred different times and have been read and quoted and sung so often that almost every body has them by heart; but for the benefit of posterity, to whom the works of Mr. Brown will probably descend when those of Dwight and Paine are forgotten. Lord Byron's pathetic Farewell to his Wife is likewise added, as is facetiously observed, 'for the *amusement* of the reader.' We will not dwell any longer on this work. Mr. Brown has fallen into a great mistake in thinking himself qualified to write a book. In the present instance, with talents of a very humble order, he has assumed a very pompous tone and made a great parade of small acquisitions.

DOCUMENT 14

Richard Henry Dana, Sr.

Picking up the inventory of American literary achievement at the point where Bryant left it, Richard Henry Dana, Sr. (1787–1879), poet and journalist and another of the founding group of the *North American,* used the appearance of Irving's *The Sketch Book* (1819–20) as an opportunity not only for a critical and appreciative study of all of Irving's work but for some general remarks on the state of American literature and its prospects. Although Dana accepted the basic literary philosophy of his Channing cousins, his temperament was more restrained and his mind more critical than theirs. In spite of his recognition of Irving as the first American man of letters who could have any pretensions to the claim of genius, he discusses carefully what he finds of good and bad in his materials and in his style, and he warns that American literary nationalism can only be self-defeating if it loses sight of literary values in the national cause. The passages here omitted discuss in detail the individual essays and sketches in *The Sketch Book.*

TEXT: from the *North American Review,* IX (September 1819), 322–39, 348–51, and 356.

Review of The Sketch Book of Geoffrey Crayon, Gent.

When Launcelot Langstaff, Will Wizard, and Anthony Evergreen first appeared before the public, they made known that 'they should not puzzle their heads to give an account of themselves, for two reasons; first, because it was nobody's business; secondly, because if it were, they did not hold themselves bound to attend to any body's business but their own;' and the most that could be gotten from them was, 'there are three of us, Bardolph, Peto and I.' This cavalier air, together with the mystery and the bold declaration, 'we care not what the public think of us,' put the public upon guessing and thinking about them and nothing else. Whether it was the sagacity of the people or that eagerness to be found out which we see in little children at hide-and-go-seek which discovered them, we cannot tell, but it was not long before the authors of Salmagundi were as well known as their writings. Probably the secrecy was a mere matter of sport and that after it had served its turn, they cared little whether they were known or not. It is now well understood who the gentlemen were and that Mr. Washington Irving was the principal contributor to the work. Knickerbocker which was published not long after was written wholly by him as are also the numbers of the Sketch Book which have just appeared.

Though the surest way of judging of a man's talents is from his writings, it is a very uncertain one by which to form an opinion of his moral character. Yet we have as little doubt about the good principles and kind-heartedness of the author before us merely from reading his works as we could have had we known him for years. The interest which he makes us feel in him is one reason why we now go back to his former productions, for we have no hesitation in saying at the outset that we consider the good papers of Salmagundi and the greater part of Knickerbocker superior to the Sketch Book. Another is the intention we have all along had of noticing most of such American books, whether of a later or earlier date, as may add to our literary character.

In doing this we hope to be free from any disposition to sneer at a book because written while our literary reputation is so low. On the other hand, we shall not care to flatter the vanity of those who think to raise themselves and the country to a high rank in authorship through much and earnest talking about it. We shall examine a work without any home feelings—our only business is with its merits and faults. We have many times forborn making amusement for ourselves and our readers from the trashy works which are daily turned out because there is little danger of their doing much harm. When one considers how pleasant and easy a thing it is to run upon the follies and vanity of our neighbours, we may be allowed to take some credit to ourselves for this self-denial, especially when it is known that we are now lying under the displeasure of a multitude of authors for this very silence, which is all from our good will towards them and regard for our country.

Though there has been much abuse abroad of our literary character and too little allowed to circumstances, yet that abuse is rather in the spirit in which facts have been stated than in a falsifying of the facts themselves. Would we give our anger time to cool—place ourselves in the situation of England—consider the number of men of learning and genius who have risen, clustering like stars, to be her light and glory since we became a nation, and then look over our own land at the few dim, blinking lights, with only here and there one of steady and bright blaze, so distant that "fire answers not fire;" we should allow something to the sound of triumph and rejoicing which is heard from the midst of her splendour—we should be moved with the spirit of forgiveness if we would consider what would be our language of boasting were our situation hers. Without any regard to this, we at once become exceeding angry—begin to talk in large and general terms of American genius and enterprise, forgetting that first-rate authors are not as easily made as prime sailors and soldiers. We do not stop to ask ourselves whether this universal talent for action in our country may not be inconsistent with that abstract, ideal, and reflective cast of mind which marks those whose lives appear to be unmixed thought—whose intellectual being seems kindled and whose passions work most violently in worlds of their own creating.—In the eagerness of defence, we urge the necessary employment of the talents of a young country upon the gainful and useful and looking forward to the time when we shall no longer be rovers through wild regions, but settled down quietly and full of wealth, we speak of that as the period when we shall have our host of scientific men, great scholars and poets, moralists and novelists, to be our boast and delight. But if the English superciliously tell us that they can furnish us with intellectual nourishment till these ends are accomplished, we forget the very argument we were using as a reason for our deficiency and deny our need of their aid—run over our small list of writers, good, bad, and indifferent, and make up with long and heated declamation for all that is wanting.

Some have been so far gone in their zeal as to utter a cry of affected mourning over the decay of learning and genius in Europe, and with that happy talent of making the future present so common to us and which has been scoffingly called our "figure of anticipation," have congratulated their country upon having become the home of the intellectual greatness of man. Others hold a lamentation over the thraldom of mind in England and talk of our letting it out from its dark, close prison-house.

We should be happy to learn of these men, what there may be in religion, politics, the sciences and literature, which has not been discussed by her authors often and freely. In political and religious freedom, we may have put in practice what they have taught, but they have left us little in the leading principles of these to discover. A short time ago, when the world was talking of discoveries in politics as familiarly as of discoveries in geography, it was curious to look into the older writers of Europe and see with how many of these new-found wonders they were acquainted. Society at large has gone forward rapidly but great minds have always reasoned and felt very much as they do now. Though their vigour of thought was sometimes turned from its right action by the prejudices and superstition of the age, still they have been our instructers in much wherein we have fancied ourselves self-taught. At any rate, we cannot as yet believe that because the people of England are living under old institutions, they are so enslaved in body or mind as to call forth our pity, but think that it will be time enough for us to give utterance to our mixed feelings of triumph and grief when the scholars, philosophers, and poets of America shall furnish study for a man's life; when their views shall be so broad and liberal that the authors of England shall become dangerous to our freedom of mind and those who have hitherto been our instructers in all that is moral, lofty, and pure within us shall be shunned as corrupting and degrading our natures. Indeed, it is not yet time to empty our shelves of European lumber to make way for American writers,—there is still room enough for them in the vacancies left. An American library would, we fancy, be rather a sorry and heart-sickening sight to a literary man.

Such notions are almost too ludicrous to be hinted at. Yet if we examine nakedly those which have so often of late been forced upon us, we shall find them the same only curiously stuffed out and dressed up. This sort of contest deserves no better name than squabbling and we are sorry to find men engaged in it who are fitted for better things.

The class of men abroad who affect this vulgar triumph over us, with an exception or two, are not those who add to the superiority of which they boast. Of those at home who will not stay to consider how much there may be of truth in charges so rudely urged, some are restless through wounded vanity and from feeling their own importance lessening with that of the order to which they belong, while others with more generosity and no less zeal enter into the contest because their country is assailed.

We do not affect to be wholly unmoved by either of these feelings; yet it is more in sorrow than in anger that we read the contemptuous reflections upon our literary character because with all their colouring there is too much of truth and because even the hope that a brighter day is breaking upon us loses something of its gladness at the thought of how small a change even literature makes in the character of its followers.

A man who cares at all for his own nature may well forget all distinctions of place in the sense of pain and disappointment that minds whose labours and joys would seem to lie apart from the confused strugglings and evil envyings of the world, who are left to love the beauties of ideal excellence and to study the deformities of vice

only to show them to the world—whose toils are for the
world's uses and whose dreams of delight give it purifying
pleasures,—that such minds should turn away from all
these to be heated and depraved in petty bickerings and
low strife. He who values literature for its moral uses, for
its cleansing of the heart and exalting of the mind, and
not from the vanity of scholarship—who loves it for its
own sake more than for its distinctions—cannot but lament
to find it degraded to the service of false pride and sour
malignity. First rate genius has but little of this and where
they are found together it is to the mind's hurt. Every
taint of vice is a dimming of intellectual brightness and
the taking away of one good feeling from the heart is
shutting out forever countless visions of beauty and delight from the mind. Could this language of boasting on
the one side and of contempt on the other be kept up
without harm, a war of words will never raise us to distinction nor make us deserving of it. We must take another
course to bring us to a level with the literary men of
Europe.

In the first place, to have learned men it would be fortunate if half our colleges or universities as they are sometimes called were turned into good schools and the funds
of the rest given to one or two large institutions for fellowships and other purposes. As this cannot be effected, men
of wealth must make their donations to those institutions
which have already the greatest advantages. Nor let them
consider this as granting a favour or conferring honour on
others. It is for their own glory, without which they will
live with no other distinction than the poor one of wealth,
and when they die, their names will go down with them
to their graves and they will sink from the memory of man
faster than they rose into his notice.

We are not of those who think mere scholars useless.
They deserve praise for the example of industry which
they set before us and for the helps which they afford not
only to the world at large but to men of genius in a thousand ways. Neither is it of good tendency to underrate
those who are thorough in any calling in a country where
each one does every thing and nothing well. True, they

have their reward; for if their merits are not understood, the mystery of their calling makes them the gods of the ignorant, and if holden lightly by some, they have a consolation in their own self-esteem. It is true that mere learning does not give a nation its great name; and what would England have been with her Bentleys and Porsons, without her Shakspeare and Milton? Neither have many of those works which make a nation's reading been written within college walls; and some of those which are most familiar to us are from men who never wore a gown or square cap. Still the influence of literary institutions upon society reaches to the uneducated author and the effect of their early discipline is felt by the educated after they go into the world. Suppose such institutions at an end, or what would be as bad, with just science enough to instruct head workmen in the mechanic arts or a sailor how to take a lunar observation or, according to a system of intellectual economics, "to teach no more than can be turned to some account"; how long would there be left any reward for mental toil or any excitement to peculiar genius? Those who are most fond of trying things by their usefulness know least of the great uses of life.

More is necessary to our literary character and changes must be wrought in society at large without which all arbitrary institutions will first become mere things of show and then decay.

If we allow society to have any effect upon first rate minds, perhaps genius is no where more likely to die at its opening than in this country. The peculiar fitness of our state for general talent and activity of character is that which is most in the way of individual genius. Men of genius are a sort of outlaws because too few as yet to form a class in our society and because, for the most part, they want that *getting-along* faculty which is naturally enough made the measure of a man's mind in a young country where every one has his fortune to make. This call for business talent may continue to put a check upon the higher kind of literature as by the division of property the sons of men of wealth are turned down from books into the order of watchful and eager men of business, and the

common way must be that the works of genius, if not
wholly laid aside, will no longer fill up hours of lonely
thoughtfulness nor keep a strong hold upon their hearts.
Men of acute minds, to be sure, yet uninformed, take place
of the learned rich and in this continual shifting, the exalted but silent movements of great minds are crossed and
broken in upon.

This, at least, seems the natural course of things. Without a rivalry which might stimulate men of newly acquired
property to raise themselves to the level with hereditary
wealth by building up some part of their character along
with that of a man of genius, they feel distinctly what has
given undisputed consequence to themselves and would
make that the rate of his importance too. The luxuries of
sense are new to them. Lofty rooms and gay furniture still
draw their attention and make their pride and it is hardly
yet forgotten how fine a thing is a fine coach. Satiety of
outward wealth has not turned them to the riches of the
mind.

Let us not be misunderstood. If there be any thing of
truth in our loose suggestions, we would hardly forego the
substantial good which our political equality has given us,
for the mere luxuries of mind. It often falls out, however,
that facts run counter to theories, and experience and
prophecy seldom meet. It may be, that with the wealth of
the country will come in a better taste and that instead of
growing more sensual we shall become more intellectual—
that we shall, one day, buy pictures as well as looking-
glasses, and that in good time an author will be set as
much by as an Argand lamp or an imported chimneypiece.
Even now, there are many well educated among the
wealthy, and some have laboured to improve themselves
later in life and in most of them there is a generosity of
character needing nothing but a right direction. All that
has been done of late for public institutions has been by
rich individuals and when they shall have learned how to
value original creative minds, these too will receive their
respect and support.

This must be brought about by a middle class—men of
improved intellects who are labouring in the different call-

ings of public life. And here the evils from change of property may, perhaps, find their cure. A young man of cultivated mind, thrown into that order of society which after all is the most efficient will have an influence over those who have succeeded him in the rank of wealth which will lead them to support and encourage those whose powers they may not clearly understand.

Our scholars, though a little apart from society, have an influence in it which might be used to the same end. Here again there is something in the way of the mere man of genius. Our scholars, though less learned than those of Europe, hold properly enough a high rank in society. They form a numerous class, and being in many ways connected with the world, have that authority which talents and acquirements always carry with them. The European scholar has only a portion of power and influence; for there, to say the least, genius has kept pace with learning and holden as wide sway. Here we begin with the learned of whom it is asking a little more self-sacrifice than is often found in humanity to give up into other hands a part of that power which they now exercise alone. The European scholar, when he has an eye to see, has nothing of this to take from his admiration when the brightness of a new mind breaks upon him; for suns have for ages been coming up in that horizon, making a noonday blaze, and never has he thought to see them quenched in his own borrowed and fainter light. But those here might not only feel that self estimation which undivided power gives, sinking away, but the fear of losing their influence might startle them to find a man of untaught powers suddenly rising to a height which they can never reach, or one like Milton with as much of other men's knowledge as they using it as the stuff of his own mind, building a temple in which they may be the worshippers but can never be the gods.

It would be a narrow prejudice to suppose men,—whose studies from childhood have been fitted to enlarge the mind, and bring them acquainted with its beauties,—so moved by selfishness as to shut the doors upon all outward excellencies and live in complacent contemplation of themselves. We speak of that which is natural to all of us, —of that which is common to the learned and the ignorant, the man of genius and the fool—a proneness in favour of our own sect which leads us unawares to judge hardly of those not of it—to be quicksighted to their defects and careless of what is good in them—to feel our own importance growing with that of those we belong to and, unconscious of our motives, if not pleased yet not sorrowing at the ill success of others.

We need not go thus far to find why mere scholars (we mean those whose reputation rests on their acquisitions and studied correctness alone and not those amongst us who have laid open to the world the rich veins of thought in their own minds) are so slow to see and acknowledge what is good in a new author. The habit of referring to certain rules makes them doubtful of every thing that cannot be tried by them; and reading under old authority with the mind at school takes away from their freedom of judgment—leads them to consider every thing new as dangerous innovation, and to look upon it with a mixed feeling of superiority and alarm. Besides this, an exclusive study of the classics is much like living in a foreign country, with which we can never become so intimate as to have the feelings of a native and must always be in some degree on the outside of its society at the same time that our old associations are fading and dropping off. The early familiarity with the thoughts and feelings of home may make them appear vulgar to such men—and from the mistaken notion that a knowledge of what is best there can be reached without toil, they let it fall into neglect. What is foreign too will always have so much of show and dress to their eyes that they cannot but look upon it as something a great deal finer than they ever saw at home, and because they cannot make themselves masters of it, they consider it superior to all they have before attained to. Giving up thus entirely, when we go to books, the delights, fears and superstitions of our infancy—all that we connect with the thoughts of our ancestors and that which has helped in forming what is peculiar in ourselves and the society in which we live,—is apt to put the mind into too

artificial a mood to perceive, even in those authors of
which we are the most fond, their greatest because their
most simple and natural beauties. And knowing little how
variously nature works, we are for bringing every thing to
our own forced state.

We have hinted at the evil effects of confining the mind
to the classics, not from a foolish wish to lessen the study
of them in this country. No man of good taste who had
begun to be acquainted with them early and has neglected
them in after life but will think of it with regret; and the
greatest consolation which he will find is that some of their
precepts are still with him and some of their images still
floating before him, and that though most of them may
be forgotten, the labour of once acquiring them has given
a lasting vigour and elasticity to his mind. If the danger
we have spoken of really exists, there is an easy and delightful way of avoiding it by adding to the classics a
thorough acquaintance not only with modern but early
English literature. Every literary man in England is familiar with it. All her poets and great prose writers who for
the most part have been classical scholars made the early
literature of their country their study. Milton, to say nothing of Gray, was as well versed in it as in that of Greece
and Rome and turned it to as good account; and Burke
the most poetical of the late prose writers, did not forget
it through all the heat and contest of political life.

If we have spoken freely of the failings of scholars, it is
not from a disposition to fault-finding, nor from a blind-
ness to their use and merit. Each class has its errors; to
the wealthy is pride, to the poor, envy—and to the favoured of mind, an impatience of the talk and a super-
cilious indifference to the opinions of ordinary men.
Through the large variety of life there never will be wanting something to put in motion the evil as well as the
good of our natures, and trusting to the strength of our
virtue, we are ever failing through its weakness.

Whatever we have said has been from anxiety for the
literary character of our country. We would warn those
who are to encourage and support it against a narrowness
of taste,—a taming down by confined notions of faultless-

ness. Original minds will be peculiar and individual and
it is not for us to haggle at every thing new but look at
it with care and see if there may not be some beauties
in its novelties, and whether what at first appeared a deformity, may not have its fair proportions and movements
no less graceful and natural because all its own. We must
be careful not to complain too much of that of which,
after allowing something to the eccentricities of genius,
we may not approve. Those who have produced what is
lasting have always been fond of working in their own
way. For the most part, we should be content with them
as we find them, lest with that perversity so common to
such minds they run more into the fault; or in the endeavour to remove it, tear away some beauty, which was
more closely connected with it than we were aware of.
Some have complained of Milton's inversions, and they
are now and then overstrained. Had he begun to correct
them, who can tell where he would have stopped—had he
listened, some pedant critic might have spoiled the loftiest
and most varied harmony of English verse. In the same
way, Cowper's rhyme might have lost all its spirit, and
had Wordsworth in the Excursion given more compactness
and vigour to his thoughts, where they are sometimes languid from being drawn out, he might have lost something
of that calm, moral sentiment, of that pure shedding of
the soul over his world of beauties, which lies upon
them like gentle and thoughtful sunset upon the earth.

The giant minds of England grew up in times when
there was less of order in society,—no critics, few rules,
and those slighted. They have their absurdities, affectations and conceits; but what are all these, when we feel
the breathing upon us of that spirit which was given to
them alone. Sir Joshua Reynolds says, "that deformity
came in with the dancing master;"—and if too great constraint upon the body's movements not only takes from
them their elegance, but gives to them an awkwardness in
its stead, it is the same thing with the mind. How would
the studied graces of Chesterfield appear by the side of
a well made savage, and who can remember without
laughter Hogarth's Frenchman with head erect and toes

turned out, telling the grand figure of Antinous, with his fine curved neck and firm set foot, to hold up his head and look like him? It is strange to see how the motions of the body give the character of the mind and there is something besides ingenuity in the remark of Sterne, "that there are a thousand unnoticed openings which let a penetrating eye at once into a man's soul, and that a man of sense does not lay down his hat on coming into a room—or take it up in going out—but something escapes which discovers him." The French tied up their writers, with the little inspiration they had, as if they were mad-men till well might Madame De Stael ask, "why all this reining of dull steeds?" At the same time, they taught the world to hold as uncouth the movements natural to man and to admire sudden, sharp, angular shootings of the limbs as the only true lines of beauty. Yet the polite world not long ago read and talked nothing but French and "went to church in a galliard, and came home in a coranto."

Our analogy, perhaps, is hardly in place and we will run it no further, but will close our general remarks by once more urging those who may have an influence over our writers to use it with liberal minds, honestly looking for what is good and not dealing harshly with what is doubt-ful. We do not mean that the eccentricities and faults of men who show some talent should be passed over in si-lence for this would be no compliment to their intellects, but that the good may be weighed against the bad fairly and openly, without bitterness or ridicule, and above all that they may not be shackled by "those rules by which little minds fancy they may be able to comprehend great things."

With the exception of a few editors of magazines and reviews, Mr. Irving is almost the only American, who has attempted to support himself by literary labours. Mr. Walsh began with a book of very respectable size and most excellent matter, but that was political, and we were all politicians then. He, too, soon thought best to under-take periodical works, but they came to the same end with others after much toil, little praise, and less money. Brown wrote novels; but was obliged to turn to the making up of political registers and magazines. It is true that the English who are slow enough in giving us praise had his novels in every tolerable circulating library in the kingdom—and that Godwin spoke of them with commendation. We at home, who talk so much about the literary character of America, knew little or nothing about them. They were read in New York and Philadelphia by his personal friends and there were some half dozen in this part of the country a few years ago who had seen one or two of his works—liked them exceedingly, but took them up and laid them down for English.—The first edition of Franklin appeared abroad and there are one or two other works of merit which are waiting for notice from the same quarter.

We must not forget, however, to make one exception from our general neglect of American authors, for therein is our boast—our very liberal patronage of the compilers of geographies in great and little, reading books, spelling books and arithmetics. It is encouraging to our literary adventurers that should they fail to please the public in works of invention, they have at last this resort and the consolation that if they are not to rank with the poets and novel writers of the day, they may be studied and admired till Pike and Webster are forgotten.

Jesting apart, we have to thank Mr. Irving for being the first to begin and persevere in works which may be called purely literary. His success has done more to remove our anxiety for the fate of such works than all we have read or heard about the disposition to encourage American genius.

Mr. Irving's success does not rest, perhaps, wholly upon his merit, however great. Salmagundi came out in numbers, and a little at a time. With a few exceptions it treated of the city—what was seen and felt and easy to be understood by those in society. It had to do with the present and real, not the distant and ideal. It was exceedingly pleasant morning or after-dinner reading, never taking up too much of a gentleman's time from his business and pleasures nor so exalted and spiritualized as to seem mystical to his far reaching vision. It was an excellent

thing in the rests between cotillions and pauses between
games at cards; and answered a most convenient purpose
in as much as it furnished those who had none of their
own with wit enough for sixpence, to talk out the sitting of an evening party. In the end, it took fast hold of
people through their vanity; for frequent use had made
them so familiar with it as to look upon it as their own;
and having retailed its good things so long, they began to
run of the notion that they were all of their own making.

It was fortunate, too, that the work made its first appearance in New York—'where the people—heaven help
them—are the most irregular, crazy-headed, quicksilver,
eccentric, whim-whamsical set of mortals that ever were
jumbled together.' Had it first shown its face in any other
part of the country, how soon would it have been looked
out of countenance and talked down by your 'honest, fair,
worthy, square, good-looking, well meaning, regular, uniform, straight forward, clock-work, clear headed, one-like-
another, salubrious, upright, kind of people!'

New York being a city of large and sudden growth,
with people from all parts of the country and many foreigners, individuals there do not feel every chance sarcasm
or light ridicule of some foible in the rank or set they belong to as a personal attack, as is the case in smaller cities
where sets must be small, too, or as in older cities where
they are more distinctly marked. Neither have they enough
of clanship in the different classes into which society will
always be in some degree divided to allow any lady or gentleman authority to dictate what a man shall be taken into
favor for and for what he shall be put down. One there,
who can do it well, may laugh at follies, as well at those in
fashion as at those out; nor will any wait to be told
whether they are to laugh too. If ladies of all sizes and
complexions in heat and cold chose to wear red, he may
ridicule it though all the rage, and that in print, too;
nor will the female patrons of Mrs. Toole and Madame
Bouchard banish him from society because he ventured
to say that muslin walking dresses in wet weather were
not quite the thing.

In hinting what there might be in accidental circumstances to help to the early popularity of Salmagundi, we must not be understood as questioning its right to all and more than it obtained. To say that it was out of all comparison the ablest work of wit and humour which we had produced would be saying very little of it; for we had done but little before this. McFingal is just enough like Hudibras to remind you that it was intended as an imitation of it, and the Foresters, though written by a man of rather uncommon talents and in a very clear, familiar, natural style, and such as we scarce meet with at home nowadays, is remarkable only for a careful ingenuity in keeping up its allegorical character. It professes to be nothing more than the application of Swift's John Bull to the concerns of this country with Great Britain. And except in the wit and quick fancy of that work, it is a close copy, but it is as guiltless of its wit as it is of its indelicacy; for there are but two or three places to shock the most sensitively refined and no more to make the merriest laugh.

Mr. Irving has taken the lead here, in the witty, humorous and playful cast of works—those suited to our happier feelings,—while Brown harasses us with anxiety and strange terror. He has not modelled himself upon any body, but has taken things just as he found them and treated them according to his own humour. So that you never feel as when looking at the works just mentioned that you have gotten a piece of second-hand furniture, scraped and varnished till made to look fine and modern that it may be put to a new use. His wit and humour do not appear to come of reading witty and humorous books; but it is the world acting upon a mind of that cast and putting those powers in motion. There are parts, it is true, which remind you of other authors, not, however, as imitations but resemblances of mind. In Knickerbocker, particularly, though it may be hard to point out in what the likeness consists, you frequently think of Sterne. It, however, would have been just the book it now is though Sterne had never written.

Amidst the abundance of his wit and drollery, you never meet with any bilious sarcasm. He turns aside from the vices of men to be amused with their affectation and foibles; and the entertainment he finds in these seems to be from a pure goodness of soul—a sense that they are seldom found in thoroughly depraved and hardened hearts. The mind is relieved when it can shake off the secret malignity, violent hate, proud oppression and unsparing selfishness of man and look at him with all his follies showing themselves with a vain but honest ostentation upon the outside of him—pleased with himself and fancying the world pleased with him too, and wishing well to it from his very error. For though foppery seems the most selfish thing in nature, yet a fop for the most part is the best tempered creature in the world; so that old fashioned censoriousness, which has lived upon the diseases of others minds—forever finding something bad in what is mainly good till tired of itself and all else,—is ready to give over its calling in despair and turn foppling too that it may be reconciled to itself and the world again.

Amiableness is so strongly marked in all Mr. Irving's writings as never to let you forget the man; and the pleasure is doubled in the same manner as it is in lively conversation with one for whom you have a deep attachment and esteem. There is in it also the gayety and airiness of a light, pure spirit—a fanciful playing with common things, and here and there beautiful touches till the ludicrous becomes half picturesque.

Though many of the characters and circumstances in Salmagundi are necessarily without such associations, yet the Cocklofts are not only the most witty and eccentric but the most thoroughly sentimental folks in the world, like some of the characters in the Spectator, and like Trim, and that best of men, my Uncle Toby. And here we would notice a resemblance in our author to Sterne. With a very few exceptions, his sentiment is in a purer taste and better sustained where it is mixed with witty and ludicrous characters and circumstances than where it stands by itself. He not only shows a contemplative, sentimental mind, but what is more rare, a power of mingling with his wit the wild, mysterious and visionary. Glimpses of this appear in his Rip Van Winkle and the same fine combination is seen in the "Two Painters" and "the Paint King" of Mr. Allston. It is a very uncommon union of qualities and one which no man who has it in him should neglect.

It looks a little like impertinent interference to advise a man to undertake subjects of a particular sort who is so well suited for variety in kind. Nor do we wish that Mr. Irving should give up entirely the purely witty or humorous for those of a mixed nature. We would only express our opinion of the deep interest which such writings excite and of his peculiar fitness for them; and at the same time suggest to him the great advantages he gains by changing from one to the other. For ourselves, we have no fear of being tired of his wit or humour so long as they come from him freely. He is much more powerful in them than in the solely sentimental or pathetic.

We give him joy of making his way so miraculously as not to offend the dignity of many stately folks and pray him go on and prosper. It was a bold undertaking in a country where we are in the habit of calling humour, buffoonery—and wit, folly. The notion is singular enough —but there are many who hold, that for a wit to be a gentleman—there is nothing more strange. It is in course that people, ignorant of its nature, should fall into this confusion. The misfortune is, that they should commit themselves by an opinion uncalled for. We have seen some curb up at a witticism let fall in their presence as at an unbecoming familiarity, and others amusingly vehement against it. So that mother wit would, in all likelihood, have been banished genteel company had not Mr. Irving in a lucky moment given her his countenance. We have our fears of being unduly sprightly, and have forborn many a good thing lest we should be taken to task for sacrificing our dignity and decorum. The commission of this offence is considered much more heinous in writing, than in conversation. For being rather raw in authorship, and feeling all the while as put upon our good behaviour and not knowing well how to distinguish between freedom and coarseness, and avoiding the former lest we fall into the latter, we become very proper and very common.

Mr. Irving's style in his lighter productions is suited to his subject. He has not thought it necessary to write the history of the family of the Giblets as he would that of the Gracchi, nor to descant upon Mustapha's Breeches in all the formality of a lecture. He is full, idiomatic and easy to an uncommon degree; and though we have observed a few grammatical errors, they are of a kind which appear to arise from the hurry in which such works are commonly written. There are likewise one or two Americanisms. Upon the whole, it is superior to any instance of the easy style in this country that we can call to mind. That of the Foresters is more free from faults than Mr. Irving's but not so rich. The principal defect in his humorous style is a multiplying of epithets which, making no new impression, weaken from diffusion. It is too much like forcing a good thing upon us till we think it good for nothing. We make no objection to a style rich with epithets, which have fitness and character, unless they are strung along so as to look like a procession. But Mr. Irving's are sometimes put upon a service for which they were never intended and only occasion confusion and delay.

Another fault, and one easily to be avoided, is the employing of certain worn out veterans in the cause of wit. Indeed, we owe it to him to say that we believe he has now dismissed them as we do not meet with them in the Sketch Book. We will mention a few, as instances. Gaffer Phœbus, Daddy Neptune, Dan Homer, Dame Nature, Dame Fortune. Also a mock gravity in the use of such antiquated phrases as, 'eftsoons, ycleped, whilome,' &c. Like the German princes, we suppose, having no further use for them, he let them out for that most unfortunate expedition up mount Parnassus, under the conduct of the famous Backwoodsman, in which fatal service we presume they perished with their leader; for as far as we were able to follow them, we found that they were put to constant and hard duty.

Another fault, which is found principally in Knickerbocker, is that of forcing wit as if from duty—running it down and then whipping and spurring it into motion

again—as in that part upon the different theories of philosophers. Wit must appear to come accidentally or the
effect is lost. The moment we see any forecasting, it is all
over with it. The great superiority of Swift lies as much in
the manner in which his good things come from him as in
the things themselves. If he keeps you in a roar of laughter
for half a score pages, you are fully persuaded that he
could no more help it than a dull man could, putting you
to sleep in the same compass. And where it is not continuous but comes in here and there amidst his fine, plain
sense, it is always a part of the fabric and never patched
on. It is needless to say, that, were this defect frequent in
Mr. Irving, it would be fatal. No doubt a good deal might
be taken from Knickerbocker which would leave it more
sustained and vivid; yet, after the witty and humorous
works of a few of the English-standard authors, there are
no books of the kind in the language half so entertaining,
in which the circumstances are so ludicrous, and the characters so well sustained and made out. . . .

It was delightful meeting once more with an old acquaintance who had been so long absent from us, and we
felt our hearts lightened and cheered when we for the first
time took the Sketch Book into our hands. Foreigners can
know nothing of the sensation, for authors are as numerous and common with them as street acquaintances. We
who have only two or three are as closely attached to
them as if they were our brothers. And this one is the
same mild, cheerful, fanciful, thoughtful, humorous being
that we parted with a few years ago though something
changed in manner by travel. We will be open with him
and tell him that we do not think the change is for the
better. He appears to have lost a little of that natural run
of style for which his lighter writings were so remarkable.
He has given up something of his direct, simple manner,
and plain phraseology for a more studied, periphrastical
mode of expression. He seems to have exchanged words
and phrases which were strong, distinct and definite, for
a genteel sort of language, cool, less definite, and general.
It is as if his mother English had been sent abroad to be
improved and in attempting to become accomplished, had

lost too many of her home qualities. We have pointed out the defects in his former style and they were no doubt violent and obvious, yet not infused into the whole but distinct and individual, and might be removed not only without injuring what remains but leaving it firmer and even more entire. It was masculine—good bone and muscle—this is feminine, *dressy*, elegant and languid. The fact is that what is idiomatic and essentially English—that which is in us and a part of us from old and familiar associations and on which, too, the eye can rest as upon a picture,—has been laid aside for a language which is learned like a foreign one and which must always be wanting to us in some degree in character, definiteness and nearness. We do not ask for a *conversational* style in books (except where the subject, or mode of treating it, is light and familiar) though it is far better than that which is always impressing us as laboriously sought after and cautiously put together. We shall save all trouble of defining and be better understood by saying at once that we want nothing more than a style as English and easy (though without the slips in grammar) as that of the often cited authority Addison—a style as unlike that which passes in this country at the present day for pure and elegant composition as it is different from the rich, gorgeous, poetic style of Jeremy Taylor or the scarcely less poetic style of Burke. There is a good deal of the fault we have spoken of in Mr. Irving's notice of Roscoe and he was not altogether free from it formerly, in what he laboured most as, for instance, in his biography of Campbell. He too often aims at effect by a stately inversion of sentences. Another and a greater error which is found principally in his serious and sentimental writings is an incorrect use of figurative language which is frequently from connecting a word, strictly an image, with one which is not so as to present a picture to the mind's eye and the next moment rub it out. This appears to be owing to a mere oversight, a want of considering that any figure was used. Another is connecting two words which are figures but quite hostile to one another so that they seem brought together for no other purpose than to put an end to each other. This is sometimes from the same cause with the former, though it is often done with such an appearance of aim at figurative writing as shows it is from the want of a clear and right perception of things,—seeing things indistinctly and confusedly. This misuse of figurative language, the inversion of sentences, and the inflated style (of which last Mr. Irving is, perhaps, never guilty,) must be put down under the head of American fine writing.

As an instance of what some may think elegant writing but which appears to us feeble and affected, we refer our readers to the paragraph in his biography of Campbell in which he speaks of our scenery as wanting poetical associations, and the one immediately following, in which the thought is continued. They are too long to quote. In the same article, he says of Campbell, 'He was left without further opposition, to the impulse of his own genius, and *the seductions of the muse*,' and again, he speaks of 'the richer and more *interesting field* of German belles-lettres.' Of Mr. Roscoe, he says, 'he has planted bowers by the way-side for the refreshment of the pilgrim and sojourner, and has *established* pure *fountains* which,' &c.— And again, 'Now dry and dusty with the *lizard and toad brooding* over the shattered marbles.' In the Broken Heart—'She is like some tender *tree*, the pride and beauty of the grove; graceful in its form, bright in its foliage, but with the worm preying at its *core*.' In Rural Life in England—'and while it has thus banded society together, has *implanted* in each intermediate *link* a *spirit* of independence.' In the same:—'various strata of society, therefore, are diffused over the whole surface of the kingdom, and the most retired neighbourhoods afford specimens of the different ranks.'

It is no matter how many figures a writer uses if his subject properly admits of them and if he seems, without forcing himself to it, to think and feel in figure. But they must not,—indeed, then they hardly can be common. If they have been used before, there will be a novelty in their application or in the language in which they are expressed which will give them an air of originality.

We have made these short remarks and given these few

instances because it is faults of this kind which make our style feeble and impure, rather than the use of Americanisms as they are called. They are faults, too, not easily corrected, because slowly discovered, not only by ordinary readers, but even by those who do not themselves fall into the use of them. This defect of vision in picturesque language is the more singular in Mr. Irving as he has an eye for nature and all his pictures from it are drawn with great truth and spirit. The Sketch Book is extremely popular and it is worthy of being so. Yet it is with surprise that we have heard its style indiscriminately praised.

We have already stated why we consider Mr. Irving's former works, though more obviously bad in places, still, as a whole, superior in point of style to the Sketch Book. The same difference holds with respect to the strength, quickness and life of the thoughts and feelings. The air about this last work is soft but there is a still languor in it. It is not breezy and fresh like that which was stirring over the others. He appears to us to have taken up some wrong notion of a subdued elegance as different from the true as in manners the elegance of fashion is from that of character. There is an appearance of too great elaboration. We see that some one has been at work trying to give form and polish to it, but its regular shape is not half so beautiful as its natural irregularity—it is no brighter than before, and rich, sparkling masses have been broken off and lost. Something of the vigour, firmness and spirit of the former works is gone, and there is too much diffusiveness in its stead. What was best done in the others was wrought in the heat of the mind and turned out glowing.

We have spoken of these defects in Mr. Irving as briefly as possible for though our duty, yet it is irksome to remark upon the faults of a writer for whom every reader of any heart must feel a personal attachment. We think, also, that he is so free from an impatience of correction and a person of so good taste that he will avoid such errors when once suggested to him. . . .

Upon looking back, it is with some pain that we find how much we have dwelt upon Mr. Irving's defects. If, however, a man may trust that the feelings which lead him to his remarks will naturally appear in his manner, we have no fear that Mr. Irving will think we took any pleasure in pointing out his faults. Had we thought less highly of his powers, we should have said less about his errors. Did we not take delight in reading him, we should have been less earnest about his mistakes. The truth is that in this part of our notice of him we have been more anxious for the literary character of our country than for his fame or our own pleasure. He is a man of genius and able to bear his faults. But then, again, he is the most popular writer in this country and for aught we can see is likely to be for years. At least he will always be a standard author amongst us. Our literary character is said to be forming. But if we have discovered some talent and industry, we have likewise shown an abundance of bad taste. We cannot have a right character till this is corrected; and the sanction of Mr. Irving to some of our errors would give them a growth which would take years of our dull toiling to root out.

Here we must at last close, looking for another Sketch Book with as pleasant articles as Rural Life in England, and other tales in the manner of Rip Van Winkle, a little longer and no less circumstantial.

PART III

The National Mind in Writing
1820–1830

No major historical events seem to mark off the decade of the twenties unless the Missouri Compromise of 1820 be taken as a measure of expansion to the West and a portent of trouble to come, and the election of Jackson as a sign of deep political and social change. In American literature, however, it was the period of coming of age. The years 1819–20 saw the publication of Irving's *The Sketch Book*, 1821 of the first collection of Bryant's *Poems* and of Cooper's *The Spy*, and 1827 Poe's *Tamerlane and Other Poems*. Halleck, Catherine Sedgwick, and Paulding established themselves as professional writers, and Timothy Flint was writing of the land beyond the Alleghenies. James Nelson Barker, John Howard Payne, and William Dunlap were among those whose plays had been produced and Daniel Webster and Edward Everett had made oratory a literary genre. The *North American* maintained its ascendancy but, with a growing conservatism, lost some of its influence as competing journals were launched in New York, Philadelphia, Baltimore and points South and West.

Meanwhile the debate on a national literature became more widespread and took a subtle turn of emphasis. With growing political and social maturity, the question of national character inevitably was raised as literary influences from overseas gradually shifted from those of the Scottish rationalists to the English and German romantics. Wordsworth and Scott became widely read and Coleridge and Carlyle made their early appearances in the English and Scottish reviews. A more organic view of the national character and of the role of the literary "genius" provoked the three principal statements on literary nationalism of the decade, those of Ingersoll, Everett, and W. E. Channing, and was reflected less dramatically in other reviewers and critics. The completion of the first edition of Webster's *Ameri-*

can Dictionary added perhaps the final touch to literary maturity.

The larger questions of just how and when the Romantic Movement came to America and how and when American critical thinking moved from the sharp logic of the Scottish rationalists to the broad syntheses and generalizations of Coleridge, Carlyle and the Germans do not fall within the limits of this volume. The Emerson of 1821 who won a Bowdoin prize for his "Dissertation on the Present State of Ethical Philosophy," was also the Emerson who left Edinburgh in 1833 to seek out Carlyle in the barren and cold retreat of Craiggenputtock. During this period the work of English romantics was increasingly reviewed in the *North American* and elsewhere, but it was not until well after 1837 that the basic principles of American romanticism were fully defined and generally accepted. The development of a concept of a national character prepared the way for the acceptance of an organic view of literary theory, even though Ingersoll, W. E. Channing, and Emerson were far from agreement as to what the American national character might be. The concept of a national mind in a people so diversified as the Americans gave the argument for a national literature new validity and new urgency.

DOCUMENT 15

Charles Jared Ingersoll

Charles Jared Ingersoll (1782–1862), although a descendant of Loyalists, was the son of a member of the Constitutional Convention and himself a liberal during a long life of public service and political writing. As a practicing lawyer, member of Congress, and District Attorney of Pennsylvania, he supported Madison, Jackson, and Van Buren and was a pioneer in introducing enabling legislation for the promotion of steam railroads. He was the author of a tragedy which was produced in Philadelphia, a pamphlet on United States commercial policies, and a personal history of the War of 1812. His most famous literary work was *Inchiquin, the Jesuit's Letters* (1809), a supposed packet of letters from a Jesuit traveler in the United States, but in reality a lively and appreciative satire of American institutions and ideas. His *Discourse Concerning the Influence of America on the Mind* (1823) was the Annual Oration of the American Philosophical Society. Accepting the basic assumption of the *North American* group that literature should be the expression of experience, but broadening it to include any written expression of intellectual achievement, he attempts a definition and defense of the national character by reviewing American achievements in all fields of intellectual activity. His tone is temperate, but there is a running comparison with British parallels which makes his position strongly patriotic as well as thoroughly informed and judicious. Later writers on literary nationalism adopted his concern for national character, but differed with his conclusion that the American mind is essentially practical and pragmatic.

TEXT: from the first edition, Philadelphia, 1823.

A *Discourse Concerning the Influence of America on the Mind*

Appointed to deliver the annual discourse of the American Philosophical Society, I propose to sketch the philosophical condition of this country and explain the influence of America on the mind. The task is not an easy one owing to the extreme dispersion of the materials. Elsewhere intellectual improvements are collected in the accessible repositories of a metropolis, absorbing most of the intelligence of a whole nation and flourishing with artificial culture long applied. In the United States we have no such emporium; the arts and sciences are but of recent and spontaneous growth, scattered over extensive regions and a sparse population.

We will begin with the base of the American pile whose aggrandisement, like the pyramids of Africa, confounds the speculations of Europe. While the summit and sides elsewhere are more wrought and finished, America excels in the foundation in which we are at least the seniors of all other nations. Public funds for the education of the whole community are endowments exclusively American, which have been in operation here for several ages, while the most improved governments of Europe are but essaying such a groundwork, which indeed some of them dread and others dare not risk. It is nearly two hundred years since school funds were established by that aboriginal and immortal hive of intelligence, piety, and self-government, the Plymouth colony. These inestimable appropriations are now incorporated with all our fundamental institutions. By the Constitution of the United States it is the duty of government to promote the progress of science and the useful arts. Not one of the eleven new States has been admitted into the Union without provision in its constitution for schools, academies, colleges, and universities. In most of the original States large sums in money are appropriated to education, and they claim a share in the great landed investments which are mortgaged to it in the new States. Reckoning all those contributions federal and local, it may be asserted that nearly as much as the whole national expenditure of the United States is set apart by laws to enlighten the people. The public patronage of learning in this country, adverting to what the value of these donations will be before the close of the present century, equals at least the ostentatious bounties conferred on it in Europe. In one State alone, with but 275,000 inhabitants, more than forty thousand pupils are instructed at the public schools. I believe we may compute the number of such pupils throughout the United States at more than half a million. In the city of Philadelphia, without counting the private or the charity schools, there are about five thousand pupils in the Commonwealth's seminaries, taught reading, writing, and arithmetic at an expense to the public of little more than three dollars a year each one. Nearly the whole minor population of the United States are receiving school education. Besides the multitudes at school, there are considerably more than three thousand under graduates always matriculated at the various colleges and universities authorised to grant academical degrees; not less than twelve hundred at the medical schools; several hundred at the theological seminaries; and at least a thousand students of law. Nearly all of these are under the tuition of professors, without sinecure support, depending for their livelihood on capacity and success in the science of instruction. In no part of these extensive realms of knowledge is there any monastic prepossession against the modern improvements. Not long since chemistry, political economy, and the other great improvements of the age were excluded from the English universities as innovations unfit to be classed with rhetoric, logic, and scholastic ethics. Oxford and Cambridge, in the fine metaphor of Dugald Stewart, are immovably moored to the same station by the strength of their cables, thereby enabling the historian of the human mind to measure the rapidity of the current by which the rest of the world are borne along. The schools are equally stationary. Notwithstanding their barbarous discipline and the barbarous privileges of the colleges, they have always produced good Latinists and Hellenists. But American education is better adapted to enlarge and strengthen the mind and prepare it for practical usefulness. In that excellent institution, the Military Academy, the dead languages are not taught, and that kind of scholarship is postponed to sciences certainly more appropriate to a military education. This is not the occasion to inquire whether those standard exercises of the faculties and roots of language may ever be supplanted without injury. But as it is certain that the many great men who have received education at the English seminaries is not a conclusive proof of their excellence, though often cited for the purpose, so it is also true that eminent individuals have appeared in literature and science without the help of that kind of scholarship. The founder of the American Philosophical Society was not a scholar in this sense; yet his vigorous and fruitful mind, teeming with sagacity and cultivated by observation, germinated many of the great discoveries which, since matured by others, have become the monuments of the age: And whether science, politics, or polite literature was the subject of which Franklin treated, he always wrote in a fine, pure style, with the power and the charm of genius.

Successive improvements in the modern languages, continually perfecting themselves under the prevalence of liberal ideas, have brought them to a degree of moral certainty and common attainment which must render the dead languages less important hereafter. Their study will be confined probably to a few and may, perhaps, in the lapse of time, perish under the mass of knowledge destined to occupy entirely the limited powers of the human understanding. While, therefore, we are discussing whether the learning of the ancient languages ought to be maintained, innovating time is settling the question in spite of unavailing efforts and regrets for the immortal authors of European literature. Thus we may understand why the Latin and Greek languages are less cultivated in America than in Europe. Unfettered by inveterate prepossessions, the mind on this continent follows in its march the new spirit that is abroad, leading the intelligence of all the world to other pursuits.

Since the career of this country began, education on the continent of Europe has severely suffered by political fluctuations and continues to be thwarted by political superintendence. Whatever science and literature accomplish there must be in spite of a perplexing and pernicious education. Wanting the stability and tranquillity and security of free institutions, their existence is in perpetual fluctuation and jeopardy. The schools are regulated by one dynasty to-day, by another on opposite principles to-morrow, as the instruments of each in its turn, employed as much in unlearning what had been taught as in learning what is to be inculcated, continually molested and convulsed by state intrusion. The arts and sciences which war requires and requites may be encouraged and advanced: and fortunately for mankind, their extensive circle embraces many in which peace also delights or may enjoy. The northern universities have best preserved both their liberality and their usefulness. But in southern Europe, learning appears to be disastrously eclipsed where it has never ceased to receive Pagan and Christian sacrifice for more than two thousand successive years.—Liberty, says Sismondi, had bestowed on Italy four centuries of grandeur and glory during which she did not need conquests to make her greatness known. The Italians were the first to study the theory of government and to set the example of liberal institutions. They restored to the world, philosophy, eloquence, poetry, history, architecture, sculpture, painting, and music. No science, art, or knowledge could be mentioned, the elements of which they did not teach to people who have since surpassed them. This universality of intelligence had developed their mind, their taste, and their manners, and lasted as long as Italian liberty. How melancholy is the modern reverse of this attractive picture! When even freedom of thought can hardly breathe and freedom of speech or writing has no existence, revolution is the only remedy for disorder; sedition infects the schools, rebellion the academies, and treason the universities. In America, where universal education is the handmaid of universal suffrage, execution has never been done on a traitor; general intelligence disarms politics of their chimerical terrors; our only revolution was but a temperate transition, without mobs, massacres, or more than a single instance of signal perfidy; every husbandman understands the philosophy of politics better than many princes in Europe. Poetry, music, sculpture, and painting may yet linger in their Italian haunts. But philosophy, the sciences, and the useful arts, must establish their empire in the modern republic of letters where the mind is free from power or fear, on this side of that great water barrier which the creator seems to have designed for the protection of their asylum. The monarchs of the old world may learn from those sovereign citizens, the ex-presidents of these United States, the worth of an educated nation: who, having made large contributions to literature and the sciences, live in voluntary retirement from supreme authority, at ages beyond the ordinary period of European existence, enjoying the noble recreations of books and benevolence, without guards for their protection or pomp for their disguise, accessible, admired, protected, and immortalised. The Egyptians pronounced posthumous judgment on their kings: we try our presidents while living in canonised resignation, and award to those deserving it an exquisite foretaste of immortality.

In adult life we may trace the effects of the causes just indicated in education. The English language makes English reading American: and a generous, especially a parental nationality, instead of disparaging a supposed deficiency in the creation of literature, should remember and rejoice that the idiom and ideas of England are also those of this country and of this continent, destined to be enjoyed and improved by millions of educated and thinking people spreading from the bay of Fundy to the mouth of the Columbia. Such is the influence of general education and self-government that already over a surface of almost two thousand miles square there are scarcely any material provincialisms or peculiarities of dialect, much less than in any nation in Europe, I believe I might say than in any hundred miles square in Europe; and, what is perhaps even more remarkable, the German, Dutch and French veins which exist in different sections are rapidly yielding to the English ascendancy by voluntary fusion, without any coercive or violent applications. Adverting to the great results from the mysterious diversity of the various languages of mankind, the anticipation is delightful in the effects of the American unity of tongue, combined with universal education throughout this vast continent,—the home of liberty at least, if not the seat of one great empire.

But speaking and writing the language of an ancient and refined people whose literature preoccupies nearly every department is, in many respects, an unexampled disadvantage in the comparative estimate. America cannot contribute in any comparative proportion to the great British stock of literature which almost supersedes the necessity of American subscriptions. Independent of this foreign oppression, the American mind has been called more to political, scientific, and mechanical than to literary exertion. And our institutions, moreover, partaking of the nature of our government, have a levelling tendency. The average of intellect and of intellectual power in the United States surpasses that of any part of Europe. But the range is not, in general, so great, either above or below the horizontal line. In the literature of imagination, our standard is considerably below that of England, France, Germany and perhaps Italy. The concession, however, may be qualified by a claim to a respectable production of poetry; and the recollection that American scenes and incidents have been wrought by American authors into successful romances, some of which have been re-published and translated and are in vogue in Europe; and that even popular dramatic performances have been composed out of these incidents. The stage, however, is indicative of many things in America, being engrossed by the English drama and English actors. But as a proof of American fondness, if not taste, for theatrical entertainment, I may mention here that an English comedian has lately received for performances before the audiences of four or five towns whose united population falls short of four hundred thousand people a much larger income than any of the actors of that country receive in which this sort of intellectual recreation is most esteemed. There would be no inducement for strolling across the Atlantic if the largest capital in Europe afforded similar encouragement, taking emolument as the test and London with 1,200,000 inhabitants as the standard. As another remarkable proof of the state of the stage in the United States, I may add that an eminent American actor appears in the same season, (and it is practicable within the same month) before audiences at Boston and New-Orleans, compassing two thousand miles from one to the other by internal conveyance. Such is the philosophical as well as natural approximation of place and the unity of speech throughout that distance.

In the literature of fact, of education, of politics, and of perhaps even science, European pre-eminence is by no means so decided. The American schools, the church, the state, the bar, the medical profession are, all but the last, largely and all of them adequately, supplied by their own literature. Respectable histories are extant by American authors of the States of Kentucky, Georgia, North Carolina, South Carolina, Virginia, Maryland, Pennsylvania, New York, New Jersey, Vermont, Maine, Massachusetts, Connecticut, and New Hampshire; besides some general histories of New England, and several geographical and topographical works on Ohio, Indiana, Illinois, and Missouri, containing histories of their settlements. Our national histories, inferior in subordinate attractions to the romantic historical fictions of Europe, are composed of much more permanent and available materials. In biography, without equal means, have we not done as much since we began as our English masters? In the literature as well as the learning of the sciences, botany, mineralogy, metallurgy, entymology, ornithology, astronomy, and navigation, there is no reason to be ashamed of our proficiency. In mathematics and chemistry, our comparative deficiency is perhaps the most remarkable. In grammatical researches, particularly in the interesting elements of the Indian languages, American erudition has preceded that of Europe, where some of the most learned and celebrated of the

German and French philologists have caught from American publications the spirit of similar inquiry. In natural and political geography our magnificent interior has produced great accomplishments, scientific and literary. The maps of America have been thought worthy of imitation in Europe. Mr. Tanner's Atlas, lately published, is the fruit of a large investment of money and time and reflects credit on every branch of art employed in its execution. The surveys of the coast now making by government will be among the most extensive, accurate, and important memorials extant. Several scientific expeditions have likewise been sent by the government at different times into the western regions whose vast rivers, steppes and deltas have been explored by learned men whose publications enrich many departments of science and are incorporated with applause into the useful literature of the age. One of the most copious and authentic statistical works in print is an American production which owes its publication to the patronage of Congress. The public libraries, particularly those of Cambridge University, of the New York Historical Society, of the American Philosophical Society, of the city of Philadelphia, of Congress, and others which might be enumerated, abound with proof and promise of the flourishing condition and rapid advances of literature and science throughout America. A single newspaper of this city contains advertisements by a single bookseller of more than one hundred and fifty recent publications by American authors from the American press, comprehending romance, travels, moral philosophy, mineralogy, political and natural geography, poetry, biography, history, various scientific inquiries, and discoveries, botany, philology, oratory, chemistry applied to the arts, statistics, agricultural and horticultural treatises, strategy, mechanics, and many other subjects. From this ample and creditable catalogue I may select for especial notice the Journal of the Academy of Natural Sciences as a work of uncommon merit; and the profound and elaborate report on Weights and Measures as a laudable specimen of official function.

The first and the present Secretaries of the Department

of State, who have both made reports on this important branch of scientific politics, rank among the foremost scholars of the age by their eminence in various literary and scientific attainments. The American state papers, generally, have received the homage of the most illustrious statesmen of England for excellence in the principles and eloquence of that philosophy which is the most extensively applied to the affairs of men: and their publications afford large contributions to its literature. Whether any policy be preferable to another is generally a merely speculative topic. But I may with propriety assert that the United States have been the most stedfast supporters of maritime liberality, of inter-national neutrality, and of the modern system of commercial equality. They were the first to out-law the slave trade and the first to declare it piratical. Great Britain is imitating their example in commercial, colonial, navigation, penal, and even financial, regulations. France, Spain, Italy, Portugal, parts of Germany, and South America, have in part adopted their political principles. And in all the branches of political knowledge, the American mind has been distinguished.

The publication of books is so much cheaper in this country than in Great Britain that nearly all we use are American editions. According to reports from the Custom-houses, made under a resolution of the Senate in 1822, it appears that the importation of books bears an extremely small proportion to the American editions. The imported books are the mere seed. It is estimated that between two and three millions of dollars worth of books are annually published in the United States. It is to be regretted, that literary property here is held by an imperfect tenure, there being no other protection for it than the provisions of an inefficient act of Congress, the impotent offspring of an obsolete English statute. The inducement to take copy-rights is therefore inadequate and a large proportion of the most valuable American books are published without any legal title. Yet there were one hundred and thirty five copy rights purchased from January 1822 to April 1823. There have been eight editions comprising 7500 copies of Stewart's Philosophy published here since its appearance in Europe thirty years ago. Five hundred thousand dollars was the capital invested in one edition of Rees' Cyclopœdia. Of a lighter kind of reading, nearly 200,000 copies of the Waverley novels, comprising 500,000 volumes, have issued from the American press in the last nine years. Four thousand copies of a late American novel were disposed of immediately on its publication. Five hundred dollars were paid by an enterprising bookseller for a single copy of one of these novels, without any copy right, merely by prompt republication to gratify the eagerness to read it. Among the curiosities of American literature, I must mention the itinerant book trade. There are, I understand, more than two hundred wagons which travel through the country loaded with books for sale. Many biographical accounts of distinguished Americans are thus distributed. Fifty thousand copies of Mr. Weem's Life of Washington have been published and mostly circulated in this way throughout the interior. I might add to these instances, but it is unnecessary and would be irksome. Education, the sciences, the learned professions, the church, politics, together with ephemeral and fanciful publications, maintain the press in respectable activity.

The modern manuals of literature and science, magazines, journals and reviews, abound in the United States, although they have to cope with a larger field of newspapers than elsewhere. The North American Review, of which about four thousand copies are circulated, is not surpassed in knowledge or learning, is not equalled in liberal and judicious criticism, by its great British models, the Edinburgh and Quarterly Reviews, of which about four thousand copies are also published in the United States. Written in a pure, old English style, and, for the most part, a fine American spirit, the North American Review, superintends with ability the literature and science of America.

Not less than a thousand newspapers, some of them with several thousand subscribers, are circulated in this country; the daily fare of nearly every meal in almost every family; so cheap and common, that, like air and water, its uses are undervalued. But a free press is the great distinction of this age and country, and as indispensable as those elements to the welfare of all free countries. Abundant and emulous accounts of remarkable occurrences concentrate and diffuse information, stimulate inquiry, dispel prejudices, and multiply enjoyments. Copious advertisements quicken commerce; rapid and pervading publicity is a cheap police. Above all the press is the palladium of liberty. An American would forego the charms of France or Italy for the luxury of a large newspaper which makes every post an epoch and provides the barrenest corners of existence with an universal succedaneum. Duly to appreciate the pleasures of it, like health or liberty, we must undergo their temporary privation. Nor is our experience of the licentiousness of the press too dear a price to pay for its freedom. It is a memorable fact in the history of American newspapers that while some of the most powerful have been consumed in the combustion of their own calumnies, on the other hand, the most permanent and flourishing are those least addicted to defamation. It is also a fact that the most licentious newspapers which have appeared in America were edited by Europeans. The American standard is equally removed from the coarse licentiousness which characterises much of the English press and the constraints of that of the rest of Europe—and this standard has been established while state prosecutions have been falling into dislike. Our newspapers are regulated by a public tact much truer and stronger than such ordeals. The same ethereal influence in a free temperature is equally effective to preserve the good from obloquy and to consign the unworthy to degradation. Where the press is perfectly free, truth is an overmatch for detraction. Many of our public men have constantly enjoyed the public favour, in spite of intense abuse, and have survived its oblivion, to receive a foretaste of posthumous veneration. Under the light of these results, the press has learned the value of temperance, and while all the avenues of private redress are open to those who choose to seek it, state prosecutions have nearly disappeared. Irreligious, obscene, and seditious publications are infinitely more common from the English than from the American press: scurrilous and libellous newspapers exist to be sure, but they are the lowest and most obscure of the vocation, whereas in England, some of the most elevated and best patronised are the most scandalous and personal. In the darker ages, dungeons, scaffolds, torture, and mutilation, were the dreadful but vain restraints put on the understanding. Can it be supposed that in this enlightened æra, punishment, however mitigated, will do more than inflame it? And what is the English law of public prosecution for libels but a milder remnant of those principles? By which, infidelity, blasphemy, sedition, treason, and individual calumny, are provoked, disseminated and infuriated. Experience has taught us that the freedom of the press is the best protection against its abuse and that its transient licentiousness is part of the very nature of the blessing itself. The splendid skies, forests and foliage of America, with which Europe has nothing of the kind to compare, are inseparable from those vicissitudes and extremities of weather and seasons which, while menacing desolation, purify and sublimate existence. This American deduction of the much apprehended postulate of the press is obviously and rapidly gaining converts in England, whence perhaps it may ultimately spread over Europe and abolish the pernicious alternatives there prevalent. Without it, the press must cause convulsions, and retard the progress of the mind. The English newspaper press, much less free by law than the American, is in practice much more licentious. A late number of the Quarterly Review, (which is no mean authority on such a point) admits, in so many words, that the occupation of the English daily press is, to 'do every thing that honor and honesty shrink from': to which character the absence of decency should be superadded. The Attorney General protects government from libels; but the Chancellor has brought about a most preposterous state of things between the right of literary property, and the want of right in obscene, blasphemous, or otherwise illegal subjects of that property. English party vituperation is much coarser and more personal than ours. But, without going into politics, it may suffice to notice the difference in other things.

There are vented in the London newspapers, regular and
perennial streams of defilement—polluting police reports,
details of inhuman amusements, pugilistic and others,
indelicate particulars of various private occurrences, the
infamous amours of the royal and noble, are catered for
every day's repast, and demanded with an eagerness which
bespeaks a vitiated appetite. It seems to be thought that
publicity, like execution, deters from crimes, when assuredly, they both stimulate their perpetration. There is
another office of the English press, extremely derogatory
to the press itself, and injurious to society. I mean the
journalising private and domestic concerns and the most
trivial transactions of social intercourse for the gratification of a vanity peculiar to the aristocracy of that kingdom. The effects of this proclamation of the common affairs of private life can hardly fail to be injurious to the
female character in particular, whose modesty and retirement are thus perpetually broken in upon. The American
newspaper press is conducted in better taste and with
more dignity.

From literature the transition is natural to the arts
which minister to usefulness, comfort and prosperity, individual and national. Under their authority to provide
for the encouragement of the arts and sciences, the United
States, in thirty years, have issued about four thousand
four hundred patent rights for new and useful inventions,
discoveries, and improvements. By the prevailing construction of the acts of Congress, American patentees must be
American inventors or improvers and are excluded from
all things before known or used in any other part or period
of the world. The English law allows English patentees
to monopolise the inventions, discoveries, and improvements of all the rest of the world when naturalised in
Great Britain. Notwithstanding this remarkable disadvantage, I believe the American list of discoveries is quite
equal to the English. The specimens and models open
to public inspection in the national repository at Washington are equal, I understand, to any similar collections
in England or France and superior to those of any other
country. It will hardly be expected that I should under-

take to mention even the most remarkable articles of this immense museum, containing every element of practical science, of mechanism, of refinement, and of skill. I may be allowed, however, to say that the cotton gin has been of more profit to the United States than ten times all they ever received by internal taxation; that our grain mill machinery, applied to the great staples of subsistence, is very superior to that of Europe; that there are in the patent office models of more than twenty different power looms of American invention, operated on and weaving solely by extraneous power, steam, water, wind, animals, and otherwise; and that the English machines for spinning have been so improved here that low-priced cottons can be manufactured cheap enough to undersell the English in England after defraying the charges of transportation. Where American ingenuity has been put to trial it has never failed. In all the useful arts and in the philosophy of comfort,—that word which cannot be translated into any other language and which, though of English origin, was reserved for maturity in America, we have no superiors. If labour saving machinery has added the power of a hundred millions of hands to the resources of Great Britain, what must be the effect of it on the population and means of the United States? Steam navigation, destined to have greater influence than any triumph of mind over matter, equal to gunpowder, to printing, and to the compass, worthy to rank in momentum with religious reformation, and civil liberty, belongs to America. A member of this Society, in his eloquent appeal to the judgment of Great Britain, has argued this claim ably on abstract reasoning. But without disputing the conceptions and experiments of England, France, and Scotland, of Worcester, Hulls, Juffrou, or Miller, or entering at all into the question of prior imagination, it has always appeared to me that there is a plain principle on which to rest the rights of this country. Steam navigation was reserved for the genius of those rivers, on a single one of which there is already more than a hundred steam-boats containing upwards of fourteen thousand tons, and in whose single sea port, fifty steam boats may be counted at one time. This was the meridian to reduce to practical results, whatever conceptions may have existed elsewhere on this subject. Necessity, the mother of this invention, was an American mother; born, perhaps, on the shores of the Potomac, the Delaware, or the Hudson, yet belonging to the Missouri, the Arkansas, the Mississippi, and the Pacific ocean. By a very useful book called the Western Navigator, (published in this city,) it appears that the entire length of the Mississippi river is 2500 miles, of the Missouri 3000, of the Arkansas 2000, of the Red 1500; and from the recent works of Major Long and Mr. Schoolcraft, it is ascertained that a large number of great tributaries unite their waters with these prodigious floods, washing altogether, according to the summary of the author of the Western Navigator, in the valley of the Ohio, 200,000 square miles, in the valley of the Mississippi proper, 180,000, in that of the Missouri, 500,000, and in that of the lower Mississippi, 330,000, giving a total of 1,210,000 miles as the area of what is termed the Mississippi basin. Most if not all of these vast streams are innavigable but by steam boats owing to the course of their currents and other circumstances. These then are the latitudes of steam boats, which have been abandoned in some parts of Europe as too large for their rivers and too expensive for their travelling.—In less than ten years from this time, steam boats may pass from the great lakes of the northwest by canals to the Atlantic, thence to the isthmus of Darien, and across that to China and New Holland. They now ply like ferry boats from New York to Pensacola, New Orleans and Havanna, with the punctuality and security and more than the accommodation of the best land carriage of Europe. Wherever this wonderful invention appears, overcoming the winds and waves by steam, measuring trackless ocean distances by the quadrant, and protected from lightning by the rod, it displays in every one of these accomplishments the genius of America.

In the ordinary art of navigation, the construction, equipment, and manipulation of vessels, commercial and belligerent, America is also conspicuous. The merchant vessels of the United States, manned with fewer hands, perform their voyages generally in one third less time than those of the only other maritime people to be compared with them. And without referring to the achievements of the American navy as credentials of courage or renown, I may with propriety remark that an intelligent and scientific fabrication and application of arms, ammunition, ships, and all the materials of maritime warfare are unquestionably demonstrated by their success in it.

The mechanics, artisans, and laborers of this country are remarkable for a disposition to learn. Asserted European superiority has been of great advantage to America in preventing habitual repugnance to improvement, so common to all mankind, especially the least informed classes. Superior aptitude, versatility and quickness in the handicrafts are the consequences of this disposition of our people. A mechanic in Europe is apt to consider it almost irreverent and altogether vain to suppose that any thing can be done better than as he was taught to do it by his father or master. A house or ship is built in much less time here than there. From a line of battle ship or a steam engine to a ten penny nail, in every thing the mechanical genius displays itself by superior productions. The success of a highly gifted American mechanical genius now in England seems to be owing in part to his adapting his improvements, by a happy ingenuity, to the preservation of machinery, for which several English mechanics have been enriched and ennobled but which would have been superseded as useless had it not been thus rescued.

If a ship, a plough and a house be taken as symbols of the primary social arts of navigation, agriculture and habitation, we need not fear comparisons with other people in any one of them. In the intellectual use of the elements, the combinations and improvements of the earth and its products, of water, of air, and of fire, no greater progress has been made in Europe within this century than in the United States. The houses, ships, carriages, tools, utensils, manufactures, implements of husbandry, conveniences, comforts, the whole circle of social refinement, are always equal, mostly superior here to those of the most improved nations. I do not speak of mere natural advantages, of being better fed, more universally housed and more comfortably clothed, than any other people; but excepting the ostentatious, and extravagant, if not degenerate and mischievous, luxuries of a few in the capitals of Europe merely; looking to the general average of civilisation, where does it bespeak more mind or display greater advancement? Internal improvements, roads, bridges, canals, water-works, and all the meliorations of intercourse, have been as extensively and as expensively made within the last ten years in the United States, as in probably any other country; notwithstanding the sparseness of a population, of which scarcely half a million is concentrated in cities, and a slender capital. Five thousand post offices distribute intelligence throughout the United States with amazing celerity and precision over eighty thousand miles of post roads. The mail travels twenty-one thousand miles every day, compassing eight millions of miles in a year. There are twelve thousand miles of turnpike roads. Our facilities and habits of intercourse are unequalled in Europe; almost annihilating the obstacles of space. Within two years from this time, when all the great canals now in progress shall be completed, an internal navigation of ten thousand miles will belt this country from the great western valley to the waters of the Hudson and the Chesapeake. The New York canal and the Philadelphia water-works are not surpassed, if equalled, by any similar improvements in Europe within the period of their construction.

The polite arts, painting, engraving, music, sculpture, architecture, the arts of recreation, amusement, and pageantry, flourish most in the seats of dense population. Few of them thrive without the forcing of great capitals, the reservoirs of the refinements of ancient, sometimes declining, empire. Architecture is an art of state, whose master works are reserved for seats of government. The public edifices of Edinburgh or Liverpool, for instance, or those erected at any other provincial town within the last twenty years, bear no comparison to the costly and magnificent capitol, built, burnt, and rebuilt within that period at Washington. Indeed, I believe that there are no public buildings which have been constructed at London during this century in so expensive and splendid a style. The Halls of the Senate and of the Representatives at Washington are in the relation of contrast with the Houses of Commons and the Lords in London, as to magnitude, magnificence and accommodation. And if I am not mistaken, the only historical paintings of national events which have ever been paid for by legislative appropriation are those executed by an American artist for the walls of the capitol.

To these imperfect views of education, literature, science, and the arts, I will add sketches of the American mind, as developed in legislation, jurisprudence, the medical profession and the church; which, in this country, may be considered as the other cardinal points of intellectual exercise.

Representation is the great distinction between ancient and modern government. Representation and confederation distinguish the politics of America, where representation is real and legislation perennial. Thousands of springs, gushing from every quarter, eddy onward the cataract of representative democracy, from primary self-constituted assemblies, to the State Legislatures and the national Congress. Three thousand chosen members represent these United States in five and twenty Legislatures. There are, moreover, innumerable voluntary associations under legislative regulations in their proceedings. I am within bounds in asserting that several hundred thousand persons assemble in this country every year, in various spontaneous convocations, to discuss and determine measures according to parliamentary routine. From bible societies to the lowest handicraft there is no impediment but every facility, by law, to their organisation: And we find not only harmless but beneficial those various self-created associations which in other countries give so much trouble and alarm. It is not my purpose to consider the political influences of these assemblies, nor even their political character. But their philosophical effect on the individuals composing them is to sharpen their wits, temper their passions, and cultivate their elocution: While this almost universal practice of political or voluntary legislation could hardly fail to familiarise a great number of persons with its proprieties. The mode of transacting business is nearly the same in them all, from the humblest debating club to Congress in the capitol. Legislation in the United States is better ordered, more deliberative, decorous, and dignified, much less tumultuous or arbitrary and more eloquent than in Europe. Continual changes of the political representatives afford not less than ten thousand individuals spread throughout the United States, practically familiar with the forms and principles of legislation, who, through the vivid medium of a free press, constitute, as it were, an auditory greatly superior to that of any other nation. A large proportion of this great number of practical legislators is qualified by the habits of discussion incident to such employment, and perfect freedom, to deliver their sentiments in public speaking which, being in greater request, of greater efficacy and at greater liberty in America than in Europe, is naturally more prevalent and powerful here than there. It is a striking view of the ideas of legislation in Europe that within the last thirty years France and Spain have waged destructive wars for legislatures consisting of single assemblies; a constitution which in America would not be thought worth so much bloodshed.

The much abused French revolution has given to that country a Legislature of two houses and a press of considerable freedom. But the peers are lost in the secrecy of their sessions and the deputies can hardly be called a deliberative assembly. Few speak, inasmuch as most of the orations are read from a pulpit: and still fewer listen, amidst the tumults that agitate the whole body. To crown these frustrations of eloquent debate, when it becomes intense and critical, as it must be, to do its offices, the proceedings are sometimes closed by an armed force, marched in to seize and expel an obnoxious orator. This is certainly not the philosophy of legislation.

In Great Britain, an excessive number is crowded into an inconvenient apartment where but few attempt to speak and few can be brought to listen: and where both speakers and hearers are disturbed by tumultuous shouts

and unseemly noises, not, according to our ideas, conso-
nant with either eloquent or deliberative legislation. In
theory, the House of Commons contains nearly 700 members: in practice the most important laws are debated and
enacted by sixty or fifty. Owing to the want of personal
accommodation, when the house is crowded, its divisions
to be counted are attended with great confusion. Most of
the bills are drafted, not by members but by clerks hired
for that purpose: to which is owing much of the inordinate
tautology and technicality of modern acts of Parliament.
In theory and principle there is no audience, and in fact,
bystanders are not permitted but occasionally, under inconvenient restrictions. Reports and publications of the
debates are unauthorised and of course imperfect, notwithstanding the exploits of stenography. Although Parliament is omnipotent, yet a member may not publish
abroad what he says in his place without incurring igno-
minious punishment as a libeller: which punishment was
actually inflicted not long ago on a peer, proceeded against
by information, for that offence. In France, the press is, in
this respect, freer than in England. The publication of
speeches in the Legislature is considered an inviolable
right which, among all the revocations of the present government, has never been molested or called in question.
By a perversion of the hours, unknown, I believe, in any
other country or age, most of the business of Parliament
is done in the dead of night, to which, probably, many
of the irregularities now mentioned are ascribable. The
great popular principles which have preserved the British
Parliament, while every other similar attempt in Europe
has failed, or nearly so, and its brilliant political performances, have recommended it to admiration, notwithstanding these disadvantages; and indeed sanctioned them as
part of the system. But unprejudiced judgment must allow that all these are imperfections which have no place
in Congress. Hence it is that there are not now, and probably never were at any one time, more than two or three
members of Parliament actuated by the great impulses
of oratory and that the talent of extemporaneous and useful eloquence always has been much more common in

Congress. Burke's inimitable orations which all ages will read with delight were delivered to an empty house. A member, now a peer, himself one of the most eloquent men of England, whose political and personal ties bound him particularly to remain during the delivery of one of these master-pieces, after nearly every body else had withdrawn, actually crawled out of the house to escape unnoticed from an intolerable scene. Johnson, the editor of Chatham's famous speeches, in a number of the Rambler treats the graces of eloquence with elaborate ridicule and contempt; and Hume, in his Essay on Eloquence, and Blair, in his Lectures on Rhetoric, acknowledge that they are not characteristics of British oratory. The printed speeches of England are among the finest specimens of the art of composition; but it is notorious that in parliament and at the bar the most celebrated speeches avail nothing with those to whom they are addressed; and eloquence, in the pulpit of the established church is, I believe, a thing unheard of. The talent of effective oratory is much more common in America where laws are made, controversies are settled, and proselytes are gained by it every day. An eloquent professor or lecturer in England is very rare, if there be any such. While it is well known that the medical school of Philadelphia owes its success, in part, to the mere eloquence of its lecturers. Crowds of listeners are continually collected in all parts of this country to hear eloquent speeches and sermons. The legislature, the court house, and the church are thronged with auditors of both sexes, attracted by that talent which was the intense study and great power of the ancient orators. Thought, speech, and action must be perfectly free to call forth the utmost powers of this mighty art. It requires difficulties but it needs hopes. Its temples in free countries are innumerable. When its rites are administered the most divine of human unctions searches the marrow of the understanding; the orator is inspired, the auditor is absorbed by the occasion.

Annual sessions of five and twenty legislatures multiply laws which produce a numerous bar, in all ages the teeming offspring of freedom. Their number in the United

States has been lately computed at six thousand; which is probably an under estimate. American lawyers and judges adhere with professional tenacity to the laws of the mother country. The absolute authority of recent English adjudications is disclaimed but they are received with a respect too much bordering on submission. British commercial law, in many respects inferior to that of the continent of Europe, is becoming the law of America. The prize law of Great Britain was made that of the U. States by judicial legislation during flagrant war between the two countries. The homage lately paid by the English prime minister to the neutral doctrines proclaimed by the American government, in the beginning of the French revolution, which declares them worthy the imitation of all neutral nations, may teach us that the American state papers contain much better principles of international jurisprudence than the passionate and time-serving, however brilliant, sophisms of the British admiralty courts. On the other hand, English jurisprudence, while silently availing itself of that of all Europe and adopting without owning it, has seldom if ever made use of an American law book, recommended by the same language, system, and subject matter. American translations of foreign jurists on subjects in which the literature of English law is extremely deficient appear to be less known in England than translations of the laws of China. This veneration on our part and estrangement on theirs are infirmities characteristic of both. Our professional bigotry has been counteracted by penal laws in some of the States against the quotation of recent British precedents, as it was once a capital offence in Spain to cite the civil law and as the English common law has always repelled that excellent code from its tribunals. I cannot think, with the learned editor of the Law Register, that late English law books are a dead expense to the American bar, or that, in his strong phrase, scarcely an important case is furnished by a bale of their reports. But I deplore the colonial acquiescence in which they are adopted, too often without probation or fitness. The use and respect of American jurisprudence in Great Britain will begin only when we cease to prefer their adjudications to our own. By the same means we shall be relieved from disadvantageous restrictions on our use of British wisdom; and our system will acquire that level to which it is entitled by the education, learning, and purity of those by whose administration it is formed.

In their national capacity, the United States have no common law, but all the original States are governed by that of England, with adaptations. In one of the new States in which the French, Spanish, and English laws happen to be all naturalised, an attempt at codification from all these stocks is making, under legislative sanction. In others, possibly all of the new States which have been carved out of the old, a great question is in agitation whether the English common law is their inheritance. Being a scheme of traditional precepts and judicial precedents, that law requires continual adjudications, with their reasons at large, to explain, replenish, and enforce it. Of these reports, as they are termed, no less than sixty four, consisting of more than two hundred volumes and a million of pages, have already been uttered in the United States, most of them in the present century and in a ratio of great increase. The camel's load of cases which is said to have been necessary to gain a point of law in the decline of the Roman empire is therefore already insufficient for that purpose in the American. Add to which, an American lawyer's library is incomplete without a thousand volumes of European legists, comprehending the most celebrated French, Dutch, Italian, and German treatises on natural, national, and maritime law, together with all the English chancery and common law. I have heard of an American lawyer of eminence whose whole property is said to consist in a large and expensive law library.

Notwithstanding this mass of literature, the law has been much simplified in transplantation from Europe to America and its professional as well as political tendency is still to further simplicity. The brutal, ferocious, and inhuman laws of the feudists, as they were termed by the civilians, (I use their own phrase,) the arbitrary rescripts of the civil law, and the harsh doctrines of the common law have all been melted down by the genial mildness of

American institutions. Most of the feudal distinctions between real and personal property, complicated tenures and primogeniture, the salique exclusion of females, the unnatural rejection of the half-blood, and ante-nuptial offspring, forfeitures for crimes, the penalties of alienage, and other vices of European jurisprudence which nothing but their existence can defend and reason must condemn are either abolished or in a course of abrogation here. Cognisance of marriage, divorce, and posthumous administration, taken from ecclesiastical, has been conferred on the civil tribunals. Voluminous conveyancing and intricate special pleading, among the costliest mysteries of professional learning in Great Britain, have given place to the plain and cheap substitutes of the old common law. With a like view to abridge and economise litigation, coercive arbitration, or equivalents for it, have been tried by legislative provision; jury trial, the great safeguard of personal security, is nearly universal and ought to be quite so for its invaluable political influences. It not only does justice between the litigant parties but elevates the understanding and enlightens the rectitude of all the community. Sanguinary and corporal punishments are yielding to the interesting experiment of penitential confinement. Judicial official tenure is mostly independent of legislative interposition and completely of executive influence. The jurisdiction of the courts is far more extensive and elevated than that of the mother country. They exercise, among other high political functions, the original and remarkable power of invalidating statutes by declaring them unconstitutional, an ascendancy over politics never before or elsewhere asserted by jurisprudence, which authorises the weakest branch of a popular government to annul the measures of the strongest. If popular indignation sometimes assails this authority, it has seldom if ever been able to crush those who have honestly exercised it; and even if it should, though an individual victim might be immolated, his very martyrdom would corroborate the system for which he suffered. Justice is openly, fairly, and purely administered, freed from the absurd costumes and ceremonies which disfigure it in England. Judicial appointment is less influenced by politics and judicial proceedings more independent of political considerations.

The education for the bar is less technical, their practice is more intellectual, the vocation is relatively at least more independent in the United States than in Great Britain. Here, as there, it is a much frequented avenue to political honours. All the chief justices of the United States have filled eminent political stations both abroad and at home. Of the five Presidents of the United States, four were lawyers; of the several candidates at present for that office, most, if not all, are lawyers. But without any public promotion, American society has no superior to the man who is advanced in any of the liberal professions. Hence there are more accomplished individuals in professional life here than where this is not the case. Under other governments, patronage will advance the unworthy and power will oppress the meritorious. Even in France, where there are and always have been lawyers of great and just celebrity, we sometimes see that for exerting the noblest and, in free countries, the most common duties of their profession, for resisting the powerful and defending the weak, they are liable to irresponsible arrest, imprisonment and degradation without the succour and sanctuary of a free press and dauntless public sympathy. In Great Britain, it is true, there is no such apprehension to deter them, and equally true that professional as well as political dignities are free to all candidates. But the ascendancy of rank, the contracted divisions of intellectual labour, the technicality of practice, combine with other causes to render even the English individuals, not perhaps inferior lawyers but subordinate men.

British jurisprudence itself, too, that sturdy and inveterate common law to which Great Britain owes many of the great popular conservative principles of her constitution—even these have been impaired by long and terrible wars, during which, shut up within their impregnable island, the offspring of Alfred and of Edward, infusing their passions, their politics, and their prejudices into their laws, have wrenched them to their occasions. The distinguishing attributes and merits of the common law are that it is popular and mutable, takes its doctrines from the people, and suits them to their views. While the American judiciary enforces this system of jurisprudence, may it never let wars or popular passions or foreign influences impair its principles.

There are about ten thousand physicians in the United States, and medical colleges for their education in Massachusetts, Rhode-Island, Connecticut, New York, Pennsylvania, Virginia and Ohio. There are also two medical universities in the state of New York, one in Pennsylvania, one in Maryland, one in Massachusetts, and one in Kentucky; containing altogether about twelve hundred students. Under the impulses of a new climate and its peculiar distempers, the medical profession has been pursued and its sciences developed with great zeal and success in this country; whose necessities have called forth a bolder and more energetic treatment of diseases, more discriminating and philosophical, as well as decisive and efficient; a more scientific assignment of their causes and ascertainments of their nature. Many medical errors and prejudices, now abandoned in Europe, were first refuted here. What is justly termed a national character has been given to the medical science of America, and American medical literature is circulated and read in Europe, where several American medical discoveries and improvements have been claimed as European. Anatomy, the most stationary of the medical sciences, is ardently cultivated and has been advanced by discoveries in the American schools. Valuable contributions have been made to physiology and more rational views inculcated of animal economy. An American discovery in chemistry has distinguished its author throughout Europe where the achievements of this master spirit of sciences, while to be sure they leave ours behind, yet encourage it to an application full of promise. It is a merit of the American schools, at least, to have accurately defined the bounds of chemistry and physiology. Our diversified soils and climates afford inexhaustible healing and balsamic plants, many of which have been adopted into the materia medica and displayed in publications creditable to the literature and some of the fine arts as well as the science of this country. And the bowels of this continent are rich with sanative minerals, some of which likewise have been extracted and made known both to science and by literature. Mr. Cleaveland's treatise on mineralogy is, I believe, used as a text book in Great Britain.

American physicians are probably unrivalled in the knowledge and use of what are termed the heroic remedies. They have introduced new and rational doctrines respecting the operation of remedies, combatting the notion of their reception into the circulation and referring it to the principle of sympathy. They deny the asserted identity of remedies, believing that they have succeeded in proving an essential difference in their operation, not only in degree but in effect. The American improvements in Surgery are too numerous and, though not the less important, too minute and technical to be generalised in a summary. Its apparatus, mechanism, and operations have been improved by a theory and practice equal in science, skill and success to any in the world. But its greatest melioration is philosophical. The founder of most of the improvements in surgery alluded to, deeming its most skilful operations but imperfections in the preserving art, reserves them for its last resort, never to be performed till all means of natural cure prove abortive. On this exalted principle the great Hunter taught and practised, uniting humanity and philosophy to science and art; a benefactor, whose original and admirable suggestions it is the merit of American physicians and surgeons to have introduced into their practice in this country before their imputed innovations were reconciled to pre-conceived opinions in his own.

Midwifery, both practical and theoretical, has also received essential improvements in the American school, some of which have been declared by high authority to mark an æra in the obstetric practice. In the theory and practice of medicine, the improvements are too many and important for my recital. The gastric pathology, the prevailing treatment and theory of hydrokephalus and of dropsies in general, the boasted European practice in marasmus, the cure of the croup, of gout by evacuations, the arrest of malignant erisipelas, and of mortification, and of inflamation of the veins; in short, a long list of remedial systems, which might be enumerated, though claimed in Europe, belong to America. The vaunted suggestion of Europe that fever originates in sympathetic irritation and that venesection and other evacuations are requisite in the primary stages of it have long been the established doctrines of America where they were first demonstrated. American medical science and skill have outstripped those of the rest of the world, Europe included, in the character and treatment of epidemics and pestilences. In this great field, Europe has done little, while the progress of America has been great. Bigoted to antiquated notions the medical science of the old world has stagnated for centuries in prejudices which have been expelled in the new, where the causes, nature, laws, and treatment of these destructive visitations have been ascertained and systematised. English critics particularly dwell with exultation on their supposed late triumphs over these distempers. Divested of the long prevalent notion of debility and putrescency, they now urge depletion as if the suggestion were their own, whereas thirty years have elapsed since the physicians of this country were in the full employment of it.

The theory and practice of medicine, the fearless and generous resistance of pestilential disease, suggest a recollection of a late medical professor here, whose works are in the libraries of the learned in many countries and in several languages, whose fascinating manners and eloquent lectures largely contributed to the foundation of a flourishing school, whose zeal, if some times excessive, was characteristic of genius, and the pioneer of success, whose services, let me add, as a patriot, and a philanthropist, shed a divine lustre on his career as a physician. The first leading man to lay down his life in battle in the American revolution was an eminent physician. The best historian of that period was also an eminent physician. And in a country which knows no grade above that of the eminent in learning and usefulness, there have been and there are many others of this profession to whom more than professional celebrity belongs. They frequently unite political with professional distinctions. Many of the members of this profession have filled various stations in every branch of our government. Many of them at this moment occupy high executive and legislative public offices. The pernicious and degrading system which subdivides labour infinitesi-mally—a system useful perhaps for pin-makers but most injurious in all the thinking occupations—has no counte-nance in America. The American physician practices phar-macy, surgery, midwifery, and is cast on his own resources for success in all he does; the consequence of which is, that he is forced to think more for himself and of course to excel. In Europe, successful physicians are too often made so by favour or chance. They are, moreover, the luxuries of the metropolis and a few great cities. Through-out the interior of England, generally, the medical attend-ant is an uneducated apothecary whose science stops at the compounding of a drug or the opening of a vein. Even in London, this class is always in reserve to succeed the preliminary and expensive visits of the doctor whose em-ployment, besides, depends too much on the recommenda-tion of these subordinates. In this country, medical skill is much more generally distributed. Every hamlet, every region abounds with educated physicians whose qualifica-tions, to be sure, ultimately depend much on their oppor-tunities, but who, at least for the most part, begin with the recommendations of diplomas.

Perhaps the most humane discovery in modern medicine is vaccination, to which America has no claim though su-perior intelligence here has given it much greater effect than among the ignorant populace of Europe. The doc-trine of non-contagion in pestilential distempers, should it be established, must also enjoy great credit as a triumph for humanity. The most distressing prejudices concerning contagion are not yet extirpated in Europe. I am not authorised to consider a disbelief in this shocking aggra-vation of any malady as a point in which the medical profession of America is quite unanimous with respect to yellow fever, but a foreign physician who lately collected their opinions ascertained the ratio of non-contagionists to be 567 to 28 contagionists. A late French ambassador in this country, who was bred a physician, has publicly claimed the merit of the discovery of non-contagion for another French physician who was in practice in this city in 1793 and is now in the service of the king of France. But in a treatise on the yellow fever by Dr. Hillary, published sixty years ago, its contagion is explicitly denied by the unqualified declaration, that 'it has nothing of a pestilential or contagious nature in it.' That this is not the sentiment prevalent in France would seem to be inferrible from recent events. A French army was stationed at the foot of the Pyrennees, as a sanitory cordon, to prevent the passage of contagion over those lofty and frost crowned mountains. Whatever may be the theories or reveries of a few, therefore, it is a remarkable proof of the actual state of the public intelligence on this subject, not only in France but throughout Europe, that all inquiries concerning the cause of this apparently warlike demonstration were silenced by assurances that its design was to repel contagious disease, under which assertion the wisdom of Europe rested till the plans thus masked were ripe for execution.

I shall conclude with some views of the American church which I hope to be able to shew is as justly entitled to that distinctive appellation as the church of Rome, the church of England, the Gallican church, the Greek church, or any others, to theirs respectively.

It is the policy or the prejudice of governments which use the church as an engine of state to decry institutions which separate them and leave religion to self-regulation. They are accused of infidelity and immorality. The want of ecclesiastical respectability is inferred from its want of political protection and influence. These Pagan doctrines have prevailed where ever Christianity has been unknown. They were Egyptian, Grecian, Roman, they are Mahometan. But they cannot endure the light of reason and truth. Whoever reads the text book of Christianity must be convinced that it is the religion of self-government. No European dogma is more unfounded than that republicanism and infidelity are coadjutors. Intelligent men in the United

States, with much more unanimity and sincerity than in Europe, believe that without religion humanity would be forlorn and barbarous. And in no country are those ecclesiastical classes and cures which have formed parts of the institutions of religion in all times better established than in this. In estimating the progress and condition of the mind in America, therefore, I have neither disposition nor occasion to deny that the condition of religion is one of the best tests of the general intellectual state. Independently of their help in the cure of souls, the clergy have always rendered the most important services to the human understanding. Learning and science were long in their exclusive care. In those periods when the mind was most depressed, the church was the chancery of its preservation. To it we owe nearly all the best relics of ancient learning; from it, we still receive much of our education, for here, as elsewhere, most of our teachers are ecclesiastics. It is therefore a very interesting inquiry how the church and its ministers, who are also the ministers of education, fare in any community.

Segregation from political connection and toleration are the cardinal principles of the American church. On the continent of Europe, toleration means, where it is said to exist, catholic supremacy suffering subordinate protestantism. In the united kingdom of Great Britain and Ireland, it means a protestant hierarchy, abetted by dissenters, excluding catholics from political privileges and subjecting them to double ecclesiastical impositions. France, Italy, Ireland, and Spain have been desolated by contests between church and state. Toleration has won at least part of these bloody fields. But a segregated church does not appear to have made any advance in Europe. In the United States, both of these principles are not only fundamental political laws but ancient, deep-seated doctrines whose bases were laid long before political sovereignty was thought of, when Williams, Penn and Baltimore, by a remarkable coincidence, implanted them in every quarter and in every creed. American toleration means the absolute independence and equality of all religious denominations. American segregation means that no human authority can in any case whatever control or interfere with the rights of conscience. Adequate trial of these great problems, not less momentous than that of political self-government, has proved their benign solution. Bigotry, intolerance, blood thirsty polemics waste themselves in harmless, if not useful, controversy when government takes no part. We enjoy a religious calm and harmony not only unknown but inconceivable in Europe. We are continually receiving accessions of their intolerance which is as constantly disarmed by being let alone. Our schools, families, legislatures, society find no embarrassment from varieties of creed which in Europe would kindle the deadliest discord.

That these consequences are not the fruits of lukewarmness and disregard to religion remains to be shewn.

I shall touch but lightly on the dissenting church, as it is called in England; not because its condition in the United States is not worthy of regard, and a great argument for my object, but because its well known prosperity renders it almost unnecessary that I should dwell on any details of it. Always democratic even in Europe, no reason can be imagined why it should not thrive in the aboriginal republicanism of America, the natural and fruitful soil of spontaneous religion. Accordingly, there are upwards of seven hundred congregational churches in the New England States alone and nearly that number of clergymen of that denomination, including pastors, unsettled ministers, and licensed preachers, from which enumeration I exclude the Baptists of that quarter, who are uniformly of the congregational order in church government. There is a theological seminary at Andover, in Massachusetts, containing about one hundred and fifty students in divinity. At Harvard college, there is a theological professor of the Anti-trinitarian faith, with whom several resident graduates commonly study. Of the two hundred and thirty congregational ministers of Massachusetts, about seventy are Anti-trinitarians. In Maine, there is a theological seminary with two professors and about forty pupils. Yale college in Connecticut has a theological department attached to it, in which there are three professors and a considerable number of students. In Cornwall, in Connecticut, there is also a Heathen mission school in which about thirty youths, born in India, on the Pacific ocean, and the western wilds of this continent, or other heathen places are educated with special reference to ministerial duties in their respective birth places.

The Presbyterian church in the United States, in addition to the congregational, contains about nine hundred ministers, one hundred and thirty five licentiates, one hundred and forty seven candidates, more than fourteen hundred churches, and last year administered the sacrament of the Lord's Supper to an hundred thousand communicants. It has theological seminaries in the States of New Jersey, New York, and Tennessee, and, as is obvious from these indications, is established on broad and flourishing endowments.

I shall also very summarily touch the condition of those enthusiastic and, for the most part, itinerant churches which, ever since their first example in the appearance of the Franciscan and Dominican friars of the thirteenth century, in a similar manner and on similar occasions, have, under various titles, interposed their austere and reviving tenets into the deserted or decaying quarters of Christianity; whose popular and rallying doctrines have a highly beneficial influence on the morals of the community. The Methodist church of America contains three dioceses, eleven hundred itinerant clergy, exclusively clerical, and about three thousand stationary ministers who attend also to other than ecclesiastical occupations. They reckon twelve conferences and more than twenty five hundred places of worship. By the report to the Baptist convention which sat in June last at Washington, the places of worship of that persuasion are stated at more than two thousand three hundred and they reckon a very large number of ministers. There are three theological seminaries of the Baptist church, one in New England, one in the interior of the State of New York, and one at the city of Washington. There were likewise two theological seminaries of the Methodist church, of whose services, however, it has been for the present deprived by accidental circumstances. It is a remarkable and most laudable characteristic of all these religious denominations that their means are applied, among other beneficial purposes, always liberally to that of education.

The Universalists have one hundred and twenty preachers, two hundred separate societies, and eight periodical publications. The Lutheran, the Dutch Reformed, and Associate Reformed, the Moravians, the Friends, in short, almost an innumerable roll of creeds, have their several seminaries of education, their many places of worship, numerous clergy or preachers, and every other attribute of secular as well as spiritual religion in prosperity.

To the clergy of some of these sects, especially the Presbyterian and Congregational, the American revolution is deeply indebted for its origin, progress, and issue. The generous, yet jealous principles of self-government, proclaimed as the motives of that event, have no more steadfast, uniform, or invincible adherents than their followers. Polemical literature, metaphysical knowledge, pulpit eloquence, philological learning, invigorating the mind and giving it power over the world, are superadded to the laborious and self-denyed lives and pure ministry of these ecclesiastics. The dissenters in England form, no doubt, a body of learned and zealous divines, but from the time when England first sent her sons to New England to learn and teach theology to the present day, the American dissenting church is at least equal to that of the mother country in intelligence and influence and much superior in eloquence.

But it is on the American church of England and the American church of Rome that we may dwell with most complacency. Here, where no political predominance, no peculiar, above all no mysterious, inquisitorial, arbitrary, or occult polity, no tythes, no titles, peerage, crown or other such appliances sustain the ministry, where the crosier is as plain as the original cross itself, and the mitre does not sparkle with a single brilliant torn from involuntary contribution,—it is here, I venture to say, that within the last century, the church of England and the church of Rome have constructed more places of worship, (relatively speaking,) endowed more dioceses, founded more religious houses, and planted a stronger pastoral influence than in any other part of the globe. It is in the United States of America under the power of American religion that the English and Roman Catholic churches are flourishing.

Until the revolution, the church of England was the established church in all the American colonies. In Maryland and Virginia, where it was most firmly seated, a sort of modus or composition for tythes was assessed by law, either on the parishes or by the polls. In Virginia there were moreover glebes annexed to the parish churches. In New York, there was also a fund taken from the public money, appropriated to the few parishes established there. Throughout New England, Pennsylvania, and the other colonies, if I am not misinformed, though the church of England was the national church, yet it languished in great infirmity, having no other support than the pew rents and voluntary assessments which now, under a very different regimen, supply adequate resources for all the occasions of an establishment which has no rich and no very poor pastorates.

The whole of these vast regions, by a gross ordinance of colonial misrule, were attached to the London diocess. Most of the incumbents, it may be supposed, those especially supported by tythes at such a distance from the diocesan, were supine and licentious. As soon as the revolution put a stop to their stipends, they generally ceased to officiate and in Maryland and Virginia particularly the Methodists and Baptists stepped in to their deserted places. The crisis for the church of England at this conjuncture was vital. Several of its ministers at first joined their compatriots for the independence declared. But few endured unto the end of the struggle. When the enemy were in possession of Philadelphia, then the capital of the country where Congress sat, and that inimitable assembly was driven to resume its deliberations at the village of Yorktown, they elected for their chaplain a clergyman of the church of England who had been expelled his home in this city by its capture. Every ingenuous mind will do justice to the predicament in which such an election placed an American pastor of the English church. The cause of independence to which he was attached was in ruin; the government forced from its seat, the army routed and disheartened, the country prostrate and nearly subdued by a triumphant enemy in undisputed occupation of the capital. The chaplain elected by Congress under such circumstances proved worthy of their confidence. Without other attendant, protection, or encouragement than the consciousness of a good cause, he repaired to the retreat of his country's abject fortunes to offer daily prayers from the bosom of that immortal assembly which never despaired of them, to the almighty providence by which they were preserved and prospered. The chaplain of Congress, at Yorktown, has been rewarded for those days of trial. Already, in the compass of his own life and ministry, he is at the head of the ten bishoprics into which the American church of England has since then expanded in the United States, with three hundred and fifty clergymen, about seven hundred churches, a theological seminary, and every other assurance of substantial prosperity. Within his life time there was but one, and at the commencement of his ministry but three episcopal churches in Philadelphia, and they in jeopardy of the desecration from which they were saved by his patriotic example and pious influence. It would be an unjust and unacceptable homage, however, to him not to declare that the intrinsic temperance and resource of popular government mainly contributed to the preservation of the English church in America, where it has since advanced far more than in the mother country during the same period, and where it is probably destined to flourish greatly beyond the English example. Of this there can be no doubt if it thrives henceforth as it has done heretofore, for under the presidency of a single prelate, still in the effective performance of all the duties of a good bishop and a good citizen, the American church of England, without a particle of political support, has, as we have seen, extended itself. Within a few years a million of pounds sterling were appropriated by parliament on the special recommendation of the crown of Great Britain for the repair and construction of churches, with views doubtless to political as much as to religious consequences. I venture to predict that within the period to elapse from that appropriation to its expenditure, a larger sum of money will have been raised in the United States by voluntary subscription and expended for similar purposes and to greater effect.

The Roman catholic church grows as vigorously as any other in the soil and atmosphere of America. The late (first) archbishop of that church likewise adhered with unshaken and zealous constancy to the cause of the American revolution and indeed, served for it in a public station. His illustrious relative is one of the three signers of a charter destined to have more influence on mankind than any uninspired writing, who have lived to enjoy its developements during half a century; in which period, all North and South America have been regenerated and the most intelligent portions of Europe quickened with the spirit of that political scripture. He periled a million of dollars when he pledged his fortune to the declaration of independence: as to the short sighted, the patriot priest might have seemed to risk his religion when he abjured European allegiance. But neither of them has had reason to regret the effects of self-government on a faith of which they have both, at all times, been the American pillars and ornaments. From a mere mission in 1790, the Roman catholic establishment in the United States has spread into an extended and imposing hierarchy consisting of a metropolitan see and ten bishoprics, containing between eighty and a hundred churches, some of them the most costly and splendid ecclesiastical edifices in the country, superintended by about one hundred and sixty clergymen. The remotest quarters of the U. States are occupied by these flourishing establishments; from the chapels at Damascotti (in Maine) and at Boston, to those of St. Augustine in Florida and St. Louis in Missouri. There are catholic seminaries at Bardstown and Frankfort in Kentucky, a catholic clerical seminary in Missouri, catholic colleges at St. Louis and New Orleans, where there is likewise a catholic Lancasterian school, two catholic charity schools at Baltimore, two in the District of Columbia, a catholic seminary and college at Baltimore, a catholic college in the District of Columbia, a catholic seminary at Emmitsburg in Maryland, a catholic free school and Orphans' asylum in Philadelphia. These large contributions to education are not, however highly respectable and cultivated as many of them are, the most remarkable characteristics of the American Roman catholic church. It is a circumstance pregnant with reflections and results, that the Jesuits, since their suppression in Europe, have been established in this country. In 1801, by a brief of pope Pius the seventh, this society, with the concurrence of the emperor Paul, was established in Russia under a general authorised to resume and follow the rule of St. Ignatius of Loyola; which power was extended in 1806, to the United States of America, with permission to preach, educate youth, administer the sacraments, &c. with the consent and approbation of the ordinary. In 1807, a noviciate was opened at Georgetown college in the District of Columbia, which continued to improve till 1814 when, being deemed sufficiently established, the congregation was formally organised by a papal bull. This society now consists of twenty-six fathers, ten scholastics in theology, seventeen scholarships in philosophy, rhetoric, and belles lettres, fourteen scholastics in the noviciate, twenty-two lay-brothers out of, and four lay-brothers in, the noviciate, some of whom are dispersed throughout the United States, occupied in missionary duties and the cure of souls. This statement is enough to prove the marvellous radication of the strongest fibres of the Roman catholic church in our soil. But the argument does not stop here. The oldest catholic literary establishment in this country is the catholic college just mentioned, which was founded immediately after the revolution by the incorporated catholic clergy of Maryland, now capable of containing two hundred resident students, furnished with an extensive and choice library, a philosophical and chemical apparatus of the latest improvement, and professorships in the Greek, Latin, French and English languages, mathematics, moral and natural philosophy, rhetoric, and belles lettres. This institution, I have mentioned, was put in 1805 under the direction of the society of Jesuits and that nothing might be wanting to the strong relief in which the subject appears, the college thus governed was, by act of Congress of the United States of America, raised to the rank of a University and empowered to confer degrees in any of the faculties. Thus, since the suppression of the order of Jesuits about the time of the origin of the American revolution, has that celebrated brotherhood of propagandists been restored in the United States and its principal and most operative institution organised and elevated by an act of our national Legislature.

In like manner, the Sulpitian monks have been incorporated by act of the legislature of the State of Maryland in the administration of the flourishing catholic seminary at Baltimore. Still more remains, however, to be made known for so silent and unobtrusive is religious progress, when neither announced nor enforced by political power, that it is probable that many of these curious details may be new to some of those who now hear them mentioned. Those religious houses and retreats which have been rended from their ancient seats in so many parts of Europe —monasteries and convents—are sprouting up and casting their uncultivated fragrance throughout the kindlier glebes and wilds of America. Even where corruption and abuse had exposed them to destruction, learning turned with sorrow from the abomination of their desolation, and charity wept over the downfall of her ancient fanes. But here, where corruption and abuse can hardly exist in self supported religious institutions—what have we to apprehend from these chaste and pious nurseries of education and alms? What may we not hope, on the contrary, for the mind, from their consecration and extension? In the oldest religious house in America, that of the female Carmelites, near Port Tobacco, in Maryland, the established number of inmates is always complete. The convent of St. Mary's, at Georgetown, in the District of Columbia, contains fifty nuns, having under their care a day school at which upwards of a hundred poor girls are educated. The convent of the Sisters of Charity of St. Joseph, incorporated by the Legislature of Maryland, at Emmitsburg in that State, consists of fifty-nine sisters, including novices, with fifty-two young ladies under their tuition and upwards of forty poor children. A convent of Ursulines, at Boston, is yet in its infancy, consisting of a prioress, six sisters, and two novices, who undertake to instruct those committed to their charge in every polite accomplishment, in addition to the useful branches of female education. The Emmitsburg Sisters of Charity have a branch of their convent for the benefit of female orphan children, established in the city of New York, where the Roman catholics are said to have increased in the last twenty years from 300 to 20,000. The church of St. Augustine, in Philadelphia, belongs to the Augustine monks, by whom it was built. There is also a branch of the Emmitsburg Sisters of Charity in this city, consisting of several pious and well informed ladies who superintend the education of orphan children. The Daughters of Charity have another branch in Kentucky, where there are likewise a house of the order of Apostolines, lately established by the Pope at Rome, a cloister of Loretto, and another convent. In the State of Missouri there is a convent of religious ladies at the village of St. Ferdinand, where a noviciate is seated, of five novices and several postulants, with a thriving seminary, largely resorted to by the young ladies of that remote region, and also a day school for the poor. In New Orleans, there is a convent of Ursuline nuns, of ancient and affluent endowment, containing fifteen or sixteen professed nuns and a number of novices and postulants. The ladies of the Heart of Jesus are about founding a second establishment for education at Opelousas. I will terminate these curious, I hope not irksome, particulars, by merely adding that in Maine and Kentucky, there are tribes of Indians attached to the Roman catholic worship, whose indefatigable ministers have always been successful in reclaiming those aborigines of this continent. Vincennes, the chief town of Indiana, where there is now a Roman catholic chapel, was once a station of the Jesuits for this purpose.

Upon the whole I do not think that we can reckon less than eight thousand places of worship and five thousand ecclesiastics in the United States, besides twelve theological seminaries and many religious houses, containing, the former, about five hundred, and the latter three hundred votaries; all self-erected and sustained by voluntary contribution and nearly all within the last half century. If this unequalled increase of churches and pastors, and worshippers attests the prosperity of religion, we may rest assured of its welfare without tythes or political support and we need not fear its decline from the ascendancy of republicanism.

In proving the existence and magnitude of the American church, I have incidentally, I hope, sufficiently explained its character. For the most part well educated, well informed, and well employed, eloquent, unpensioned, self-sustained, trusting to their own good works, and relying on no court favour or individual interest for advancement, exempt from that parasite worldly-mindedness which the honest Massillon, even when preaching before Louis XIV, denounced as the canker of political religion, the American clergy are necessarily called upon to think, to read, to write, to preach, and officiate more than the European. Accordingly the divinity of the American church, if I am not mistaken, is much more active at this time and its literature more efficient than that of England. Indeed it is hardly to be accounted for that with the great inducements, means and opportunities of the dignitaries of the English church, the mind is at present so little benefited by their contributions to its enlargement. I by no means design to speak disrespectfully of personages of whom I know little more than their titles; nor do I call in question their learning, their piety, or even their partial usefulness. But assuredly it is fair to infer some radical defect in the system when of all the modern English bench of bishops and arch-bishops there are very few, I believe, at present in any way known to literature, not one distinguished for eloquence, and on that noble theatre, the house of peers, who ever heard of their performances? Relying on political protection, they seem to have lost the stimulus which urges their American brethren to incessant labours for the furtherance of religion by eloquent sermons, by contributions to clerical literature, and by the ardent exercise of all their duties. The Roman catholics boast of numerous converts from protestantism in Europe. Where is the spirit of Tillotson and Sherlock, the English successors of the Chrysostoms and the Bazils? Not in England at present. The works of the great fathers of the English church, those wells of doctrine as of language undefiled appear to be much more likely to be replenished and perpetuated in America.

In this review, I have of course abstained from all polemic and various other delicate considerations connected with it, confining myself to the actual progress of religion as indicative of the tendency of the mind on that subject in this country. Anti-trinitarians and Jesuits, convents and quakers, all grow and thrive together. The most imposing Roman catholic cathedral and a considerable Unitarian church are built within the sound of each others service; and neither the intelligence nor the tranquillity of the community has suffered by their neighbourhood. There may be those who think indeed that the growth is inordinate, that the establishments are on a scale of expense and influence disproportioned to our numbers, our principles, and even our independence. But to all such suggestions the answer is that while the whole is spontaneous, there can be nothing to apprehend.

My undertaking will be unfinished, if I do not explain the political and physical causes of the results to which attention has been invited. But that task I may not attempt on this occasion, if ever. It is said to be the American fault to expend itself in details instead of reasoning by generalisation. I am very sensible of this, with many other faults, in this discourse, in which scarcely any thing more is attempted than the collection of facts. But, however imperfect the performance, my views will be accomplished if the glimpses thus afforded should induce some qualified person to examine and explain the subject philosophically. The operations of American institutions on the human understanding are a noble study for the labours of a life. The most intelligent portions of mankind are animated by their impulses, which already actuate, and before long must regulate the destinies of the world. The first settlement of this continent was from England, in a state of revolution, when all minds were exercised with new ideas of religious and political liberty. The associates of Pym and Hampden, and Raleigh, Penn and Locke, founded our institutions. A republican empire, really representative, always as it were in a state of temperate revolution, has been ever since exciting and evolving the great principles of free agency. Our simple and peaceable but irresistible religion and politics are inoffensively reforming the brilliant abuses which feudal and chivalric barbarism have rivetted on the nations of Europe. This rouses detraction against the whole elements, moral, physical, and intellectual, as well as political, of our existence. Naturalists, and statists, philosophers, historians, ambassadors, poets, priests, nobles, tourists, journalists—I speak with precision to this catalogue—have in vain sentenced this country to degradation. It already ranks with communities highly refined before America was discovered. France and England were enjoying Augustan ages when the place where we are met to discourse of literature and science was a wilderness. But one hundred and forty years have elapsed since the patriarch of Pennsylvania first landed on these shores and sowed them with the germs of peace, toleration, and self-government. Since when, a main employment has been to reclaim the forests for habitation. It is not yet half a century since the United States were politically emancipated; it is only since the late war that they have begun to be intellectually independent. Colonial habits and reverence still rebuke and counteract intellectual enterprise. Education, the learned professions, the arts, scientific and mechanical, legislation, jurisprudence, literature, society—the mind in a word—require time to be freed from European pupilage.

It was not in a spirit of hostility to any other country that I undertook to shew what has been already done in this but by that review to encourage further and keener exertions.

To those who will inquire and reflect, the encouragement of philosophy is as strong as the instinct of patriotism. But the empire of habit and of prejudice is in strong opposition to the supremacy of thought and reason. There was a time when it was not considered disaffection to be ashamed of our country, nor disloyalty to despair of it when we re-colonised ourselves. But within the last ten years, especially, the mind of America, has thought for itself, piercing the veil of European beau ideal.

Still less, however, than national disparagement was national vanity the shrine of my sacrifice. Comparative views are indispensable. I might have compared America now with America forty years ago, which would have presented a striking and enlivening contrast. But I preferred the bolder view of America compared with Europe, disclaiming, however, invidious comparisons which have been studiously avoided. The cause asserted is of too high respect to be defended by panegyric, or avenged by invective. The truth is an ample vindication. Let us strive to refute discredit by constant improvement. Let our intellectual motto be, that naught is done while aught remains to be done, and our study to prove to the world, that the best patronage of religion, science, literature, and the arts, of whatever the mind can achieve, is SELF-GOVERNMENT.

Document 16

Edward Everett

Another of Emerson's Harvard professors, Edward Everett (1794–1865), in 1824 delivered the Phi Beta Kappa oration at Cambridge, in the presence of Lafayette—probably the most distinguished of the series prior to that of 1837. The theme of literary nationalism was not new to him; as the Phi Beta Kappa poet in 1812, he had versified the basic problem of putting America into poetry, with such unpoetic place names as Massa-chu-setts, Bunker, Memphremagog, and Connecticut:

> Would he one verse of easy movement frame,
> The map will meet him with a hopeless name;

but in this first of his major orations (of which there were to be many) he looked upon the problem in a larger perspective. Accepting Ingersoll's premise that the problem was basically one of national character, this former editor of the *North American Review* defined, against the background of Greek literature which he knew as a specialist, "the peculiar motives to intellectual exertion in America" as, with Ingersoll, the principle of self-government and individual sovereignty of the people, the extent and uniformity of a common language, and the rapid increase of population with the corresponding development of civilization. These were new and vital ideas which might have been expressed in fewer pages, but their influence in their day was not altogether because of the oratorical powers of their speaker. Everett's subsequent career, which was brilliant in politics and public life but was marred, as was Daniel Webster's, by compromise and, unlike Webster's, rewarded with high station and final acclaim, need not concern us here. Although this oration is titled by Duyckinck, "The Circumstances Favorable to the Prog-

ress of Literature in America," Everett's own statement of
his purpose is here used as a title.

TEXT: from the first edition, Boston, 1824.

Oration on the Peculiar Motives to
Intellectual Exertion in America

In discharging the honorable trust of being the public
organ of your sentiments on this occasion, I have been
anxious that the hour which here pass together should
be occupied by those reflections exclusively which belong
to us as scholars. Our association in this fraternity is academical; we engaged in it before our alma mater dismissed
us from her venerable roof to wander in the various paths
of life; and we have now come together in the academical
holidays, from every variety of pursuit, from almost every
part of our country, to meet on common ground as the
brethren of one literary household. The professional cares
of life, like the conflicting tribes of Greece, have proclaimed to us a short armistice, that we may come up in
peace to our Olympia.

But from the wide field of literary speculation and the
innumerable subjects of meditation which arise in it a
selection must be made. And it has seemed to me proper
that we should direct our thoughts, not merely to a subject
of interest to scholars, but to one which may recommend
itself as peculiarly appropriate to us. If 'that old man
eloquent, whom the dishonest victory at Cheronæa killed
with report' could devote fifteen years to the composition
of his Panegyric on Athens, I shall need no excuse to a
society of American scholars, in choosing for the theme of
an address on an occasion like this, *the peculiar motives
to intellectual exertion in America*. In this subject that
curiosity which every scholar feels in tracing and comparing the springs of mental activity is heightened and
dignified by the important connexion of the inquiry with
the condition and prospects of our native land.

In the full comprehension of the terms, the motives to

intellectual exertion in a country embrace the most important springs of national character. Pursued into its details, the study of these springs of national character is often little better than fanciful speculation. The questions why Asia has almost always been the abode of despotism and Europe more propitious to liberty; why the Egyptians were abject and melancholy, the Greeks inventive, elegant, and versatile; the Romans stern, saturnine, and, in matters of literature, for the most part servile imitators of a people whom they conquered, despised, and never equalled; why tribes of barbarians from the north and east, not known to differ essentially from each other at the time of their settlement in Europe, should have laid the foundation of national characters so dissimilar as those of the Spanish, French, German, and English nations; these are questions to which a few general answers may be attempted that will probably be just and safe only in proportion as they are vague and comprehensive. Difficult as it is, even in the individual man, to point out precisely the causes under the influence of which members of the same community and of the same family, placed apparently in the same circumstances, grow up with characters the most diverse; it is infinitely more difficult to perform the same analysis on a subject so vast as a nation where it is first not a small question what the character is before you touch the inquiry into the circumstances by which it was formed.

But as in the case of individual character, there are certain causes of undisputed and powerful operation; there are also in national character causes equally undisputed of improvement and excellence on the one hand, and of degeneracy and decline on the other. The philosophical student of history, the impartial observer of man, may often fix on circumstances which in their operation on the minds of the people, in furnishing the motives and giving the direction to intellectual exertion, have had the chief agency in making them what they were or are. Nor are there many exercises of the speculative principle more elevated than this. It is in the highest degree curious to trace physical facts into their political, intellectual, and moral consequences; and to show how the climate, the geographical position, and even the particular topography of a region connect themselves by evident association with the state of society, its predominating pursuits, and characteristic institutions.

In the case of other nations, particularly of those which in the great drama of the world have long since passed from the stage, these speculations are often only curious. The operation of a tropical climate in enervating and fitting a people for despotism; the influence of a broad river or a lofty chain of mountains in arresting the march of conquest or of emigration and thus becoming the boundary not merely of governments but of languages, literature, institutions, and character; the effect of a quarry of fine marble on the progress of the liberal arts; the agency of popular institutions in promoting popular eloquence and the tremendous reaction of popular eloquence on the fortunes of a state; the comparative destiny of colonial settlements, of insular states, of tribes fortified in nature's Alpine battlements, or scattered over a smiling region of olive gardens and vineyards; these are all topics indeed of rational curiosity and liberal speculation but important only as they may illustrate the prospects of our own country.

It is therefore when we turn the inquiry to our country, when we survey its features, search its history, and contemplate its institutions to see what the motives are which are to excite and guide the minds of the people; when we dwell not on a distant, an uncertain, an almost forgotten past but on an impending future, teeming with life and action, toward which we are rapidly and daily swept forward and with which we stand in the dearest connexion, which can bind the generations of man together; a future, which our own characters, our own actions, our own principles will do something to stamp with glory or shame; it is then that the inquiry becomes practical, momentous, and worthy the attention of every patriotic scholar. We then strive, as far as it is in the power of philosophical investigation to do it, to unfold our country's reverend auspices, to cast its great horoscope in the national sky where many stars are waning and many have set; to ascertain whether the soil which we love as that where our fathers are laid and we shall presently be laid with them, will be trod in times to come by a people virtuous, enlightened, and free.

The first of the circumstances which are acting and will continue to act with a strong peculiarity among us and which must prove one of the most powerful influences in exciting and directing the intellect of the country is the new form of civil society which has here been devised and established. I shall not wander so far from the *literary* limits of this occasion, nor into a field so oft trodden, as the praises of free political institutions. But the direct and appropriate influence on mental effort of institutions like ours has not yet, perhaps, received the attention which, from every American scholar, it richly deserves. I have ventured to say that a new form of civil society has here been devised and established. The ancient Grecian republics, indeed, were free enough within the walls of the single city of which most of them were wholly or chiefly composed; but to these single cities the freedom, as well as the power, was confined. Toward the confederated or tributary states the government was generally a despotism, more capricious and not less stern than that of a single tyrant. Rome as a state was never free; in every period of her history, authentic and dubious, royal, republican, and imperial, her proud citizens were the slaves of an artful, accomplished, wealthy aristocracy; and nothing but the hard fought battles of her stern tribunes can redeem her memory to the friends of liberty. In ancient and modern history there is no example before our own of a purely elective and representative system. It is therefore, on an entirely novel plan that, in this country, the whole direction and influence of affairs, all the trusts and honors of society, the power of making, abrogating, and administering the laws, the whole civil authority and sway, from the highest post in the government to the smallest village trust, are put directly into the market of merit. Whatsoever efficacy there is in high station and exalted honors to call out and exercise the powers, either by awakening the emulation of the aspirants or exciting the efforts of the incumbents, is here directly exerted on the largest mass of men with the smallest possible deductions. Nothing is bestowed on the chance of birth, nothing depends on proximity to the fountain of honor, nothing is to be acquired by espousing hereditary family interests, but whatever is desired must be sought in the way of a broad, fair, personal competition. It requires little argument to show that such a system must most widely and most powerfully have the effect of appealing to whatever of energy the land contains; of searching out, with magnetic instinct, in the remotest quarters, the latent ability of its children.

It may be objected, and it has been, that for want of a hereditary government, we lose that powerful spring of action which resides in the patronage of such a government and must emanate from the crown. With many individuals, friendly to our popular institutions, it is nevertheless an opinion that we must consent to lose something of the genial influence of princely and royal patronage on letters and arts and find our consolation in the political benefits of our free system. It may be doubted, however, whether this view be not entirely false. A crown is in itself a strip of velvet set with jewels; the dignity which it imparts and the honor with which it is invested depend on the numbers, resources, and intelligence of the people who permit it to be worn. The crown of the late emperor of Hayti is said to have been one of the most brilliant in the world; and Theodore of Corsica, while confined for debt in the fleet in London, sat on as high a throne as the king of England. Since then the power and influence of the crown are really in the people, it seems preposterous to say, that what increases the importance of the people can diminish the effect of that which proceeds from them, depends upon them, and reverts to them. Sovereignty, in all its truth and efficacy, exists here as much as ever it did at London, at Paris, at Rome, or at Susa. It exists, it is true, in an equal proportionate diffusion; a part of it belongs to the humblest citizen. The error seems to be in confounding the idea of sovereignty with the quality of an individual sovereign. Wheresoever Providence gathers into a nation the tribes of men, there a social life, with its energies and functions, is conferred; and this social life is sovereignty. By the healthful action of our representative system, it is made to pervade the empire like the air; to reach the farthest, descend to the lowest, and bind the distant together; it is made not only to cooperate with the successful and assist the prosperous, but to cheer the remote, 'to remember the forgotten, to attend to the neglected, to visit the forsaken.' Before the rising of our republic in the world, the faculties of men have had but one weary pilgrimage to perform—to travel up to court. By an improvement on the Jewish polity, which enjoined on the nation a visit thrice a year to the holy city, the great, the munificent, the enlightened states of the ancient and modern world have required a constant residence on the chosen spot. *Provincial* has become another term for inferior and rude; and *unpolite*, which once meant only *rural*, has got to signify, in all our languages, something little better than barbarous. But since, in the nature of things, a small part only of the population of a large state can, by physical possibility, be crowded within the walls of a city and there receive the genial beams of metropolitan favor, it follows that the great mass of men are cut off from the operation of some of the strongest excitements to exertion. It is rightfully urged then, as a great advantage of our system, that the excitements of society go down as low as its burdens and search out and bring forward whatsoever of ability and zeal are comprehended within the limits of the land. This is but the beginning of the benefit, or rather it is not yet the benefit. It is the effect of this diffusion of privileges that is precious. Capacity and opportunity, the twin sisters who can scarce subsist but with each other, are now brought together. The people who are to choose and from whose number are to be chosen by their neighbors the highest officers of state, infallibly feel an impulse to mental activity; they read, think, and compare; they found village schools, they collect social libraries, they prepare their children for the higher establishments of education. The world, I think, has been abused on the tendency of institutions perfectly popular.

From the ill-organized states of antiquity, terrific examples of license and popular misrule are quoted to prove that man requires to be protected from himself, without asking who is to protect him from the protector, himself also a man. While from the very first settlement of America to the present day, the most prominent trait of our character has been to cherish and diffuse the means of education. The village schoolhouse and the village church are the monuments which the American people have erected to their freedom; to read, and write, and think are the licentious practices which have characterised our democracy.

But it will be urged perhaps that, though the effect of our institutions be to excite the intellect of the nation, they excite it too much in a political direction; that the division and subdivision of the country into states and districts and the equal diffusion throughout them of political privileges and powers, whatever favorable effect in other ways they may produce, are attended by this evil,— that they kindle a political ambition where it would not and ought not be felt; and particularly that they are unfriendly in their operation on literature as they call the aspiring youth from the patient and laborious vigils of the student to plunge prematurely into the conflicts of the Forum. It may, however, be doubted whether there be any foundation whatever for a charge like this; and whether the fact, so far as it is one, that the talent and ambition of the country incline at present to a political course be not owing to causes wholly unconnected with the free character of our institutions. It need not be said that the administration of the government of a country, whether it be liberal or despotic, is the first thing to be provided for. Some persons must be employed in making and administering the laws before any other interest can receive attention. Our fathers, the pilgrims, before they left the vessel in which for five months they had been tossed on the ocean, before setting foot on the new world of their desire, drew up a simple constitution of government. As this is the first care in the order of nature, it ever retains its paramount importance. Society must be preserved in its constituted forms or there is no safety for life, no security for property, no permanence for any institution civil, moral, or religious. The first efforts then of social men are of necessity political. Apart from every call of ambition, honorable or selfish, of interest enlarged or mercenary, the care of the government is the first care of a civilised community. In the early stages of social progress, where there is little property and a scanty population, the whole strength of the society must be employed in its support and defence. Though *we* are constantly receding from these stages we have not wholly left them. Even our rapidly increasing population is and will for some time remain small compared with the space over which it is diffused; and this, with the total absence of large hereditary fortunes, will create a demand for political services on the one hand, and a necessity of rendering them on the other. There is then no ground for ascribing the political tendency of the talent and activity of this country to an imagined incompatibility of popular institutions with the profound cultivation of letters. Suppose our government were changed tomorrow; that the five points of a stronger government were introduced, a hereditary sovereign, an order of nobility, an established church, a standing army, and a vigilant police; and that these should take place of that admirable system which now, like the genial air, pervades all, supports all, cheers all, and is nowhere seen. Suppose this change made and other circumstances to remain the same; our population no more dense, our boundaries as wide, and the accumulation of private wealth no more abundant. Would there, in the new state of things, be less interest in politics? By the terms of the supposition, the leading class of the community, the nobles, are to be politicians by birth. By the nature of the case, a large portion of the remainder who gain their livelihood by their industry and talents would be engrossed, not indeed in the free political competition which now prevails, but in pursuing the interests of rival court factions. One class only, the peasantry, would remain which would take less interest in politics than the corresponding class in a free state; or rather, this is a new class, which invariably comes in with a strong government; and no one can seriously think the cause of science and literature would be promoted by substituting a European peasantry in the place of, perhaps, the most substantial uncorrupted population on earth, the American yeomanry. Moreover the evil in question is with us a self-correcting evil. If the career of politics be more open and the temptation to crowd it stronger, competition will spring up, numbers will engage in the pursuit; the less able, the less industrious, the less ambitious must retire and leave the race to the swift and the battle to the strong. But in hereditary governments no such remedy exists. One class of society by the nature of its position must be rulers, magistrates, or politicians. Weak or strong, willing or unwilling they must play the game, though they as well as the people pay the bitter forfeit. The obnoxious king cannot [*sic*] seldom shake off the empoisoned purple; he must wear the crown of thorns till it is struck off at the scaffold; and the same artificial necessity has obliged generations of nobles, in all the old states of Europe, to toil and bleed for a

Power too great to keep or to resign.

Where the compulsion stops short of these afflicting extremities, still, under the governments in question, a large portion of the community is unavoidably destined to the calling of the courtier, the soldier, the party retainer; to a life of service, intrigue, and court attendance; and thousands, and those the prominent individuals in society, are brought up to look on a livelihood gained by private industry as base; on study as the pedant's trade, on labor as the badge of slavery. I look in vain in institutions like these for any thing essentially favorable to intellectual progress. On the contrary, while they must draw away the talent and ambition of the country quite as much as popular institutions can do it into pursuits foreign from the culture of the intellect, they necessarily doom to obscurity no small part of the mental energy of the land. For that mental energy has been equally diffused by sterner levellers than ever marched in the van of a Revolution; the nature of man and the Providence of God. Native character, strength and quickness of mind, are not of the number of distinctions and accomplishments that human institutions can monopolize within a city's walls. In quiet times, they remain and perish in the obscurity to which a false organization of society consigns them. In dangerous, convulsed, and trying times, they spring up in the fields, in the village hamlets, and on the mountain tops, and teach the surprised favorites of human law, that bright eyes, skilful hands, quick perceptions, firm purpose, and brave hearts are not the exclusive *appanage* of courts. Our popular institutions are favorable to intellectual improvement because their foundation is in dear nature. They do not consign the greater part of the social frame to torpidity and mortification. They send out a vital nerve to every member of the community, by which its talent and power, great or small, are brought into living conjunction and strong sympathy with the kindred intellect of the nation; and every impression on every part vibrates with electric rapidity through the whole. They encourage nature to perfect her work; they make education, the soul's nutriment, cheap; they bring up remote and shrinking talent into the cheerful field of competition; in a thousand ways they provide an audience for lips which nature has touched with persuasion; they put a lyre into the hands of genius; they bestow on all who deserve it or seek it the only patronage worth having, the only patronage that ever struck out a spark of 'celestial fire,'—the patronage of fair opportunity. This is a day of improved education; new systems of teaching are devised; modes of instruction, choice of studies, adaptation of text books, the whole machinery of means have been brought in our day under severe revision. But were I to attempt to point out the most efficacious and comprehensive improvement in education, the engine by which the greatest portion of mind could be brought and kept under cultivation, the discipline which would reach farthest, sink deepest, and cause the word of instruction not to spread over the surface like an artificial hue carefully laid on, but to penetrate to the heart and soul of its objects, it would be popular institutions. Give the people an object in promoting education and the best methods will infallibly be suggested by that instinctive ingenuity of our nature which provides means for great and precious ends. Give the people an object in promoting education and the worn hand of labor will be opened to the last farthing that its children may enjoy means denied to itself. This great contest about black boards and sand tables will then lose something of its importance, and even the exalted names of Bell and Lancaster may sink from that very lofty height where an over hasty admiration has placed them.

But though it be conceded to us that the tendency which is alleged to exist in this country toward the political career is not a vicious effect of our free institutions, still it may be inquired whether the new form of social organization among us is at least to produce no corresponding modification of our literature? As the country advances, as the population becomes denser, as wealth accumulates, as the various occasions of a large, prosperous, and polite community call into strong action and vigorous competition the literary talent of the country, will no peculiar form or direction be given to its literature, by the nature of its institutions? To this question an answer must without hesitation be given in the affirmative. Literature as well in its origin as in its true and only genuine character, is but a more perfect communication of man with man and mind with mind. It is a grave, sustained, deliberate utterance of fact, of opinion, and feeling; or a free and happy reflection of nature, of character, or of manners; and if it be not these it is poor imitation. It may, therefore, be assumed as certain, that the peculiarity of our condition and institutions will be reflected in some peculiarity of our literature; but what that shall be it is as yet too early to say.[1] Literary history informs us of many stud-

[1] The peculiar natural features of the American Continent are of themselves sufficient to produce some strong peculiarity in its literature, but this topic is comprehensive and curious enough for a separate Essay. It has, I am permitted to say, been made the subject of one, by M. de Salazar the minister from the Colombian Republic to the United States, which will shortly be presented to the friends of American letters. An essay on such a subject, from an accomplished citizen of a free State, established in the kingdom of Nueva Granada, is itself an admirable illustration of

ies which have been neglected as dangerous to existing governments; and many others which have been cultivated because they were prudent and safe. We have hardly the means of settling from analogy what direction the mind will most decisively take when left under strong excitements to action wholly without restraint from the arm of power. It is impossible to anticipate what garments our native muses will weave for themselves. To foretell our literature would be to create it. There was a time before an epic poem, a tragedy, or a historical composition had ever been produced by the wit of man. It was a time of vast and powerful empires, of populous and wealthy cities. But these new and beautiful forms of human thought and feeling all sprang up in Greece, under the stimulus of her free institutions. Before they appeared in the world, it would have been idle for the philosopher to form conjectures as to the direction which the kindling genius of the age was to assume. He who could form, could and would realise the anticipation and it would cease to be an anticipation. Assuredly epic poetry was invented then and not before, when the gorgeous vision of the Iliad, not in its full detail of circumstance but in the dim conception of its leading scenes and sterner features, burst into the soul of Homer. Impossible, indeed, were the task fully to read the auspices of the mind under the influence of institutions as new, as peculiar, and far more animating than those of Greece. But if, as no one will deny, our political system bring more minds into action on equal terms, if it provide a prompter circulation of thought throughout the community, if it give weight and emphasis to more voices, if it swell to tens of thousands and millions those 'sons of emulation, who crowd the narrow strait where honor travels,' then it seems not too much to foretell some peculiarity at least, if we may not call it improvement, in that literature which is but the voice and utterance of all this mental action. There is little doubt that the instrument of communication itself will receive great improvements;

the genial influence of popular institutions on Intellectual Improvement.

that the written and spoken language will acquire force and power; possibly, that forms of address, wholly new, will be struck out to meet the universal demand for new energy. When the improvement and the invention (whatever it be) comes, it will come unlooked for as well to its happy author as the world. But where great interests are at stake, great concerns rapidly succeeding each other, depending on almost innumerable wills, and yet requiring to be apprehended in a glance, and explained in a word; where movements are to be given to a vast empire, not by transmitting orders, but by diffusing opinions, exciting feelings, and touching the electric chord of sympathy, there language and expression will become intense, and the old processes of communication must put on a vigor and a directness adapted to the aspect of the times. Our country is called, as it is, practical; but this is the element for intellectual action. No strongly marked and high toned literature; poetry, eloquence, or ethics; ever appeared but in the pressure, the din, and crowd of great interests, great enterprises, perilous risks, and dazzling rewards. Statesmen, and warriors, and poets, and orators, and artists, start up under one and the same excitement. They are all branches of one stock. They form, and cheer, and stimulate, and, what is worth all the rest, understand each other; and it is as truly the sentiment of the student, in the recesses of his cell, as of the soldier in the ranks, which breathes in the exclamation;

> To all the sons of sense proclaim,
> One glorious hour of *crowded life*
> Is worth an age without a name.

But we are brought back to the unfavorable aspect of the subject by being reminded out of history of the splendid patronage which arbitrary governments have bestowed on letters and which, from the nature of the case, can hardly be extended even to the highest merit under institutions like our own. We are told of the munificent pensions, the rich establishments, the large foundations; of the museums erected, the libraries gathered, the endowments granted by Ptolemies, Augustuses, and Louises of ancient and modern days. We are asked to remark the fruit of this noble patronage; wonders of antiquarian or scientific lore, Thesauruses and Corpuses, efforts of erudition from which the emulous student who would read all things, weigh all things, surpass all things, recoils in horror; volumes and shelves of volumes before which meek-eyed patience folds her hands in despair.

When we have contemplated these things and turn our thoughts back to our poor republican land, to our frugal treasury, and the caution with which it is dispensed; to our modest fortunes, and the thrift with which they are hoarded; to our scanty public libraries and the plain brick walls within which they are deposited: we may be apt to form gloomy auguries of the influence of free political institutions on our literature. It is important then that we examine more carefully the experience of former ages and see how far their institutions, as they have been more or less popular, have been more or less associated with displays of intellectual excellence. When we make this examination, we shall be gratified to find that the precedents are all in favor of liberty. The greatest efforts of human genius have been made where the nearest approach to free institutions has taken place. There shone not forth one ray of intellectual light to cheer the long and gloomy ages of the Memphian and Babylonian despots. Not a historian, not an orator, not a poet is heard of in their annals. When you ask, what was achieved by the generations of thinking beings, the millions of men, whose natural genius was as bright as that of the Greeks, nay, who forestalled the Greeks in the first invention of many of the arts, you are told that they built the pyramids of Memphis, the temples of Thebes, and the tower of Babylon, and carried Sesostris and Ninus upon their shoulders from the West of Africa to the Indus. Mark the contrast in Greece. With the first emerging of that country into the light of political liberty the poems of Homer appear. Some centuries of political misrule and literary darkness follow, and then the great constellation of their geniuses seems to rise at once. The stormy eloquence and the deep philosophy, the impassioned drama and the grave history, were all produced for the entertainment of that 'fierce democratie' of Athens. Here then the genial influence of liberty on letters is strongly put to the test. Athens was certainly a free state; free to licentiousness, free to madness. The rich were arbitrarily pillaged to defray the expenses of the state, the great were banished to appease the envy of their rivals, the wise sacrificed to the fury of the populace. It was a state, in short, where liberty existed with most of the imperfections which have led men to love and praise despotism. Still, however, it was for this lawless, merciless people, that the most chastised and accomplished literature which the world has known was produced. The philosophy of Plato was the attraction which drew to a morning's walk in the olive gardens of the academy the young men of this factious city. Those tumultuous assemblies of Athens, the very same which rose in their wrath and to a man, and clamored for the blood of Phocion, required to be addressed, not in the cheap extemporaneous rant of modern demagogues, but in the elaborate and thrice repeated orations of Demosthenes. No! the noble and elegant arts of Greece grew up in no Augustan age, enjoyed neither royal nor imperial patronage. Unknown before in the world, strangers on the Nile and strangers on the Euphrates, they sprang at once into life in a region not unlike our own New England—iron bound, sterile, and free. The imperial astronomers of Chaldæa went up almost to the stars in their observatories; but it was a Greek who first foretold an eclipse and measured the year. The nations of the East invented the alphabet, but not a line has reached us of profane literature in any of their languages; and it is owing to the embalming power of Grecian genius that the invention itself has been transmitted to the world. The Egyptian architects could erect structures which after three thousand five hundred years are still standing in their uncouth original majesty; but it was only on the barren soil of Attica that the beautiful columns of the Parthenon and the Theseum could rest, which are standing also. With the decline of liberty in Greece began the decline of all her letters and all her arts; though her tumultuous democracies were succeeded by liberal and accomplished princes.

Compare the literature of the Alexandrian with that of the Periclean age; how cold, pedantic, and imitative! Compare, I will not say, the axes, the eggs, the altars, and the other frigid devices of the pensioned wits in the museum at Alexandria, but compare their best spirits with those of independent Greece; Callimachus with Pindar, Lycophron with Sophocles, Aristophanes of Byzantium with Aristotle, and Apollonius the Rhodian with Homer. When we descend to Rome, to the Augustan age, the exalted era of Mæcenas, we find one uniform work of imitation, often of translation. The choicest geniuses seldom rise beyond a happy transfusion of the Grecian masters. Horace translates Alcæus, Terence translates Menander, Lucretius translates Epicurus, Virgil translates Homer, and Cicero —I had almost said, translates Demosthenes and Plato. But the soul of liberty did burst forth from the lips of Cicero, 'her form had not yet lost all its original brightness,' her inspiration produced in him the only specimens of a purely original literature which Rome has transmitted to us. After him, their literary history is written in one line of Tacitus; gliscente adulatione, magna ingenia deterrebantur. The fine arts revived a little under the princes of the Flavian house, but never rose higher than a successful imitation of the waning excellence of Greece. With the princes of this line, the arts of Rome expired and Constantine the great was obliged to tear down an arch of Trajan for sculptures wherewithal to adorn his own. In modern times civilized states have multiplied; political institutions have varied in different states and at different times in the same state; some liberal institutions have existed in the bosom of societies otherwise despotic; and a great addition of new studies has been made to the encyclopædia, which have all been cultivated by great minds and some of which, as the physical and experimental sciences, have little or no direct connexion with the state of liberty. These circumstances perplex, in some degree, the inquiry into the effect of free institutions on intellectual improvement in modern times. There are times and places where it would seem that the muses, both the gay and the severe, had been transformed into court ladies. Upon the whole, however, the modern history of literature bears but a cold testimony to the genial influence of the governments under which it has grown up. Dante and Petrarch composed their beautiful works in exile; Boccaccio complains in the most celebrated of his that he was transfixed with the darts of envy and calumny; Machiavelli was pursued by the party of the Medici for resisting their tyrannical designs; Guicciardini retired in disgust to compose his history in voluntary exile; Galileo confessed in the prisons of the Inquisition that the earth did not move; Ariosto lived in poverty; and Tasso died in want and despair.[2] Cervantes, after he had immortalized himself in his great work, was obliged to write on for bread. The whole French academy was pensioned to crush the great Corneille. Racine, after living to see his finest pieces derided as cold and worthless, died of a broken heart. The divine genius of Shakspeare raised him to no higher rank than that of a subaltern actor in his own and Ben Jonson's plays. The immortal Chancellor was sacrificed to the preservation of a worthless minion and is said, (falsely I trust) to have begged a cup of beer in his old age, and begged it in vain. The most valuable of the pieces of Selden were written in that famous resort of great minds, the tower of London. Milton, surprised by want in his infirm old age, sold the first production of the human mind for five pounds. The great boast of English philosophy was expelled from his place in Oxford and kept in banishment, 'the king having been given to understand' to use the words of Lord Sunderland who ordered the expulsion, 'that *one Locke* has, upon several occasions, behaved himself very factiously against the government'. Dryden sacrificed his genius to the spur of immediate want. Otway was choked with a morsel of bread, too ravenously swallowed after a long fast. Johnson was taken to prison for a debt of five shillings; and Burke petitioned for a Professorship at Glasgow and was denied. When we survey these facts and the innumerable others of which these are not even an adequate specimen, we may perhaps

[2] Martinelli, in his Edition of the Decamerone, cited in the Introduction to Sidney's Discourses on Government, Edition of 1751, p. 34.

conclude that, in whatever way the arbitrary governments of Europe have encouraged letters, it has not been in that of a steady cheering patronage. We may think there is abundant reason to acknowledge that the ancient lesson is confirmed by modern experience and that popular institutions are most propitious to the full and prosperous growth of intellectual excellence.

If the perfectly organized system of liberty which here prevails be thus favorable to intellectual progress, various other conditions of our national existence are not less so, particularly the extension of one language, government, and character over so vast a space as the United States of America. Hitherto, in the main, the world has seen but two forms of social existence, free governments in small states, and arbitrary governments in large ones. Though various shades of both have appeared at different times in the world, yet on the whole, the political ingenuity of man has never found out the mode of extending liberal institutions beyond small districts, or of governing large empires by any other means than the visible demonstration and exercise of absolute power. The effect in either case has been unpropitious to the growth of intellectual excellence. Free institutions, though favorable to the growth of intellectual excellence, are not the only thing needed. The wandering savage is free, but most of the powers of his mind lie dormant under the severe privations of a barbarous life. An infant colony on a distant coast may be free, but for want of the necessary mental aliment and excitement may be unable to rise above the limits of material existence. In order then that free institutions may have their full and entire effect in producing the highest attainable degree of intellectual improvement, they require to be established in an extensive region and over a numerous people. This constitutes a state of society entirely new among men; a vast empire whose institutions are wholly popular. While we experience the genial influence of those principles which belong to all free states, and in proportion as they are free; independence of thought and the right of expressing it; we are to feel in this country, we and those who succeed us, all that excitement which, in various ways, arises from the reciprocal action upon each other of the parts of a great empire. Literature, as has been partly hinted, is the voice of the age and the state. The character, energy, and resources of the country are reflected and imaged forth in the conceptions of its great minds. They are the organs of the time; they speak not their own language, they scarce think their own thoughts; but under an impulse like the prophetic enthusiasm of old, they must feel and utter the sentiments which society inspires. They do not create, they obey the Spirit of the Age; the serene and beautiful spirit descended from the highest heaven of liberty, who laughs at our little preconceptions and with the breath of his mouth sweeps before him the men and the nations that cross his path. By an unconscious instinct, the mind in the strong action of its powers adapts itself to the number and complexion of the other minds with which it is to enter into communion or conflict. As the voice falls into the key which is suited to the space to be filled, the mind, in the various exercises of its creative faculties, strives with curious search for that master-note which will awaken a vibration from the surrounding community and which, if it do not find, it is itself too often struck dumb.

For this reason, from the moment in the destiny of nations that they descend from their culminating point and begin to decline, from that moment the voice of creative genius is hushed, and at best the age of criticism, learning, and imitation, succeeds. When Greece ceased to be independent, the forum and the stage became mute. The patronage of Macedonian, Alexandrian, and Pergamean princes was lavished in vain. They could not woo the healthy Muses of Hellas, from the cold mountain tops of Greece, to dwell in their gilded halls. Nay, though the fall of greatness, the decay of beauty, the waste of strength, and the wreck of power, have ever been among the favorite themes of the pensive muse, yet not a poet arose in Greece to chant her own elegy; and it is, after near three centuries and from Cicero and Sulpicius, that we catch the first notes of pious and pathetic lamentation

over the fallen land of the arts. The freedom and genius
of a country are invariably gathered into a common tomb,
and there

> Can only strangers breathe
> The name of that which was beneath.

It is when we reflect on this power of an auspicious future that we realize the prospect which smiles upon the
intellect of America. It may justly be accounted the great
peculiarity of ancient days, compared with modern, that
in antiquity there was, upon the whole, but one civilized
and literary nation at a time in the world. Art and refinement followed in the train of political ascendency, from
the East to Greece and from Greece to Rome. In the
modern world, under the influence of various causes, intellectual, political, and moral, civilization has been diffused throughout the greater part of Europe and America.
Now mark a singular fatality as regards the connexion of
this enlarged and diffused civilization with the progress of
letters and the excitement to intellectual exertion in any
given state. Instead of one sole country, as in antiquity,
where the arts and refinements find a home, there are, in
modern Europe, seven or eight equally entitled to the general name of cultivated nations, and in each of which some
minds of the first order have appeared. And yet, by the
unfortunate multiplication of languages, an obstacle all
but insuperable has been thrown in the way of the free
progress of genius, in its triumphant course from region
to region. The muses of Shakspeare and Milton, of
Camoens, of Lope de Vega and Calderon, of Corneille and
Racine, of Dante and Tasso, of Gœthe and Schiller, are
strangers to each other.

This evil was so keenly felt in the sixteenth and seventeenth centuries that the Latin language was widely
adopted as a dialect common to scholars. We see men like
Luther, Calvin, and Erasmus, Bacon, Grotius, and Thu-
anus, who could scarce have written a line without exciting the admiration of their contemporaries, driven to
the use of a tongue which none but the learned could
understand. For the sake of addressing the scholars of

other countries, these great men and others like them, in many of their writings were obliged to cut themselves off from all sympathy with the mass of those whom as patriots they must have wished most to instruct. In works of pure science and learned criticism this is of the less consequence; for being independent of sentiment, it matters less how remote from real life the symbols in which their ideas are conveyed. But when we see a writer like Milton, who, more than any other whom England ever produced, was a master of the music of his native tongue, who, besides all the eloquence of thought and imagery, knew better than any other man how to clothe them according to his own beautiful expression,

> In notes, with many a winding bout
> Of linked sweetness, long drawn out,
> With wanton heed and giddy cunning,
> The melting voice through mazes running,
> Untwisting all the chains that tie
> The hidden soul of harmony;

when we see a master of English eloquence thus gifted, choosing a dead language, the dialect of the closet, a tongue without an echo from the hearts of the people as the vehicle of his defence of that people's rights; asserting the cause of Englishmen in the language, as it may be truly called, of Cicero; we can only measure the incongruity, by reflecting what Cicero would himself have thought and felt, if called to defend the cause of Roman freedom, not in the language of the Roman citizen but in that of the Chaldeans or Assyrians or some people still farther remote in the history of the world. There is little doubt that the prevalence of the Latin language among modern scholars was a great cause not only of the slow progress of letters among the lower ranks, but of the stiffness and constraint formerly visible in the vernacular style of most scholars themselves. That the reformation in religion advanced with such rapidity is doubtless in no small degree to be attributed to the translations of the Scriptures and the use of liturgies in the modern tongues. While the preservation in England of a strange language—I will not sin against the majesty of Rome by calling it Latin—in legal acts down to so late a period as 1730, may be one cause that the practical forms of administering justice have not been made to keep pace with the popular views that have triumphed in other things. With the erection of popular institutions under Cromwell, among various other legal improvements,[3] very many of which were speedily adopted by our plain dealing forefathers, the records of the law were ordered to be kept in English; 'A novelty,' says the learned commentator on the English laws, 'which at the restoration was no longer continued, practisers having found it very difficult to express themselves so *concisely* or significantly in any other language but Latin;'[4] an argument for the use of that language whose soundness it must be left to clients to estimate.

Nor are the other remedies more efficacious which have been attempted for the evil of a multiplicity of tongues. Something is done by translations and something by the acquisition of foreign languages. But that no effectual transfusion of the higher literature of a country can take place in the way of translation is matter of notoriety; and it is a remark of one of the few who could have courage to make such a remark, Madame de Stael, that it is impossible fully to comprehend the literature of a foreign tongue. The general preference given to Young's Night Thoughts and Ossian over all the other English poets in many parts of the continent of Europe seems to confirm the justice of the observation. There is, indeed, an influence of exalted genius coextensive with the earth. Something of its power will be felt, in spite of the obstacles of different languages, remote regions, and other times. But its true empire, its lawful sway, are at home and over the hearts of kindred men. A charm which nothing can borrow, nothing counterfeit, nothing dispense with, resides in the simple sound of our mother tongue. Not analyzed nor reasoned upon, it unites the earliest associations of life with the maturest conceptions of the understanding.

[3] See a number of them in Lord Somers' Tracts, vol. i.
[4] Blackstone's Commentaries, vol. iii. 422.

The heart is willing to open all its avenues to the language, in which its infantile caprices were soothed; and by the curious efficacy of the principal association, it is this echo from the feeble dawn of life, which gives to eloquence much of its manly power, and to poetry much of its divine charm. This feeling of the music of our native language is the first intellectual capacity that is developed in children, and when by age or misfortune,

> 'The ear is all unstrung,
> Still, still, it loves the lowland tongue.'

What a noble prospect is opened in this connexion for the circulation of thought and sentiment in our country! Instead of that multiplicity of dialect by which mental communication and sympathy are cut off in the old world a continually expanding realm is opened and opening to American intellect in the community of our language throughout the wide spread settlements of this continent. The enginery of the press will here for the first time be brought to bear with all its mighty power on the minds and hearts of men in exchanging intelligence and circulating opinions, unchecked by the diversity of language, over an empire more extensive than the whole of Europe.

And this community of language, all important as it is, is but a part of the manifold brotherhood which unites and will unite the growing millions of America. In Europe, the work of international alienation, which begins in diversity of language, is carried on and consummated by diversity of government, institutions, national descent, and national prejudices. In crossing the principal rivers, channels, and mountains, in that quarter of the world, you are met, not only by new tongues, but by new forms of government, new associations of ancestry, new and generally hostile objects of national boast and gratulation. While on the other hand, throughout the vast regions included within the limits of our Republic, not only the same language, but the same laws, the same national government, the same republican institutions, and a common ancestral association prevail, and will diffuse themselves. Mankind will here exist, move, and act in a kindred mass such as

was never before congregated on the earth's surface. The
necessary consequences of such a cause overpower the
imagination. What would be the effect on the intellectual
state of Europe at the present day were all her nations
and tribes amalgamated into one vast empire, speaking the
same tongue, united into one political system, and that a
free one, and opening one broad unobstructed pathway for
the interchange of thought and feeling from Lisbon to
Archangel. If effects are to bear a constant proportion to
their causes; if the energy of thought is to be commensurate with the masses which prompt it and the masses it
must penetrate; if eloquence is to grow in fervor with the
weight of the interests it is to plead and the grandeur of
the assemblies it addresses; if efforts rise with the glory
that is to crown them; in a word, if the faculties of the
human mind as we firmly believe are capable of tension
and achievement altogether indefinite;

Nil actum reputans, dum quid superesset agendum,

then it is not too much to say that a new era will open on
the intellectual world in the fulfilment of our country's
auspices. By the sovereign efficacy of the partition of powers between the national and state governments, in virtue
of which the national government is relieved from all the
odium of internal administration and the state governments are spared the conflicts of foreign politics, all
bounds seem removed from the possible extension of our
country but the geographical limits of the continent. Instead of growing cumbrous as it increases in size, there
never was a moment since the first settlement in Virginia
when the political system of America moved with so firm
and bold a step as at the present day. If there is any faith
in our country's auspices, this great continent in no remote futurity will be filled up with a homogeneous population; with the mightiest kindred people known in history;
our language will acquire an extension which no other ever
possessed; and the empire of the mind, with nothing to
resist its sway, will attain an expansion of which as yet
we can but partly conceive. The vision is too magnificent
to be fully borne;—a mass of two or three hundred mil-

lions, not chained to the oar like the same number in China by a brutalizing despotism, but held in their several orbits of nation and state by the grand representative attraction; bringing to bear on every point the concentrated energy of such a host; calling into competition so many minds; uniting into one great national feeling the hearts of so many freemen; all to be guided, persuaded, moved, and swayed, by the master spirits of the time!

Let me not be told that this is a chimerical imagination of a future indefinitely removed; let me not hear repeated the ribaldry of an anticipation of 'two thousand years,'—of a vision that requires for its fulfilment a length of ages beyond the grasp of any reasonable computation. It is the last point of peculiarity in our condition to which I invite your attention, as affecting the progress of intellect in the country, that it is growing with a rapidity hitherto entirely without example in the world. For the two hundred years of our existence, the population has doubled itself in periods of less than a quarter of a century. In the infancy of the country and while our numbers remained within the limits of a youthful colony, a progress so rapid as this, however important in the principle of growth disclosed, was not yet a circumstance strongly to fix the attention. But arrived at a population of ten millions, it is a fact of the most overpowering interest that, within less than twenty five years, these ten millions will have swelled to twenty; that the younger members of this audience will be citizens of the largest civilized state on earth; that in a few years more than one century, the American population will equal the fabulous numbers of the Chinese empire. This rate of increase has already produced the most striking phenomena. A few weeks after the opening of the Revolutionary drama at Lexington, the momentous intelligence that the first blood was spilt reached a party of hunters beyond the Alleghanies who had wandered far into the western wilderness. In prophetic commemoration of the glorious event, they gave the name of Lexington to the spot of their encampment in the woods. That spot is now the capital of a state larger than Massachusetts; it is the seat of an university as fully attended as our venerable

Alma Mater; nay more it is the capital of a state from which, in the language of one of her own citizens whose eloquence is the ornament of his country, the tide of emigration still farther westward is more fully pouring than from any other in the union.[5]

I need not say that this astonishing increase of numbers is by no means the limit and measure of our country's growth. Arts, agriculture, all the great national interests, all the sources of national wealth are growing in a ratio still more rapid. In our cities the intensest activity is apparent; in the country every spring of prosperity from the smallest improvement in husbandry to the construction of canals across the continent is in vigorous action; abroad our vessels are beating the pathways of the ocean white; on the inland frontier, the nation is journeying on like a healthy giant, with a pace more like romance than reality.

These facts and thousands like them form one of those peculiarities in our country's condition which will have the most powerful influence on the minds of its children. The population of several states of Europe has reached its term. In some it is declining, in some stationary, and in the most prosperous, under the extraordinary *stimulus* of the last part of the eighteenth century, it doubles itself but about once in seventy five years. In consequence of this, the process of social transmission is heavy and slow. Men not adventitiously favored come late into life, and the best years of existence are exhausted in languishing competition. The man grows up, and in the stern language of one of their most renowned economists,[6] finds no cover laid for him at Nature's table. The smallest official provision is a boon at which great minds are not ashamed to grasp; the assurance of the most frugal subsistence commands the brightest talents and the most laborious studies; poor wages pay for the unremitted labor of the most curious hands; and it is the smallest part of the population only that is within the reach even of these humiliating

[5] Mr Clay's late Speech on Internal Improvements.
[6] Mr Malthus.

springs of action. We need not labor to contrast this state of things with the teeming growth and noble expansion of all our institutions and resources. Instead of being shut up, as it were, in the prison of a stationary or a very slowly progressive community, the emulation of our countrymen is drawn out and tempted on by a horizon constantly receding before them. New nations of kindred freemen are springing up in successive periods, shorter even than the active portion of the life of man. 'While we spend our time,' says Burke on this topic, 'in deliberating on the mode of governing two millions in America, we shall find we have millions more to manage.[7] Many individuals are in this house who were arrived at years of discretion when these words of Burke were uttered, and the two millions which Great Britain was then to manage have grown into ten, exceedingly unmanageable. The most affecting view of this subject is that it puts it in the power of the wise, and good, and great to gather, while they live, the ripest fruits of their labors. Where in human history is to be found a contrast like that which the last fifty years have crowded into the lives of those favored men who raising their hands or their voices when our little bands were led out to the perilous conflict with one of the most powerful empires on earth, have lived to be crowned with the highest honors of the Republic which they established? Honor to their grey hairs and peace and serenity to the evening of their eventful days!

Though it may never again be the fortune of our country to bring within the compass of half a century a contrast so dazzling as this, yet in its grand and steady progress, the career of duty and usefulness will be run by all its children under a constantly increasing *stimulus*. The voice which, in the morning of life, shall awaken the patriotic sympathy of the land, will be echoed back by a community incalculably swelled in all its proportions before it shall be hushed in death. The writer by whom the noble features of our scenery shall be sketched with a glowing pencil, the traits of our romantic early history

[7] Speech on Conciliation with America, March 22, 1775.

gathered up with filial zeal, and the peculiarities of our character seized with delicate perception, cannot mount so entirely and rapidly to success but that ten years will add new millions to the numbers of his readers. The American statesman, the orator, whose voice is already heard in its supremacy from Florida to Maine, whose intellectual empire already extends beyond the limits of Alexander's, has yet new states and new nations starting into being, the willing tributaries to his sway.

This march of our population westward has been attended with consequences in some degree novel in the history of the human mind. It is a fact somewhat difficult of explanation that the refinement of the ancient nations seemed almost wholly devoid of an elastic and expansive principle. The arts of Greece were enchained to her islands and her coasts; they did not penetrate the interior. The language and literature of Athens were as unknown to the north of Pindus, at a distance of two hundred miles from the capital of Grecian refinement, as they were in Scythia. Thrace, whose mountain tops may almost be seen from the porch of the temple of Minerva at Sunium, was the proverbial abode of barbarism. Though the colonies of Greece were scattered on the coasts of Italy, of France, of Spain, and of Africa, no extension of their population toward the interior took place, and the arts did not penetrate beyond the walls of the cities where they were cultivated. How different is the picture of the diffusion of the arts and improvements of civilization from the coast to the interior of America! Population advances westward with a rapidity which numbers may describe indeed but cannot represent with any vivacity to the mind. The wilderness which one year is impassable is traversed the next by the caravans of the industrious emigrants who go to follow the setting sun, with the language, the institutions, and the arts of civilized life. It is not the irruption of wild barbarians, come to visit the wrath of God on a degenerate empire; it is not the inroad of disciplined banditti, marshalled by the intrigues of ministers and kings. It is the human family led out to possess its broad patrimony. The states and nations which are springing up in the valley of the Missouri are bound to us by the dearest ties of a common language, a common government, and a common descent. Before New-England can look with coldness on their rising myriads, she must forget that some of the best of her own blood is beating in their veins; that her hardy children, with their axes on their shoulders, have been literally among the pioneers in this march of humanity; that young as she is, she has become the mother of populous states. What generous mind would sacrifice to a selfish preservation of local preponderance the delight of beholding civilized nations rising up in the desert; and the language, the manners, the institutions to which he has been reared, carried with his household gods to the foot of the Rocky Mountains? Who can forget that this extension of our territorial limits is the extension of the empire of all we hold dear; of our laws, of our character, of the memory of our ancestors, of the great achievements in our history? Whithersoever the sons of the thirteen states shall wander, to southern or western climes, they will send back their hearts to the rocky shores, the battle fields, and the intrepid councils of the Atlantic coast. These are placed beyond the reach of vicissitude. They have become already matter of history, of poetry, of eloquence:

> The love, where death has set his seal,
> Nor age can chill, nor rival steal,
> Nor falsehood disavow.

Divisions may spring up, ill blood arise, parties be formed, and interests may seem to clash; but the great bonds of the nation are linked to what is passed. The deeds of the great men to whom this country owes its origin and growth are a patrimony, I know, of which its children will never deprive themselves. As long as the Mississippi and the Missouri shall flow, those men and those deeds will be remembered on their banks. The sceptre of government may go where it will; but that of patriotic feeling can never depart from Judah. In all that mighty region which is drained by the Missouri and its tributary streams—the valley coextensive with the temperate zone—will there be, as long as the name of America shall last, a father that will not take his children on his knee and recount to them the events of the twentieth of December, the nineteenth of April, the seventeenth of June, and the fourth of July?

This then is the theatre on which the intellect of America is to appear, and such the motives to its exertion; such the mass to be influenced by its energies, such the crowd to witness its efforts, such the glory to crown its success. If I err in this happy vision of my country's fortunes, I thank God for an error so animating. If this be false, may I never know the truth. Never may you, my friends, be under any other feeling, than that a great, a growing, an immeasurably expanding country is calling upon you for your best services. The name and character of our Alma Mater have already been carried by some of our brethren thousands of miles from her venerable walls; and thousands of miles still farther westward, the communities of kindred men are fast gathering whose minds and hearts will act in sympathy with yours.

The most powerful motives call on us as scholars for those efforts which our common country demands of all her children. Most of us are of that class who owe whatever of knowledge has shone into our minds to the free and popular institutions of our native land. There are few of us who may not be permitted to boast that we have been reared in an honest poverty or a frugal competence and owe every thing to those means of education which are equally open to all. We are summoned to new energy and zeal by the high nature of the experiment we are appointed in Providence to make and the grandeur of the theatre on which it is to be performed. When the old world afforded no longer any hope, it pleased Heaven to open this last refuge of humanity. The attempt has begun and is going on, far from foreign corruption, on the broadest scale, and under the most benignant auspices; and it certainly rests with us to solve the great problem in human society, to settle, and that forever, the momentous question—whether mankind can be trusted with a purely popular system? One might almost think, without extravagance,

that the departed wise and good of all places and times
are looking down from their happy seats to witness what
shall now be done by us; that they who lavished their
treasures and their blood of old, who labored and suffered,
who spake and wrote, who fought and perished, in the one
great cause of Freedom and Truth, are now hanging from
their orbs on high over the last solemn experiment of humanity. As I have wandered over the spots, once the scene
of their labors, and mused among the prostrate columns
of their Senate Houses and Forums, I have seemed almost
to hear a voice from the tombs of departed ages; from the
sepulchres of the nations which died before the sight.
They exhort us, they adjure us to be faithful to our trust.
They implore us, by the long trials of struggling humanity,
by the blessed memory of the departed; by the dear faith
which has been plighted by pure hands to the holy cause
of truth and man; by the awful secrets of the prison
houses where the sons of freedom have been immured;
by the noble heads which have been brought to the block;
by the wrecks of time, by the eloquent ruins of nations,
they conjure us not to quench the light which is rising on
the world. Greece cries to us, by the convulsed lips of her
poisoned, dying Demosthenes; and Rome pleads with us
in the mute persuasion of her mangled Tully. They address us each and all in the glorious language of Milton,
to one who might have canonized his memory in the
hearts of the friends of liberty but who did most shame-
fully betray the cause, 'Reverere tantam de te expecta-
tionem, spem patriæ de te unicam. Reverere vultus et
vulnera tot fortium virorum, quotquot pro libertate tam
strenue decertârunt, manes etiam eorum qui in ipso cer-
tamine occubuerunt. Reverere exterarum quoque civita-
tum existimationem de te atque sermones; quantas res de
libertate nostra tam fortiter partâ, de nostra republica tam
gloriose exorta sibi polliceantur; quæ si tam cito quasi
aborta evanuerit, profecto nihil æque dedecorosum huic
genti atque periculosum fuerit.[8]

Yes, my friends, such is the exhortation which calls on

[8] Milton's Defensio Secunda.

us to exert our powers, to employ our time and consecrate our labors in the cause of our native land. When we engage in that solemn study, the history of our race, when we survey the progress of man from his cradle in the East to these last limits of his wandering; when we behold him forever flying westward from civil and religious thraldom, bearing his household gods over mountains and seas, seeking rest and finding none but still pursuing the flying bow of promise to the glittering hills which it spans in Hesperian climes, we cannot but exclaim with Bishop Berkeley, the generous prelate of England, who bestowed his benefactions as well as blessings on our country

> Westward the Star of Empire takes its way;
> The four first acts already past,
> The fifth shall close the drama with the day;
> Time's noblest offspring is the last.

In that high romance, if romance it be, in which the great minds of antiquity sketched the fortunes of the ages to come, they pictured to themselves a favored region beyond the ocean, a land of equal laws and happy men. The primitive poets beheld it in the islands of the blest; the Doric bards surveyed it in the Hyperborean regions; the sage of the academy placed it in the lost Atlantis; and even the sterner spirit of Seneca could discern a fairer abode of humanity in distant regions then unknown. We look back upon these uninspired predictions and almost recoil from the obligation they imply. By us must these fair visions be realized, by us must be fulfilled these high auspices which burst in trying hours from the longing hearts of the champions of truth. There are no more continents or worlds to be revealed; Atlantis hath arisen from the ocean, the farthest Thule is reached, there are no more retreats beyond the sea, no more discoveries, no more hopes. Here then a mighty work is to be fulfilled, or never, by the race of mortals. The *man* who looks with tenderness on the sufferings of good men in other times; the *descendant* of the pilgrims who cherishes the memory of his fathers; the *patriot* who feels an honest glow at the majesty of the system of which he is a member; the *scholar* who beholds with rapture the long sealed book of unprejudiced truth expanded to all to read; these are they by whom these auspices are to be accomplished. Yes, brethren, it is by the intellect of the country that the mighty mass is to be inspired; that its parts are to communicate and sympathise, its bright progress to be adorned with becoming refinements, its strong sense uttered, its character reflected, its feelings interpreted to its own children, to other regions, and to after ages.

Meantime the years are rapidly passing away and gathering importance in their course. With the present year will be completed the half century from that most important era in human history, the commencement of our revolutionary war. The jubilee of our national existence is at hand. The space of time that has elapsed from that momentous date has laid down in the dust which the blood of many of them had already hallowed most of the great men to whom, under Providence, we owe our national existence and privileges. A few still survive among us, to reap the rich fruits of their labors and sufferings; and One has yielded himself to the united voice of a people and returned in his age, to receive the gratitude of the nation to whom he devoted his youth. It is recorded on the pages of American history that when this friend of our country applied to our commissioners at Paris in 1776 for a passage in the first ship they should despatch to America, they were obliged to answer him, (so low and abject was then our dear native land) that they possessed not the means nor the credit sufficient for providing a single vessel in all the ports of France. Then, exclaimed the youthful hero, 'I will provide my own;' and it is a literal fact that when all America was too poor to offer him so much as a passage to her shores, he left, in his tender youth, the bosom of home, of happiness, of wealth, of rank, to plunge in the dust and blood of our inauspicious struggle.

Welcome, friend of our fathers, to our shores! Happy are our eyes that behold those venerable features. Enjoy a triumph such as never conqueror or monarch enjoyed, the assurance that throughout America there is not a bosom which does not beat with joy and gratitude at the sound of your name. You have already met and saluted, or will soon meet, the few that remain of the ardent patriots, prudent counsellors, and brave warriors with whom you were associated in achieving our liberty. But you have looked round in vain for the faces of many who would have lived years of pleasure on a day like this with their old companion in arms and brother in peril. Lincoln, and Greene, and Knox, and Hamilton, are gone; the heroes of Saratoga and Yorktown have fallen, before the only foe they could not meet. Above all, the first of heroes and of men, the friend of your youth, the more than friend of his country, rests in the bosom of the soil he redeemed. On the banks of his Potomac he lies in glory and peace. You will revisit the hospitable shades of Mount Vernon, but him whom you venerated as we did you will not meet at its door. His voice of consolation which reached you in the Austrian dungeons cannot now break its silence, to bid you welcome to his own roof. But the grateful children of America will bid you welcome in his name. Welcome, thrice welcome to our shores; and whithersoever throughout the limits of the continent your course shall take you, the ear that hears you shall bless you, the eye that sees you shall bear witness to you, and every tongue exclaim, with heartfelt joy, welcome, welcome La Fayette!

Robert Walsh (?)

Robert Walsh (1784–1859), Baltimore lawyer, turned in 1809 to political writing and became in his own day an authority on international politics with books on Napoleonic France, on Russia, and on Europe in general. His *An Appeal from the Judgments of Great Britain respecting the United States of America* (1819) was perhaps the best-informed and most effective answer by an American to the attacks of reviewers and travelers which harassed the young republic in its formative years. Encouraged by the new and firmer spirit of nationalism in American letters, he established, in 1827 in Philadelphia, after several earlier failures, a new periodical which he called the *American Quarterly Review*. In the third issue there appeared a review of plays by William Dunlap and James Nelson Barker which opens with a discussion of the state of the American theatre (here quoted) and pleads for a national drama in terms of simple patriotism that harks back to an earlier phase of the nationalistic literary movement and forward to some of the problems of the theatre today. "National character" here means the diversity of types that make for dramatic interest rather than the basic sense of an evolving nationality which Ingersoll and Everett had in mind. Walsh had a large circle of literary friends and as the articles in his periodical have not been identified, he may have been merely the editor rather than the author of this review.

TEXT: from the *American Quarterly Review*, I (June 1827), 331–57.

American Drama

It might perhaps be a question with some whether it be more indicative of a want of genius in the dramatic writers or a want of taste in the readers, of these United States that a large portion of the latter have, we believe, remained to this day ignorant of the very existence of the former. To the frequenters of the theatre, it is known that some such strange monsters did once and perhaps do still inhabit this barren wilderness of literature, unless perchance they have been starved to death or become extinct like the mammoth and various other animals whose remains sometimes rise up in judgment against them. But to a vast proportion of our readers, they are as if they had never been—not forgotten, for that would be something—but never known.

For this reason, it will no doubt surprise the reader to learn that we have actually in our possession nearly sixty American dramas, consisting of tragedies, comedies, operas, serious and comic, melo-dramas and farces, besides others that baffle all our attempts at "codification." These last cannot be called by any name, Christian or Pagan, with which we are acquainted and, like certain equivocal substances which belong neither to the animal nor vegetable kingdom, must be left to be defined when they shall become sufficiently numerous to merit the distinction.

To those who have had occasion to observe and to regret the prevalence of a certain colonial spirit which equally affects our legal and literary tribunals, and, by a natural consequence, the opinions of the public, it will probably occur that this total oblivion of our dramatic productions is entirely owing to the accident of their not being worth remembering or even meriting a passing notice. A perusal of the plays in our possession has, however, satisfied us that this is not altogether the fact. Unless we are greatly mistaken, there are some among them not entirely unworthy of being read and which, if represented on our stage, with the advantage of good scenery and good acting, would or at least ought to be successful. They are, we really think, to say the least of them, quite equal to the productions of the present race of London playwrights, which are regularly brought out at our theatres and to which the certificate of having been performed a hundred nights with unbounded applause gives all the efficacy of a quack medicine.

Before, however, we proceed to notice some of these domestic wonders more particularly, it may perhaps be no uninteresting or useless task to glance at a few of the leading causes which have brought about that decline in the dignity and usefulness of the stage which is now acknowledged on all hands to be notorious in England, and as an almost inevitable consequence in this country. For ourselves, we cannot but lament it most deeply as one of those indications that point with unerring finger to the absence of that wholesome, manly and vigorous taste which may be said always to mark the best periods in the history of every civilized country. Notwithstanding all that has been said and written since the days of Jeremy Collier, we cannot but bear in our heads as well as our hearts a love and respect for an art which, in its purity, administers so delightfully to our taste as well as to our best feelings. Of all popular amusements ever devised, dramatic exhibitions are, when properly conducted, the most elegant and instructive. They address themselves both to the understanding and the senses, and carry with them the force of precept and example. In witnessing them, we are excited by the passions of others instead of our own, as is the case in the real transactions of life; and that stimulus which may be pronounced to be one of the actual wants of our nature is thus afforded to us without any of the evil consequences resulting from an indulgence of the passions in our own proper persons.

It is by this mode of giving play and excitement to the mind, by mimic representations, that the force of the operations of the passions in real life is unquestionably tempered and restrained; and hence it has always been held with justice that the stage, in its legitimate and proper state, is a most powerful agent in humanizing and refining mankind. It operates also in other ways in bringing about this salutary result. It allures the people from an attendance upon barbarous and brutifying spectacles—from brawls, boxing-matches, and bull-baitings;—it accustoms them, in a certain degree, to intellectual enjoyments and rational recreations and substitutes innocent amusement, if not actual instruction, in the place of those which afford neither one nor the other. A theatre where the price of admittance is within the means of the ordinary classes of people is a substitute, and a most salutary one, for tavern brawls and low debauchery. Those whose faculties are too obtuse to relish or comprehend the intrinsic excellence of a plot, the lofty morality or classic ease of the dialogue, are still instructed and amused through the medium of their eyes and actually see before them examples to imitate or avoid. If it be said that these examples are too far removed from the ordinary sphere of those who witness them to be of any use, still it may be replied that chastity, fortitude, patriotism, and magnanimity are virtues of all classes of mankind, and that all can feel and comprehend them, though they may be exercised in circumstances and situations in which they never expect to be placed. That the Drama may be, has been, and actually now is, in some degree diverted from its proper and most important purposes will hardly be denied by those who have the misfortune to like a good play; and though it cannot exactly be said of the infirmities of intellect as it is of the maladies of the body that when once the causes are known they are half cured; still it is certain, that a knowledge of the source of a defect is indispensable to the finding of an adequate remedy. For this reason, the ensuing remarks may not be entirely without utility.

It is generally, we believe, considered a sufficient apology in behalf of the persons who preside over this most delightful of all intellectual banquets that the degradation of the stage originated in the necessity of administering to a taste already vitiated. The public must be pleased that the manager may live. If the people require the attractions of a menagerie and a puppet-show combined, and will relish nothing living but horses, dogs, dromedaries, and elephants prancing in the midst of pasteboard pageantry, conflagrations, bombardments, springing of mines, blowing up of castles and such like accumulations of awful nursery horrors, it is alleged that there is no help for it. This taste must be gratified, like the appetites of other animals that chance to prefer raw meat and offals to the highest delicacies of the table. This may be true to a certain extent; but we are, notwithstanding, satisfied in our own judgment that it is very materially in the power of the managers of theatres, to give a better direction to the public taste; and that it would eventually lead to the most profitable results, were they to take equal pains and incur equal expense to cater for a good taste that they do to pamper a bad one.

We are quite sure, that a theatre, devoted to the exhibition of none but legitimate dramas, in the hands of competent actors, would prove permanently attractive, rally around it almost all the more enlightened portions of society and, by a natural consequence, all the inferior classes; and finally prove far more profitable to the manager than one devoted to expensive spectacles, one of which it costs more to get up than a dozen first-rate tragedies and comedies. If one-half of the sums laid out on pasteboard, tinsel, and trumpery were offered as a premium for good actors, a first-rate company might be collected, permanently, and fully adequate to give effect to the finest efforts of the dramatist. There would then be no necessity to depend upon perpetual novelty which supplies the place of good acting; and perpetual shows substituted for the beautiful creations of genius.

It is not attempted to be denied that a large portion of the attendants on the theatres, and on whom they are in a considerable degree dependent for its support, are of that order of people which, however worthy in other respects, is not distinguished either for a correct taste or a well disciplined judgment as to authors or actors. But still, there is always in every civilized country a sufficient number of persons better educated and of a more refined taste to give the tone to the others. Those who cannot feel like them or comprehend and relish the same beauties in literature and the arts are at first ashamed to dissent from their decisions, and at length partake in the enjoyment of the same beauties with an equal relish, since it is only necessary to become a little accustomed to what is good to be disgusted with what is bad. The example descends to those in the next degree below, until finally all will partake of its influence; and even the gods in the gallery will be ashamed not to be pleased with what they see applauded by their masters and mistresses in the pit and boxes.

We are therefore of opinion that no small portion of this bad taste which we deplore in relation to the stage may be fairly laid to the charge of the managers who, if we mistake not, have been at least accomplices in producing that very state of things which they now offer as an apology for persevering in the same course by which it was brought about. After having vitiated the public taste for more delicate viands by affording us nothing better, they make this an excuse for offering us still worse; like the bumpkin, who having fed his ass upon nothing but husks for a long while, took occasion afterwards to reproach him with his indifference to corn.

There certainly was a time when a sterling play, in the hands of sterling actors, was a sufficient attraction to ensure a good house. The public neither required the excitement of wild beasts nor the allurements of pasteboard mimicry of what nature every day presented to view in all the attractions of her own inimitable grace and beauty. Can it be pretended that it would not be so now, if the same motives were held out to the public? It is the boast of the present age that within the very period that has been marked by the decay of the stage, mankind have made greater advances in the general diffusion of knowledge and an improvement in taste than during any similar portion of time for many generations past. No one, it is presumed, will be disposed to deny that this improvement in almost every thing else would, if not counteracted by some cause peculiarly applicable to this art, have been accompanied by a similar advancement of theatrical taste and consequently in theatrical exhibitions, if not theatrical productions. That such "counteracting principles," as Mr. Owen calls them, have operated peculiarly against the stage is therefore, we think, undeniable. It may be worth while to advert to some of the most powerful of these.

The perpetual exhibition of shows possessing no other merit but that of imitating or rather caricaturing nature most vilely has by degrees rendered the more refined classes of society quite indifferent to the stage, which has of consequence fallen in a great measure into the occupation of those who relish "Tom and Jerry" better than Shakspeare or Sheridan. The fashionable people have, for this reason, decided the theatre to be unfashionable; and, one and all, prefer eating ice-cream and pickled oysters at parties to visting a place which is not only not fashionable but where there is neither ice-cream nor pickled oysters. One of the first results of this abandonment or indifference to the stage is the deterioration of both plays and actors. There is no use in writing a good play to please people who have neither taste nor capacity to admire it; and no occasion for first-rate actors to please an audience whose keenest relish is for dogs, horses, and opera dancers.

The standard plays of a better era will, therefore, remain without any reinforcement from the contributions of later bards; and if any attempt is occasionally made by a manager to bring forward a legitimate drama for the purpose of exhibiting a *star*, it is taken from a class of productions, excellent indeed, but so destitute of novelty as to be almost indifferent. We have seen it so often that its very beauties have become stale, and we are fain to follow the universal instinct which prefers indifferent novelty to worn-out excellence. For this reason it is that a succession of new plays of merit is indispensable to maintain the stage upon a proper basis. We ourselves are free to confess, that we have so often witnessed the performance of Hamlet, Macbeth, Othello, and Venice Preserved as to require the concomitants of new actors and new acting to give them a proper relish. But the divinity of Genius is too often a golden calf, set up in the intellectual deserts of fashionable saloons. The expectation of rewards from those who have the means of rewarding and the hope of being

praised and admired by those whose notice is the height
of our ambition are often the indispensable stimulants by
which the morbid sensibilities and proud indolence of
bards are quickened and inflamed into action. That effort
of inspiration, so necessary to all poetical excellence and
which communicates such a glow to every thought and
such a rich redundancy of ideas, is very often but the
wish and the hope of being admired by the world. An
indifference to any one species of literature with a decided
preference for another on the part of the public is the
almost certain precursor of decay in the one and improvement in the other. Hence it has happened, that the talent
which, under different circumstances, would have developed itself in dramatic excellence, has, of late, expended
itself in novels, simply because all the world reads novels
and but a very small portion of it goes to the theatre.

Another reason probably why so few writers attempt the
stage of late is the utter hopelessness of seeing justice done
to their productions by the actors. Large as are our modern
theatres, they can accommodate but one good performer
at a time. The world was not big enough for Alexander;
and the mimic world of the stage is not sufficiently ca-
pacious for the strut of more than one mimic hero. Only
one sun can blaze in the heavens and but one *star*, of all
the galaxy of stars, can display its nightly glories and twin-
kle us blind at the theatres. If it should, therefore, unfortunately happen that the author has developed more
than one character in his piece which requires something
beyond the ordinary talent of a candle-snuffer to personate,
it will almost inevitably happen that the piece is condemned. The really good actors belonging to the company
are kept in reserve, while the *star* is exhibiting its splen-
dours; or if brought forward at all, are condemned to toil
through their parts neglected and unapplauded while the
course of the *star*, however wayward and eccentric, is
hailed with shouts of admiration. In such situations, actors
have no motive for exertion and consequently no exertions
will be made. Hence it has become supremely important
for a dramatic writer to have but one real character in his
piece. The rest must be walking ladies and gentlemen,

mere necessary implements or speaking automata to afford the *catch-word* and answer as foils to set off the glories of the *star*.

These *stars*, or as they may justly be denominated, malignant planets of the stage, it will be noticed, are generally very confined in their excellence. They are, for the most part, incapable of performing more than half a dozen characters with any extraordinary degree of talent, after which they shoot to some other sphere and coruscate there awhile until their lustre is extinguished. If, therefore, an author wishes to produce a successful piece, he must devote it exclusively to the bringing out and exhibiting the peculiar excellencies of the *star*. If the illustrious itinerant Roscius excels in starts, shrugs, and grimaces, the author must devote his talents to the production of opportunities for the unceasing display of this prominent excellence. If Roscius is great at the single rapier, he must be kept fighting his way through the whole dramatis personæ. If he is great at enacting the beast, let him be drunk the whole evening. If inimitable at cold sarcasm, our author must be most bitterly sarcastic. If dignified hauteur be his forte, the play must be stiff as buckram. If his voice happens to be peculiarly loud and sonorous, our author must give him scope and occasion and "restrain and aggravate" his muse till she roars throughout like honest Nic Bottom's lion: if, on the contrary, it is especially touching, your play must dissolve in perpetual dews of lachrymal tenderness. In short, the piece must accommodate itself to the actor, not the actor to the piece; and the genius of the author becomes the mere slave of the peculiarities, perhaps the very defects, of the performer. This is assuredly reversing the natural order. The genius that creates ought to take precedence of the genius which merely exhibits beauties.

The custom of *starring*, as it is now technically called, is without doubt highly injurious to the best interests of the stage, the public, and even the managers. From having been at first the privilege only of such as stood decidedly at the head of their profession and who merely took advantage of the temporary closing of the theatre to which they were attached to make a summer excursion through the provincial towns, it has become the ordinary privilege of every actor who can attempt one or two of Shakspeare's heroes. They come upon us from all points of the compass —glimmering for a few moments—attracting perhaps one or two full houses, and staying till the imposture is detected and then pass on to delude some other simple community which naturally believes they must be great performers because they travel from place to place and make such a figure in the play-bills, where their names are always put in great capitals. It is sufficient if these impostors deceive for one night only and attract a single full house. The spoil of public credulity is shared between the actor and the manager. He passes on, another and another succeeds, and thus the public is kept alive by the excitement of perpetual expectation and perpetual disappointment. Yet, still—

"Hope travels on, nor quits us when we die."

Really, and seriously, it is quite provoking to witness the exhibition of not a few of these *starring* performers who, if the truth must be told, are, for the most part, utterly inadequate to sustain the ordinary characters of a respectable drama with any tolerable degree of propriety. We are informed, it has become almost impossible to engage the permanent services of a tolerable actor even by the most liberal offers. By the prevalence of this absurd vanity on the part of the actors and the equally absurd credulity of the public, our theatres are deprived of any permanent attractions other than those of gorgeous spectacles, prodigious dancers, and prodigious wild beasts. It is beneath the dignity of the theatrical stars to shine in constellations; and the lovers of the true drama are consequently condemned to behold a noble production of genius marred and murdered by negligent or incapable actors who, if they were ever so capable, have no heart to exert themselves from a consciousness that their best efforts will receive little attention from an audience so accustomed to the glories of the *stars* that taper luminaries offer no attraction. The best if not the only remedy for this evil would be for the managers to enter into an association not to engage any performers but those unquestionably at the head of the profession for less than a season. This mode would secure to the principal cities of the United States the services of respectable actors, since it is in these alone that the public patronage is sufficient for a permanent support which will remunerate the managers for the expense of retaining a good company. By being thus stationary for a certain period and to a certain degree dependent on the support of a single community, every actor would then feel the necessity of exertion and improvement to supply the place of mere novelty, and those who were capable of it would improve accordingly. On the contrary, under the present system of *starring*, a performer goes from place to place, affording no opportunity for a comparison of one effort with another, careless of improvement from a consciousness that novelty and puffing will afford all that is necessary to a temporary success and that he will be gone before the audience has had time to study his defects. Every other part of the theatre is impoverished to pamper the illustrious itinerant—the orchestra is a desert—the stationary performers are put upon the shortest possible allowance—poor *John* is stript of his livery —and the very play-bills are stinted in their customary allowance of paper. All this is to enable the manager to conciliate the benign influence of a *star*, fill his house some half dozen nights, and make it a desert for the rest of the season. We ourselves have seen the rats playing about the pit of one of our theatres which, only the night before, was thronged by hundreds of spectators attracted thither by one of these theatrical *stars*.

There are many other causes which have, without doubt, cooperated with the preceding to bring down the stage to its present dead level of degradation. Our limits will not permit us to enumerate them, and having thus far confined ourselves to those which equally apply to this country and England, we will now revert to such as peculiarly belong to the former.

The want of a National Drama is the first thing that strikes us in this inquiry. By a national drama, we mean, not merely a class of dramatic productions written by Americans, but one appealing directly to the national feelings; founded upon domestic incidents—illustrating or satirizing domestic manners—and, above all, displaying a generous chivalry in the maintenance and vindication of those great and illustrious peculiarities of situation and character by which we are distinguished from all other nations. We do not hesitate to say that, next to the interests of eternal truth, there is no object more worthy the exercise of the highest attributes of the mind than that of administering to the just pride of national character, inspiring a feeling for the national glory, and inculcating a love of country. It is this which we would call a national literature; and, unless we greatly err, it is these characteristics which must eventually constitute the principal materials of one. We have no peculiar language to create an identity of our own; and it must, in a great measure, be in its apt and peculiar application to ourselves, our situation, character, government and institutions that our literature would seem destined to become national.

We do not wish to be understood as making an appeal to the national feeling, an indispensable requisite in all American productions; but we do mean to say, that such appeals, when introduced with genuine sentiment and without affectation, are proper and praiseworthy. They are equally advantageous to the author and his readers. They give to the productions of the former all that peculiar and decisive interest derived from an association of the efforts of the mind with manners, incidents, and local affections; and they instil into the latter a more powerful feeling of patriotism. Every man contemplates his country with a greater degree of affection and pride when he sees its happiness, virtues, or glories commemorated by genius in a manner which evinces that he who thus celebrates them is himself worthy of admiration. There are so few writers of powerful creative imagination that it savours of a base desertion to withdraw their genius from the service of their country and devote those powers which were bestowed by Providence for higher purposes to themes and exploits having no connexion with her situation or history.

The best and most permanent foundation for fame is our native soil; and a man who is admired or beloved by his own countrymen may almost dispense with the praises of the rest of the world.

There are two points essential to the existence and growth of this patriotic spirit of literature. The one is a proper degree of susceptibility on the part of the nation; the other, sufficient power in a writer to appeal to it successfully. It would be a hopeless attempt to appeal to a common feeling which had no existence, on the one hand, and on the other, the feeling would remain latent if there were no one to make the appeal. For many years subsequent to the establishment of our independence, an American writer laboured under the worst species of discouragement to an aspiring mind. There were comparatively but few general readers, and those were so accustomed to the productions of the mother country that they viewed the appearance of an American work pretty much in the light a Parisian coterie would the intrusion of a half-civilized Indian. A gentleman of that day would as soon have thought of wearing a homespun coat as of reading a book of home manufacture. The sense of inferiority in consequence kept down and discouraged the restless aspirations of actual or imagined genius; and if by chance a daring adventurer desperately invaded these barren regions of Parnassus, it was in the disguise of a foreigner or behind the leaden shield of abject imitation. He dared not attempt originality for fear of being stigmatized as a barbarian or select a purely native subject lest he should be laughed at by those who presided over the public taste as a dabbler in "Indian poetry,"—the favourite phrase of the day.

But times have changed and are daily changing for the better. Abroad, the public curiosity is excited towards the new world; and at home, there is a growing taste for historical truths and romantic fictions connected or associated with the progress of this nation. The public mind and taste have been and now are in a state to encourage and reward the successful efforts of genius employed on domestic subjects; and although it must be confessed that some considerable leaven of the old colonial vassalage still remains to embarrass and discourage, yet still it may be fairly asserted that no native writer can now justly plead the fact of the discouragements to which we have just alluded in extenuation of his indolence or in explanation of his ill success. By a proper choice of his subjects, and a tolerably happy mode of treating them he may reasonably calculate upon a moderate success. We do not say that he will actually add another to the wonders peculiar to the present times; to wit, rich authors—but he will bid fair to escape oblivion and a jail. We cannot offer a more apt and honourable example of the success attending such a course as we recommend than that of Mr. Cooper, the author of the Pioneers and other works, whose various and acknowledged excellence has received a peculiar and happy aid from the nature of the subjects which appeal directly to our early associations, local impressions, and sectional feelings. He displayed the same talent in his novel of "Precaution," but falling into the error of laying the *venue*, as the lawyers say, in the wrong place, his first work fell into oblivion and was only brought to light again by its connexion with the author of the Spy, and the Pioneers.

The remarks we made in relation generally to American literature may, we think, be specially applied to the drama which appeals most strongly to popular feelings. Were it not for the obstacles and discouragements we have previously noticed, among which are conspicuous a want of taste in the audience and a want of proper management in the conductors of theatres, we think there is little doubt that successful efforts could and would be made in this branch of literature. This land is full of materials—such as novelty of incident, character, and situation. Like the forests of our country which have never been cut down, those materials remain unemployed and unexhausted— fresh and novel, with all the bold features of primeval strength and vigour. It only requires a brave, original intellect, to convert them into the materials of excellence. It has been often imagined as one of the obstacles which stand in the way of a national drama that we lack variety in our national character. No idea, we think, can possibly be more erroneous than this. There is, probably, no country in the world which affords more numerous and distinct characters than the United States. Our cities are full of bipeds from every quarter of the old world, bringing with them all their peculiarities to be exhibited in a new sphere. From the city on the sea-side to the frontier settler—from him to the white hunter more than half savage—to the savage himself—there are continual gradations in the characters and situation of mankind; and every state in the Union is a little world by itself, exhibiting almost the same degrees of difference that we observe in the English, the Scotch, and the Irish. Their manners, habits, occupations, prejudices, and opinions, are equally various and dissimilar. For these reasons, we believe that there is no want of sufficient varieties of character in the United States, to afford ample materials for a diversified drama. We rather fear the obstacle has hitherto arisen from the habit of imitation we have noticed. The author perhaps did not catch any original characters because he did not think of looking for them and complained in consequence of the scarcity of what he never took the pains to find. But even conceding, for one moment only, that complaints of a want of variety of character are just, still no one will deny that there is an abundant field for novelty of situation, and novelty of situation is the best possible substitute for novelty of character if it does not in reality create it. . . .

Whatever talent there may be among us, it will unless encouraged lie inactive like those seeds which are buried in the forests perhaps for ages and which only vegetate into fruits and flowers when the warm rays of the sun awaken their dormant energy and vivify the chill bosom of the earth. The first requisite for producing a National Drama is national encouragement. We do not mean pensions and premiums—but liberal praise and rewards to success—and a liberal allowance for failures. The second is a little more taste and liberality in the managers of our theatres; and the third is the presence of competent performers, collected in companies of sufficient strength to give effectual support to a new piece and sufficient talent to personate an original character without resorting to some hacknied model which has descended from generation to generation and, like all copies, lost something of the original in the hands of each succeeding imitator.

Let not, however, our youthful aspirants after honest fame be discouraged by the obstacles we have placed before them. Genius has often a divinity within itself, a sort of prophetic consciousness, a daring insight into futurity, an irrepressible impulse, which animates and supports it in the midst of discouragements and neglect. But one man out of millions is a hero, a saint, or a sage. Yet this should be no obstacle to the pursuit of glory, virtue, or wisdom. If but one man out of millions attain the summit of Parnassus, let it be recollected that his reward is immortality.

DOCUMENT 18

Noah Webster

The position of Noah Webster on the problem of
an American language had softened rather than changed
in the thirty-nine years since he first expressed them in
his *Dissertations* (Document 4). His years of comparative study of the use of words in a variety of languages
had given him a surer knowledge of the language process itself, and therefore a sounder basis for his distinctions between American and British English. Further,
he now understood that American variations may be
attributed not only to accidental local usage, but to
fundamental institutions, qualities, and customs attrib-
utable to the national character. He now is content to
record and explain these differences rather than to urge
radical reform in spelling and usage. His Preface to the
first edition of the definitive form of his *Dictionary* is
the statement of a scholarly lexicographer rather than of
an inventive reformer.

TEXT: from Volume I of *An American Dictionary of the English
Language*, 2 vols., New York, 1828.

An American Dictionary of the English Language

PREFACE

In the year 1783, just at the close of the revolution, I
published an elementary book for facilitating the acquisition of our vernacular tongue and for correcting a vicious
pronunciation which prevailed extensively among the common people of this country. Soon after the publication of
that work, I believe in the following year, that learned
and respectable scholar, the Rev. Dr. Goodrich of Dur-

ham, one of the trustees of Yale College, suggested to me the propriety and expediency of my compiling a dictionary which should complete a system for the instruction of the citizens of this country in the language. At that time, I could not indulge the thought, much less the hope, of undertaking such a work; as I was neither qualified by research, nor had I the means of support during the execution of the work had I been disposed to undertake it. For many years therefore, though I considered such a work as very desirable, yet it appeared to me impracticable; as I was under the necessity of devoting my time to other occupations for obtaining subsistence.

About twenty seven years ago, I began to think of attempting the compilation of a Dictionary. I was induced to this undertaking, not more by the suggestion of friends, than by my own experience of the want of such a work while reading modern books of science. In this pursuit, I found almost insuperable difficulties, from the want of a dictionary for explaining many new words which recent discoveries in the physical sciences had introduced into use. To remedy this defect in part, I published my Compendious Dictionary in 1806; and soon after made preparations for undertaking a larger work.

My original design did not extend to an investigation of the origin and progress of our language; much less of other languages. I limited my views to the correcting of certain errors in the best English Dictionaries and to the supplying of words in which they are deficient. But after writing through two letters of the alphabet, I determined to change my plan. I found myself embarrassed at every step for want of a knowledge of the origin of words which Johnson, Bailey, Junius, Skinner and some other authors do not afford the means of obtaining. Then laying aside my manuscripts and all books treating of language except lexicons and dictionaries, I endeavored, by a diligent comparison of words having the same or cognate radical letters, in about twenty languages, to obtain a more correct knowledge of the primary sense of original words, of the affinities between the English and many other languages, and thus to enable myself to trace words to their source.

I had not pursued this course more than three or four years before I discovered that I had to unlearn a great deal that I had spent years in learning, and that it was necessary for me to go back to the first rudiments of a branch of erudition which I had before cultivated, as I had supposed, with success.

I spent ten years in this comparison of radical words and in forming a synopsis of the principal words in twenty languages, arranged in classes, under their primary elements or letters. The result has been to open what are to me new views of language, and to unfold what appear to be the genuine principles on which these languages are constructed.

After completing this synopsis, I proceeded to correct what I had written of the Dictionary and to complete the remaining part of the work. But before I had finished it, I determined on a voyage to Europe with the view of obtaining some books and some assistance which I wanted; of learning the real state of the pronunciation of our language in England, as well as the general state of philology in that country; and of attempting to bring about some agreement or coincidence of opinions in regard to unsettled points in pronunciation and grammatical construction. In some of these objects I failed; in others, my designs were answered.

It is not only important but in a degree necessary that the people of this country should have an *American Dictionary* of the English Language; for, although the body of the language is the same as in England and it is desirable to perpetuate that sameness, yet some differences must exist. Language is the expression of ideas; and if the people of one country cannot preserve an identity of ideas, they cannot retain an identity of language. Now an identity of ideas depends materially upon a sameness of things or objects with which the people of the two countries are conversant. But in no two portions of the earth, remote from each other, can such identity be found. Even physical objects must be different. But the principal differences between the people of this country and of all others arise from different forms of government, different laws, institutions and customs. Thus the practice of hawking and hunting, the institution of heraldry, and the feudal system of England originated terms which formed, and some of which now form, a necessary part of the language of that country; but, in the United States, many of these terms are no part of our present language,—and they cannot be, for the things which they express do not exist in this country. They can be known to us only as obsolete or as foreign words. On the other hand, the institutions in this country which are new and peculiar give rise to new terms or to new applications of old terms, unknown to the people of England, which cannot be explained by them and which will not be inserted in their dictionaries unless copied from ours. Thus the terms, *land-office*; *land-warrant*; *location of land*; *consociation* of churches; *regent* of a university; *intendant* of a city; *plantation, selectmen, senate, congress, court, assembly, escheat,* &c. are either words not belonging to the language of England, or they are applied to things in this country which do not exist in that. No person in this country will be satisfied with the English definitions of the words *congress, senate* and *assembly, court,* &c. for although these are words used in England, yet they are applied in this country to express ideas which they do not express in that country. With our present constitutions of government, *escheat* can never have its feudal sense in the United States.

But this is not all. In many cases, the nature of our governments and of our civil institutions requires an appropriate language in the definition of words, even when the words express the same thing as in England. Thus the English Dictionaries inform us that a *Justice* is one deputed by the *King* to do right by way of judgment—he is a *Lord* by his office—Justices of the peace are appointed by the *King's commission*—language which is inaccurate in respect to this officer in the United States. So *constitutionally* is defined by Todd or Chalmers, *legally,* but in this country the distinction between *constitution* and *law* requires a different definition. In the United States, a *plantation* is a very different thing from what it is in England. The word *marshal,* in this country, has one important application unknown in England or in Europe.

A great number of words in our language require to be defined in a phraseology accommodated to the condition and institutions of the people in these states, and the people of England must look to an American Dictionary for a correct understanding of such terms.

The necessity therefore of a Dictionary suited to the people of the United States is obvious; and I should suppose that this fact being admitted, there could be no difference of opinion as to the *time* when such a work ought to be substituted for English Dictionaries.

There are many other considerations of a public nature, which serve to justify this attempt to furnish an American Work which shall be a guide to the youth of the United States. Most of these are too obvious to require illustration.

One consideration however which is dictated by my own feelings, but which I trust will meet with approbation in correspondent feelings in my fellow citizens, ought not to be passed in silence. It is this. "The chief glory of a nation," says Dr. Johnson, "arises from its authors." With this opinion deeply impressed on my mind, I have the same ambition which actuated that great man when he expressed a wish to give celebrity to Bacon, to Hooker, to Milton and to Boyle.

I do not indeed expect to add celebrity to the names of *Franklin, Washington, Adams, Jay, Madison, Marshall, Ramsay, Dwight, Smith, Trumbull, Hamilton, Belknap, Ames, Mason, Kent, Hare, Silliman, Cleaveland, Walsh, Irving,* and many other Americans distinguished by their writings or by their science; but it is with pride and satisfaction, that I can place them, as authorities, on the same page with those of *Boyle, Hooker, Milton, Dryden, Addison, Ray, Milner, Cowper, Davy, Thomson* and *Jameson.*

A life devoted to reading and to an investigation of the origin and principles of our vernacular language, and especially a particular examination of the best English writers, with a view to a comparison of their style and phraseology with those of the best American writers and with our colloquial usage, enables me to affirm with confidence that the genuine English idiom is as well preserved by the unmixed English of this country as it is by the best *English* writers. Examples to prove this fact will be found in the Introduction to this work. It is true that many of our writers have neglected to cultivate taste and the embellishments of style; but even these have written the language in its genuine *idiom*. In this respect, Franklin and Washington, whose language is their hereditary mother tongue unsophisticated by modern grammar, present as pure models of genuine English as Addison or Swift. But I may go farther and affirm, with truth, that our country has produced some of the best models of composition. The style of President Smith; of the authors of the Federalist; of Mr. Ames; of Dr. Mason; of Mr. Harper; of Chancellor Kent; [the prose] of Mr. Barlow; of the legal decisions of the Supreme Court of the United States; of the reports of legal decisions in some of the particular states; and many other writings; in purity, in elegance and in technical precision is equaled only by that of the best British authors and surpassed by that of no English compositions of a similar kind.

The United States commenced their existence under circumstances wholly novel and unexampled in the history of nations. They commenced with civilization, with learning, with science, with constitutions of free government and with that best gift of God to man, the christian religion. Their population is now equal to that of England; in arts and sciences, our citizens are very little behind the most enlightened people on earth; in some respects, they have no superiors; and our language, within two centuries, will be spoken by more people in this country than any other language on earth except the Chinese, in Asia, and even that may not be an exception.

It has been my aim in this work, now offered to my fellow citizens, to ascertain the true principles of the language, in its orthography and structure; to purify it from some palpable errors and reduce the number of its anomalies, thus giving it more regularity and consistency in its forms, both of words and sentences; and in this manner, to furnish a standard of our vernacular tongue which we shall not be ashamed to bequeath to *three hundred millions of people* who are destined to occupy and, I hope, to adorn the vast territory within our jurisdiction.

If the language can be improved in regularity so as to be more easily acquired by our own citizens and by foreigners, and thus be rendered a more useful instrument for the propagation of science, arts, civilization and christianity; if it can be rescued from the mischievous influence of sciolists and that dabbling spirit of innovation which is perpetually disturbing its settled usages and filling it with anomalies; if, in short, our vernacular language can be redeemed from corruptions and our philology and literature from degradation; it would be a source of great satisfaction to me to be one among the instruments of promoting these valuable objects. If this object cannot be effected and my wishes and hopes are to be frustrated, my labor will be lost and this work must sink into oblivion.

This Dictionary, like all others of the kind, must be left, in some degree, imperfect; for what individual is competent to trace to their source and define in all their various applications, popular, scientific and technical, *sixty* or *seventy thousand* words! It satisfies my mind that I have done all that my health, my talents and my pecuniary means would enable me to accomplish. I present it to my fellow citizens, not with frigid indifference, but with my ardent wishes for their improvement and their happiness; and for the continued increase of the wealth, the learning, the moral and religious elevation of character and the glory of my country.

To that great and benevolent Being who, during the preparation of this work, has sustained a feeble constitution amidst obstacles and toils, disappointments, infirmities and depression; who has twice borne me and my manuscripts in safety across the Atlantic and given me strength and resolution to bring the work to a close, I would present the tribute of my most grateful acknowledgments. And if the talent which he entrusted to my care has not been put to the most profitable use in his service, I hope it has not been "kept laid up in a napkin," and that any misapplication of it may be graciously forgiven.

DOCUMENT 19

William Ellery Channing

It was seven years before William Ellery Channing (1780–1842) took up the challenge of C. J. Ingersoll and, in what started as a review of his essay on "The Influence of America on the Mind," in *The Christian Examiner* for January 1830, developed the theory of literature as the expression of national character to perhaps its farthest and most idealistic limits. The eldest of the Channing brothers, he broke with orthodox Calvinism with his "Baltimore Sermon" of 1819 and became virtually the founder of American Unitarianism. Emerson as a boy heard him preach in Boston many times and others felt the strong influence of his many liberal essays and tracts on religious, social, and literary topics. Channing and Ingersoll, as well as Everett, agreed on the basic proposition that great literature is the expression of great minds and that therefore a national literature, to be great, must be the expression of a lofty and distinctive national mind, but he differed sharply with Ingersoll on the relative value of practical and professional vs. religious and moral qualities of achievement. He also differed from him and anticipated Emerson in the value which he put on the spiritual qualities of the individual and in the ultimately religious rather than worldly tests of character, whether individual or national.

TEXT: from the first printing in *The Christian Examiner*, XXXVI (January 1830), 269–94. The essay was called, "Remarks on National Literature" when it was republished in his collected works, 1841–45.

Remarks on National Literature

We shall use the work prefixed to this article as ministers are sometimes said to use their texts. We shall make it a point to start from, not the subject of our remarks. Our purpose is to treat of the importance and means of a National Literature. The topic seems to us a great one, and to have intimate connexions with morals and religion as well as with all our public interests. Our views will be given with great freedom, and if they serve no other purpose than to recommend the subject to more general attention, one of our principal objects will be accomplished.

We begin with stating what we mean by national literature. We mean the expression of a nation's mind in writing. We mean the production among a people of important works in philosophy and in the departments of imagination and taste. We mean the contribution of new truths to the stock of human knowledge. We mean the thoughts of profound and original minds, elaborated by the toil of composition and fixed and made immortal in books. We mean the manifestation of a nation's intellect in the only forms by which it can multiply itself at home and send itself abroad. We mean that a nation shall take a place, by its authors, among the lights of the world. It will be seen, that we include under literature all the writings of superior minds, be the subjects what they may. We are aware that the term is often confined to compositions which relate to human nature and human life; that it is not generally extended to physical science; that mind, not matter, is regarded as its main subject and sphere. But the worlds of matter and mind are too intimately connected to admit of exact partition. All the objects of human thought flow into one another. Moral and physical truths have many bonds and analogies, and whilst the former are the chosen and noblest themes of literature, we are not anxious to divorce them from the latter, or to shut them up in a separate department. The expression of superior mind in writing, we regard then, as a nation's literature. We regard its gifted men, whether devoted to the exact sciences, to mental and ethical philosophy, to history and legislation, or to fiction and poetry, as forming a noble intellectual brotherhood, and it is for the purpose of quickening all to join their labors for the public good that we offer the present plea in behalf of a national literature.

To show the importance which we attach to the subject, we begin with some remarks on what we deem the distinction which a nation should most earnestly covet. We believe that more distinct apprehensions on this point are needed, and that for want of them, the work of improvement is carried on with less energy, consistency, and wisdom than may and should be brought to bear upon it. The great distinction of a country, then, is that it produces superior men. Its natural advantages are not to be disdained. But they are of secondary importance. No matter what races of animals a country breeds. The great question is, does it breed a noble race of men. No matter what its soil may be. The great question is, how far is it prolific of moral and intellectual power. No matter how stern its climate is if it nourish force of thought and virtuous purpose. These are the products by which a country is to be tried, and institutions have value only by the impulse which they give to the mind. It has sometimes been said that the noblest men grow where nothing else will grow. This we do not believe, for mind is not the creature of climate or soil. But were it true, we should say that it were better to live among rocks and sands than in the most genial and productive region on the face of the earth.

As yet, the great distinction of a nation on which we have insisted has been scarcely recognised. The idea of forming a superior race of men has entered little into schemes of policy. Invention and effort have been expended on matter much more than on mind. Lofty piles have been reared; the earth has groaned under pyramids and palaces. The thought of building up a nobler order of intellect and character has hardly crossed the most adventurous statesman. We beg that we may not be misapprehended. We offer these remarks to correct what we deem a disproportioned attention to physical good and not at all to condemn the expenditure of ingenuity and strength on the outward world. There is a harmony between all our great interests, between inward and outward improvements; and by establishing among them a wise order, all will be secured. We have no desire to shut up man in his own spiritual nature. The mind was made to act on matter, and it grows by expressing itself in material forms. We believe, too, that in proportion as it shall gain intellectual and moral power, it will exert itself with increased energy and delight on the outward creation; will pour itself forth more freely in useful and ornamental arts; will rear more magnificent structures, and will call forth new beauties in nature. An intelligent and resolute spirit in a community perpetually extends its triumphs over matter. It can even subject to itself the most unpromising region. Holland, diked from the ocean, Venice, rising amidst the waves, and New England, bleak and rock bound New England, converted by a few generations from a wilderness into smiling fields and opulent cities, point us to the mind as the great source of physical good and teach us that in making the culture of man our highest end, we shall not retard but advance the cultivation of nature.

The question which we most solicitously ask about this country is, what race of men it is likely to produce. We consider its liberty of value only as far as it favors the growth of men. What is liberty? The removal of restraint from human powers. Its benefit is that it opens new fields for action and a wider range for the mind. The only freedom worth possessing is that which gives enlargement to a people's energy, intellect, and virtues. The savage makes his boast of freedom. But what is its worth? Free as he is, he continues for ages in the same ignorance, leads the same comfortless life, sees the same untamed wilderness spread around him. He is indeed free from what he calls the yoke of civil institutions. But other and worse chains bind him. The very privation of civil government is in effect a chain; for, by withholding protection from property, it virtually shackles the arm of industry and forbids exertion for the melioration of his lot. Progress, the growth of power, is the end and boon of liberty; and without this, a people may have the name but want the substance and spirit of freedom.

We are the more earnest in enlarging on these views because we feel that our attachment to our country must be very much proportioned to what we deem its tendency to form a generous race of men. We pretend not to have thrown off national feeling; but we have some stronger feelings. We love our country much, but mankind more. As men and Christians, our first desire is to see the improvement of human nature. We desire to see the soul of man, wiser, firmer, nobler, more conscious of its imperishable treasures, more beneficent and powerful, more alive to its connexion with God, more able to use pleasure and prosperity aright, and more victorious over poverty, adversity, and pain. In our survey of our own and other countries, the great question which comes to us is this; Where and under what institutions are men most likely to advance? Where are the soundest minds and the purest hearts formed? What nation possesses in its history, its traditions, its government, its religion, its manners, its pursuits, its relations to other communities, and especially in its private and public means of education, the instruments and pledges of a more resolute virtue and devotion to truth than we now witness? Such a nation, be it where it may, will engage our warmest interest. We love our country but not blindly. In all nations we recognise one great family, and our chief wish for our native land is that it may take the first rank among the lights and benefactors of the human race.

These views will explain the vast importance which we attach to a national literature. By this, as we have said, we understand the expression of a nation's mind in writing. It is the action of the most gifted understandings on the community. It throws into circulation through a wide sphere the most quickening and beautiful thoughts which have grown up in men of laborious study or creative genius. It is a much higher work than the communication of a gifted intellect in discourse. It is the mind giving to multitudes whom no voice can reach its compressed and selected thoughts in the most lucid order and attractive forms which it is capable of inventing. In other words, literature is the concentration of intellect for the purpose of spreading itself abroad and multiplying its energy.

Such being the nature of literature, it is plainly among the most powerful methods of exalting the character of a nation, of forming a better race of men. In truth, we apprehend that it may claim the first rank among the means of improvement. We know nothing so fitted to the advancement of society as to bring its higher minds to bear upon the multitude; as to establish close connexions between the more and less gifted; as to spread far and wide the light which springs up in meditative, profound, and sublime understandings. It is the ordinance of God, and one of his most benevolent laws, that the human race should be carried forward by impulses which originate in a few minds, perhaps in an individual; and in this way the most interesting relations and dependences of life are framed. When a great truth is to be revealed, it does not flash at once on the race, but dawns and brightens on a superior understanding from which it is to emanate and to illumine future ages. On the faithfulness of great minds to this awful function, the progress and happiness of men chiefly depend. The most illustrious benefactors of the race have been men who, having risen to great truths, have held them as a sacred trust for their kind, and have borne witness to them amidst general darkness, under scorn and persecution, perhaps in the face of death. Such men, indeed, have not always made contributions to literature, for their condition has not allowed them to be authors; but we owe the transmission, perpetuity, and immortal power of their new and high thoughts to kindred spirits which have concentrated and fixed them in books.

The quickening influences of literature need not be urged on those who are familiar with the history of modern Europe and who of course know the spring given to the human mind by the revival of ancient learning. Through their writings the great men of antiquity have exercised a sovereignty over these later ages not enjoyed in their own. It is more important to observe that the influence of literature is perpetually increasing; for, through the press and the spread of education, its sphere is indefinitely enlarged. Reading, once the privilege of a few, is now the occupation of multitudes and is to become one of the chief gratifications of all. Books penetrate everywhere, and some of the works of genius find their way to obscure dwellings which, a little while ago, seemed barred against all intellectual light. Writing is now the mightiest instrument on earth. Through this, the mind has acquired a kind of omnipresence. To literature we then look as the chief means of forming a better race of human beings. To superior minds, which may act through this, we look for the impulses by which their country is to be carried forward. We would teach them that they are the depositaries of the highest power on earth, and that on them the best hopes of society rest.

We are aware that some may think that we are exalting intellectual above moral and religious influence. They may tell us that the teaching of moral and religious truth, not by philosophers and boasters of wisdom, but by the comparatively weak and foolish, is the great means of renovating the world. This truth we indeed regard as 'the power of God unto salvation.' But let none imagine that its chosen temple is an uncultivated mind, and that it selects, as its chief organs, the lips of the unlearned. Religious and moral truth is indeed appointed to carry forward mankind; but not as conceived and expounded by narrow minds, not as darkened by the ignorant, not as debased by the superstitious, not as subtilized by the visionary, not as thundered out by the intolerant fanatic, not as turned into a drivelling cant by the hypocrite. Like all other truths, it requires for its full reception and powerful communication a free and vigorous intellect. Indeed, its grandeur and infinite connexions demand a more earnest and various use of our faculties than any other subject. As a single illustration of this remark, we may observe that all moral and religious truth may be reduced to one great and central thought, Perfection of Mind; a thought which comprehends all that is glorious in the Divine nature and which reveals to us the end and happiness of our own existence. This perfection has as yet only dawned on the most gifted human beings, and the great purpose of our present and future existence is to enlarge our conceptions of it without end, and to embody and make them manifest in character and life. And is this sublime thought to grow within us, to refine itself from error and impure mixture, to receive perpetual accessions of brightness from the study of God, man, and nature, and especially to be communicated powerfully to others without the vigorous exertion of our intellectual nature? Religion has been wronged by nothing more than by being separated from intellect; than by being removed from the province of reason and free research into that of mystery and authority, of impulse and feeling. Hence it is, that the prevalent forms or exhibitions of Christianity are comparatively inert, and that most which is written on the subject is of little or no worth. Christianity was given, not to contradict and degrade the rational nature, but to call it forth, to enlarge its range and its powers. It admits of endless developement. It is the last truth which should remain stationary. It ought to be so explored and so expressed as to take the highest place in a nation's literature, as to exalt and purify all other literature. From these remarks it will be seen that the efficacy which we have ascribed to literary or intellectual influence in the work of human improvement is consistent with the supreme importance of moral and religious truth.

If we have succeeded in conveying the impressions which we have aimed to make, our readers are now prepared to inquire with interest into the condition and prospects of literature among ourselves. Do we possess, indeed, what may be called a national literature? Have we produced eminent writers in the various departments of intellectual effort? Are our chief resources of instruction and literary enjoyment furnished from ourselves? We regret that the reply to these questions is so obvious. The few standard works which we have produced and which promise to live can hardly, by any courtesy, be denominated a national literature. On this point, if marks and proofs of our real condition were needed, we should find them in the current apologies for our deficiencies. Our writers are accustomed to plead in our excuse our youth, the necessities of a newly settled country, and the direction of our best talents to practical life. Be the pleas sufficient or not, one thing they prove, and that is, our consciousness of having failed to make important contributions to the interests of the intellect. We have few names to place by the side of the great names in science and literature on the other side of the ocean. We want those lights which make a country conspicuous at a distance. Let it not be said that European envy denies our just claims. In an age like this, when the literary world forms a great family and the products of mind are circulated more rapidly than those of machinery, it is a nation's own fault if its name be not pronounced with honor beyond itself. We have ourselves heard, and delighted to hear, beyond the Alps, our country designated as the land of Franklin. This name had scaled that mighty barrier and made us known where our institutions and modes of life were hardly better understood than those of the natives of our forests.

We are accustomed to console ourselves for the absence of a commanding literature by urging our superiority to other nations in our institutions for the diffusion of elementary knowledge through all classes of the community. We have here just cause for boasting, though perhaps less than we imagine. That there are gross deficiencies in our common schools, and that the amount of knowledge which they communicate, when compared with the time spent in its acquisition, is lamentably small, the community begin to feel. There is a crying need for a higher and more quickening kind of instruction than the laboring part of society have yet received, and we rejoice that the cry begins to be heard. But allowing our elementary institutions to be ever so perfect, we confess that they do not satisfy us. We want something more. A dead level of intellect, even if it should rise above what is common in other nations, would not answer our wishes and hopes for our country. We want great minds to be formed among us, minds which shall be felt afar, and through which we may act on the world. We want the human intellect to do its utmost here. We want this people to obtain a claim on the gratitude of the human race by adding strength to the foundations and fulness and splendor to the developement of moral and religious truth; by originality of thought, by discoveries of science, and by contributions to the refining pleasures of taste and imagination.

With these views we do and must lament that, however we surpass other nations in providing for and spreading elementary instruction, we fall behind many in provision for the liberal training of the intellect, for forming great scholars, for communicating that profound knowledge and that thirst for higher truths which can alone originate a commanding literature. The truth ought to be known. There is among us much superficial knowledge but little severe, persevering research; little of that consuming passion for new truth which makes outward things worthless; little resolute devotion to a high intellectual culture. There is nowhere a literary atmosphere or such an accumulation of literary influence as determines the whole strength of the mind to its own enlargement and to the manifestation of itself in enduring forms. Few among us can be said to have followed out any great subject of thought patiently, laboriously, so as to know thoroughly what others have discovered and taught concerning it, and thus to occupy a ground from which new views may be gained. Of course exceptions are to be found. This country has produced original and profound thinkers. We have named Franklin, and we may name Edwards, one of the greatest men of his age, though unhappily his mind was lost, in a great degree, to literature and, we fear, to religion, by vassalage to a false theology. His work on the Will throws, indeed, no light on human nature and, notwithstanding the nobleness of the subject, gives no great or elevated thoughts; but as a specimen of logical acuteness and controversial power, it certainly ranks in the very highest class of metaphysical writings. We might also name living authors who do honor to their country. Still, we must say, we chiefly prize what has been done among us as a promise of higher and more extensive effort. Patriotism as well as virtue forbids us to burn incense to national vanity. The truth should be seen and felt. In an age of great intellectual activity, we rely chiefly for intellectual excitement and enjoyment on foreign minds, nor is our own mind felt abroad. Whilst clamoring against dependence on European manufactures, we contentedly rely on Europe for the nobler and more important fabrics of the intellect. We boast of our political institutions and receive our chief teachings, books, impressions, from the school of monarchy. True, we labor under disadvantages. But if our liberty deserve the praise which it receives, it is more than a balance for these. We believe that it is. We believe that it does open to us an indefinite intellectual progress. Did we not so regard it, we should value it little. If hereditary governments minister most to the growth of the mind, better restore them than to cling to a barren freedom. Let us not expose liberty to this reproach. Let us prove, by more generous provisions for the diffusion of elementary knowledge, for the training of great minds, and for the joint culture of the moral and intellectual powers, that we are more and more instructed by freedom in the worth and greatness of human nature and in the obligation of contributing to its strength and glory.

We have spoken of the condition of our literature. We now proceed to the consideration of the causes which obstruct its advancement; and we are immediately struck by one so prevalent as to deserve distinct notice. We refer to the common doctrine that we need, in this country, useful knowledge rather than profound, extensive, and elegant literature, and that this last, if we covet it, may be imported from abroad in such variety and abundance as to save us the necessity of producing it among ourselves. How far are these opinions just? This question we purpose to answer.

That useful knowledge should receive our first and chief care, we mean not to dispute. But in our views of utility, we may differ from some who take this position. There are those who confine this term to the necessaries and comforts of life and to the means of producing them. And is it true that we need no knowledge but that which clothes and feeds us? Is it true that all studies may be dispensed with but such as teach us to act on matter and to turn it to our use? Happily, human nature is too stubborn to yield to this narrow utility. It is interesting to observe how the very mechanical arts, which are especially designed to minister to the necessities and comforts of life, are perpetually passing these limits; how they disdain to stop at mere convenience. A large and increasing proportion of mechanical labor is given to the gratification of an elegant taste. How simple would be the art of building if it limited itself to the construction of a comfortable shelter. How many ships should we dismantle and how many busy trades put to rest were dress and furniture reduced to the standard of convenience. This 'utility' would work great changes in town and country, would level to the dust the wonders of architecture, would annihilate the fine arts, and blot out innumerable beauties which the hand of taste has spread over the face of the earth. Happily, human nature is too strong for the utilitarian. It cannot satisfy itself with the convenient. No passion unfolds itself sooner than the love of the ornamental. The savage decorates his person and the child is more struck with the beauty than the uses of its raiment. So far from limiting ourselves to convenient food and raiment, we enjoy but little a repast which is not arranged with some degree of order and taste, and a man who should consult comfort alone in his wardrobe would find himself an unwelcome guest in circles which he would very reluctantly forego. We are aware that the propensity to which we have referred often breaks out in extravagance and ruinous luxury. We know that the love of ornament is often vitiated by vanity and that when so perverted, it impairs, sometimes destroys, the soundness and simplicity of the mind and the relish for true glory. Still, it teaches, even in its excesses, that the idea of beauty is an indestructible principle of our nature, and this single truth is enough to put us on our guard against vulgar notions of utility.

We have said that we prize, as highly as any, useful knowledge. But by this we mean knowledge which answers and ministers to our complex and various nature; we mean that which is useful, not only to the animal man, but to the intellectual, moral, and religious man; useful to a being of spiritual faculties whose happiness is to be found in their free and harmonious exercise. We grant that there is a primary necessity for that information and skill by which subsistence is earned and life is preserved; for it is plain that we must live in order to act and improve. But life is the means; action and improvement the end; and who will deny that the noblest utility belongs to that knowledge by which the chief purpose of our creation is accomplished? According to these views, a people should honor and cultivate, as unspeakably useful, that literature which corresponds to and calls forth the highest faculties; which expresses and communicates energy of thought, fruitfulness of invention, force of moral purpose, a thirst for the true, and a delight in the beautiful. According to these views, we attach special importance to those branches of literature which relate to human nature and which give it a consciousness of its own powers. History has a noble use, for it shows us human beings in various and opposite conditions, in their strength and weakness, in their progress and relapses, and thus reveals the causes and means by which the happiness and virtue of the race may be enlarged. Poetry is useful, by touching deep springs in the human soul, by giving voice to its more delicate feelings, by breathing out and making more intelligible, the sympathy which subsists between the mind and the outward universe, by creating beautiful forms or manifestations for great moral truths. Above all, that higher philosophy which treats of the intellectual and moral constitution of man, of the foundation of knowledge, of duty, of perfection, of our relations to the spiritual world, and especially to God; this has a usefulness so peculiar as to throw other departments of knowledge into obscurity; and a people among whom this does not find honor has little ground to boast of its superiority to uncivilized tribes. It will be seen from these remarks that utility, with us, has a broad meaning. In truth, we are slow to condemn as useless any researches or discoveries of original and strong minds, even when we discern in them no bearing on any interests of mankind;

for all truth is of a prolific nature and has connexions not immediately perceived; and it may be that what we call vain speculations, may, at no distant period, link themselves with some new facts or theories, and guide a profound thinker to the most important results. The ancient mathematician, when absorbed in solitary thought, little imagined that his theorems, after the lapse of ages, were to be applied by the mind of Newton to the solution of the mysteries of the universe, and not only to guide the astronomer through the heavens, but the navigator through the pathless ocean. For ourselves we incline to hope much from truths, which are particularly decried as useless; for the noblest and most useful truth is of an abstract or universal nature; and yet the abstract, though susceptible of infinite application, is generally, as we know, opposed to the practical.

We maintain that a people which has any serious purpose of taking a place among improved communities should studiously promote within itself every variety of intellectual exertion. It should resolve strenuously to be surpassed by none. It should feel that mind is the creative power through which all the resources of nature are to be turned to account, and by which a people is to spread its influence and establish the noblest form of empire. It should train within itself men able to understand and to use whatever is thought and discovered over the whole earth. The whole mass of human knowledge should exist among a people, not in neglected libraries, but in its higher minds. Among its most cherished institutions should be those which will insure to it ripe scholars, explorers of ancient learning, profound historians and mathematicians, intellectual laborers devoted to physical and moral science and to the creation of a refined and beautiful literature.

Let us not be misunderstood. We have no desire to rear in our country a race of pedants, of solemn triflers, of laborious commentators on the mysteries of a Greek accent or a rusty coin. We would have men explore antiquity, not to bury themselves in its dust, but to learn its spirit, and so to commune with its superior minds as to accumulate on the present age the influences of whatever was great and wise in former times. What we want is, that those among us whom God has gifted to comprehend whatever is now known and to rise to new truths, may find aids and institutions to fit them for their high calling, and may become at once springs of a higher intellectual life to their own country, and joint workers with the great of all nations and times in carrying forward their race.

We know that it will be said that foreign scholars, bred under institutions which this country cannot support, may do our intellectual work and send us books and learning to meet our wants. To this we have much to answer. In the first place, we reply that to avail ourselves of the higher literature of other nations, we must place ourselves on a level with them. The products of foreign machinery we can use, without any portion of the skill which produced them. But works of taste and genius and profound investigations of philosophy can only be estimated and enjoyed through a culture and power corresponding to that from which they sprung.

In the next place, we maintain that it is an immense gain to a people to have in its own bosom, among its own sons, men of distinguished intellect. Such men give a spring and life to a community by their presence, their society, their fame; and what deserves remark, such men are nowhere so felt as in a republic like our own; for here the different classes of society flow together and act powerfully on each other, and a free communication, elsewhere unknown, is established between the gifted few and the many. It is one of the many good fruits of liberty that it increases the diffusiveness of intellect; and accordingly a free country is above all others false to itself in withholding from its superior minds the means of enlargement.

We next observe, and we think the observation important, that the facility with which we receive the literature of foreign countries, instead of being a reason for neglecting our own, is a strong motive for its cultivation. We mean not to be paradoxical, but we believe that it would be better to admit no books from abroad than to make them substitutes for our own intellectual activity. The more we receive from other countries, the greater the need of an original literature. A people into whose minds the thoughts of foreigners are poured perpetually needs an energy within itself to resist, to modify this mighty influence, and without it, will inevitably sink under the worst bondage, will become intellectually tame and enslaved. We have certainly no desire to complete our restrictive system by adding to it a literary non-intercourse law. We rejoice in the increasing intellectual connexion between this country and the old world. But sooner would we rupture it than see our country sitting passively at the feet of foreign teachers. Better have no literature than form ourselves unresistingly on a foreign one. The true sovereigns of a country are those who determine its mind, its modes of thinking, its tastes, its principles; and we cannot consent to lodge this sovereignty in the hands of strangers. A country, like an individual, has dignity and power only in proportion as it is self-formed. There is a great stir to secure to ourselves the manufacturing of our own clothing. We say, let others spin and weave for us, but let them not think for us. A people whose government and laws are nothing but the embodying of public opinion should jealously guard this opinion against foreign dictation. We need a literature to counteract and to use wisely the literature which we import. We need an inward power proportionate to that which is exerted on us as the means of self-subsistence. It is peculiarly true of a people whose institutions demand for their support a free and bold spirit that they should be able to subject to a manly and independent criticism, whatever comes from abroad. These views seem to us to deserve serious attention. We are more and more a reading people. Books are already among the most powerful influences here. The question is, Shall Europe, through these, fashion us after its pleasure? Shall America be only an echo of what is thought and written under the aristocracies beyond the ocean?

Another view of the subject is this. A foreign literature will always, in a measure, be foreign. It has sprung from the soul of another people which, however like, is still not our own soul. Every people has much in its own character and feelings which can only be embodied by its own writers, and which, when transfused through literature, makes it touching and true, like the voice of our earliest friend.

We now proceed to an argument in favor of native literature which, if less obvious, is, we believe, not less sound than those now already adduced. We have hitherto spoken of literature as the expression, the communication of the higher minds in a community. We now add, that it does much more than is commonly supposed to *form* such minds so that without it, a people wants one of the chief means of educating or perfecting talent and genius. One of the great laws of our nature, and a law singularly important to social beings, is, that the intellect enlarges and strengthens itself by expressing worthily its best views. In this, as in other respects, it is more blessed to give than to receive. Superior minds are formed, not merely by solitary thought, but almost as much by communication. Great thoughts are never fully possessed till he who has conceived them, has given them fit utterance. One of the noblest and most invigorating labors of genius is to clothe its conceptions in clear and glorious forms, to give them existence in other souls. Thus literature creates, as well as manifests, intellectual power, and without it, the highest minds will never be summoned to the most invigorating action.

We doubt whether a man ever brings his faculties to bear with their whole force on a subject until he writes upon it for the instruction or gratification of others. To place it clearly before others, he feels the necessity of viewing it more vividly himself. By attempting to seize his thoughts and fix them in an enduring form, he finds them vague and unsatisfactory to a degree which he did not suspect, and toils for a precision and harmony of views of which he never before felt the need. He places his subject in new lights; submits it to a searching analysis; compares and connects with it his various knowledge; seeks for it new illustrations and analogies; weighs objections, and through these processes often arrives at higher truths than he first aimed to illustrate. Dim conceptions grow bright. Glorious thoughts which had darted as meteors through the mind are arrested, and gradually shine with a sunlike splendor, with prolific energy, on the intellect and heart. It is one of the chief distinctions of a great mind that it is prone to rush into twilight regions and to catch faint glimmerings of distant and unbounded prospects; and nothing perhaps aids it more to pierce the shadows which surround it, than the labor to unfold to other minds the indistinct conceptions which have dawned on its own. Even where composition yields no such fruits, it is still a great intellectual help. It always favors comprehensive and systematical views. The laborious distribution of a great subject so as to assign to each part or topic its just position and due proportion is singularly fitted to give compass and persevering force of thought.

If we confine ourselves simply to the consideration of style, we shall have reason to think that a people among whom this is neglected wants one important intellectual aid. In this, great power is exerted, and by exertion increased. To the multitude, indeed, language seems so natural an instrument that to use it with clearness and energy seems no great effort. It is framed, they think, to the writer's hand, and so continually employed as to need little thought or skill. But in nothing is the creative power of a gifted writer seen more than in his style. True, his words may be found in the dictionary. But there they lie disjointed and dead. What a wonderful life does he breathe into them by compacting them into his sentences. Perhaps he uses no term which has not been hackneyed by ordinary writers; and yet with these vulgar materials what miracles does he achieve. What a world of thought does he condense into a phrase. By new combinations of common words, what delicate hues or what a blaze of light does he pour over his subject. Power of style depends very little on the structure or copiousness of the language which the writer of genius employs, but chiefly, if not wholly, on his own mind. The words arranged in his dictionary, are no more fitted to depict his thoughts than the block of marble in the sculptor's shop to show forth the conceptions which are dawning in his mind. Both are inert materials. The power which pervades them comes from the soul; and the same creative energy is manifested in the production of a noble style as in extracting beautiful forms from the lifeless stone. How unfaithful, then, is a nation to its own intellect, in which grace and force of style receive no culture.

The remarks now made on the importance of literature as a means of educating talent and genius, we are aware, do not apply equally to all subjects or kinds of knowledge. In the exact or physical sciences, a man may acquire much without composition, and may make discoveries without registering them. Even here, however, we believe that, by a systematic developement of his views in a luminous style, he will bring great aid to his own faculties as well as to others'. It is on the vast subjects of morals and human nature that the mind especially strengthens itself by elaborate composition; and these, let it be remembered, form the staple of the highest literature. Moral truth, under which we include everything relating to mind and character, is of a refined and subtle as well as elevated nature, and requires the joint and full exercise of discrimination, invention, imagination, and sensibility, to give it effectual utterance. A writer who would make it visible and powerful must strive to join an austere logic to a fervent eloquence; must place it in various lights; must create for it interesting forms; must wed it to beauty; must illuminate it by similitudes and contrasts; must show its correspondence with the outward world, perhaps must frame for it a vast machinery of fiction. How invigorating are these efforts! Yet it is only in writing, in elaborate composition, that they are deliberately called forth and sustained, and without literature they would almost cease. It may be said of many truths that greater intellectual energy is required to express them with effect than to conceive them; so that a nation which does not encourage this expression impoverishes, so far, its own mind. Take for example, Shakspeare's Hamlet. This is a developement of a singularly interesting view of human nature. It shows us a mind to which life is a burden; in which the powers of meditation and feeling are disproportioned to the active powers; which sinks under its own weight, under the consciousness of wanting energies commensurate with its visions of good, with its sore trials, and with the solemn task which is laid upon it. To conceive clearly this form of human nature shows indeed the genius of the writer. But what a new power is required to bring it out in such a drama as Shakspeare's; to give it life and action; to invent for it circumstances and subordinate characters fitted to call it forth; to give it tones of truth and nature; to show the hues which it casts over all the objects of thought. This intellectual energy we all perceive; and this was not merely *manifested* in Shakspeare's work, but without such a work, it would not have been awakened. His invention would have slumbered had he not desired to give forth his mind in a visible and enduring form. Thus literature is the nurse of genius. Through this, genius learns its own strength and continually accumulates it; and of course, in a country without literature, genius, however liberally bestowed by the Creator, will languish and will fail to fulfil its great duty of quickening the mass amidst which it lives.

We come now to our last, and what we deem a weighty argument in favor of a native literature. We desire and would cherish it because we hope from it important aids to the cause of truth and human nature. We believe that a literature springing up in this new soil would bear new fruits and, in some respects, more precious fruits than are elsewhere produced. We know that our hopes may be set down to the account of that national vanity which, with too much reason, is placed by foreigners among our besetting sins. But we speak from calm and deliberate conviction. We are inclined to believe that, as a people, we occupy a position from which the great subjects of literature may be viewed more justly than from those which most other nations hold. Undoubtedly we labor under disadvantages. We want the literary apparatus of Europe; her libraries, her universities, her learned institutions, her race of professed scholars, her spots consecrated by the memory of sages, and a thousand stirring associations which hover over ancient nurseries of learning. But the mind is not a local power. Its spring is within itself, and under the inspiration of liberal and high feeling, it may attain and worthily express nobler truth than outward helps could reveal.

The great distinction of our country is, that we enjoy some peculiar advantages for understanding our own nature. Man is the great subject of literature, and juster and profounder views of man may be expected here than elsewhere. In Europe, political and artificial distinctions have, more or less, triumphed over and obscured our common nature. In Europe, we meet kings, nobles, priests, peasants. How much rarer is it to meet *men*; by which we mean, human beings conscious of their own nature and conscious of the utter worthlessness of all outward distinctions compared with what is treasured up in their own souls. Man does not value himself as man. It is for his blood, his rank, or some artificial distinction, and not for the attributes of humanity that he holds himself in respect. The institutions of the old world all tend to throw obscurity over what we most need to know, and that is the worth and claims of a human being. We know that great improvements in this respect are going on abroad. Still the many are too often postponed to the few. The mass of men are regarded as instruments to work with, as materials to be shaped for the use of their superiors. That consciousness of our own nature which contains, as a germ, all noble thoughts, which teaches us at once self-respect and respect for others, and which binds us to God by filial sentiment and hope, this has been repressed, kept down by establishments founded in force; and literature, in all its departments, bears, we think, the traces of this inward degradation. We conceive that our position favors a juster and profounder estimate of human nature. We mean not to boast, but there are fewer obstructions to that moral consciousness, that consciousness of humanity, of which we have spoken. Man is not hidden from us by as many disguises as in the old world. The essential equality of all human beings, founded on the possession of a spiritual, progressive, immortal nature, is, we hope, better understood; and nothing more than this single conviction is needed to work the mightiest changes in every province of human life and of human thought.

We have stated what seems to us our most important distinction. But our position has other advantages. The mere circumstance of its being a new one gives reason to hope for some new intellectual activity, some fresher views of nature and life. We are not borne down by the weight of antiquated institutions, time-hallowed abuses, and the remnants of feudal barbarism. The absence of a religious establishment is an immense gain as far as originality of mind is in question; for an establishment, however advantageous in other respects, is, by its nature, hostile to discovery and progress. To keep the mind where it is, to fasten the notions of one age on all future time, is its aim and proper business; and if it happened, as has generally been the case, to grow up in an age of strife and passion when, as history demonstrates, the church was overrun with error, it cannot but perpetuate darkness and mental bondage. Among us, intellect, though far from being free, has broken some of the chains of other countries, and is more likely, we conceive, to propose to itself its legitimate object, truth, everlasting and universal truth.

We have no thought of speaking contemptuously of the literature of the old world. It is our daily nutriment. We feel our debt to be immense to the glorious company of pure and wise minds which in foreign lands have bequeathed us in writing their choicest thoughts and holiest feelings. Still we feel that all existing literature has been produced under influences which have necessarily mixed with it much error and corruption, and that the whole of it ought to pass, and must pass, under rigorous review. For example, we think that the history of the human race is to be rewritten. Men imbued with the prejudices which thrive under aristocracies and state religions cannot understand it. Past ages, with their great events, and great men are to undergo, we think, a new trial and to yield new results. It is plain that history is already viewed under new aspects, and we believe that the true principles for studying and writing it are to be unfolded here, at least as rapidly as in other countries. It seems to us that in literature an immense work is yet to be done. The most interesting questions to mankind are yet in debate. Great principles are yet to be settled in criticism, in morals, in politics; and above all, the true character of religion is to be rescued from the disguises and corruptions of ages. We want a reformation. We want a literature in which genius will pay supreme, if not undivided homage, to truth and virtue; in which the childish admiration of what has been called greatness will give place to a wise moral judgment; which will breathe reverence for the mind and elevating thoughts of God. The part which this country is to bear in this great intellectual reform, we presume not to predict. We feel, however, that if true to itself, it will have the glory and happiness of giving new impulses to the human mind. This is our cherished hope. We should have no heart to encourage native literature did we not hope that it would become instinct with a new spirit. We cannot admit the thought that this country is to be only a repetition of the old world. We delight to believe that God in the fulness of time has brought a new continent to light in order that the human mind should move here with a new freedom, should frame new social institutions, should explore new paths, and reap new harvests. We are accustomed to estimate nations by their creative energies, and we shall blush for our country if, in circumstances so peculiar, original, and creative, it shall satisfy itself with a passive reception and mechanical reiteration of the thoughts of strangers.

We have now completed our remarks on the importance of a native literature. The next great topic is the means of producing it; and here our limits forbid us to enlarge; yet we cannot pass it over in silence. A primary and essential means of the improvement of our literature is, that, as a people, we should feel its value, should desire it, should demand it, should encourage it, and should give it a hearty welcome. It will come if called for, and under this conviction, we have now labored to create a want for it in the community. We say that we must call for it; by which we mean, not merely that we must invite it by good wishes and kind words, but must make liberal provision for intellectual education. We must enlarge our literary institutions, secure more extensive and profound teaching, and furnish helps and resources to men of superior talent for continued, laborious research. As yet, intellectual labor devoted to a thorough investigation and a full developement of great subjects is almost unknown among us; and without it, we shall certainly rear few lasting monuments of thought. We boast of our primary schools. We want universities worthy of the name where a man of genius and literary zeal may possess himself of all that is yet known and may strengthen himself by intercourse with kindred minds. We know it will be said that we cannot afford these. But it is not so. We are rich enough for ostentation, for intemperance, for luxury. We can lavish millions on fashion, on furniture, on dress, on our palaces, on our pleasures; but we have nothing to spend for the mind. Where lies our poverty? In the purse, or in the soul?

We have spoken of improved institutions as essential to an improved literature. We beg, however, not to be misunderstood as if these were invested with a creating power, or would necessarily yield the results which we desire. They are the means, not causes of advancement. Literature depends on individual genius, and this, though fostered, cannot be created by outward helps. No human mechanism can produce original thought. After all the attempts to explain by education the varieties of intellect, we are compelled to believe that minds, like all the other products of nature, have original and indestructible differences, that they are not exempted from that great and beautiful law which joins with strong resemblances as strong diversities; and, of consequence, we believe, that the men who are to be the lights of the world bring with them their commission and power from God. Still, whilst institutions cannot create, they may and do unfold genius; and for want of them, great minds often slumber or run to waste, whilst a still larger class who want genius but possess admirable powers, fail of that culture through which they might enjoy and approach their more gifted brethren.

A people, as we have said, are to give aid to literature by founding wise and enlarged institutions. They may do much more. They may exert a nobler patronage. By cherishing in their own breasts the love of truth, virtue, and freedom, they may do much to nurse and kindle genius in its favored possessors. There is a constant reaction between a community and the great minds which spring up within it, and they form one another. In truth, great minds are developed more by the spirit and character of the people to which they belong than by all other causes. Thus, a free spirit, a thirst for new and higher knowledge in a community, does infinitely more for literature than the most splendid benefactions under despotism. A nation under any powerful excitement becomes fruitful of talent. Among a people called to discuss great questions, to contend for great interests, to make great sacrifices for the public weal, we always find new and unsuspected energies of thought brought out. A mercenary, selfish, luxurious, sensual people, toiling only to secure the pleasures of sloth, will often communicate their own softness and baseness to the superior minds which dwell among them. In this impure atmosphere, the celestial spark burns dim, and well will it be, if God's great gift of genius be not impiously prostituted to lust and crime.

In conformity with the views now stated, we believe that literature is to be carried forward, here and elsewhere, chiefly by some new and powerful impulses communicated to society; and it is a question naturally suggested by this discussion, from what impulse, principle, excitement, the highest action of the mind may now be expected. When we look back, we see that literature has been originated and modified by a variety of principles; by patriotism and national feeling, by reverence for antiquity, by the spirit of innovation, by enthusiasm, by scepticism, by the passion for fame, by romantic love, and by political and religious convulsions. Now we do not expect from these causes, any higher action of the mind than they have yet produced. Perhaps most of them have spent their force. The very improvements of society seem to forbid the manifestation of their former energy. For example the patriotism of antiquity and the sexual love of chivalrous ages, which inspired so much of the old literature, are now seen to be feverish and vicious excesses of natural principles, and have gone, we trust, never to return.

Are we asked then to what impulse or power we look for a higher literature than has yet existed. We answer, to a new action or developement of the religious principle. This remark will probably surprise not a few of our readers. It seems to us that the energy with which this principle is to act on the intellect is hardly suspected. Men identify religion with superstition, with fanaticism, with the common forms of Christianity; and seeing it arrayed against intellect, leagued with oppression, fettering inquiry, and incapable of being blended with the sacred dictates of reason and conscience, they see in its progress only new encroachments on free and enlightened thinking. Still, man's relation to God is the great quickening truth, throwing all other truths into insignificance, and a truth which, however obscured and paralysed by the many errors which ignorance and fraud have hitherto linked with it, has ever been a chief spring of human improvement. We look to it as the true life of the intellect. No man can be just to himself, can comprehend his own existence, can put forth all his powers with an heroic confidence, can deserve to be the guide and inspirer of other minds, till he has risen to communion with the Supreme Mind; till he feels his filial connexion with the Universal Parent; till he regards himself as the recipient and minister of the Infinite Spirit; till he feels his consecration to the ends which religion unfolds; till he rises above human opinion and is moved by a higher impulse than fame.

From these remarks it will be seen, that our chief hopes of an improved literature rest on our hopes of an improved religion. From the prevalent theology, which has come down to us from the dark ages, we hope nothing. It has done its best. All that can grow up under its sad shade has already been brought forth. It wraps the Divine nature and human nature in impenetrable gloom. It overlays Christianity with technical, arbitrary dogmas. True faith is of another lineage. It comes from the same source with reason, conscience, and our best affections, and is in harmony with them all. True faith is essentially a moral conviction; a confidence in the reality and immutableness of moral distinctions; a confidence in disinterested virtue or in spiritual excellence as the supreme good; a confidence in God as its fountain and almighty friend, and in Jesus Christ as having lived and died to breathe it into the soul; a confidence in its power, triumphs, and immortality; a confidence through which outward changes, obstructions, disasters, sufferings, are overcome, or rather made instruments of perfection. Such a faith, unfolded freely and powerfully, must 'work mightily' on the intellect as well as on practice. By revealing to us the supreme purpose of the Creator, it places us, as it were, in the centre of the universe, from which the harmonies, true relations, and brightest aspects of things are discerned. It unites calmness and enthusiasm, and the concord of these seemingly hostile elements is essential to the full and healthy action of the creative powers of the soul. It opens the eye to beauty and the heart to love. Literature, under this influence, will become more ingenuous and single-hearted; will penetrate farther into the soul; will find new interpretations of nature and life; will breathe a martyr's love of truth, tempered with a never failing charity; and, whilst sympathizing with all human suffering, will still be pervaded by a healthful cheerfulness, and will often break forth in tones of irrepressible joy, responsive to that happiness which fills God's universe.

We cannot close our remarks on the means of an improved literature without offering one suggestion. We earnestly recommend to our educated men a more extensive acquaintance with the intellectual labors of continental Europe. Our reading is confined too much to English books, and especially to the more recent publications of Great Britain. In this we err. We ought to know the different modes of viewing and discussing great subjects in different nations. We should be able to compare the writings of the highest minds in a great variety of circumstances. Nothing can favor more our own intellectual independence and activity. Let English literature be ever so fruitful and profound, we should still impoverish ourselves by making it our sole nutriment. We fear, however, that at the present moment English books want much which we need. The intellect of that nation is turned now to what are called practical and useful subjects. Physical science goes forward, and what is very encouraging, it is spread with unexampled zeal through all classes of the community. Abuses of government, of the police, of the penal code, of charity, of poor laws, and corn laws are laboriously explored. General education is improved. Science is applied to the arts with brilliant success. We see much good in progress. But we find little profound or fervid thinking, expressed in the higher forms of literature. The noblest subjects of the intellect receive little attention. We see an almost total indifference to intellectual and moral science. In England there is a great want of philosophy, in the true sense of that word. If we examine her reviews, in which much of the intellectual power of the nation is expended, we meet perpetually a jargon of criticism which shows a singular want of great and general principles in estimating works of art. We have no ethical work of any living English writer to be compared with that of Degerando, entitled, '*Du Moral Perfectionnement;*' and although we have little respect for the rash generalizations of the bold and eloquent Cousin, yet the interest which his metaphysics awaken in Paris is in our estimation a better presage than the lethargy which prevails on such topics in England. In these remarks we have no desire to depreciate the literature of England which, taken as a whole, we regard as the noblest monument of the human mind. We rejoice in our descent from England and esteem our free access to her works of science and genius as among our high privileges. Nor do we feel as if her strength were spent. We see no wrinkles on her brow, no decrepitude in her step. At this moment she has authors, especially in poetry and fiction, whose names are 'familiar in our mouths as household words,' and who can never perish but with her language. Still we think that at present her intellect is laboring more for herself than for mankind, and that our scholars, if they would improve our literature, should cultivate an intimacy not only with that of England, but of continental Europe.

We have now finished our remarks on the importance
and means of an improved literature among ourselves.
Are we asked what we hope in this particular. We answer, much. We see reasons for anticipating an increased
and more efficient direction of talent to this object. But
on these we cannot enlarge. There is, however, one ground
of expectation, to which we will call a moment's attention. We apprehend that literature is to make progress
through an important change in society which civilization and good institutions are making more and more
apparent. It seems to us that, through these causes, political life is less and less regarded as the only or chief
sphere for superior minds, and that influence and honor
are more and more accumulated in the hands of literary
and thinking men. Of consequence more and more of the
intellect of communities is to be drawn to literature. The
distinction between antiquity and the present times, in
respect to the importance attached to political life, seems
to us striking; and it is not an accidental difference, but
founded on permanent causes which are to operate with
increased power. In ancient times, everything abroad and
at home threw men upon the public and generated an
intense thirst for political power. On the contrary, the
improvements of later periods incline men to give importance to literature. For example, the instability of the
ancient republics, the unsettled relations of the different
classes of society, the power of demagogues and orators,
the intensity of factions, the want of moral and religious
restraints, the want of some regular organ for expressing
the public mind, the want of precedents and precise laws
for the courts of justice, these and other circumstances
gave to the ancient citizen a feeling as if revolutions and
convulsions were inseparable from society, turned his mind
with unremitting anxiety to public affairs, and made a
participation of political power an important, if not an
essential means of personal safety.—Again, the ancient citizen had no home, in our sense of the word. He lived in the
market, the forum, the place of general resort, and of
course his attention was very much engrossed by affairs
of state.—Again, religion, which now more than all things

throws a man upon himself, was in ancient times a public concern and turned men to political life. The religion of the heart and closet was unknown. The relation of the gods to particular states was their most prominent attribute, and to conciliate their favor to the community the chief end of worship. Accordingly religion consisted chiefly in public and national rites. In Rome the highest men in the state presided at the altar, and adding to their other titles that of Supreme Pontiff, performed the most solemn functions of the priesthood. Thus the whole strength of the religious principle was turned into political channels. The gods were thought to sustain no higher office than a political one, and of consequence this was esteemed the most glorious for men.—Once more, in ancient times political rank was vastly more efficient, whether for good or for evil, than at present, and of consequence was the object of a more insatiable ambition. It was almost the only way of access to the multitude. The public man held a sway over opinion, over his country, perhaps over foreign states, now unknown. It is the influence of the press and of good institutions to reduce the importance of the man of office. In proportion as private individuals can act on the public mind; in proportion as a people read, think, and have the means of expressing and enforcing their opinions; in proportion as laws become fixed, known, and sanctioned by the moral sense of the community; in proportion as the interests of the state, the principles of administration, and all public measures, are subjected to free and familiar discussion, government becomes a secondary influence. The power passes into the hands of those who think, write, and spread their minds far and wide. Accordingly literature is to become more and more the instrument of swaying men, of doing good, of achieving fame. The contrast between ancient and modern times, in the particulars now stated, is too obvious to need illustration, and our great inference is equally clear. The vast improvements which in the course of ages have taken place in social order, in domestic life, in religion, in knowledge, all conspire to one result, all tend to introduce other and higher influences than political power, and to give to that form of intellectual effort which we call literature, dominion over human affairs. Thus truth, we apprehend, is more and more felt, and from its influence, joined with our peculiar condition and free institutions, we hope for our country the happiness and glory of a pure, deep, rich, beautiful, and ennobling literature.

PART IV

The American Man of Letters
1819–1837

While the debate on literary nationalism billowed and
rolled through the first two decades of the nineteenth
century, a native American literature was gradually coming into being. The early years of the century saw the
further expansion of popular and higher education and
the development of instruments of culture. Bookstores
and libraries were set up in most of the larger communities, theatres became more numerous, and books and
magazines, both domestic and imported, became more
available. The times were getting ready for the professional American writer and his readers.

One does not normally look for well-formulated aesthetic philosophies to professional novelists, dramatists,
or even essayists or poets, unless they are also literary
critics; but many authors discuss at length their own
aims, methods, and accomplishments as well as their
difficulties. The earliest successful men of letters were
no exceptions to this rule. For all of them, the primary
problem was how to express their own experience
(which was of course mainly an American one) in linguistic and literary forms and modes which had been
developed by an alien rather than a native tradition.
For some like Irving, Paulding, Cooper, and Longfellow, the problem was little more than a practical one,
motivated by varying degrees of patriotic enthusiasm;
for others, like Bryant, Poe, and Emerson, who were
all literary critics as well as creative writers, the theoretical aspects of the problem came in for varying degrees of ethical and aesthetic consideration. On the
other hand, as the documents in this volume have already demonstrated, the existence and development of
a broadly based and generally accepted concept of
literature as a major aspect of general culture helped
to provide the motivation, the underlying theory of aesthetic expression, the instruments of production and

communication, and the receptivity of a sufficiently large reading public to make possible a professional career in letters. Without the running debate on literary nationalism which the documents in this volume illustrate, the emergence of the Romantic Movement in America as an indigenous phase of our literary history would probably not have occurred.

DOCUMENT 20

Washington Irving

Washington Irving (1783–1859) probably said less and did more about American literary nationalism than any American author of his day. Except for some sly remarks on the English attitude toward America (as in this sketch), and an essay or two which were mild enough to offend no one, he sought refuge in conformity to the English literary fashion of his day and then wrote about what he pleased. That fashion was dictated by the publisher John Murray and the St. James Square group like Samuel Rogers or Tom Moore, rather than by the radicals out in Hampstead like Keats or Hunt. His first two ventures into literature, the *Salmagundi* papers, which he did with his Knickerbocker friends, and the *Knickerbocker's History of New York*, were tinged with an American freshness which his compatriots missed in his later work. "The Author's Account of Himself" (here quoted) introduces his mature literary personality, Geoffrey Crayon, Gent., the supposed author of *The Sketch Book* (1819–20). It conforms to and echoes every English essayist from Addison to Goldsmith without losing its integrity. Irving was the first American to conquer both the American and the British reading publics; this was an accomplishment. And, by a careful attention to the copyright laws of both countries, he managed to be, with intervals of statesmanship and historical writing, the first American professional man of letters.

TEXT: from the first edition (2 vols.), New York, 1819.

The Author's Account of Himself

"I am of this mind with Homer, that as the snaile that crept out of her shel was turned eftsoones into a toad, and thereby was forced to make a stoole to sit on; so the traveller that stragleth from his owne country is in a short time transformed into so monstrous a shape, that he is faine to alter his mansion with his manners, and to live where he can, not where he would."—*Lyly's Euphues.*

I was always fond of visiting new scenes, and observing strange characters and manners. Even when a mere child I began my travels, and made many tours of discovery into foreign parts and unknown regions of my native city, to the frequent alarm of my parents and the emolument of the town-crier. As I grew into boyhood, I extended the range of my observations. My holiday afternoons were spent in rambles about the surrounding country. I made myself familiar with all its places famous in history or fable. I knew every spot where a murder or robbery had been committed, or a ghost been seen. I visited the neighbouring villages, and added greatly to my stock of knowledge, by noting their habits and customs and conversing with their sages and great men. I even journeyed one long summer's day to the summit of the most distant hill, from whence I stretched my eye over many a mile of terra incognita, and was astonished to find how vast a globe I inhabited.

This rambling propensity strengthened with my years. Books of voyages and travels became my passion, and in devouring their contents, I neglected the regular exercises of the school. How wistfully would I wander about the pier heads in fine weather, and watch the parting ships, bound to distant climes—with what longing eyes would I gaze after their lessening sails, and waft myself in imagination to the ends of the earth.

Farther reading and thinking, though they brought this vague inclination into more reasonable bounds, only served to make it more decided. I visited various parts of my own country; and had I been merely a lover of fine scenery, I should have felt little desire to seek elsewhere for its gratification: for on no country have the charms of nature been more prodigally lavished. Her mighty lakes, like oceans of liquid silver; her mountains, with their bright aërial tints; her valleys, teeming with wild fertility; her tremendous cataracts, thundering in their solitudes; her boundless plains, waving with spontaneous verdure; her broad deep rivers, rolling in solemn silence to the ocean; her trackless forests, where vegetation puts forth all its magnificence; her skies, kindling with the magic of summer clouds and glorious sunshine:—no, never need an American look beyond his own country for the sublime and beautiful of natural scenery.

But Europe held forth all the charms of storied and poetical association. There were to be seen the masterpieces of art, the refinements of highly cultivated society, the quaint peculiarities of ancient and local custom. My native country was full of youthful promise; Europe was rich in the accumulated treasures of age. Her very ruins told the history of times gone by, and every mouldering stone was a chronicle. I longed to wander over the scenes of renowned achievement—to tread, as it were, in the footsteps of antiquity—to loiter about the ruined castle—to meditate on the falling tower—to escape, in short, from the commonplace realities of the present, and lose myself among the shadowy grandeurs of the past.

I had, beside all this, an earnest desire to see the great men of the earth. We have, it is true, our great men in America: not a city but has an ample share of them. I have mingled among them in my time, and been almost withered by the shade into which they cast me; for there is nothing so baleful to a small man as the shade of a great one, particularly the great man of a city. But I was anxious to see the great men of Europe; for I had read in the works of various philosophers, that all animals degenerated in America, and man among the number. A great man of Europe, therefore, thought I, must be as superior to a great man of America, as a peak of the Alps to a highland of the Hudson; and in this idea I was confirmed, by observing the comparative importance and swelling magnitude of many English travellers among us; who, I was assured, were very little people in their own country. I will visit this land of wonders, therefore, thought I, and see the gigantic race from which I am degenerated.

It has been either my good or evil lot to have my roving passion gratified. I have wandered through different countries, and witnessed many of the shifting scenes of life. I cannot say that I have studied them with the eye of a philosopher, but rather with the sauntering gaze with which humble lovers of the picturesque stroll from the window of one print shop to another; caught sometimes by the delineations of beauty, sometimes by the distortions of caricature, and sometimes by the loveliness of landscape. As it is the fashion for modern tourists to travel pencil in hand, and bring home their port folios filled with sketches, I am disposed to get up a few for the entertainment of my friends. When I look over, however, the hints and memorandums I have taken down for the purpose, my heart almost fails me to find how my idle humour has led me aside from the great objects studied by every regular traveller who would make a book. I fear I shall give equal disappointment with an unlucky landscape painter, who had travelled on the continent, but following the bent of his vagrant inclination, had sketched in nooks, and corners, and by-places. His sketch book was accordingly crowded with cottages, and landscapes, and obscure ruins; but he had neglected to paint St. Peter's, or the Coliseum; the cascade of Terni, or the bay of Naples; and had not a single glacier or volcano in his whole collection.

James Kirke Paulding

James Kirke Paulding (1778–1860), essayist and novelist, was an early friend of Washington Irving, with whom he was associated in the first series of *Salmagundi* papers (1807–8). After Irving went abroad, Paulding alone issued a second series (1819–20) in which this essay on "National Literature" appeared. His literary nationalism took the forms of direct attacks on British criticism in satires like *The Diverting History of John Bull and Brother Jonathan* (1812) as well as regional and historical novels about the upstate New York Dutch, the Kentucky pioneers, the New England Puritans, the Swedes on the Delaware, and the Revolution. A professional man of letters throughout his long life and a violently anti-British Jeffersonian agrarian, his devotion to the cause is more evident in his persistent use of American materials than in any depth of literary philosophy.

TEXT: from the collected edition of his *Works*, II, New York (1835), 265–72.

National Literature

It has been often observed by such as have attempted to account for the scarcity of romantic fiction among our native writers, that the history of the country affords few materials for such works, and offers little in its traditionary lore to warm the heart or elevate the imagination. The remark has been so often repeated that it is now pretty generally received with perfect docility as an incontrovertible truth, though it seems to me without the shadow of a foundation. It is in fact an observation that never did nor ever will apply to any nation, ancient or modern.

Wherever there are men, there will be materials for romantic adventure. In the misfortunes that befall them; in the sufferings and vicissitudes which are everywhere the lot of human beings; in the struggles to counteract fortune, and in the conflicts of the passions, in every situation of life, he who studies nature and draws his pictures from her rich and inexhaustible sources of variety, will always find enough of those characters and incidents which give a relish to works of fancy. The aid of superstition, the agency of ghosts, fairies, goblins, and all that antiquated machinery which till lately was confined to the nursery, is not necessary to excite our wonder or interest our feelings; although it is not the least of incongruities that in an age which boasts of having by its scientific discoveries dissipated almost all the materials of superstition, some of the most popular fictions should be founded upon a superstition which is now become entirely ridiculous, even among the ignorant.

The best and most perfect works of imagination appear to me to be those which are founded upon a combination of such characters as every generation of men exhibits, and such events as have often taken place in the world and will again. Such works are only fictions because the tissue of events which they record never perhaps happened in precisely the same train and to the same number of persons as are exhibited and associated in the relation. Real life is fraught with adventures to which the wildest fictions scarcely afford a parallel; and it has this special advantage over its rival, that these events, however extraordinary, can always be traced to motives, actions, and passions arising out of circumstances no way unnatural and partaking of no impossible or supernatural agency.

Hence it is that the judgment and the fancy are both equally gratified in the perusal of this class of fictions if they are skilfully conducted; while in those which have nothing to recommend them but appeals to the agency of beings in whose existence nobody believes and whose actions of course can have no alliance either with nature or probability, it is the imagination alone that is satisfied, and that only by the total subjection of every other faculty of the mind.

It must be acknowledged, however, that these probable and consistent fictions are by far the most difficult to manage. It is easy enough to bring about the most improbable, not to say impossible catastrophe by the aid of beings whose power is without limit and whose motives are inscrutable, though in my opinion it is always a proof of want of power in the writer when he is thus compelled to call upon Hercules to do what he cannot perform himself. It is either an indication that his judgment is inadequate to the arrangement of his materials and the adjustment of his plans, or that he is deficient in the invention of rational means to extricate himself from his difficulties.

On the contrary, nothing is more easy than the management of this machinery of ghosts, goblins, and fairies, who are subject neither to Longinus, Quinctilian, or Dryden (whom I look upon as the best critic of modern times); who are always within call and can be made active or passive without the trouble of putting them or the author to the inconvenience of being governed by any rational motive whatever. Events that would be extraordinary, if they were not impossible, are thus brought about in a trice without any preparatory and laborious arrangements of causes and effects, and the fiction becomes thus complete in its kind by being equally elevated beyond our comprehension and belief.

The rare and happy combination of invention, judgment, and experience, requisite to produce such a work as *Tom Jones*, is seldom twice found in the same country while thousands of mere romance-writers flourish and are forgotten in every age.

In the raw material for the latter species of fiction, it must be acknowledged this country is quite deficient. Fairies, giants, and goblins are not indigenous here, and with the exception of a few witches that were soon exterminated, our worthy ancestors brought over with them not a single specimen of Gothic or Grecian mythology. The only second-sight they possessed was founded on the solid basis of a keen recollection of the past, a rational anticipation of the future. They acknowledged no agency above that of the physical and intellectual man, except that of the Being that created him; and they relied for protection and support on their own resolute perseverance, aided by the blessings of God. But if I mistake not, there is that in the peculiarities of their character; in the motives which produced the resolution to emigrate to the wilderness; in the courage and perseverance with which they consummated this gallant enterprise; and in the wild and terrible peculiarities of their intercourse, their adventures, and their contests with the savages, amply sufficient for all the purposes of those higher works of imagination which may be called Rational Fictions.

That these materials have as yet been little more than partially interwoven into the few fictions which this country has given birth to is not owing to their being inapplicable to that purpose, but to another cause entirely. We have been misled by bad models or the suffrages of docile critics who have bowed to the influence of rank and fashion and given testimony in favour of works which their better judgment must have condemned. We have cherished a habit of looking to other nations for examples of every kind, and debased the genius of this new world by making it the ape and the tributary of that of the old. We have imitated where we might often have excelled; we have overlooked our own rich resources, and sponged upon the exhausted treasury of our empoverished neighbours; we were born rich, and yet have all our lives subsisted by borrowing. Hence it has continually occurred that those who might have gone before had they chosen a new path, have been content to come last, merely by following the old track. Many a genius that could and would have attained an equal height in some new and unexplored region of fancy has dwindled into insignificance and contempt by stooping to track some inferior spirit to whom fashion had assigned a temporary elevation. They ought to be told that though fashion may give a momentary popularity to works that neither appeal to national attachments, domestic habits, or those feelings which are the same yesterday, to-day, for ever, and everywhere, still it is not by imitation they can hope to equal any thing great. It appears to me that the young candidate for the prize of genius in the regions of invention and fancy has but one path open to fame. He cannot hope to wing his way above those immortal works that have stood the test of ages and are now with one consent recognised as specimens beyond which the intellect of man is not permitted to soar. But a noble prize is yet within his grasp, and worthy of the most aspiring ambition.

By freeing himself from a habit of servile imitation; by daring to think and feel, and express his feelings; by dwelling on scenes and events connected with our pride and our affections; by indulging in those little peculiarities of thought, feeling, and expression which belong to every nation; by borrowing from nature and not from those who disfigure or burlesque her—he may and will in time destroy the ascendency of foreign taste and opinions and elevate his own in the place of them. These causes lead to the final establishment of a national literature, and give that air and character of originality which it is sure to acquire, unless it is debased and expatriated by a habit of servile imitation.

The favourite yet almost hopeless object of my old age is to see this attempt consummated. For this purpose, it is my delight to furnish occasionally such hints as may turn the attention of those who have leisure, health, youth, genius, and opportunities, to domestic subjects on which to exercise their powers. Let them not be disheartened, even should they sink into a temporary oblivion in the outset. This country is not destined to be always behind in the race of literary glory. The time will assuredly come when that same freedom of thought and action which has given such a spur to our genius in other respects will achieve similar wonders in literature. It is then that our early specimens will be sought after with avidity, and that those who led the way in the rugged discouraging path will be honoured as we begin to honour the adventurous spirits who first sought, explored, and cleared this western wilderness.

These remarks will, we think, most especially apply to the fictions of the late Mr. Charles Brockden Brown, which are among the most vigorous and original efforts of our native literature. Indeed, it appears to us that few if any writers of the present day exceed or even approach him in richness of imagination, depth of feeling, command of language, and the faculty of exciting a powerful and permanent interest in the reader. They constitute a class of fictions standing alone by themselves; they are the product of our soil, the efforts of one of our most blameless and esteemed fellow-citizens, and they would do honour to any country. Yet they want the stamp of fashion and notoriety; they have never been consecrated by the approbation of foreign criticism; and, in all probability, a large portion of our readers are ignorant that they were ever written.

Yet we hazard little in predicting that the period is not far distant when they will be rescued from oblivion by the hand of some kindred spirit, and the people of the United States become sufficiently independent to dare to admire and to express their admiration of a writer who will leave many followers, but few equals; and whose future fame will furnish a bright contrast to the darkness in which he is now enveloped.

Henry Wadsworth Longfellow

Like Paulding, Henry Wadsworth Longfellow (1807–82) early committed himself to experimentation with American materials, and adapted native tales to the literary forms and rhythms of Chaucer, Homer, and the Finnish *Kalevala*. In his novel *Kavanagh* (1849) he justifies his ardent literary nationalism in much the same terms that he had used when, in 1825 at the age of eighteen, he delivered a graduation oration at Bowdoin on "Our Native Writers."

TEXT: from the first printing, from manuscript, in *Every Other Saturday*, I (April 12, 1884), 116–17.

Our Native Writers

To an American there is something endearing in the very sounds—Our Native Writers. Like the music of our native tongue when heard in a foreign land, they have power to kindle up within him the tender memory of his home and fireside;—and more than this, they foretell that whatever is noble and attractive in our national character will one day be associated with the sweet magic of Poetry. Is then our land to be indeed the land of song? Will it one day be rich in romantic associations? Will poetry, that hallows every scene, that renders every spot classical, and pours out on all things the soul of its enthusiasm, breathe over it that enchantment which lives in the isles of Greece, and is more than life amid the "woods, that wave o'er Delphi's steep." Yes!—and palms are to be won by our native writers!—by those that have been nursed and brought up with us in the civil and religious freedom of our country. Already has a voice been lifted up in this land, already a spirit and a love of literature are springing up in the shadow of our free political institutions.

But as yet we can boast of nothing farther than a first beginning of a national literature: a literature associated and linked in with the grand and beautiful scenery of our country—with our institutions, our manners, our customs, in a word, with all that has helped to form whatever there is peculiar to us and to the land in which we live. We cannot yet throw off our literary allegiance to Old England, we cannot yet remove from our shelves every book which is not strictly and truly American. English Literature is a great and glorious monument, built up by those master-spirits of old time that had no peers, and rising bright and beautiful until its summit is hid in the mists of antiquity.

Of the many causes which have hitherto retarded the growth of polite literature in our country, I have not time to say much. The greatest which now exists is doubtless the want of that exclusive attention which eminence in any profession so imperiously demands. Ours is an age and a country of great minds, though perhaps not of great endeavors. Poetry with us has never yet been anything but a pastime. The fault however is not so much that of our writers as of the prevalent modes of thinking which characterize our country and our times. We are a plain people that have had nothing to do with the mere pleasures and luxuries of life: and hence there has sprung up within us a quick-sightedness to the failings of literary men, and an aversion to everything that is not practical, operative, and thorough-going. But if we would ever have a national literature, our native writers must be patronized. Whatever there may be in letters, over which time shall have no power, must be "born of great endeavors," and those endeavors are the offspring of a liberal patronage. Putting off, then, what Shakspeare calls "the visage of the times," we must become hearty well-wishers to our native authors: and with them there must be a deep and thorough conviction of the glory of their calling, an utter abandonment of everything else, and a noble self-devotion to the cause of literature. We have indeed much to hope from these things: for our hearts are already growing warm towards literary adventurers, and a generous spirit has gone abroad in our land, which shall liberalize and enlighten.

In the vanity of scholarship, England has reproached us that we have no finished scholars. But there is reason for believing that men of mere learning, men of sober research and studied correctness, do not give to a nation its great name. Our very poverty in this respect will have a tendency to give a national character to our literature. Our writers will not be constantly toiling and panting after classical allusions to the vale of Tempe and the Etrurian river, nor to the Roman fountains shall

"The emulous nations of the West repair
To kindle their quenched urns, and drink fresh
spirit there."

We are thus thrown upon ourselves: and thus shall our native hills become renowned in song, like those of Greece and Italy. Every rock shall become a chronicle of storied allusions: and the tomb of the Indian prophet be as hallowed as the sepulchres of ancient kings, or the damp vault and perpetual lamp of the Saracen monarch.

Having briefly mentioned one circumstance which is retarding us in the way of our literary prosperity, I shall now mention one from which we may hope a happy and glorious issue: It is the influence of natural scenery in forming the poetical character. Genius, to be sure, must be born with a man; and it is its high prerogative to be free, limitless, irrepressible. Yet how is it moulded by the plastic hand of Nature! how are its attributes shaped and modulated, when a genius like Canova's failed in the bust of the Corsican, and amid the splendor of the French metropolis languished for the sunny skies and vine-clad hills of Italy? Men may talk of sitting down in the calm and quiet of their libraries and of forgetting, in the eloquent companionship of books, all the vain cares that beset them in the crowded thoroughfares of life: but, after all, there is nothing which so frees us from the turbulent ambition and bustle of the world, nothing which so fills the mind with great and glowing conceptions and at the same time so warms the heart with love and tenderness, as a frequent and close communion with natural scenery. The scenery of our own country, too, so rich as it is in everything beautiful and magnificent, and so full of quiet loveliness or of sublime and solitary awe, has for our eyes enchantment, for our ears an impressive and unutterable eloquence. Its language is in high mountains, and in the pleasant valleys scooped out between them, in the garniture which the fields put on, and in the blue lake asleep in the hollow of the hills. There is an inspiration, too, in the rich sky that "brightens and purples" o'er our earth when lighted up with the splendor of morning, or when the garment of the clouds comes over the setting sun.

Our poetry is not in books alone. It is in the hearts of those men whose love for the world's gain, for its business and its holiday has grown cold within them, and who have gone into the retirements of nature, and have found there that sweet sentiment, and pure devotion of feeling can spring up and live in the shadow of a low and quiet life, and amid those that have no splendor in their joys, and no parade in their griefs.

Thus shall the mind take color from things around us: from them shall there be a genuine birth of enthusiasm, a rich development of poetic feeling that shall break forth in song. Though the works of art must grow old and perish away from earth, the forms of nature shall keep forever their power over the human mind, and have their influence upon the literature of a people.

We may rejoice, then, in the hope of beauty and sublimity in our national literature, for no people are richer than we are in the treasures of nature. And well may each of us feel a glorious and high-minded pride in saying, as he looks on the hills and vales, on the woods and waters of New England,

"This is my own, my native land."

Document 23

James Fenimore Cooper

By 1828 there was probably no one in America who knew more about the total situation confronting the aspiring American author, its incentives, its possibilities, its materials, its means, and its obstacles, than James Fenimore Cooper (1789–1851). By that time he had experimented with novels of English domestic life, the American Revolution, the frontier settlement, the sea, and the wilderness life of the Indian; he was widely read and greeted with mixed criticism both at home and abroad; he was already under attack for his political and social ideas; and he had gone to Europe to broaden the education of his children and to try to arrange for the profitable foreign publication and translation of his writings. His *Notions of the Americans, Picked up by a Travelling Bachelor* of that year was a thinly disguised defense of American ideas and institutions against the attacks of British travelers and critics. His fictional device was an international club of traveling gentlemen of whom the author was one, Cooper himself was his American host in the person of John Cadwallader of upstate New York, and the addressee of these two letters was the Abbate Giromachi of Florence, Italy. He speaks here with the authority of the practitioner rather than the theorist, and his initial enthusiasm for the literary life was still running high although, as the first American to make a profession of the novel of American life, he already recognized the difficulties and problems that lay in his path.

TEXT: from the first American edition, 2 vols., Philadelphia, 1828.

FROM *Notions of the Americans*

I. LETTER #23

As respects authorship, there is not much to be said. Compared to the books that are printed and read, those of native origin are few indeed. The principal reason of this poverty of original writers is owing to the circumstance that men are not yet driven to their wits for bread. The United States are the first nation that possessed institutions and, of course, distinctive opinions of its own that was ever dependent on a foreign people for its literature. Speaking the same language as the English, and long in the habit of importing their books from the mother country, the revolution effected no immediate change in the nature of their studies or mental amusements. The works were re-printed, it is true, for the purposes of economy, but they still continued English. Had the latter nation used this powerful engine with tolerable address, I think they would have secured such an ally in this country as would have rendered their own decline not only more secure, but as illustrious as had been their rise. There are many theories entertained as to the effect produced in this country by the falsehoods and jealous calumnies which have been undeniably uttered in the mother country, by means of the press, concerning her republican descendant. It is my own opinion that, like all other ridiculous absurdities, they have defeated themselves, and that they are now more laughed at and derided, even here, than resented. By all that I can learn, twenty years ago the Americans were, perhaps, far too much disposed to receive the opinions and to adopt the prejudices of their relatives; whereas, I think it is very apparent that they are now beginning to receive them with singular distrust. It is not worth our while to enter further into this subject, except as it has had, or is likely to have, an influence on the national literature.[1]

[1] The writer might give, in proof of this opinion, one fact. He

It is quite obvious that, so far as taste and forms alone are concerned, the literature of England and that of America must be fashioned after the same models. The authors, previously to the revolution, are common property, and it is quite idle to say that the American has not just as good a right to claim Milton, and Shakspeare, and all the old masters of the language, for his countrymen, as an Englishman. The Americans having continued to cultivate, and to cultivate extensively, an acquaintance with the writers of the mother country since the separation, it is evident they must have kept pace with the trifling changes of the day. The only peculiarity that can or ought to be expected in their literature is that which is connected with the promulgation of their distinctive political opinions. They have not been remiss in this duty, as any one may see who chooses to examine their books. But we will devote a few minutes to a more minute account of the actual condition of American literature.

The first, and the most important though certainly the most familiar branch of this subject, is connected with the public journals. It is not easy to say how many newspapers are printed in the United States. The estimated number varies from six hundred to a thousand. In the State of New-York there are more than fifty counties. Now, it is rare that a county, in a State as old as that of New-York, (especially in the more northern parts of the country), does not possess one paper at least. The cities have many. The smaller towns sometimes have three or four, and very many of the counties four or five. There cannot be many less than one hundred and fifty journals in the State of New-York alone. Pennsylvania is said to possess eighty. But we will suppose that these two States publish two hundred journals. They contain about 3,000,

is led to believe that, so lately as within ten years, several English periodical works were re-printed, and much read in the United States, and that now they patronize their own, while the former are far less sought, though the demand, by means of the increased population, should have been nearly doubled. Some of the works are no longer even re-printed. [The reference is probably to the *Quarterly, Edinburgh* and *North American Reviews.*]

ooo of inhabitants. As the former is an enlightened State, and the latter rather below the scale of the general intelligence of the nation, it may not be a very bad average of the whole population. This rate would give eight hundred journals for the United States, which is probably something within the truth. I confess, however, this manner of equalizing estimates in America is very uncertain in general, since a great deal, in such a question, must depend on the progress of society in each particular section of the country.

As might be expected, there is nearly every degree of merit to be found in these journals. No one of them has the benefit of that collected talent which is so often enlisted in the support of the more important journals of Europe. There is not often more than one editor to the best; but he is usually some man who has seen, in his own person, enough of men and things to enable him to speak with tolerable discretion on passing events. The usefulness of the American journals, however, does not consist in their giving the tone to the public mind, in politics and morals, but in imparting facts. It is certain that, could the journals agree, they might, by their united efforts, give a powerful inclination to the common will. But, in point of fact, they do not agree on any one subject or set of subjects except, perhaps, on those which directly affect their own interests. They, consequently, counteract, instead of aiding each other, on all points of disputed policy; and it is in the bold and sturdy discussions that follow that men arrive at the truth. The occasional union in their own favour is a thing too easily seen through to do either good or harm. So far, then, from the journals succeeding in leading the public opinion astray, they are invariably obliged to submit to it. They serve to keep it alive by furnishing the means for its expression, but they rarely do more. Of course, the influence of each particular press is in proportion to the constancy and the ability with which it is found to support what is thought to be sound principles; but those principles must be in accordance with the private opinions of men, or most of their labour is lost.

The public press in America is rather more decent than that of England, and less decorous than that of France. The tone of the nation, and the respect for private feelings which are, perhaps, in some measure, the consequence of a less artificial state of society, produce the former; and the liberty, which is a necessary attendant of fearless discussion, is, I think, the cause of the latter. The affairs of an individual are rarely touched upon in the journals of this country; never, unless it is thought they have a direct connexion with the public interests or from a wish to do him good. Still there is a habit, getting into use in America no less than in France, that is borrowed from the English, which proves that the more unworthy feelings of our nature are common to men under all systems, and only need opportunity to find encouragement. I allude to the practice of repeating the proceedings of the courts of justice, in order to cater to a vicious appetite for amusement in the public.

It is pretended that, as a court of justice is open to the world, there can be no harm in giving the utmost publicity to its proceedings. It is strange the courts should act so rigidly on the principle that it is better a dozen guilty men should go free than that one innocent man should suffer, and yet permit the gross injustice that is daily done by means of this practice. One would think that if a court of justice is so open to the world, that it should be the business of the people of the world to enter it, in order that they might be certain that the information they crave should be without colouring or exaggeration. It is idle to say that the reports are accurate, and that he who reads is enabled to do justice to the accused, by comparing the facts that are laid before him. A reporter may give the expression of the tongue; but can he convey that of the eye, of the countenance, or of the form?—without regarding all of which, no man is perfectly master of the degree of credibility that is due to any witness of whose character he is necessarily ignorant. But every man has an infallible means of assuring himself of the value of these reports. Who has ever read a dozen of them without meeting with one (or perhaps more,) in which the decision of the court and jury is to him a matter of surprise? It is true he assumes that those who were present knew best, and as he has no great interest in the matter, he is commonly satisfied. But how is it with the unfortunate man who is wrongfully brought out of his retirement to repel an unjust attack against his person, his property, or his character? If he be a man of virtue, he is a man of sensibility; and not only he, but, what is far worse, those tender beings whose existence is wrapped up in his own are to be wounded daily and hourly, for weeks at a time, in order that a depraved appetite should be glutted. It is enough for justice that her proceedings should be so public as to prevent the danger of corruption; but we pervert a blessing to a curse in making that which was intended for our protection, the means of so much individual misery. It is an unavoidable evil of the law that it necessarily works some wrong, in order to do much good; but it is cruel that even the acquittal of a man should be unnecessarily circulated, in a manner to make all men remember that he had been accused. We have proof of the consequences of this practice in England. Men daily shrink from resistance to base frauds rather than expose themselves to the observations and comments of those who enliven their breakfasts by sporting with these exhibitions of their fellow-creatures. There are, undoubtedly, cases of that magnitude which require some sacrifice of private feelings, in order that the community should reap the advantage; but the regular books are sufficient for authorities—the decisions of the courts are sufficient for justice—and the utmost possible oblivion should prove as nearly sufficient as may be to serve the ends of a prudent and a righteous humanity.

Nothing can be more free than the press of this country on all subjects connected with politics. Treason cannot be written, unless by communicating with an open enemy. There is no other protection to a public man than that which is given by an independent jury, which punishes, of course, in proportion to the dignity and importance of the injured party. But the utmost lenity is always used in construing the right of the press to canvass the public acts of public men. Mere commonplace charges defeat themselves and get into discredit so soon as to be lost, while graver accusations are met by grave replies. There is no doubt that the complacency of individuals is sometimes disturbed by these liberties; but they serve to keep the officers of the government to their work, while they rarely do any lasting, or even temporary injury. Serious and criminal accusations against a public man, if groundless, are, by the law of reason, a crime against the community, and, as such, they are punished. The general principle observed in these matters is very simple. If A. accuse B. of an act that is an offence against law, he may be called on for his proof, and if he fail he must take the consequences. But an editor of a paper or any one else who should bring a criminal charge, no matter how grave, against the President, and who could prove it, is just as certain of doing it with impunity as if he held the whole power in his own hands. He would be protected by the invincible shield of public opinion, which is not only in consonance with the law, but which, in this country, makes law.

Actions for injuries done by the press, considering the number of journals, are astonishingly rare in America. When one remembers the usual difficulty of obtaining legal proof, which is a constant temptation even to the guilty to appeal to the courts; and, on the other hand, the great freedom of the press, which is a constant temptation to abuse the trust, this fact, in itself, furnishes irresistible evidence of the general tone of decency which predominates in this nation. The truth is that public opinion, among its other laws, has imperiously prescribed that, amidst the utmost latitude of discussion, certain limits shall not be passed; and public opinion, which is so completely the offspring of a free press, must be obeyed in this, as well as in other matters.

Leaving the journals, we come to those publications which make their appearance periodically. Of these there are a good many, some few of which are well supported. There are several scientific works that are printed monthly, or quarterly, of respectable merit, and four or five reviews.

Magazines of a more general character are not much encouraged. England, which is teeming with educated men who are glad to make their bread by writing for these works, still affords too strong a competition for the success of any American attempts in this species of literature. Though few, perhaps no English magazine is actually republished in America, a vast number are imported and read in the towns, where the support for any similar original production must first be found.

The literature of the United States has, indeed, two powerful obstacles to conquer before (to use a mercantile expression) it can ever enter the markets of its own country on terms of perfect equality with that of England. Solitary and individual works of genius may, indeed, be occasionally brought to light, under the impulses of the high feeling which has conceived them; but, I fear, a good, wholesome, profitable and continued pecuniary support is the applause that talent most craves. The fact that an American publisher can get an English work without money must, for a few years longer, (unless legislative protection shall be extended to their own authors,) have a tendency to repress a national literature. No man will pay a writer for an epic, a tragedy, a sonnet, a history, or a romance when he can get a work of equal merit for nothing. I have conversed with those who are conversant on the subject, and, I confess, I have been astonished at the information they imparted.

A capital American publisher has assured me that there are not a dozen writers in this country whose works he should feel confidence in publishing at all, while he reprints hundreds of English books without the least hesitation. This preference is by no means so much owing to any difference in merit as to the fact that, when the price of the original author is to be added to the uniform hazard which accompanies all literary speculations, the risk becomes too great. The general taste of the reading world in this country is better than that of England.[2] The fact is

[2] The writer does not mean that the best taste of America is better than that of England; perhaps it is not quite so good; but,

both proved and explained by the circumstance that thousands of works that are printed and read in the mother country are not printed and read here. The publisher on this side of the Atlantic has the advantage of seeing the reviews of every book he wishes to print, and, what is of far more importance, he knows, with the exception of books that he is sure of selling by means of a name, the decision of the English critics before he makes his choice. Nine times in ten, popularity, which is all he looks for, is a sufficient test of general merit. Thus, while you find every English work of character or notoriety on the shelves of an American book-store, you may ask in vain for most of the trash that is so greedily devoured in the circulating libraries of the mother country, and which would be just as eagerly devoured here, had not a better taste been created by a compelled abstinence. That taste must now be overcome before such works could be sold at all.

When I say that books are not rejected here from any want of talent in the writers, perhaps I ought to explain. I wish to express something a little different. Talent is sure of too many avenues to wealth and honours in America, to seek, unnecessarily, an unknown and hazardous path. It is better paid in the ordinary pursuits of life than it would be likely to be paid by an adventure in which an extraordinary and skilful, because practised, foreign competition is certain. Perhaps high talent does not often make the trial with the American bookseller; but it is precisely for the reason I have named.

The second obstacle against which American literature has to contend is in the poverty of materials. There is scarcely an ore which contributes to the wealth of the author that is found here in veins as rich as in Europe. There are no annals for the historian; no follies (beyond the most vulgar and commonplace) for the satirist; no manners for the dramatist; no obscure fictions for the writer of romance; no gross and hardy offences against decorum for the moralist; nor any of the rich artificial auxiliaries

as a whole, the American reading world requires better books than the whole of the English reading world.

of poetry. The weakest hand can extract a spark from the flint, but it would baffle the strength of a giant to attempt kindling a flame with a pudding-stone. I very well know there are theorists who assume that the society and institutions of this country are, or ought to be, particularly favourable to novelties and variety. But the experience of one month, in these States, is sufficient to show any observant man the falsity of their position. The effect of a promiscuous assemblage any where is to create a standard of deportment; and great liberty permits every one to aim at its attainment. I have never seen a nation so much alike in my life as the people of the United States, and what is more, they are not only like each other, but they are remarkably like that which common sense tells them they ought to resemble. No doubt, traits of character that are a little peculiar, without, however, being either very poetical or very rich, are to be found in remote districts; but they are rare, and not always happy exceptions. In short, it is not possible to conceive a state of society in which more of the attributes of plain good sense, or fewer of the artificial absurdities of life, are to be found than here. There is no costume for the peasant, (there is scarcely a peasant at all,) no wig for the judge, no baton for the general, no diadem for the chief magistrate. The darkest ages of their history are illuminated by the light of truth; the utmost efforts of their chivalry are limited by the laws of God; and even the deeds of their sages and heroes are to be sung in a language that would differ but little from a version of the ten commandments. However useful and respectable all this may be in actual life, it indicates but one direction to the man of genius.

It is very true there are a few young poets now living in this country who have known how to extract sweets from even these wholesome, but scentless native plants. They have, however, been compelled to seek their inspiration in the universal laws of nature, and they have succeeded precisely in proportion as they have been most general in their application. Among these gifted young men, there is one (Halleck) who is remarkable for an exquisite vein of ironical wit, mingled with a fine, poetical, and, frequently, a lofty expression. This gentleman commenced his career as a satirist in one of the journals of New-York. Heaven knows, his materials were none of the richest; and yet the melody of his verse, the quaintness and force of his comparisons, and the exceeding humour of his strong points, brought him instantly into notice. He then attempted a general satire, by giving the history of the early days of a *belle*. He was again successful, though every body, at least every body of any talent, felt that he wrote in leading-strings. But he happened, shortly after the appearance of the little volume just named, (Fanny,) to visit England. Here his spirit was properly excited, and, probably on a rainy day he was induced to try his hand at a *jeu d'esprit*, in the mother country. The result was one of the finest semi-heroic ironical descriptions to be found in the English language.[3] This simple fact, in itself, proves the truth of a great deal of what I have just been writing, since it shows the effect a superiority of material can produce on the efforts of a man of true genius.

Notwithstanding the difficulties of the subject, talent has even done more than in the instance of Mr. Halleck. I could mention several other young poets of this country of rare merit. By mentioning Bryant, Percival, and Sprague, I shall direct your attention to the names of those whose works would be most likely to give you pleasure. Unfortunately they are not yet known in Italian, but I think even you would not turn in distaste from the task of translation which the best of their effusions will invite.

The next, though certainly an inferior branch of imaginative writing, is fictitious composition. From the facts just named, you cannot expect that the novelists or romance writers of the United States should be very successful. The same reason will be likely, for a long time to come, to repress the ardour of dramatic genius. Still, tales and plays are no novelties in the literature of this country. Of the former, there are many as old as soon after the revolution; and a vast number have been published within the last five years. One of their authors of romance, who

[3] This little *morceau* of pleasant irony is called Alnwick Castle.

curbed his talents by as few allusions as possible to actual society, is distinguished for power and comprehensiveness of thought. I remember to have read one of his books (Wieland) when a boy, and I take it to be a never-failing evidence of genius that, amid a thousand similar pictures which have succeeded, the images it has left still stand distinct and prominent in my recollection. This author (Mr. Brockden Brown) enjoys a high reputation among his countrymen, whose opinions are sufficiently impartial, since he flattered no particular prejudice of the nation in any of his works.

The reputation of Irving is well known to you. He is an author distinguished for a quality (humour) that has been denied his countrymen; and his merit is the more rare that it has been shown in a state of society so cold and so restrained. Besides these writers, there are many others of a similar character who enjoy a greater or less degree of favour in their own country. The works of two or three have even been translated (into French) in Europe, and a great many are reprinted in England. Though every writer of fiction in America has to contend against the difficulties I have named, there is a certain interest in the novelty of the subject which is not without its charm. I think, however, it will be found that they have all been successful, or the reverse, just as they have drawn warily, or freely, on the distinctive habits of their own country. I now speak of their success purely as writers of romance. It certainly would be possible for an American to give a description of the manners of his own country, in a book that he might choose to call a romance, which should be read because the world is curious on the subject, but which would certainly never be read for that nearly indefinable poetical interest which attaches itself to a description of manners less bald and uniform. All the attempts to blend history with romance in America have been comparatively failures, (and perhaps fortunately,) since the subjects are too familiar to be treated with the freedom that the imagination absolutely requires. Some of the descriptions of the progress of society on the borders have had a rather better success, since there is a positive, though no very poetical, novelty in the subject; but, on the whole, the books which have been best received are those in which the authors have trusted most to their own conceptions of character, and to qualities that are common to the rest of the world and to human nature. This fact, if its truth be admitted, will serve to prove that the American writer must seek his renown in the exhibition of qualities that are general, while he is confessedly compelled to limit his observations to a state of society that has a wonderful tendency not only to repress passion, but to equalize humours.

The Americans have always been prolific writers on polemics and politics. Their sermons and fourth of July orations are numberless. Their historians, without being very classical or very profound, are remarkable for truth and good sense. There is not, perhaps, in the language a closer reasoner in metaphysics than Edwards; and their theological writers find great favour among the sectarians of their respective schools.

The stage of the United States is decidedly English. Both plays and players, with few exceptions, are imported. Theatres are numerous, and they are to be found in places where a traveller would little expect to meet them. Of course they are of all sizes, and of every degree of decoration and architectural beauty known in Europe, below the very highest. The façade of the principal theatre in Philadelphia is a chaste specimen in marble, of the Ionic, if my memory is correct. In New-York, there are two theatres about as large as the Théatre Français (in the interior), and not much inferior in embellishments. Besides these, there is a very pretty little theatre, where lighter pieces are performed, and another with a vast stage for melodramas. There are also one or two other places of dramatic representation in this city, in which horses and men contend for the bays.

The Americans pay well for dramatic talent. Cooke, the greatest English tragedian of our age, died on this side of the Atlantic; and there are few players of eminence in the mother country who are not tempted, at some time or other, to cross the ocean. Shakspeare is, of course, the

great author of America, as he is of England, and I think
he is quite as well relished here as there. In point of taste,
if all the rest of the world be any thing against England,
that of America is the best, since it unquestionably approaches nearest to that of the continent of Europe. Nearly
one-half of the theatrical taste of the English is condemned by their own judgments, since the stage is not
much supported by those who have had an opportunity
of seeing any other. You will be apt to ask me how it
happens, then, that the American taste is better? Because
the people, being less exaggerated in their habits, are less
disposed to tolerate caricatures, and because the theatres
are not yet sufficiently numerous (though that hour is
near) to admit of a representation that shall not be subject to the control of a certain degree of intelligence. I
have heard an English player complain that he never saw
such a dull audience as the one before which he had just
been exhibiting; and I heard the same audience complain
that they never listened to such dull jokes. Now, there
was talent enough in both parties; but the one had formed
his taste in a coarse school, and the others had formed
theirs under the dominion of common sense. Independently of this peculiarity, there is a vast deal of acquired,
travelled taste in this country. English tragedy, and high
English comedy, both of which, you know, are excellent,
never fail here, if well played; that is, they never fail under the usual limits of all amusement. One will cloy of
sweets. But the fact of the taste and judgment of these
people, in theatrical exhibitions, is proved by the number
of their good theatres compared to their population.

Of dramatic writers there are none, or next to none.
The remarks I have made in respect to novels apply with
double force to this species of composition. A witty and
successful American comedy could only proceed from extraordinary talent. There would be less difficulty, certainly,
with a tragedy; but still, there is rather too much foreign
competition, and too much domestic employment in other
pursuits, to invite genius to so doubtful an enterprise.
The very baldness of ordinary American life is in deadly
hostility to scenic representation. The character must be

supported solely by its intrinsic power. The judge, the
footman, the clown, the lawyer, the belle, or the beau, can
receive no great assistance from dress. Melo-dramas, except
the scene should be laid in the woods, are out of the
question. It would be necessary to seek the great clock,
which is to strike the portentous twelve blows, in the nearest church; a vaulted passage would degenerate into a
cellar; and, as for ghosts, the country was discovered since
their visitations have ceased. The smallest departure from
the incidents of ordinary life would do violence to every
man's experience; and, as already mentioned, the passions
which belong to human nature must be delineated, in
America, subject to the influence of that despot—common
sense.

Notwithstanding the overwhelming influence of British
publications, and all the difficulties I have named, original
books are getting to be numerous in the United States.
The impulses of talent and intelligence are bearing down a
thousand obstacles. I think the new works will increase
rapidly, and that they are destined to produce a powerful
influence on the world. We will pursue this subject another time.—Adieu.

II. LETTER #24

You will be satisfied with these reasons for the abrupt
conclusion of my last. I shall now tax your patience for a
short continuation of the subject.

Although there are so many reasons why an imaginative
literature should not be speedily created in this country,
there is none but that general activity of employment
which is not favourable to study why science and all the
useful arts should not be cultivated here, perhaps, more
than any where else. Great attention is already paid to the
latter. Though there is scarce such a thing as a capital
picture in this whole country, I have seen more beautiful,
graceful, and convenient ploughs in positive use here than
are probably to be found in the whole of Europe united.
In this single fact may be traced the history of the character of the people, and the germ of their future greatness.

Their axe is admirable for form, for neatness, and precision of weight, and it is wielded with a skill that is next to incredible. Reapers are nearly unknown; but I have seen single individuals enter a field of grain in the morning, and clear acres of its golden burthen, by means of the *cradle*,[4] with a rapidity that has amazed me. The vast multitude of their inventions, as they are exhibited in the Patent Office in this city, ought to furnish food for grave reflection to every stranger. Several large rooms are filled with the models, many of which give evidence of the most acute ingenuity. When one recollects the average proportion of adults to which the population must have been confined during the last thirty-five years,[5] the number of their inventions is marvellous. A great many of these models contain no new principle nor any new application of an old principle; but, as in such cases money has been paid by those who deposit them there without an object, it is fair to presume that they were inventions so far as the claimants were concerned. There are so few means by which men in remote districts of this country can profit by the ideas of other people in these matters, that it is probable there are not a dozen machines lodged in the office, of which the parties concerned did not honestly believe themselves the inventors. You may estimate the activity of thought which distinguishes the mass of this nation from all other people by this fact. It is in itself a prodigious triumph to a young people to have given form and useful existence to the greatest improvement of our age; but the steam-boats are not the only gift of this nature, by many, that Europe has already received from the western hemisphere.

The general accumulation of science in this country is exceedingly great, though it is quite likely that few men have yet attained to a very eminent degree of knowledge in any one particular branch. Still it is probable that the amount of science in the United States, at this day, com-

---

[4] The writer does not know whether this implement is an American invention or not.
[5] The whole period that the Patent Office has been in existence.

pared to what it was even fifteen years ago, and without reference to the increase of the population, is as five to one, or even in a still much greater proportion. Like all other learning, it is greatly on the advance.

In architecture the Americans have certainly no great reason to exult. They appear to have inherited the peculiarity of their ancestors in all matters of mere taste. Their houses are mostly built of wood in the country and in the villages, and of bricks in the towns. There are, however, exceptions, in all cases, which reverse the rule. There are many farm-houses, seats, churches, court-houses, &c. in the country and smaller towns, which are of stone. Marble and granite are getting a good deal into use, too, in the more northern cities. The principal motive which controls their taste is economy. It is commonly cheapest to build of wood in the country, but where stone is at hand and of a good quality, it begins to be preferred, in what may be called the second and third stages of the settlements. As the materials are cheap, the buildings are in common much larger than would be occupied by men of the same wealth in Europe. A house of forty or of forty-five feet front, and of thirty or thirty-five feet in depth, of two stories, with cellars, and garret, and with offices attached, is a usual dwelling for the owner of one or of two hundred acres of land, in a part of the country that has been under cultivation thirty or forty years. Such a man may be worth from five to ten thousand dollars. He has his growing orchard; fifty sheep; some eight or ten cows; a stock of young cattle; three or four horses; one or two yoke of oxen; hogs, poultry, and all the other provisions of a small farm. He grows his own maize; fattens his own pork; makes his own cider; kills his own beef; raises his own wheat, rye, and flax; and, in short, lives as much as possible on the articles of his own production. There are thousands and tens of thousands of these sturdy, independent yeomen in the eastern, middle and north-western States.

The villas and country-seats are commonly pretty, without ever attaining much elegance of size. A better sort of American country-house will cover perhaps sixty or seventy feet of ground in length, and from fifty to sixty in depth. There are some of twice this size; but I should say the first was a fair average. There are a great many a size smaller. The expense of building is, of course, in proportion to the general cost of every article in the particular place where the house is erected. I am told the best buildings in New-York cost from thirty to forty thousand dollars. A few are even much more expensive. But the townhouses, occupied by a majority of their gentlemen (those who own their own dwellings), cost probably something under twenty thousand.[6] These are the habitations of the rich, exclusively. They are every where exceedingly neat, prettily furnished, frequently with great elegance, and are always comfortable.

As some general idea of the state of the useful arts must have been obtained in the course of my previous letters to the fraternity, I shall now pass to those which are intended exclusively to embellish life.

The United States, considered with reference to their means and opportunities, have been exceedingly prolific in painters. It is rather remarkable that, in a country where active and less hazardous employments are so open to talent, men should take an inclination to a pursuit that is rarely profitable, and in which mediocrity is as annoying as success is triumphant. I cannot say that the majority of these gentlemen acknowledge that the fine arts are greatly encouraged in America, nor has it yet been my happy lot to enter a country in which artists and authors were very generally of opinion that the pen and the pencil received the rewards and honours which no one will deny they merit. A very great majority of the American artists are portrait painters. Some of them are highly esteemed by their own countrymen, and certainly there are a few of a good deal of merit. They are generally more dis-

---

[6] The writer afterwards saw a row of buildings in New-York of the following cost and dimensions; twenty-five feet front, (in marble) fifty-five feet deep, and of three stories, besides the basement. The lots were two hundred feet in depth. The buildings were about as well finished as a third-rate London town-house. The cost of the whole was ten thousand dollars, and the rent six hundred dollars a-year. These houses were in the dearest city of America, but not in the dearest part of the town.

tinguished for spirit and character than for finish or grace; but it is quite evident that, as a class, they are rapidly improving. Drawing is the point in which they chiefly fail; and this, too, is probably an inherited defect, since most of them are disciples of the English school.

There are some highly respectable professional land-scape painters. One of them (a Mr. Cole) possesses the rare faculty of giving to his pictures the impression of nature, to a degree so extraordinary that he promises to become eminent. You know my eye is only for nature. I have heard both high eulogiums and sneering critiques on the powers of this young man as an artist; some declaring that he has reached a point far beyond that attained by any of his competitors, and others denying that he knows how to make a sky look blue, *secundum artem.* To me his scenery is like the scenery from which he drew; and as he has taste and skill enough to reject what is disagreeable, and to arrange the attractive parts of his pictures, I only hope he will continue to study the great master from whom he has drawn his first inspirations. America has pro-duced several historical painters. West, though a native of this country, and, perhaps with a pardonable vanity, claimed as such by these people, was, to all intents and purposes an English artist. There are one or two of his pupils who practise their skill here, and a few others have aspired to the highest branch of their art. One of them (Mr. Allston) is said to be employed on a great and elabo-rate picture (the handwriting on the wall;) and as his taste and merit are universally admitted, a good deal is expected from his pencil. It may serve to give you a better idea of the taste for pictures in this country, or rather of the desire which exists to encourage talent, if I mention the price he is to receive for this work. A company of gen-tlemen are said to have bought the picture, in advance, by agreeing to pay ten thousand dollars. I believe it is their intention to remunerate themselves by exhibiting it, and then to deposit the work in some public place. Cabinet pieces by this artist are readily sold for prices of between three hundred and a thousand dollars, and the pencil of Cole is employed as much as he pleases. There are many

other artists that paint portraits and landscapes, who seldom want orders. The government of the United States
has paid Trumbull thirty-two thousand dollars for the four
historical paintings that are destined to fill as many com-
partments in the rotunda, or the great hall of the Capitol.

It is plain that the system of elementary education pursued by this country must bring an extraordinary quantity
of talent within the influence of those causes which lead to
renown. If we suppose one hundred men in America to
possess the same amount of native talent as one hundred
men in any other part of the world, more of it will, of
necessity, be excited to action, since more individuals are
placed in situations to feel and to improve their infant
powers. Although a certain degree of excellence in the
higher branches of learning and of art may yet be necessary to create a standard, and even for the establishments
of higher schools or real universities, still the truth of this
position is proved by the fact that there already exists,
among this people, a far more advanced state of improvement in all that relates to the familiar interests of life
than among any other. It is true that a division of labour,
and vast competition, may create a degree of minute perfection in many articles of European manufacture that is
not known in the same articles manufactured here; but I
think it will be commonly found, in all such cases, that
these wary people have counted the profit and the cost
with sufficient accuracy. As circumstances vary, they instantly improve; and, once induced to persevere, they soon
fearlessly challenge competition.

The purely intellectual day of America is yet in its
dawn. But its sun will not arise from darkness, like those
of nations with whose experience we are familiar; nor is
the approach of its meridian to be calculated by the known
progress of any other people. The learned professions are
now full to overflowing, not so much with learning as with
incumbents, certainly, but so much so as to begin to give
a new direction to education and talents. Writers are already getting to be numerous, for literature is beginning
to be profitable. Those authors who are successful receive
prices for their labours which exceed those paid to the

authors of any country, England alone excepted; and which exceed even the prices paid to the most distinguished authors of the mother country if the difference in the relative value of money in the two countries, and in the luxury of the press, be computed. The same work which is sold in England for six dollars is sold in the United States for two. The profit to the publisher is obtained out of a common rate of per centage. Now, as thirty-three and a third per cent. on six thousand dollars, is two thousand,[7] and on two thousand dollars, only six hundred and sixty-six, it is quite evident that if both parties sell one thousand copies of a work, the English publisher pockets three times the most profit. And yet, with one or two exceptions, and notwithstanding the great difference in the population of the two countries, the English bookseller rarely sells more, if he does as many, copies of a book than the American. It is the extraordinary demand which enables the American publisher to pay so well, and which, provided there was no English competition, would enable him to pay still better, or rather still more generally, than he does at present.

The literature of the United States is a subject of the highest interest to the civilized world; for when it does begin to be felt, it will be felt with a force, a directness, and a common sense in its application, that has never yet been known. If there were no other points of difference between this country and other nations, those of its political and religious freedom, alone, would give a colour of the highest importance to the writings of a people so thoroughly imbued with their distinctive principles, and so keenly alive to their advantages. The example of America has been silently operating on Europe for half a century; but its doctrines and its experience, exhibited with the understanding of those familiar with both, have never yet been pressed on our attention. I think the time for the experiment is getting near.

A curious inquiry might be raised as to the probable

[7] This calculation supposes one-third of the price to go to the trade in discount, one-third to the expenses, and the other third to constitute the joint profit of the author and publisher.

fate of the English language among so many people having equal claims to its possession. I put this question to my friend, who has kindly permitted me to give you the substance of his reply. You will at once understand that this is a subject which requires a greater knowledge of the matter in dispute than what I, as a foreigner, can claim:—

"In order to decide which nation speaks the English language best, it becomes necessary to refer to some standard. If it be assumed that the higher classes in London are always to set the fashion in pronunciation, and the best living writers in England are to fix the meaning of words, the point is clearly decided in their favour, since one cannot see on what principle they are to be put in the wrong. That the better company of London must set the fashion for the pronunciation of words in England, and indeed for the whole English empire, is quite plain; for, as this very company comprises all those whose manners, birth, fortune, and political distinction make them the objects of admiration, it becomes necessary to imitate their affectations, whether of speech or air, in order to create the impression that one belongs to their society. It is absurd to think that either parliament, or the stage, or the universities, or the church, can produce any very serious effect on the slighter forms of utterance adopted by this powerful caste. The player may hint at the laws of prosody for ever, unless his rule happens to suit the public ear, it becomes no more than the pronunciation of the stage. The fellow, when he gets beyond his cloisters, is glad to conceal the habits of retirement in the language of the world; and as for the member of Parliament, if he happen to be of the caste, he speaks like the rest of them; and if not, he is no better than a vulgar fellow, who is very glad to conceal his provincialisms by having as little said about them as possible. In short, the bishop might just as well expect to induce the exquisite to wear a copy of his wig, or the representative of Othello, to set the fashion of smooty faces, as either of them to think of giving the tone to pronunciation, or even to the meaning of words. A secret and lasting influence is no doubt produced by education; but fashion is far more imperious than even the laws of the schools. It is, I think, a capital mistake, to believe that either of the professions named produce any great impression on the spoken language of England. They receive more from fashion than they give to it; and they each have their particular phrases, but they rarely go any farther than their own limits. This is more or less the case in all other European nations. The rule is more absolute, however, in England than in France, for instance, because the former has no academy, and because men of letters have far less circulation, and, of course, far less influence in society there, than in the neighbouring kingdom. The tendency of every thing in England is to aristocracy. I can conceive that the King of England might very well set a fashion in the pronunciation of a word because, being the greatest aristocrat of the nation, the smaller ones might be ambitious of showing that they kept enough of his company to catch his imperfections of speech; but, as for the King of France, he sits too much on a pinnacle for men to presume to imitate his blunders. A powerful, wealthy, hereditary, but subsidizing aristocracy rules all things in England; but, while wit gives up to the King and *la charte* the control of politics in France, it asserts its own prerogative over every other interest of the empire, religion, perhaps, a little excepted.

"There exists a very different state of things in America. If we had a great capital like London, where men of leisure, and fortune, and education, periodically assembled to amuse themselves, I think we should establish a fashionable aristocracy, too, which should give the mode to the forms of speech, as well as to that of dress and deportment. Perhaps the influence of talent and wit would be as much felt in such a town as in Paris; for it is the great peculiarity of our institutions to give more influence to talents than to any one other thing. But we have no such capital, nor are we likely, for a long time to come, to have one of sufficient magnitude to produce any great effect on the language. In those States where many men of leisure and education are to be found, there are large towns, in which they pass their winters, and where, of course, they observe all those forms which are more or less peculiar to themselves. The habits of polite life, and even the pronunciation of Boston, of New-York, of Baltimore, and of Philadelphia, vary in many things, and a practised ear may tell a native of either of these places from a native of any one of the others by some little peculiarity of speech. There is yet no predominating influence to induce the fashionables of these towns to wish to imitate the fashionables of any other. If any place is to possess this influence, it will certainly be New-York; but I think, on an examination of the subject, that it can be made to appear that an entirely different standard for the language must be established in the United States from that which governs so absolutely in England.

"If the people of this country were like the people of any other country on earth, we should be speaking at this moment a great variety of nearly unintelligible patois; but, in point of fact, the people of the United States, with the exception of a few of German and French descent, speak, as a body, an incomparably better English than the people of the mother country. There is not, probably, a man (of English descent) born in this country who would not be perfectly intelligible to all whom he should meet in the streets of London, though a vast number of those he met in the streets of London would be nearly unintelligible to him. In fine, we speak our language, as a nation, better than any other people speak their language.[8] When one reflects on the immense surface of country that we occupy, the general accuracy, in pronunciation and in the use of words, is quite astonishing. This resemblance in speech can only be ascribed to the great diffusion of intelligence, and to the inexhaustible activity of the population, which, in a manner, destroys space.

"It is another peculiarity of our institutions that the language of the country, instead of becoming more divided into provincial dialects, is becoming, not only more assimilated to itself as a whole, but more assimilated to a standard which sound general principles, and the best au-

[8] Of course the writer calls Italy one nation, and all Germany one nation, so far as language is concerned.

thorities among our old writers, would justify. The distinctions in speech between New-England and New-York, or Pennsylvania, or any other State, were far greater twenty years ago than they are now. Emigration alone would produce a large portion of this change; but emigration would often introduce provincialisms without correcting them, did it not also, by bringing acute men together, sharpen wits, provoke comparisons, challenge investigations, and, finally, fix a standard. . . ."

DOCUMENT 24

Edgar Allan Poe

Edgar Allan Poe (1809–49) entered the debate on literary nationalism in 1836 with his review in the *Southern Literary Messenger* of the collected poems of Joseph Rodman Drake and Fitz-Greene Halleck. Basing his definition of *good* poetry on his understanding of Coleridge's distinction between the Imagination and the Fancy, he calls to account those American critics who welcome the work of an American poet merely because it is American in setting and sentiment and reveals what Poe considers an inferior brand of the "poetic sentiment." His distinction between poetry which is based on a mere comparison with nature, and poetry which reveals a higher moral or poetic truth, takes little account of the Associationist emphasis on the value of immediate experience. Poe worked perhaps harder than any other American author to write original verse and prose and thus enhance American literature, but his criteria were all "universal" rather than "national." His arguments against literary nationalism as such did not prevent him from making a major contribution to the new national literature.

In this printing, the passages of specific comment on Halleck's poems and on the poems of Drake other than *The Culprit Fay* are omitted, as not being immediately relevant to the issue of literary nationalism. The passage in which the outline of the poem is given in some detail is also omitted.

TEXT: from the *Southern Literary Messenger* (April 1836), 326–33.

FROM A *Review of the Poems of Drake and Halleck*

Before entering upon the detailed notice which we propose of the volumes before us, we wish to speak a few words in regard to the present state of American criticism.

It must be visible to all who meddle with literary matters that of late years a thorough revolution has been effected in the censorship of our press. That this revolution is infinitely for the worse we believe. There was a time, it is true, when we cringed to foreign opinion—let us even say when we paid a most servile deference to British critical dicta. That an American book could, by any possibility, be worthy perusal was an idea by no means extensively prevalent in the land; and if we were induced to read at all the productions of our native writers, it was only after repeated assurances from England that such productions were not altogether contemptible. But there was, at all events, a shadow of excuse, and a slight basis of reason for a subserviency so grotesque. Even now, perhaps, it would not be far wrong to assert that such basis of reason may still exist. Let us grant that in many of the abstract sciences—that even in Theology, in Medicine, in Law, in Oratory, in the Mechanical Arts, we have no competitors whatever, still nothing but the most egregious national vanity would assign us a place, in the matter of Polite Literature, upon a level with the elder and riper climes of Europe, the earliest steps of whose children are among the groves of magnificently endowed Academies, and whose innumerable men of leisure, and of consequent learning, drink daily from those august fountains of inspiration which burst around them every where from out the tombs of their immortal dead, and from out their hoary and trophied monuments of chivalry and song. In paying then, as a nation, a respectful and not undue deference to a supremacy rarely questioned but by prejudice or ignorance, we should, of course, be doing nothing more than acting in a rational manner. The *excess* of our subserviency was blameable—but, as we have before said, this very excess might have found a shadow of excuse in the strict justice, if properly regulated, of the principle from which it issued. Not so, however, with our present follies. We are becoming boisterous and arrogant in the pride of a too speedily assumed literary freedom. We throw off, with the most presumptuous and unmeaning hauteur, *all* deference whatever to foreign opinion—we forget, in the puerile inflation of vanity, that *the world* is the true thea-tre of the biblical histrio—we get up a hue and cry about the necessity of encouraging native writers of merit—we blindly fancy that we can accomplish this by indiscrimi-nate puffing of good, bad, and indifferent, without taking the trouble to consider that what we choose to denominate encouragement is thus, by its general application, rendered precisely the reverse. In a word, so far from being ashamed of the many disgraceful literary failures to which our own inordinate vanities and misapplied patriotism have lately given birth, and so far from deeply lamenting that these daily puerilities are of home manufacture, we adhere pertinaciously to our original blindly conceived idea, and thus often find ourselves involved in the gross paradox of liking a stupid book the better, because, sure enough, its stupidity is American.[1]

Deeply lamenting this unjustifiable state of public feel-ing, it has been our constant endeavor, since assuming the Editorial duties of this Journal, to stem, with what little abilities we possess, a current so disastrously undermining the health and prosperity of our literature. We have seen our efforts applauded by men whose applauses we value. From all quarters we have received abundant private as well as public testimonials in favor of our *Critical Notices*, and, until very lately, have heard from no respectable source one word impugning their integrity or candor. In

[1] This charge of indiscriminate puffing will, of course, only apply to the *general* character of our criticism—there are some noble exceptions. We wish also especially to discriminate between those *notices* of new works which are intended merely to call public attention to them, and deliberate criticism on the works themselves.

looking over, however, a number of the New York Commercial Advertiser, we meet with the following paragraph.

The last number of the Southern Literary Messenger is very readable and respectable. The contributions to the Messenger are much better than the original matter. The critical department of this work—much as it would seem to boast itself of impartiality and discernment,—is in our opinion decidedly *quacky*. There is in it a great assumption of acumen, which is completely unsustained. Many a work has been slashingly condemned therein, of which the critic himself could not write a page, were he to die for it. This affectation of eccentric sternness in criticism, without the power to back one's suit withal, so far from deserving praise, as some suppose, merits the strongest reprehension.—*Philadelphia Gazette.*

We are entirely of opinion with the Philadelphia Gazette in relation to the Southern Literary Messenger, and take this occasion to express our total dissent from the numerous and lavish encomiums we have seen bestowed upon its critical notices. Some few of them have been judicious, fair and candid; bestowing praise and censure with judgment and impartiality; but by far the greater number of those we have read, have been flippant, unjust, untenable and uncritical. The duty of the critic is to act as judge, not as enemy, of the writer whom he reviews; a distinction of which the Zoilus of the Messenger seems not to be aware. It is possible to review a book severely, without bestowing opprobrious epithets upon the writer: to condemn with courtesy, if not with kindness. The critic of the Messenger has been eulogized for his scorching and scarifying abilities, and he thinks it incumbent upon him to keep up his reputation in that line, by sneers, sarcasm, and downright abuse; by straining his vision with microscopic intensity in search of faults, and shutting his eyes, with all his might, to beauties. Moreover, we have detected him, more than once, in blunders quite as gross as those on which it was his pleasure to descant.[2]

[2] In addition to these things we observe, in the New York Mirror, what follows: "Those who have read the Notices of American books in a certain Southern Monthly, which is striving to gain notoriety by the loudness of its abuse, may find amusement in the sketch on another page, entitled 'The Successful Novel.' The Southern Literary Messenger knows ☞ *by experience* ☜ what it is to write a successless novel." We have, in this case, only to deny, flatly, the assertion of the Mirror. The Editor of the Messenger never in his life wrote or published, or attempted to publish, a novel either successful or *successless.*

In the paragraph from the Philadelphia Gazette, (which is edited by Mr. Willis Gaylord Clark, one of the Editors of the Knickerbocker) we find nothing at which we have any desire to take exception. Mr. C. has a right to think us *quacky* if he pleases, and we do not remember having assumed for a moment that we could write a single line of the works we have reviewed. But there is something equivocal, to say the least, in the remarks of Col. Stone. He acknowledges that "*some* of our notices have been judicious, fair, and candid, bestowing praise and censure with judgment and impartiality." This being the case, how can he reconcile his *total* dissent from the public verdict in our favor, with the dictates of justice? We are accused too of bestowing "opprobrious epithets" upon writers whom we review, and in the paragraph so accusing us we are called nothing less than "flippant, unjust, and uncritical."

But there is another point of which we disapprove. While in our reviews we have at all times been particularly careful *not* to deal in generalities, and have never, if we remember aright, advanced in any single instance an unsupported assertion, our accuser has forgotten to give us any better evidence of our flippancy, injustice, personality, and gross blundering, than the solitary *dictum* of Col. Stone. We call upon the Colonel for assistance in this dilemma. We wish to be shown our blunders that we may correct them—to be made aware of our flippancy, that we may avoid it hereafter—and above all to have our personalities pointed out that we may proceed forthwith with a repentant spirit, to make the *amende honorable*. In default of this aid from the Editor of the Commercial we shall take it for granted that we are neither blunderers, flippant, personal, nor unjust.

Who will deny that in regard to individual poems no definitive opinions can exist, so long as to Poetry in the abstract we attach no definitive idea? Yet it is a common thing to hear our critics, day after day, pronounce, with a positive air, laudatory or condemnatory sentences, *en masse*, upon metrical works of whose merits and demerits they have, in the first place, virtually confessed an utter ignorance, in confessing ignorance of all determinate principles by which to regulate a decision. Poetry has never been defined to the satisfaction of all parties. Perhaps, in the present condition of language it never will be. Words cannot hem it in. Its intangible and purely spiritual nature refuses to be bound down within the widest horizon of mere sounds. But it is not, therefore, misunderstood—at least, not by all men is it misunderstood. Very far from it. If, indeed, there be any one circle of thought distinctly and palpably marked out from amid the jarring and tumultuous chaos of human intelligence, it is that evergreen and radiant Paradise which the true poet knows, and knows alone, as the limited realm of his authority—as the circumscribed Eden of his dreams. But a definition is a thing of words—a conception of ideas. And thus while we readily believe that Poesy, the term, it will be troublesome, if not impossible to define—still, with its image vividly existing in the world, we apprehend no difficulty in so describing Poesy, the Sentiment, as to imbue even the most obtuse intellect with a comprehension of it sufficiently distinct for all the purposes of practical analysis.

To look upwards from any existence, material or immaterial, to its *design*, is, perhaps, the most direct, and the most unerring method of attaining a just notion of the nature of the existence itself. Nor is the principle at fault when we turn our eyes from Nature even to Nature's God. We find certain faculties implanted within us, and arrive at a more plausible conception of the character and attributes of those faculties, by considering, with what finite judgment we possess, the *intention* of the Deity in so implanting them within us, than by any actual investigation of their powers, or any speculative deductions from their visible and material effects. Thus, for example, we discover in all men a disposition to look with reverence upon superiority, whether real or supposititious. In some, this disposition is to be recognized with difficulty and, in very peculiar cases, we are occasionally even led to doubt its existence altogether until circumstances beyond the common routine bring it accidentally into development. In others again it forms a prominent and distinctive feature of character, and is rendered palpably evident in its excesses. But in all human beings it is, in a greater or less degree, finally perceptible. It has been, therefore, justly considered a primitive sentiment. Phrenologists call it Veneration. It is, indeed, the instinct given to man by God as security for his own worship. And although, preserving its nature, it becomes perverted from its principal purpose, and although, swerving from that purpose, it serves to modify the relations of human society—the relations of father and child, of master and slave, of the ruler and the ruled—its primitive essence is nevertheless the same, and by a reference to primal causes, may at any moment be determined.

Very nearly akin to this feeling, and liable to the same analysis, is the Faculty of Ideality—which is the sentiment of Poesy. This sentiment is the sense of the beautiful, of the sublime, and of the mystical.[3] Thence spring immediately admiration of the fair flowers, the fairer forests, the bright valleys and rivers and mountains of the Earth— and love of the gleaming stars and other burning glories of Heaven—and, mingled up inextricably with this love and this admiration of Heaven and of Earth, the unconquerable desire—*to know*. Poesy is the sentiment of Intellectual Happiness here, and the Hope of a higher Intellectual Happiness hereafter.[4] Imagination is its Soul.[5] With the *passions* of mankind—although it may modify them greatly —although it may exalt, or inflame, or purify, or control them—it would require little ingenuity to prove that it

[3] We separate the sublime and the mystical—for, despite of high authorities, we are firmly convinced that the latter *may* exist, in the most vivid degree, without giving rise to the sense of the former.

[4] The consciousness of this truth was possessed by no mortal more fully than by Shelley, although he has only once especially alluded to it in his *Hymn to Intellectual Beauty*.

[5] Imagination is, possibly, in man, a lesser degree of the creative power in God. What the Deity imagines, *is*, but *was not* before. What man imagines, *is*, but *was* also. The mind of man cannot imagine what *is not*. This latter point may be demonstrated.—*See Les Premiers Traits de L'Erudition Universelle*, *par* M. Le Baron de Bielfield, 1767.

has no inevitable, and indeed no necessary co-existence. We have hitherto spoken of Poetry in the abstract: we come now to speak of it in its every-day acceptation—that is to say, of the practical result arising from the sentiment we have considered.

And now it appears evident, that since Poetry, in this new sense, *is* the practical result, expressed in language, of this Poetic Sentiment in certain individuals, the only proper method of testing the merits of a poem is by measuring its capabilities of exciting the Poetic Sentiment in others. And to this end we have many aids—in observation, in experience, in ethical analysis, and in the dictates of common sense. Hence the *Poeta nascitur*, which is indisputably true if we consider the Poetic Sentiment, becomes the merest of absurdities when we regard it in reference to the practical result. We do not hesitate to say that a man highly endowed with the powers of Causality—that is to say, a man of metaphysical acumen—will, even with a very deficient share of Ideality, compose a finer poem (if we test it, as we should, by its measure of exciting the Poetic Sentiment) than one who, without such metaphysical acumen, shall be gifted, in the most extraordinary degree, with the faculty of Ideality. For a poem is not the Poetic faculty, but *the means* of exciting it in mankind. Now these means the metaphysician may discover by analysis of their effects in other cases than his own, without even conceiving the nature of these effects—thus arriving at a result which the unaided Ideality of his competitor would be utterly unable, except by accident, to attain. It is more than possible that the man who, of all writers, living or dead, has been most successful in writing the purest of all poems—that is to say, poems which excite most purely, most exclusively, and most powerfully the imaginative faculties in men—owed his extraordinary and almost magical pre-eminence rather to metaphysical than poetical powers. We allude to the author of Christabel, of the Rime of the Auncient Mariner, and of Love—to Coleridge—whose head, if we mistake not its character, gave no great phrenological tokens of Ideality, while the organs of Causality and Comparison were most singularly developed.

Perhaps at this particular moment there are no American poems held in so high estimation by our countrymen as the poems of Drake and of Halleck. The exertions of Mr. George Dearborn have no doubt a far greater share in creating this feeling than the lovers of literature for its own sake and spiritual uses would be willing to admit. We have indeed seldom seen more beautiful volumes than the volumes now before us. But an adventitious interest of a loftier nature—the interest of the living in the memory of the beloved dead—attaches itself to the few literary remains of Drake. The poems which are now given to us with his name are nineteen in number; and whether all, or whether even the best of his writings, it is our present purpose to speak of these alone, since upon this edition his poetical reputation to all time will most probably depend.

It is only lately that we have read *The Culprit Fay*. This is a poem of six hundred and forty irregular lines, generally iambic, and divided into thirty six stanzas, of unequal length. . . .

It is more than probable that from among ten readers of the *Culprit Fay*, nine would immediately pronounce it a poem betokening the most extraordinary powers of imagination, and of these nine, perhaps five or six, poets themselves, and fully impressed with the truth of what we have already assumed, that Ideality is indeed the soul of the Poetic Sentiment, would feel embarrassed between a half-consciousness that they *ought* to admire the production, and a wonder that they *do not*. This embarrassment would then arise from an indistinct conception of the results in which Ideality is rendered manifest. Of these results some few are seen in the *Culprit Fay*, but the greater part of it is utterly destitute of any evidence of imagination whatever. The general character of the poem will, we think, be sufficiently understood by any one who may have taken the trouble to read our foregoing compendium of the narrative. It will be there seen that what is so frequently termed the imaginative power of this story, lies especially—we should have rather said is thought to lie—in the passages we have quoted, or in others of a precisely similar nature. These passages embody, principally, mere specifications of qualities, of habiliments, of punishments, of occupations, of circumstances &c, which the poet has believed in unison with the size, firstly, and secondly with the nature of his Fairies. To all which may be added specifications of other animal existences (such as the toad, the beetle, the lance-fly, the fire-fly and the like) supposed also to be in accordance. An example will best illustrate our meaning upon this point—we take it from page 20.

> He put his acorn helmet on;
> It was plumed of the silk of the thistle down:
> The corslet plate that guarded his breast
> Was once the wild bee's golden vest;
> His cloak of a thousand mingled dyes,
> Was formed of the wings of butterflies;
> His shield was the shell of a lady-bug queen,
> Studs of gold on a ground of green;[6]
> And the quivering lance which he brandished bright
> Was the sting of a wasp he had slain in fight.

We shall now be understood. Were any of the admirers of the *Culprit Fay* asked their opinion of these lines, they would most probably speak in high terms of the *imagination* they display. Yet let the most stolid and the most confessedly unpoetical of these admirers only try the experiment, and he will find, possibly to his extreme surprise, that he himself will have no difficulty whatever in substituting for the equipments of the Fairy, as assigned by the poet, other equipments equally comfortable, no doubt, and equally in unison with the preconceived size, character, and other qualities of the equipped. Why we could accoutre him as well ourselves—let us see.

[6] Chesnut color, or more slack,
Gold upon a ground of black. *Ben Jonson.*

His blue-bell helmet, we have heard,
Was plumed with the down of the humming-bird,
The corslet on his bosom bold
Was once the locust's coat of gold,
His cloak, of a thousand mingled hues,
Was the velvet violet, wet with dews,
His target was the crescent shell
Of the small sea Sidrophel,
And a glittering beam from a maiden's eye
Was the lance which he proudly wav'd on high.

The truth is that the only requisite for writing verses of this nature, *ad libitum*, is a tolerable acquaintance with the qualities of the objects to be detailed, and a very moderate endowment of the faculty of Comparison—which is the chief constituent of *Fancy* or the powers of combination. A thousand such lines may be composed without exercising in the least degree the Poetic Sentiment, which is Ideality, Imagination, or the creative ability. And, as we have before said, the greater portion of the *Culprit Fay* is occupied with these, or similar things, and upon such depends very nearly, if not altogether, its reputation. We select another example from page 25.

But oh! how fair the shape that lay
    Beneath a rainbow bending bright,
She seem'd to the entranced Fay
    The loveliest of the forms of light;
Her mantle was the purple rolled
    At twilight in the west afar;
'Twas tied with threads of dawning gold,
    And button'd with a sparkling star.
Her face was like the lily roon
    That veils the vestal planet's hue;
Her eyes, two beamlets from the moon
    Set floating in the welkin blue.
Her hair is like the sunny beam,
And the diamond gems which round it gleam
Are the pure drops of dewy even,
That ne'er have left their native heaven.

Here again the faculty of Comparison is alone exercised, and no mind possessing the faculty in any ordinary degree would find a difficulty in substituting for the materials employed by the poet other materials equally as good. But viewed as mere efforts of the Fancy and without reference to Ideality, the lines just quoted are much worse than those which were taken from page 20. A congruity was observable in the accoutrements of the Ouphe, and we had no trouble in forming a distinct conception of his appearance when so accoutred. But the most vivid powers of Comparison can attach no definitive idea to even "the loveliest form of light," when habited in a mantle of "rolled purple tied with threads of dawn and buttoned with a star," and sitting at the same time under a rainbow with "beamlet" eyes and a visage of "lily roon."

But if these things evince no Ideality in their author, do they not excite it in others?—if so, we must conclude that without being himself imbued with the Poetic Sentiment, he has still succeeded in writing a fine poem—a supposition as we have before endeavored to show, not altogether paradoxical. Most assuredly we think not. In the case of a great majority of readers the only sentiment aroused by compositions of this order is a species of vague wonder at the writer's *ingenuity*, and it is this indeterminate sense of wonder which passes but too frequently current for the proper influence of the Poetic power. For our own parts we plead guilty to a predominant sense of the ludicrous while occupied in the perusal of the poem before us—a sense whose promptings we sincerely and honestly endeavored to quell, perhaps not altogether successfully, while penning our compend of the narrative. That a feeling of this nature is utterly at war with the Poetic Sentiment will not be disputed by those who comprehend the character of the sentiment itself. This character is finely shadowed out in that popular although vague idea so prevalent throughout all time, that a species of melancholy is inseparably connected with the higher manifestations of the beautiful. But with the numerous and seriously-adduced incongruities of the Culprit Fay, we find it generally impossible to connect other ideas than those

of the ridiculous. We are bidden, in the first place, and in
a tone of sentiment and language adapted to the loftiest
breathings of the Muse, to imagine a race of Fairies in the
vicinity of West Point. We are told, with a grave air, of
their camp, of their king, and especially of their sentry,
who is a wood-tick. We are informed that an Ouphe of
about an inch in height has committed a deadly sin in
falling in love with a mortal maiden, who may, very possibly, be six feet in her stockings. The consequence to the
Ouphe is—what? Why, that he has "dyed his wings,"
"broken his elfin chain," and "quenched his flame-wood
lamp." And he is therefore sentenced to what? To catch a
spark from the tail of a falling star, and a drop of water
from the belly of a sturgeon. What are his equipments
for the first adventure? An acorn helmet, a thistle-down
plume, a butterfly cloak, a lady-bug shield, cockle-seed
spurs, and a fire-fly horse. How does he ride to the second?
On the back of a bull-frog. What are his opponents in
the one? "Drizzly mists," "sulphur and smoke," "shadowy
hands" and "flame-shot tongues." What in the other?
"Mailed shrimps," "prickly prongs," "blood-red leeches,"
"jellied quarls," "stony star fishes," "lancing squabs" and
"soldier crabs." Is that all? No—Although only an inch high
he is in imminent danger of seduction from a "sylphid
queen," dressed in a mantle of "rolled purple," "tied with
threads of dawning gold," "buttoned with a sparkling star,"
and sitting under a rainbow with "beamlet eyes" and a
countenance of "lily roon." In our account of all this matter we have had reference to the book—and to the book
alone. It will be difficult to prove us guilty in any degree
of distortion or exaggeration. Yet such are the puerilities
we daily find ourselves called upon to admire, as among
the loftiest efforts of the human mind, and which not to
assign a rank with the proud trophies of the matured and
vigorous genius of England, is to prove ourselves at once
a fool, a maligner, and no patriot.[7]

[7] A review of Drake's poems, emanating from one of our
proudest Universities, does not scruple to make use of the following language in relation to the *Culprit Fay*. "It is, to say the
least, an elegant production, the purest specimen of Ideality we*

As an instance of what may be termed the sublimely ridiculous we quote the following lines from page 17.

> With sweeping tail and quivering fin,
>   Through the wave the sturgeon flew,
> And like the heaven-shot javelin,
>   He sprung above the waters blue.
>
> Instant as the star-fall light,
>   He plunged into the deep again,
> But left an arch of silver bright
>   The rainbow of the moony main.
>
> *It was a strange and lovely sight*
>   *To see the puny goblin there;*
> *He seemed an angel form of light*
>   *With azure wing and sunny hair,*
>   *Throned on a cloud of purple fair*
> *Circled with blue and edged with white*
>   *And sitting at the fall of even*
>   *Beneath the bow of summer heaven.*

The verses here italicized, if considered without their context, have a certain air of dignity, elegance, and chastity of thought. If however we apply the context, we are immediately overwhelmed with the grotesque. It is impossible to read without laughing such expressions as "It was a strange and lovely sight"—"He seemed an angel form of light"—"And sitting at the fall of even, beneath the bow of summer heaven" to a Fairy—a goblin—an Ouphe—half an inch high, dressed in an acorn helmet and butterfly-cloak, and sitting on the water in a muscle-shell, with a "brown-backed sturgeon" turning somersets over his head.

In a world where evil is a mere consequence of good, and good a mere consequence of evil—in short where all of which we have any conception is good or bad only by comparison—we have never yet been fully able to appreciate the validity of that decision which would debar the

---

have ever met with, sustaining in each incident a most bewitching interest. Its very title is enough," &c. &c. We quote these expressions as a fair specimen of the general unphilosophical and adulatory tenor of our criticism.

critic from enforcing upon his readers the merits or demerits of a work by placing it in juxta-position with another. It seems to us that an adage based in the purest
ignorance has had more to do with this popular feeling
than any just reason founded upon common sense. Thinking thus, we shall have no scruple in illustrating our opinion in regard to what *is not* Ideality or the Poetic Power,
by an example of what *is*.[8] We have already given the
description of the Sylphid Queen in the *Culprit Fay*. In
the *Queen Mab* of Shelley a Fairy is thus introduced—

> Those who had looked upon the sight,
>   Passing all human glory,
> Saw not the yellow moon,
> Saw not the mortal scene,
> Heard not the night wind's rush,
> Heard not an earthly sound,
> Saw but the fairy pageant,
> Heard but the heavenly strains
> That filled the lonely dwelling—

and thus described—

> The Fairy's frame was slight; yon fibrous cloud
> That catches but the palest tinge of even,
> And which the straining eye can hardly seize
> When melting into eastern twilight's shadow,
> Were scarce so thin, so slight; but the fair star
> That gems the glittering coronet of morn,
> *Sheds not a light so mild, so powerful,*
> *As that which, bursting from the Fairy's form,*
> *Spread a purpureal halo round the scene,*
>   *Yet with an undulating motion,*
>   *Swayed to her outline gracefully.*

[8] As examples of entire poems of the purest ideality, we would
cite the *Prometheus Vinctus* of Æschylus, the *Inferno* of Dante,
Cervantes' *Destruction of Numantia*, the *Comus* of Milton,
Pope's *Rape of the Lock*, Burns' *Tam O'Shanter*, the *Auncient
Mariner*, the *Christabel*, and the *Kubla Khan* of Coleridge; and
most especially the *Sensitive Plant* of Shelley, and the *Nightingale*
of Keats. We have seen American poems evincing the faculty in
the highest degree.

In these exquisite lines the Faculty of mere Comparison is but little exercised—that of Ideality in a wonderful degree. It is probable that in a similar case the poet we are now reviewing would have formed the face of the Fairy of the "fibrous cloud," her arms of the "pale tinge of even," her eyes of the "fair stars," and her body of the "twilight shadow." Having so done, his admirers would have congratulated him upon his *imagination*, not taking the trouble to think that they themselves could at any moment *imagine* a Fairy of materials equally as good, and conveying an equally distinct idea. Their mistake would be precisely analogous to that of many a schoolboy who admires the imagination displayed in *Jack the Giant-Killer*, and is finally rejoiced at discovering his own imagination to surpass that of the author since the monsters destroyed by Jack are only about forty feet in height, and he himself has no trouble in imagining some of one hundred and forty. It will be seen that the Fairy of Shelley is not a mere compound of incongruous natural objects, inartificially put together, and unaccompanied by any *moral* sentiment—but a being, in the illustration of whose nature some physical elements are used collaterally as adjuncts, while the main conception springs immediately *or thus apparently springs*, from the brain of the poet, enveloped in the moral sentiments of grace, of color, of motion—of the beautiful, of the mystical, of the august—in short of *the ideal*.[9]

It is by no means our intention to deny that in the *Culprit Fay* are passages of a different order from those to which we have objected—passages evincing a degree of imagination not to be discovered in the plot, conception, or general execution of the poem. The opening stanza will afford us a tolerable example.

'Tis the middle watch of a summer's night—
The earth is dark, but the heavens are bright

[9] Among things, which not only in our opinion, but in the opinion of far wiser and better men, are to be ranked with the mere prettinesses of the Muse, are the positive similes so abundant in the writings of antiquity, and so much insisted upon by the critics of the reign of Queen Anne.

Naught is seen in the vault on high
But the moon, and the stars, and the cloudless sky,
And the flood which rolls its milky hue
A river of light on the welkin blue.
The moon looks down on old Cronest,
She mellows the shades of his shaggy breast,
And seems his huge grey form to throw
In a silver cone on the wave below;
His sides are broken by spots of shade,
By the walnut bough and the cedar made,
And through their clustering branches dark
Glimmers and dies the fire-fly's spark—
Like starry twinkles that momently break
Through the rifts of the gathering tempest rack.

There is Ideality in these lines—but except in the case
of the words italicized—it is Ideality *not of a high order*.
We have it is true, a collection of natural objects, each
individually of great beauty, and, if actually seen as in
nature, capable of exciting in any mind, through the
means of the Poetic Sentiment more or less inherent in
all, a certain sense of the beautiful. But to view such natural objects as they exist, and to behold them through the
medium of words, are different things. Let us pursue the
idea that such a collection as we have here will produce,
of necessity, the Poetic Sentiment, and we may as well
make up our minds to believe that a catalogue of such
expressions as moon, sky, trees, rivers, mountains &c, shall
be capable of exciting it,—it is merely an extension of the
principle. But in the line "the earth is dark, *but* the heavens are bright" besides the simple mention of the "dark
earth" and the "bright heaven," we have, directly, the
moral sentiment of the brightness of the sky compensating
for the darkness of the earth—and thus, indirectly, of the
happiness of a future state compensating for the miseries
of a present. All this is effected by the simple introduction
of the word *but* between the "dark heaven" and the "bright
earth"—this introduction, however, was prompted by the
Poetic Sentiment, and by the Poetic Sentiment alone. The
case is analogous in the expression "glimmers and dies,"

where the imagination is exalted by the moral sentiment of beauty heightened in dissolution.

In one or two shorter passages of the *Culprit Fay* the poet will recognize the purely ideal, and be able at a glance to distinguish it from that baser alloy upon which we have descanted. We give them without farther comment.

> The winds *are whist,* and the owl is still
>   The bat in the shelvy rock *is hid*
> And naught is heard on the *lonely* hill
> But the cricket's chirp and the answer *shrill*
>   Of the gauze-winged katy-did;
> And the plaint of the *wailing* whippoorwill
>   Who mourns *unseen,* and ceaseless sings
> Ever a note of wail and wo—
>
> Up to the vaulted firmament
> His path the fire-fly courser bent,
> And at every gallop on the wind
> *He flung a glittering spark behind.*
>
> He blessed the force of the charmed line,
>   And he banned the water-goblins' spite,
> For he saw around *in the sweet moonshine,*
> *Their little wee faces above the brine;*
> *Giggling and laughing with all their might*
> At the piteous hap of the Fairy wight. . . .

DOCUMENT 25

Ralph Waldo Emerson

Ralph Waldo Emerson (1803–82) was invited, in his turn, to deliver the Phi Beta Kappa address at Cambridge in 1837. Building upon the foundations laid by his predecessors, he carried the argument for a national literature to its extreme point: the freedom and integrity of the individual soul. "We have listened too long to the courtly muses of Europe," he told his listeners, "The spirit of the American freeman is already suspected to be timid, imitative, tame." But he also admonished them, each and all, that "The world is nothing, the man is all; . . . it is for you to dare all." So that "a nation of men will for the first time exist, because each believes himself inspired by the Divine Soul which also inspires all men." The argument for literary nationalism had gone full cycle; the imminent achievement of a national literature (1837–60) had made irrelevant the debate on how to bring such a literature into being.

TEXT: from *Nature, Addresses, and Lectures*, Boston, 1849; later Volume I of the Centenary Edition of the *Works*, Boston, 1903.

The American Scholar

I greet you on the re-commencement of our literary year. Our anniversary is one of hope, and, perhaps, not enough of labor. We do not meet for games of strength or skill, for the recitation of histories, tragedies, and odes, like the ancient Greeks; for parliaments of love and poesy, like the Troubadours; nor for the advancement of science, like our cotemporaries in the British and European capitals. Thus far, our holiday has been simply a friendly sign of the survival of the love of letters amongst a people too busy to give to letters any more. As such it is precious as the sign of an indestructible instinct. Perhaps the time is already come when it ought to be, and will be, something else; when the sluggard intellect of this continent will look from under its iron lids and fill the postponed expectation of the world with something better than the exertions of mechanical skill. Our day of dependence, our long apprenticeship to the learning of other lands, draws to a close. The millions that around us are rushing into life, cannot always be fed on the sere remains of foreign harvests. Events, actions arise, that must be sung, that will sing themselves. Who can doubt that poetry will revive and lead in a new age, as the star in the constellation Harp, which now flames in our zenith, astronomers announce, shall one day be the pole-star for a thousand years?

In this hope I accept the topic which not only usage but the nature of our association seem to prescribe to this day,—the AMERICAN SCHOLAR. Year by year we come up hither to read one more chapter of his biography. Let us inquire what light new days and events have thrown on his character and his hopes.

It is one of those fables which out of an unknown antiquity, convey an unlooked-for wisdom, that the gods, in the beginning, divided Man into men, that he might be more helpful to himself; just as the hand was divided into fingers, the better to answer its end.

The old fable covers a doctrine ever new and sublime; that there is One Man,—present to all particular men only partially, or through one faculty; and that you must take the whole society to find the whole man. Man is not a farmer, or a professor, or an engineer, but he is all. Man is priest, and scholar, and statesman, and producer, and soldier. In the *divided* or social state these functions are parcelled out to individuals, each of whom aims to do his stint of the joint work, whilst each other performs his. The fable implies that the individual, to possess himself, must sometimes return from his own labor to embrace all the other laborers. But unfortunately, this original unit, this fountain of power, has been so distributed to multitudes, has been so minutely subdivided and peddled out, that it is spilled into drops, and cannot be gathered. The state of society is one in which the members have suffered amputation from the trunk, and strut about so many walking monsters,—a good finger, a neck, a stomach, an elbow, but never a man.

Man is thus metamorphosed into a thing, into many things. The planter, who is Man sent out into the field to gather food, is seldom cheered by any idea of the true dignity of his ministry. He sees his bushel and his cart, and nothing beyond, and sinks into the farmer, instead of Man on the farm. The tradesman scarcely ever gives an ideal worth to his work, but is ridden by the routine of his craft, and the soul is subject to dollars. The priest becomes a form; the attorney a statute-book; the mechanic a machine; the sailor a rope of a ship.

In this distribution of functions the scholar is the delegated intellect. In the right state he is *Man Thinking*. In the degenerate state, when the victim of society, he tends to become a mere thinker, or still worse, the parrot of other men's thinking.

In this view of him, as Man Thinking, the theory of his office is contained. Him nature solicits with all her placid, all her monitory pictures; him the past instructs; him the future invites. Is not indeed every man a student, and do not all things exist for the student's behoof? And, finally, is not the true scholar the only true master? But the old oracle said, 'All things have two handles: beware of the wrong one.' In life, too often, the scholar errs with mankind and forfeits his privilege. Let us see him in his school, and consider him in reference to the main influences he receives.

I. The first in time and the first in importance of the influences upon the mind is that of nature. Every day, the sun; and, after sunset, night and her stars. Ever the winds blow; ever the grass grows. Every day, men and women, conversing, beholding and beholden. The scholar is he of all men whom this spectacle most engages. He must settle its value in his mind. What is nature to him? There is never a beginning, there is never an end, to the inexplicable continuity of this web of God, but always circular power returning into itself. Therein it resembles his own spirit, whose beginning, whose ending, he never can find, —so entire, so boundless. Far too as her splendors shine, system on system shooting like rays, upward, downward, without centre, without circumference,—in the mass and in the particle, nature hastens to render account of herself to the mind. Classification begins. To the young mind every thing is individual, stands by itself. By and by, it finds how to join two things, and see in them one nature; then three, then three thousand; and so, tyrannized over by its own unifying instinct, it goes on tying things together, diminishing anomalies, discovering roots running under ground whereby contrary and remote things cohere and flower out from one stem. It presently learns that since the dawn of history there has been a constant accumulation and classifying of facts. But what is classification but the perceiving that these objects are not chaotic, and are not foreign, but have a law which is also a law of the human mind? The astronomer discovers that geometry, a pure abstraction of the human mind, is the measure of planetary motion. The chemist finds proportions and intelligible method throughout matter; and science is nothing but the finding of analogy, identity, in the most remote parts. The ambitious soul sits down before each refractory fact; one after another reduces all strange constitutions, all new powers, to their class and their law, and goes on for ever to animate the last fibre of organization, the outskirts of nature, by insight.

Thus to him, to this school-boy under the bending dome of day, is suggested that he and it proceed from one root; one is leaf and one is flower; relation, sympathy, stirring in every vein. And what is that Root? Is not that the soul of his soul? A thought too bold, a dream too wild. Yet when this spiritual light shall have revealed the law of more earthly natures—when he has learned to worship the soul, and to see that the natural philosophy that now is, is only the first gropings of its gigantic hand, he shall look

forward to an ever expanding knowledge as to a becoming
creator. He shall see that nature is the opposite of the
soul, answering to it part for part. One is seal and one
is print. Its beauty is the beauty of his own mind. Its
laws are the laws of his own mind. Nature then becomes
to him the measure of his attainments. So much of nature as he is ignorant of, so much of his own mind does
he not yet possess. And, in fine, the ancient precept,
"Know thyself," and the modern precept, "Study nature,"
become at last one maxim.

II. The next great influence into the spirit of the scholar
is the mind of the Past—in whatever form, whether of
literature, of art, of institutions, that mind is inscribed.
Books are the best type of the influence of the past, and
perhaps we shall get at the truth—learn the amount of
this influence more conveniently—by considering their
value alone.

The theory of books is noble. The scholar of the first
age received into him the world around; brooded thereon;
gave it the new arrangement of his own mind, and uttered
it again. It came into him life; it went out from him
truth. It came to him short-lived actions; it went out from
him immortal thoughts. It came to him business; it went
from him poetry. It was dead fact; now, it is quick
thought. It can stand, and it can go. It now endures, it
now flies, it now inspires. Precisely in proportion to the
depth of mind from which it issued, so high does it soar,
so long does it sing.

Or, I might say, it depends on how far the process had
gone of transmuting life into truth. In proportion to the
completeness of the distillation, so will the purity and
imperishableness of the product be. But none is quite perfect. As no air-pump can by any means make a perfect
vacuum, so neither can any artist entirely exclude the con-
ventional, the local, the perishable from his book, or write
a book of pure thought, that shall be as efficient, in all
respects, to a remote posterity, as to cotemporaries, or
rather to the second age. Each age, it is found, must write

its own books; or rather, each generation for the next succeeding. The books of an older period will not fit this.

Yet hence arises a grave mischief. The sacredness which attaches to the act of creation, the act of thought, is transferred to the record. The poet chanting was felt to be a divine man: henceforth the chant is divine also. The writer was a just and wise spirit: henceforward it is settled, the book is perfect; as love of the hero corrupts into worship of his statue. Instantly the book becomes noxious: the guide is a tyrant. The sluggish and perverted mind of the multitude, slow to open to the incursions of Reason, having once so opened, having once received this book, stands upon it, and makes an outcry if it is disparaged. Colleges are built on it. Books are written on it by thinkers, not by Man Thinking; by men of talent, that is, who start wrong, who set out from accepted dogmas, not from their own sight of principles. Meek young men grow up in libraries, believing it their duty to accept the views which Cicero, which Locke, which Bacon, have given, forgetful that Cicero, Locke, and Bacon were only young men in libraries when they wrote these books.

Hence, instead of Man Thinking, we have the bookworm. Hence, the book-learned class, who value books, as such; not as related to nature and the human constitution, but as making a sort of Third Estate with the world and the soul. Hence, the restorers of readings, the emendators, the bibliomaniacs of all degrees.

Books are the best of things, well used; abused, among the worst. What is the right use? What is the one end, which all means go to effect? They are for nothing but to inspire. I had better never see a book than to be warped by its attraction clean out of my own orbit, and made a satellite instead of a system. The one thing in the world of value is the active soul. This every man is entitled to; this every man contains within him, although, in almost all men obstructed and as yet unborn. The soul active sees absolute truth and utters truth, or creates. In this action it is genius; not the privilege of here and there a favorite, but the sound estate of every man. In its essence it is progressive. The book, the college, the school of art, the institution of any kind, stop with some past utterance of genius. This is good, say they, let us hold by this. They pin me down. They look backward and not forward. But genius looks forward: the eyes of man are set in his forehead, not in his hindhead: man hopes: genius creates. Whatever talents may be, if the man create not, the pure efflux of the Deity is not his;—cinders and smoke there may be, but not yet flame. There are creative manners, there are creative actions, and creative words; manners, actions, words, that is, indicative of no custom or authority, but springing spontaneous from the mind's own sense of good and fair.

On the other part, instead of being its own seer, let it receive from another mind its truth, though it were in torrents of light, without periods of solitude, inquest, and self-recovery, and a fatal disservice is done. Genius is always sufficiently the enemy of genius by over influence. The literature of every nation bear me witness. The English dramatic poets have Shakspearized now for two hundred years.

Undoubtedly there is a right way of reading, so it be sternly subordinated. Man Thinking must not be subdued by his instruments. Books are for the scholar's idle times. When he can read God directly, the hour is too precious to be wasted in other men's transcripts of their readings. But when the intervals of darkness come, as come they must,—when the sun is hid, and the stars withdraw their shining,—we repair to the lamps which were kindled by their ray, to guide our steps to the East again, where the dawn is. We hear, that we may speak. The Arabian proverb says, "A fig tree, looking on a fig tree, becometh fruitful."

It is remarkable, the character of the pleasure we derive from the best books. They impress us with the conviction that one nature wrote and the same reads. We read the verses of one of the great English poets, of Chaucer, of Marvell, of Dryden, with the most modern joy,—with a pleasure, I mean, which is in great part caused by the abstraction of all *time* from their verses. There is some awe mixed with the joy of our surprise when this poet, who lived in some past world, two or three hundred years ago, says that which lies close to my own soul, that which I also had wellnigh thought and said. But for the evidence thence afforded to the philosophical doctrine of the identity of all minds, we should suppose some preëstablished harmony, some foresight of souls that were to be, and some preparation of stores for their future wants, like the fact observed in insects, who lay up food before death for the young grub they shall never see.

I would not be hurried by any love of system, by any exaggeration of instincts, to underrate the Book. We all know that, as the human body can be nourished on any food, though it were boiled grass and the broth of shoes, so the human mind can be fed by any knowledge. And great and heroic men have existed who had almost no other information than by the printed page. I only would say that it needs a strong head to bear that diet. One must be an inventor to read well. As the proverb says, "He that would bring home the wealth of the Indies, must carry out the wealth of the Indies." There is then creative reading as well as creative writing. When the mind is braced by labor and invention, the page of whatever book we read becomes luminous with manifold allusion. Every sentence is doubly significant, and the sense of our author is as broad as the world. We then see, what is always true, that as the seer's hour of vision is short and rare among heavy days and months, so is its record, perchance, the least part of his volume. The discerning will read, in his Plato or Shakspeare, only that least part,—only the authentic utterances of the oracle;—all the rest he rejects, were it never so many times Plato's and Shakspeare's.

Of course, there is a portion of reading quite indispensable to a wise man. History and exact science he must learn by laborious reading. Colleges, in like manner, have their indispensable office,—to teach elements. But they can only highly serve us when they aim not to drill, but to create; when they gather from far every ray of various genius to their hospitable halls, and by the concentrated fires, set the hearts of their youth on flame. Thought and knowledge are natures in which apparatus and pretension avail nothing. Gowns and pecuniary foundations, though of towns of gold, can never countervail the least sentence or syllable of wit. Forget this, and our American colleges will recede in their public importance, whilst they grow richer every year.

III. There goes in the world a notion that the scholar should be a recluse, a valetudinarian,—as unfit for any handiwork or public labor as a penknife for an axe. The so-called 'practical men' sneer at speculative men, as if, because they speculate or *see*, they could do nothing. I have heard it said that the clergy,—who are always, more universally than any other class, the scholars of their day, —are addressed as women; that the rough, spontaneous conversation of men they do not hear, but only a mincing and diluted speech. They are often virtually disfranchised; and indeed there are advocates for their celibacy. As far as this is true of the studious classes, it is not just and wise. Action is with the scholar subordinate, but it is essential. Without it, he is not yet man. Without it thought can never ripen into truth. Whilst the world hangs before the eye as a cloud of beauty, we cannot even see its beauty. Inaction is cowardice, but there can be no scholar without the heroic mind. The preamble of thought, the transition through which it passes from the unconscious to the conscious, is action. Only so much do I know as I have lived. Instantly we know whose words are loaded with life and whose not.

The world,—this shadow of the soul, or *other me*, lies wide around. Its attractions are the keys which unlock my thoughts and make me acquainted with myself. I run eagerly into this resounding tumult. I grasp the hands of those next me, and take my place in the ring to suffer and to work, taught by an instinct that so shall the dumb abyss be vocal with speech. I pierce its order; I dissipate its fear; I dispose of it within the circuit of my expanding life. So much only of life as I know by experience, so much of the wilderness have I vanquished and planted, or so far have I extended my being, my dominion. I do not see how any man can afford, for the sake of his nerves and his nap, to spare any action in which he can partake. It is pearls and rubies to his discourse. Drudgery, calamity, exasperation, want, are instructers in eloquence and wisdom. The true scholar grudges every opportunity of action past by as a loss of power.

It is the raw material out of which the intellect moulds her splendid products. A strange process too, this by which experience is converted into thought, as a mulberry leaf is converted into satin. The manufacture goes forward at all hours.

The actions and events of our childhood and youth are now matters of calmest observation. They lie like fair pictures in the air. Not so with our recent actions,—with the business which we now have in hand. On this we are quite unable to speculate. Our affections as yet circulate through it. We no more feel or know it than we feel the feet, or the hand, or the brain of our body. The new deed is yet a part of life,—remains for a time immersed in our unconscious life. In some contemplative hour it detaches itself from the life like a ripe fruit, to become a thought of the mind. Instantly, it is raised, transfigured; the corruptible has put on incorruption. Henceforth it is an object of beauty, however base its origin and neighborhood. Observe too the impossibility of antedating this act. In its grub state, it cannot fly, it cannot shine, it is a dull grub. But suddenly, without observation, the selfsame thing unfurls beautiful wings, and is an angel of wisdom. So is there no fact, no event, in our private history, which shall not, sooner or later, lose its adhesive, inert form, and astonish us by soaring from our body into the empyrean. Cradle and infancy, school and playground, the fear of boys, and dogs, and ferules, the love of little maids and berries, and many another fact that once filled the whole sky, are gone already; friend and relative, profession and party, town and country, nation and world, must also soar and sing.

Of course, he who has put forth his total strength in fit actions, has the richest return of wisdom. I will not shut myself out of this globe of action, and transplant an oak into a flower-pot, there to hunger and pine; nor trust the revenue of some single faculty, and exhaust one vein of thought, much like those Savoyards who, getting their livelihood by carving shepherds, shepherdesses, and smoking Dutchmen for all Europe, went out one day to the mountain to find stock, and discovered that they had whittled up the last of their pine-trees. Authors we have, in numbers, who have written out their vein, and who, moved by a commendable prudence, sail for Greece or Palestine, follow the trapper into the prairie, or ramble round Algiers, to replenish their merchantable stock.

If it were only for a vocabulary, the scholar would be covetous of action. Life is our dictionary. Years are well spent in country labors; in town,—in the insight into trades and manufactures; in frank intercourse with many men and women; in science; in art; to the one end of mastering in all their facts a language by which to illustrate and embody our perceptions. I learn immediately from any speaker how much he has already lived, through the poverty or the splendor of his speech. Life lies behind us as the quarry from whence we get tiles and copestones for the masonry of to-day. This is the way to learn grammar. Colleges and books only copy the language which the field and the work-yard made.

But the final value of action, like that of books, and better than books, is, that it is a resource. That great principle of Undulation in nature, that shows itself in the inspiring and expiring of the breath; in desire and satiety; in the ebb and flow of the sea; in day and night; in heat and cold; and as yet more deeply ingrained in every atom and every fluid, is known to us under the name of Polarity,—these "fits of easy transmission and reflection," as Newton called them, are the law of nature because they are the law of spirit.

The mind now thinks, now acts, and each fit reproduces the other. When the artist has exhausted his materials, when the fancy no longer paints, when thoughts are no longer apprehended and books are a weariness,— he has always the resource *to live*. Character is higher than intellect. Thinking is the function. Living is the functionary. The stream retreats to its source. A great soul will be strong to live, as well as strong to think. Does he lack organ or medium to impart his truths? He can still fall back on this elemental force of living them. This is a total act. Thinking is a partial act. Let the grandeur of justice shine in his affairs. Let the beauty of affection cheer his lowly roof. Those 'far from fame,' who dwell and act with him, will feel the force of his constitution in the doings and passages of the day better than it can be measured by any public and designed display. Time shall teach him that the scholar loses no hour which the man lives. Herein he unfolds the sacred germ of his instinct, screened from influence. What is lost in seemliness is gained in strength. Not out of those on whom systems of education have exhausted their culture comes the helpful giant to destroy the old or to build the new, but out of unhandselled savage nature, out of terrible Druids and Berserkirs, come at last Alfred and Shakspeare.

I hear therefore with joy whatever is beginning to be said of the dignity and necessity of labor to every citizen. There is virtue yet in the hoe and the spade, for learned as well as for unlearned hands. And labor is everywhere welcome; always we are invited to work; only be this limitation observed, that a man shall not for the sake of wider activity sacrifice any opinion to the popular judgments and modes of action.

I have now spoken of the education of the scholar by nature, by books, and by action. It remains to say somewhat of his duties.

They are such as become Man Thinking. They may all be comprised in self-trust. The office of the scholar is to cheer, to raise, and to guide men by showing them facts amidst appearances. He plies the slow, unhonored, and unpaid task of observation. Flamsteed and Herschel, in their glazed observatories, may catalogue the stars with the praise of all men, and the results being splendid and useful, honor is sure. But he, in his private observatory, cataloguing obscure and nebulous stars of the human mind, which as yet no man has thought of as such,— watching days and months sometimes for a few facts; correcting still his old records;—must relinquish display and immediate fame. In the long period of his preparation, he must betray often an ignorance and shiftlessness in popular arts, incurring the disdain of the able who shoulder him aside. Long he must stammer in his speech; often forego the living for the dead. Worse yet, he must accept, —how often! poverty and solitude. For the ease and pleasure of treading the old road, accepting the fashions, the education, the religion of society, he takes the cross of making his own and, of course, the self-accusation, the faint heart, the frequent uncertainty and loss of time, which are the nettles and tangling vines in the way of the self-relying and self-directed; and the state of virtual hostility in which he seems to stand to society, and especially to educated society. For all this loss and scorn, what offset? He is to find consolation in exercising the highest functions of human nature. He is one who raises himself from private considerations and breathes and lives on public and illustrious thoughts. He is the world's eye. He is the world's heart. He is to resist the vulgar prosperity that retrogrades ever to barbarism, by preserving and communicating heroic sentiments, noble biographies, melodious verse, and the conclusions of history. Whatsoever oracles the human heart, in all emergencies, in all solemn hours, has uttered as its commentary on the world of actions,— these he shall receive and impart. And whatsoever new verdict Reason from her inviolable seat pronounces on the passing men and events of to-day,—this he shall hear and promulgate.

These being his functions, it becomes him to feel all confidence in himself, and to defer never to the popular cry. He and he only knows the world. The world of any moment is the merest appearance. Some great decorum, some fetish of a government, some ephemeral trade, or war, or man, is cried up by half mankind and cried down by the other half, as if all depended on this particular up or down. The odds are that the whole question is not worth the poorest thought which the scholar has lost in listening to the controversy. Let him not quit his belief that a popgun is a popgun, though the ancient and honorable of the earth affirm it to be the crack of doom. In silence, in steadiness, in severe abstraction, let him hold by himself; add observation to observation, patient of neglect, patient of reproach; and bide his own time,—happy enough if he can satify himself alone that this day he has seen something truly. Success treads on every right step. For the instinct is sure that prompts him to tell his brother what he thinks. He then learns that in going down into the secrets of his own mind, he has descended into the secrets of all minds. He learns that he who has mastered any law in his private thoughts, is master to that extent of all men whose language he speaks, and of all into whose language his own can be translated. The poet, in utter solitude remembering his spontaneous thoughts and recording them, is found to have recorded that which men in crowded cities find true for them also. The orator distrusts at first the fitness of his frank confessions,—his want of knowledge of the persons he addresses,—until he finds that he is the complement of his hearers;—that they drink his words because he fulfils for them their own nature; the deeper he dives into his privatest, secretest presentiment, to his wonder he finds this is the most acceptable, most public, and universally true. The people delight in it; the better part of every man feels, This is my music; this is myself.

In self-trust, all the virtues are comprehended. Free should the scholar be,—free and brave. Free even to the definition of freedom, "without any hindrance that does not arise out of his own constitution." Brave; for fear is a thing, which a scholar by his very function puts behind him. Fear always springs from ignorance. It is a shame to him if his tranquillity, amid dangerous times, arise from the presumption that, like children and women, his is a protected class; or if he seek a temporary peace by the diversion of his thoughts from politics or vexed questions, hiding his head like an ostrich in the flowering bushes, peeping into microscopes, and turning rhymes, as a boy whistles to keep his courage up. So is the danger a danger still; so is the fear worse. Manlike let him turn and face it. Let him look into its eye and search its nature, inspect its origin,—see the whelping of this lion,—which lies no great way back; he will then find in himself a perfect comprehension of its nature and extent; he will have made his hands meet on the other side, and can henceforth defy it and pass on superior. The world is his who can see through its pretension. What deafness, what stone-blind custom, what overgrown error you behold, is there only by sufferance,—by your sufferance. See it to be a lie, and you have already dealt it its mortal blow.

Yes, we are the cowed,—we the trustless. It is a mischievous notion that we are come late into nature; that the world was finished a long time ago. As the world was plastic and fluid in the hands of God, so it is ever to so much of his attributes as we bring to it. To ignorance and sin, it is flint. They adapt themselves to it as they may; but in proportion as a man has any thing in him divine, the firmament flows before him and takes his signet and form. Not he is great who can alter matter, but he who can alter my state of mind. They are the kings of the world who give the color of their present thought to all nature and all art, and persuade men by the cheerful serenity of their carrying the matter, that this thing which they do, is the apple which the ages have desired to pluck, now at last ripe, and inviting nations to the harvest. The great man makes the great thing. Wherever Macdonald sits, there is the head of the table. Linnæus makes botany the most alluring of studies, and wins it from the farmer and the herb-woman; Davy, chemistry; and Cuvier, fossils. The day is always his who works in it with serenity and great aims. The unstable estimates of men crowd to him whose mind is filled with a truth, as the heaped waves of the Atlantic follow the moon.

For this self-trust, the reason is deeper than can be fathomed,—darker than can be enlightened. I might not carry with me the feeling of my audience in stating my own belief. But I have already shown the ground of my hope, in adverting to the doctrine that man is one. I believe man has been wronged; he has wronged himself. He has almost lost the light that can lead him back to his prerogatives. Men are become of no account. Men in history, men in the world of to-day are bugs, are spawn, and are called 'the mass' and 'the herd.' In a century, in a millennium, one or two men; that is to say,—one or two approximations to the right state of every man. All the rest behold in the hero or the poet their own green and crude being,—ripened; yes, and are content to be less, so *that* may attain to its full stature. What a testimony,—full of grandeur, full of pity, is borne to the demands of his own nature, by the poor clansman, the poor partisan, who rejoices in the glory of his chief. The poor and the low find some amends to their immense moral capacity, for their acquiescence in a political and social inferiority. They are content to be brushed like flies from the path of a great person, so that justice shall be done by him to that common nature which it is the dearest desire of all to see enlarged and glorified. They sun themselves in the great man's light, and feel it to be their own element. They cast the dignity of man from their downtrod selves upon the shoulders of a hero, and will perish to add one drop of blood to make that great heart beat, those giant sinews combat and conquer. He lives for us, and we live in him.

Men such as they are, very naturally seek money or power; and power because it is as good as money,—the "spoils," so called, "of office." And why not? for they aspire to the highest, and this, in their sleep-walking, they dream is highest. Wake them and they shall quit the false good and leap to the true, and leave governments to clerks and desks. This revolution is to be wrought by the gradual domestication of the idea of Culture. The main enterprise of the world for splendor, for extent, is the upbuilding of a man. Here are the materials strown along the ground. The private life of one man shall be a more illustrious monarchy, more formidable to its enemy, more sweet and serene in its influence to its friend, than any kingdom in history. For a man, rightly viewed, comprehendeth the particular natures of all men. Each philosopher, each bard, each actor, has only done for me, as by a delegate, what one day I can do for myself. The books which once we valued more than the apple of the eye, we have quite exhausted. What is that but saying that we have come up with the point of view which the universal mind took through the eyes of one scribe; we have been that man, and have passed on. First one; then another; we drain all cisterns, and, waxing greater by all these supplies, we crave a better and more abundant food. The man has never lived that can feed us ever. The human mind cannot be enshrined in a person who shall set a barrier on any one side to this unbounded, unboundable empire. It is one central fire which, flaming now out of the lips of Etna, lightens the capes of Sicily; and now out of the throat of Vesuvius, illuminates the towers and vineyards of Naples. It is one light which beams out of a thousand stars. It is one soul which animates all men.

But I have dwelt perhaps tediously upon this abstraction of the Scholar. I ought not to delay longer to add what I have to say, of nearer reference to the time and to this country.

Historically, there is thought to be a difference in the ideas which predominate over successive epochs, and there are data for marking the genius of the Classic, of the Romantic, and now of the Reflective or Philosophical age. With the views I have intimated of the oneness or the identity of the mind through all individuals, I do not much dwell on these differences. In fact, I believe each individual passes through all three. The boy is a Greek; the youth, romantic; the adult, reflective. I deny not, however, that a revolution in the leading idea may be distinctly enough traced.

Our age is bewailed as the age of Introversion. Must that needs be evil? We, it seems, are critical; we are embarrassed with second thoughts; we cannot enjoy any thing for hankering to know whereof the pleasure consists; we are lined with eyes; we see with our feet; the time is infected with Hamlet's unhappiness,—

"Sicklied o'er with the pale cast of thought."

Is it so bad then? Sight is the last thing to be pitied. Would we be blind? Do we fear lest we should outsee nature and God, and drink truth dry? I look upon the discontent of the literary class as a mere announcement of the fact that they find themselves not in the state of mind of their fathers, and regret the coming state as untried; as a boy dreads the water before he has learned that he can swim. If there is any period one would desire to be born in, is it not the age of Revolution; when the old and the new stand side by side, and admit of being compared; when the energies of all men are searched by fear and by hope; when the historic glories of the old can be compensated by the rich possibilities of the new era? This time, like all times, is a very good one, if we but know what to do with it.

I read with joy some of the auspicious signs of the coming days, as they glimmer already through poetry and art, through philosophy and science, through church and state.

One of these signs is the fact that the same movement which effected the elevation of what was called the lowest class in the state, assumed in literature a very marked and as benign an aspect. Instead of the sublime and beautiful; the near, the low, the common, was explored and poetized. That which had been negligently trodden under foot by those who were harnessing and provisioning themselves for long journeys into far countries, is suddenly found to be richer than all foreign parts. The literature of the poor, the feelings of the child, the philosophy of the street, the meaning of household life, are the topics of the time. It is a great stride. It is a sign,—is it not?—of new vigor, when the extremities are made active, when currents of warm life run into the hands and the feet. I ask not for the great, the remote, the romantic; what is doing in Italy or Arabia; what is Greek art, or Provençal minstrelsy; I embrace the common, I explore and sit at the feet of the familiar, the low. Give me insight into to-day, and you may have the antique and future worlds. What would we really know the meaning of? The meal in the firkin; the milk in the pan; the ballad in the street; the news of the boat; the glance of the eye; the form and the gait of the body;—show me the ultimate reason of these matters;

show me the sublime presence of the highest spiritual cause lurking, as always it does lurk, in these suburbs and extremities of nature; let me see every trifle bristling with the polarity that ranges it instantly on an eternal law; and the shop, the plough, and the leger referred to the like cause by which light undulates and poets sing;—and the world lies no longer a dull miscellany and lumber-room, but has form and order; there is no trifle; there is no puzzle; but one design unites and animates the farthest pinnacle and the lowest trench.

This idea has inspired the genius of Goldsmith, Burns, Cowper, and, in a newer time, of Goethe, Wordsworth, and Carlyle. This idea they have differently followed and with various success. In contrast with their writing, the style of Pope, of Johnson, of Gibbon, looks cold and pedantic. This writing is blood-warm. Man is surprised to find that things near are not less beautiful and wondrous than things remote. The near explains the far. The drop is a small ocean. A man is related to all nature. This perception of the worth of the vulgar is fruitful in discoveries. Goethe, in this very thing the most modern of the moderns, has shown us, as none ever did, the genius of the ancients.

There is one man of genius, who has done much for this philosophy of life, whose literary value has never yet been rightly estimated;—I mean Emanuel Swedenborg. The most imaginative of men, yet writing with the precision of a mathematician, he endeavored to engraft a purely philosophical Ethics on the popular Christianity of his time. Such an attempt of course must have difficulty which no genius could surmount. But he saw and showed the connection between nature and the affections of the soul. He pierced the emblematic or spiritual character of the visible, audible, tangible world. Especially did his shade-loving muse hover over and interpret the lower parts of nature; he showed the mysterious bond that allies moral evil to the foul material forms, and has given in epical parables a theory of insanity, of beasts, of unclean and fearful things.

Another sign of our times, also marked by an analogous

political movement, is the new importance given to the single person. Every thing that tends to insulate the individual,—to surround him with barriers of natural respect, so that each man shall feel the world is his, and man shall treat with man as a sovereign state with a sovereign state;—tends to true union as well as greatness. "I learned," said the melancholy Pestalozzi, "that no man in God's wide earth is either willing or able to help any other man." Help must come from the bosom alone. The scholar is that man who must take up into himself all the ability of the time, all the contributions of the past, all the hopes of the future. He must be an university of knowledges. If there be one lesson more than another which should pierce his ear, it is, The world is nothing, the man is all; in yourself is the law of all nature, and you know not yet how a globule of sap ascends; in yourself slumbers the whole of Reason; it is for you to know all, it is for you to dare all. Mr. President and Gentlemen, this confidence in the unsearched might of man belongs, by all motives, by all prophecy, by all preparation, to the American Scholar. We have listened too long to the courtly muses of Europe. The spirit of the American freeman is already suspected to be timid, imitative, tame. Public and private avarice make the air we breathe thick and fat. The scholar is decent, indolent, complaisant. See already the tragic consequence. The mind of this country, taught to aim at low objects, eats upon itself. There is no work for any but the decorous and the complaisant. Young men of the fairest promise, who begin life upon our shores, inflated by the mountain winds, shined upon by all the stars of God, find the earth below not in unison with these, but are hindered from action by the disgust which the principles on which business is managed inspire, and turn drudges, or die of disgust,—some of them suicides. What is the remedy? They did not yet see, and thousands of young men as hopeful now crowding to the barriers for the career, do not yet see, that if the single man plant himself indomitably on his instincts, and there abide, the huge world will come round to him. Patience, —patience; with the shades of all the good and great for company; and for solace, the perspective of your own infinite life; and for work the study and the communication of principles, the making those instincts prevalent, the conversion of the world. Is it not the chief disgrace in the world not to be an unit;—not to be reckoned one character;—not to yield that peculiar fruit which each man was created to bear, but to be reckoned in the gross, in the hundred, or the thousand, of the party, the section, to which we belong; and our opinion predicted geographically, as the north, or the south? Not so, brothers and friends,—please God, ours shall not be so. We will walk on our own feet; we will work with our own hands; we will speak our own minds. The study of letters shall be no longer a name for pity, for doubt, and for sensual indulgence. The dread of man and the love of man shall be a wall of defence and a wreath of joy around all. A nation of men will for the first time exist, because each believes himself inspired by the Divine Soul which also inspires all men.

PART V

Circumstantial Evidence

DOCUMENT 26

The United States Copyright Act of 1790

By limiting copyright protection to American residents, the Copyright Act of the First Congress of 1790 paved the way for the reprinting of English literary works without recompense to the authors. This created a competitive situation for the American author which left him the choice of either selling his books at a higher price than that of the works with which he was already in unequal competition, or taking no return for his work whatsoever. Cooper and Irving, in their discovery that British common law copyright afforded them equal protection abroad with their foreign competitors if the work were published first in England, somewhat overcame this handicap by publishing first in England from American sheets.

TEXT: *The Public Statutes at Large of the United States of America, from the organization of the Government in 1789 to March 3, 1845.* Edited by Richard Peters. Boston, 1845, I, 124–26.

Original Copyright Act of May 31, 1790. First Congress, Second Session

AN ACT for the encouragement of learning, by securing the copies of maps, charts, and books, to the authors and proprietors of such copies, during the times therein mentioned.

SECTION 1. *Be it enacted by the Senate and House of Representatives of the United States of America in Congress assembled,* That from and after the passing of this act, the author and authors of any map, chart, book or

books already printed within these United States, being a
citizen or citizens thereof, or resident within the same,
his or their executors, administrators or assigns, who hath
or have not transferred to any other person the copyright
of such map, chart, book or books, share or shares thereof;
and any other person or persons, being a citizen or citizens
of these United States, or residents therein, his or their
executors, administrators or assigns, who hath or have purchased or legally acquired the copyright of any such map,
chart, book or books, in order to print, reprint, publish
or vend the same, shall have the sole right and liberty of
printing, reprinting, publishing and vending such map,
chart, book or books, for the term of fourteen years from
the recording the title thereof in the clerk's office, as is
herein after directed: And that the author and authors of
any map, chart, book or books already made and composed, and not printed or published, or that shall hereafter be made and composed, being a citizen or citizens of
these United States, or resident therein, and his or their
executors, administrators or assigns, shall have the sole
right and liberty of printing, reprinting, publishing and
vending such map, chart, book or books, for the like term
of fourteen years from the time of recording the title
thereof in the clerk's office as aforesaid. And if, at the expiration of the said term, the author or authors, or any
of them, be living, and a citizen or citizens of these United
States, or resident therein, the same exclusive right shall
be continued to him or them, his or their executors, administrators or assigns, for the further term of fourteen
years: *Provided,* He or they shall cause the title thereof
to be a second time recorded and published in the same
manner as is herein after directed, and that within six
months before the expiration of the first term of fourteen
years aforesaid.

SEC. 2. *And be it further enacted,* That if any other
person or persons, from and after the recording the title
of any map, chart, book or books, and publishing the same
as aforesaid, and within the times limited and granted
by this act, shall print, reprint, publish, or import, or

cause to be printed, reprinted, published, or imported from any foreign Kingdom or State, any copy or copies of such map, chart, book or books, without the consent of the author or proprietor thereof, first had and obtained in writing, signed in the presence of two or more credible witnesses; or knowing the same to be so printed, reprinted, or imported, shall publish, sell, or expose to sale, or cause to be published, sold, or exposed to sale, any copy of such map, chart, book or books, without such consent first had and obtained in writing as aforesaid, then such offender or offenders shall forfeit all and every copy and copies of such map, chart, book or books, and all and every sheet and sheets, being part of the same, or either of them, to the author or proprietor of such map, chart, book or books, who shall forthwith destroy the same: And every such offender and offenders shall also forfeit and pay the sum of fifty cents for every sheet which shall be found in his or their possession, either printed or printing, published, imported or exposed to sale, contrary to the true intent and meaning of this act, the one moiety thereof to the author or proprietor of such map, chart, book or books who shall sue for the same, and the other moiety thereof to and for the use of the United States, to be recovered by action of debt in any court of record in the United States, wherein the same is cognizable. *Provided always,* That such action be commenced within one year after the cause of action shall arise, and not afterwards.

SEC. 3. *And be it further enacted,* That no person shall be entitled to the benefit of this act, in cases where any map, chart, book or books, hath or have been already printed and published, unless he shall first deposit, and in all other cases, unless he shall before publication deposit a printed copy of the title of such map, chart, book or books, in the clerk's office of the district court where the author or proprietor shall reside: And the clerk of such court is thereby directed and required to record the same forthwith, in a book to be kept by him for that purpose, in the words following, (giving a copy thereof to the said author or proprietor, under the seal of the court, if he shall require the same). "District of   to wit: *Be it re-membered*, that on the   day of   in the year of the independence of the United States of America, A. B. of the said district, hath deposited in this office the title of a map, chart, book or books, (as the case may be) the right whereof he claims as author or proprietor, (as the case may be) in the words following, to wit: [here insert the title] in conformity to the act of the Congress of the United States, intituled 'An act for the encouragement of learning, by securing the copies of maps, charts, and books, to the authors and proprietors of such copies, during the times therein mentioned.' C. D. clerk of the district of   ." For which the said clerk shall be entitled to receive sixty cents from the said author or proprietor, and sixty cents for every copy under seal actually given to such author or proprietor as aforesaid. And such author or proprietor shall, within two months from the date thereof, cause a copy of the said record to be published in one or more of the newspapers printed in the United States, for the space of four weeks.

SEC. 4. *And be it further enacted*, That the author or proprietor of any such map, chart, book or books, shall, within six months after the publishing thereof, deliver, or cause to be delivered to the Secretary of State a copy of the same, to be preserved in his office.

SEC. 5. *And be it further enacted*, That nothing in this act shall be construed to extend to prohibit the importation or vending, reprinting or publishing within the United States, of any map, chart, book or books, written, printed, or published by any person not a citizen of the United States, in foreign parts or places without the jurisdiction of the United States.

SEC. 6. *And be it further enacted*, That any person or persons who shall print or publish any manuscript, without the consent and approbation of the author or proprietor thereof, first had and obtained as aforesaid, (if such author or proprietor be a citizen of or resident in these United States) shall be liable to suffer and pay to the said author or proprietor all damages occasioned by such injury, to be recovered by a special action on the case founded upon this act, in any court having cognizance thereof.

SEC. 7. *And be it further enacted*, That if any person or persons shall be sued or prosecuted for any matter, act or thing done under or by virtue of this act, he or they may plead the general issue, and give the special matter in evidence.

Approved, May 31, 1790.

Book-order Lists from the Archives of The Library Company of Philadelphia

Founded in 1731, The Library Company of Philadelphia is the oldest circulating library in the United States. It was and still is owned and managed by stockholders who represent the cultural and intellectual elite of the city. During the eighteenth century it bought most of its books through a London agent. Two of these lists of shipments on order are here printed with omission only of prices and shipping details, one for 1790 and another for 1800. The marked increase in books reflecting literary and cultural interests in this decade may be taken as an index to the changing taste of this particular reading public.

TEXT: Manuscript Records of The Library Company [with abbreviations retained as in copy].

London Book Orders

I. 1790

Joseph Woods and William Dillwyn

Respected Friends

We have to thank you for the Continuance of your friendly Care in forwarding a parcel of Books for the Library Co. by the Pigou Capt. Collett, which arrived in good Order. . . . The Expenses attending the building of the new House which is now nearly finish'd, prevents our importing as largely as we could wish, still we think it proper to have a few Books twice a year to feed the

Hopes of our Members; for that purpose we trespass again on you. . . .

Mordecai Lewis
Thomas Parke

London 21st of 7th month 1790

The Library of Philada. Dr.
To Joseph Woods

Benyowski's Memoirs & Travels 2 vol
Burney's History of Music vols. 3 & 4
Campbell's Transl. of the 4 Gospels 2 vols
Enquiry into the principles of Taxation
Pennant's London
Polwhele's English Orator 4 parts
Prats Humanity
Sinclair's Histy. of the Public Revenue part 3
Anecdotes of Henry the 4th
Art of Dying Wool, Silk & Cotton
Beckford's Histy. of Jamaica 2 vol
Blair's Sermons vol. 3
Buffon's Nat. Histy. vol. 9
Cockburn on the Mosaic Deluge
DeNon's Travels
Franklin's Tour
Goldsmith's poetical Works 2 vols
Gustavus Vasa's Life 2 vols
Letters on Agriculture by the Bath Society vols. 3 4 & 5
Manuscripts in the King of France's Library 2 vols
History of Peter the Cruel 2 vols
Pinkerton's Histy. of Scotland 2 vols
History of Quadrapeds
Sutherlands Tour of the Straits
Vaillants Travels 2 vols.
Life of Elnes
Brisson's Shipwreck
Nisbet on the Capacity of Negroes
Volney's considerations on the Turkish War
Cunningham on the Copernican System

II.   1800

London 18 Aug. 1800

The Library Compa of Philadelphia
To Joseph Wood

Adventurer 3 vols
Ansons voyage
Adolphus memrs. of fr. revol. 2 v
Annual Register—Dodsley's
Annual anthology
Aikin's Letters to his son
Apocalypse revealed
Anderson's recreations 1 & 2 vol
Brewster's meditations
Boy's works 2 v
Brydone's tour 2 v
Beatson's campn. in India
Blacklock's poems
Burton's anatomy of melancholy 2 vols
Beauties of history
Burn's works
Brown's dictionary of the Bible
Bingley's tour in Wales
Boucher on Americn Revolutn
British Critick vol 15th
Cooper's Letter on the irish
Cogan on the passions
Colquhon on the police of Thames
Dryden's prose works 4 v
Darwin's phytologia 4 v
Derham's physicotheology new Editn
Eloisa 3 vols
Easton's human Longevity
Enchanted plants
    Nivernois fables
Flowers of history 2 vols
Garnet's tour in Hebrides
Grave on the Apostles

Hist. of Suwarrow's Campn 2 vols.
Hawkesworth's Telemachus
Jesse on the scriptures
Jackson' Journey, India to Engd.
Inspector (The)
Lives of Gregory Hume & Kaims
Life of Kotzebue
Laing's history of Scotland 2 v.
Magazine of Knowlge
Mede's works
Murray's guide to Scotld
Mosely on sugar
Memoirs on Egypt
Montaigne (selections)
Maurie's poems
Memoirs of Europe
Magazine, european v 37th 2 sets
      "   , univers v 106th
      "   , monthly v 9th 2 sets
      "   , philosoph v 6th
Narrative of voyage in search of Perouse
Nicholson's Journal of Chemistry 2 vol
Peeper, the
Planta's helvetie Confed. 2 v.
Polnitz' memoirs
Parliamenty Register 4 vols
Repertory of arts vol 12th
Rede's anecdotes
Ramsay's poems 2 vols
Review monthly vol 31st
      "   critical vol 28th
Scientific Dialogues 2 v
Summary of history 9 v
Scott's Tales
Turner's Embassy to Thibet
Wigstead's tour in Wales
      "   voyage to Hanno
      "   hieroglyphickey
Williams poems &c
Watkin's biog. Dicty

Wakefield's Discourses
Walsh's expedn to Holland
Young on humanity to anims
Young's Lincolnshire

Earl Strongbow	2 v
Evelina	2 v
Fool of Quality	5 v
Cecelia	5 v
Orell's Quixote	4 v
Italian	3 v
Scarron's works	2 v
Castle of Otranto	
Incas of Peru	2 v
Beggar girl	5 v
West's poems	2 v
Mysteries of black tower	
Castle rack-rent	
Memn of modn Philosophers	3 v
Physiognomical travels	3 v

Crt. rev May & June July
mo.rev. May June July
mo.mag. July
British critr. July

Periodical Lists of New Publications

The *Monthly Anthology* may be taken as the immediate predecessor of the *North American Review* as both were founded and sponsored by the same group of intellectual Bostonians, including the Rev. William Emerson, William Tudor, and the Channings. From the start both periodicals published lists of new American imprints. The list for January 1810 in the *Anthology* (being a monthly) covers a shorter period than do those of the quarterly *North American Review* for January 1820 and January 1830, but it may serve, with them, as an indication of the reading interests, at decade intervals, of the intelligent American public during these years. Items are here listed only by title and author.

TEXTS: Book lists as originally printed, with omission of publication details.

(a) The *Monthly Anthology*, VIII
(January 1810) 72–74

NEW WORKS

A Compendium and Digest of the Laws of Massachusetts. By William Charles White.

A Compendious Lexicon of the Hebrew Language. By Clement C. Moore.

Reports of Cases Argued and Determined in the Supreme Judicial Court of the Commonwealth of Massachusetts. By Dudley Atkins Tyng. Vol. IV, Part II.

The Anti-Gallician Centinel. By Don Antonio Capmany. Translated from the Spanish by a gentleman of the city of New York.

An Address delivered before the Mechanick Association. By Benjamin Russel, President of the Association.

A Sermon delivered to Dr. Spring's Society in Newburyport, Thanksgiving evening, November 30, 1809. By the Rev. Ethan Smith.

The Life of Thomas Paine. By James Cheetham.

A Letter on the Genius and Dispositions of the French government. Addressed to a friend, by an American recently returned from Europe.

NEW EDITIONS

First volume of a New Translation from the original Greek, of all the Apostolic Epistles. With a Commentary, etc. by James MacKnight, D.D.

1st Volume Hume's History of England.

A series of Discourses on the principles of Religious Belief. By the Rev. R. Morehead, A.M. of Baliol college, Oxford.

Letters and Reflections of the Austrian Field Marshal Prince de Ligne. Edited by the Baroness de Stael Holstein. Translated from the French by D. Boileau.

Letters from an elder to a younger brother, on the conduct to be pursued in life. Dedicated to the Rev. William Vincent, D.D.

A new Geographical, Historical and Commercial Grammar. By William Guthrie, Esq.

A Key to the New Testament.

A new system of Modern Geography. By Elijah Parish, D.D.

Vol. I of Tales of Fashionable Life. By Miss Edgeworth.

WORKS PROPOSED AND IN PRESS

The American New Dispensatory. By James Thatcher, A.A. & M.M.S.S.

An Attempt toward an Improved Version, or Metrical Arrangement, and an Explanation of the Twelve Minor Prophets. By William Newcome, D.D.

Newcome's Observations on the conduct of our Lord as Divine Instructor.

A Course of Lectures on Rhetorick, delivered to the two senior classes in Harvard college. By John Q. Adams, Esq.

(b) The *North American Review*, X
(Jan. 1820) 218–222

HISTORY

Collections of the Massachusetts Historical Society. Vol. VIII, second series.

GEOGRAPHY

The American Universal Geography. By Jedidiah Morse, D. D.

Introduction to Ancient and Modern Geography. With an Atlas. By J. A. Cummings. 7th edition.

NATURAL HISTORY AND CHEMISTRY

A Geological Section of the west bank of the Hudson river, from Sandy Hook to Newburgh.

Exposition of the Atomic Theory of chemistry and the doctrine of Definite Proportion. By W. J. Macnevin, M. D.

A System of Chemistry, for the use of students in medicine. By Franklin Bache, M. D.

LAW

Reports of Cases Argued and Determined in the Supreme Court of Judicature of the state of New Jersey. By Samuel L. Souttard.

Reports of Cases Argued and Determined in the Circuit Court of the United States, for the Third Circuit. Vol. I. By Richard Peters Jr.

Reports of Cases Argued and Determined in the Superior Court of Judicature, for the state of New Hampshire, from Sept. 1816 to Feb. 1819. By Nathaniel Adams.

Reports of Cases Argued and Determined in the Supreme Judicial Court of Massachusetts. Vol. XV. By Dudley Atkins Tyng.

Reports of Judicial Decisions in the Constitutional Court of South Carolina, 1817 and 1818.

The Magistrate's Guide and Citizen's Counsellor; adapted to the state of Maryland. Second edition. By J. B. Calvin Esq.

MEDICINE

A statement of the occurrences during a malignant yellow fever in the city of New York in 1819, with a list of cases.

Reflections on Yellow Fever Periods. By Lyman Spalding, M. D.

A Discourse on Medical Education. By Samuel Bard, M. D. LL. D.

A history of the introduction and use of Sartellaria Lateriflora, as a remedy for hydrophobia. By Lyman Spalding, M. D.

Medical and Philosophical Essays. By J. L. E. W. Sheart.

DIVINITY

A farewell sermon. By Rev. Jesse H. Turner.

The Christian's Vade Mecum. By Hooper Cumming, A. M.

Sabbath School Catechism. By Nathan Perkins, D. D.

The Claims of Seamen; a sermon before the New York Marine Missionary Society. By E. D. Griffin, D. D.

Letters to the Rev. William E. Channing, containing remarks on his sermon. By Moses Stuart. Third edition.

The Widow and her Mites; a sermon preached Nov. 7. 1819. By Rev. James Milnor, D. D.

POETRY

The Fatal Jest, a tale, and other poems. By Moses Y. Scott.

Fanny, a poem.

The Deaf and Dumb, a poem. By Moses Y. Scott.

The Art of Penmanship, in verse, with numerous plates. By J. M'Cready.

The Exile's Return, a tale, in three cantos; with other pieces. By a South Carolinian.

Mississippian Scenery. 12mo. Philadelphia.

POLITICS

Considerations in favour of the appointment of Rufus King to the senate of the United States.

The North American United States constitution explained. By William Davis Robertson.

An Examination of the Expediency and Constitutionality of prohibiting Slavery in the State of Missouri. By Mavor.

An appeal from the Judgments of Great Britain respecting the United States. By Robert Walsh Jr.

A Review of the Administration and Civil Police of the State of New York, from 1807 to 1819. By Ferris Pell.

An Appeal to the people of the State of New York, on the expediency of abolishing the Council of appointment. By Charles G. Haines, Esq.

Thoughts on the Constitution of the State of South Carolina. By one of the people.

COMMERCE

A Memoir on the Commerce and Navigation of the Black Sea. By Henry A. S. Dearborn.

A treatise on impost duties and prohibitions of Foreign merchandize. By M. le Comte Chaptal.

VOYAGES AND TRAVELS

A voyage to South America. By H. M. Brackenridge, Esq.
Travels through the Western Country. By David Thomas.

MISCELLANEOUS

The metaphysics and philosophy of language. By Peter
S. Charotte.

Sketches of the life, ministry, and writings of the Rev.
Stephen West, D. D. By Rev. Alvan Hyde, D. D.

Essays on Agriculture, from the Raleigh Register. By
Agricola.

Address to British Emigrants, July 13, 1819, and Reply
to William Cobbett. By Morris Birkbeck.

The Sketch Book. By Geoffrey Crayon, Gent. No. 4.

Inaugural Discourse, delivered in the University in Cambridge, December 8, 1819. By Edward T. Channing,
Boylston Professor of Rhetoric and Oratory.

An Address delivered before the Massachusetts Agricultural Society, Oct. 12, 1819. By the Hon. Josiah Quincy.

Address of the Philadelphia Society for the Promotion of
Domestic Industry.

Report to the Managers of the Society for the Prevention
of Pauperism in New York.

SCHOOL BOOKS

The Pronouncing Spelling Book. By J. A. Cummings.
A Compendious System of Geography. By Jacob Willetts.

AMERICAN EDITIONS OF ENGLISH WORKS

The London Medical Dictionary. By Bartholomew Parr,
M. D.

Roman Antiquities. By Alexander Adam, LL. D. Revised
by P. Wilson, LL. D.

The Poetical Works of Alexander Pope.

Oakwood Hall, a novel. By Catherine Hutton.

Fredolfo, a tragedy in five acts. By C. B. Maturin.

European Commerce, or Complete Mercantile Guide to the Continent of Europe. By C. W. Rördansz.

Elements of Experimental Chemistry. By William Henry, M. D. F. R. S. from the 8th London edition.

Decision, a tale. By the author of Correction.

Moral Sketches of prevailing Opinions and Manners. By Hannah More. 2 editions.

Reflections on Prayer. By Hannah More.

British Encyclopedia. vol. I to VI.

The British Poets, a New Collection, in fifty volumes.

Johnson's Dictionary, with Walker's Pronunciation. Part 4th.

(c) The *North American Review*, XXX (January 1830), 285–292

ARTS AND SCIENCES

A Text Book of Chemical Philosophy. By Jacob Green, M. D.

ANNUAL PUBLICATIONS

The Atlantic Souvenir, for 1830.

Youths' Keepsake; a Christmas and New Year's Present for Young People.

The Token, a Christmas and New Year's Present. Edited by S. G. Goodrich.

The Talisman, for 1830.

The Pearl, for 1830.

The American Almanac and Repository of Useful Knowledge for the Year 1830, vol. 1.

ASTRONOMY

Mécanique Céleste. By the Marquis de la Place. Translated, with a Commentary, by Nathaniel Bowditch, LL. D. Vol. 1.

BIOGRAPHY

Memoir of Thomas Addis Emmet. By Charles Glidden Haines. With a Biographical Notice of Mr. Haines.

Life of Arthur Lee, LL. D. By Richard Henry Lee, A. M.

Memoir of Samuel John Mills. By Gardiner Spring, D. D.

Life of the Rev. Jeremiah Hallock, late Pastor of the Congregational Church in Canton, Connecticut. By Cyrus Yale.

Memoirs of the Life and Ministry of the Rev. John Summerfield, A. M. By John Holland.

BOTANY

Familiar Lectures on Botany. By Mrs. Almira H. Lincoln.

DRAMA

Eskah, a Tragedy, in five Acts. By B. B. Curtis.

The Haunted Inn, a Farce, in two Acts.

EDUCATION

Titi Livii Patavini Historiarum Liber Primus et Selecta quædam Capita.

The Latin Translator. By Mariano Cubi i Soler.

Caii Julii Cæsaris Commentarii de Bello Gallico. Curavit Fred. P. Leverett.

First Lessons in Intellectual Philosophy. By the Rev. Silas Blaisdale.

An Introduction to the Greek Language; with a Key. By W. R. Johnson.

A New Pronouncing French Primer. By Bernard Pronchin.

The Elocutionist. By Jonathan Barber.

A Book for Massachusetts Children, in Familiar Letters from a Father, for the Use of Families and Schools.

Lectures on School-Keeping. By Samuel R. Hall.

The North American Arithmetic. Part 1st. By Frederick Emerson.

Lectures on Rhetoric and Belles Lettres. By Hugh Blair, D. D.

Suggestions respecting Improvements in Education presented to the Trustees of the Hartford Female Seminary. By Catharine E. Beecher.

Inductive Grammar. By an Instructer.

Sequel to Easy Lessons: A Selection of Reading Lessons for Common Schools.

A Spelling-Book for the United States of America. By Samuel Worcester.

The Practical Arithmetic. By T. H. Babcock.

Letters to Congress, on National Free Schools.

Elements of Astronomy, Descriptive and Physical. By Hervey Wilbur, A. M.

A Geography of New Hampshire, with a Sketch of its Natural History, for Schools. By Cranmore Wallace.

Peter Parley's Method of telling about Geography to Children.

Elements of Geometry upon the Inductive Method. By James Hayward, A. M.

HISTORY

An Historical and Statistical Account of Nova-Scotia. By Thomas C. Haliburton, Esq.

Philosophical and Antiquarian Researches concerning the Aboriginal History of America. By J. H. McCulloh, Jr., M. D.

LAW

Reports of Cases argued and determined in the Supreme Court of Massachusetts. By Octavius Pickering. Vol. VI. No. 3.

Reports of Cases argued and determined in the Court of Appeals of Maryland, in 1827, 1828, and 1829. By Thomas Harris and Richard W. Gill. Vol. 2.

Cases argued and determined in the Superior Court of Judicature in the State of New Hampshire. Vol. I. Part

I.; containing the Cases from January to November, 1827.

The Law of Executors and Administrators. By Sir Samuel Toller, Knight.

Reports of Cases argued and determined in the Supreme Judicial Court of the State of Maine. By Simon Greenleaf. Vol. 5.

The New Hampshire Town Officer. By William M. Richardson.

The Law of Pleading and Evidence in Civil Actions. By John Simcoe Saunders, Esq. 2 vols.

Militia Laws of the United States and the Commonwealth of Massachusetts. By William Summer. Second edition.

The Form Book; containing nearly three hundred of the most approved Precedents. By a Member of the Philadelphia Bar.

MEDICINE AND SURGERY

A Treatise on Pathological Anatomy. By William E. Horner, M. D.

Elements of Operative Surgery. Translated from the French of A. Tavernier, with copious Notes and Additions, by S. D. Gross, M. D.

Memoria Medica. A Medical Common-Place-Book.

MISCELLANEOUS

New Views of Penitentiary Discipline, and Moral Education and Reform. By Charles Caldwell, M. D.

Sabbath-School Teacher's Visits. By the Author of Sabbath School Scenes.

A Catechism of Natural Theology. [By the Rev. Dr. Nichols.]

The Sabbath School.

The Morals of Pleasure. Illustrated by Stories designed for Young Persons. By a Lady.

Conversations on the Sandwich Island Mission; designed for Sabbath School Libraries. By a Lady.

A Dictionary of Important Names, Objects, and Terms,

found in the Holy Scriptures, intended principally for Youth. By Howard Malcolm, A. M.

Principles of Currency and Banking. By E. Lord.

Classical Journal and Scholars' Album; conducted by John P. Lathrop. No. 1.

Youths' Magazine; or Spirit of the Juvenile Miscellany. No. 1.

Practical Instructions for the Culture of Silk and the Mulberry Tree. Vol. 1.

American Turf Register, and Sporting Magazine. No. 1. Edited by J. S. Skinner.

General Index to the North American Review, from its Commencement in 1815, to 1827.

Encyclopædia Americana. Edited by Dr. Francis Lieber, Vol. 1.

Russel Jarvis *vs.* Duff Greene, addressed to the Public.

The Letters of Columbus.

Journal of Health. No. 1. Conducted by an Association of Physicians.

The Boy's Own Book, a complete Encyclopædia of all the Diversions of Boyhood and Youth.

Antediluvian Antiquities. Translated by an American Traveller in the East. Vol. 1.

A Genealogical Register of the First Settlers of New-England.

A Letter on Speculative Free Masonry. By Charles P. Sumner.

Sabbath Miscellany. By Amicus Sabbati.

Instructions and Observations concerning the Use of the Chlorides of Soda and Lime. By A. G. Labarroque. Translated by Jacob Porter.

Tales from American History.

Autobiography of an almost Septuagenarian with Remarks on the Opinions and Manners of the Age.

An Introductory Lecture, delivered before the Lexington Mechanics' Institution, June 20, 1829. By Rev. Benjamin O. Peers.

Selections from the Writings of Fenelon, with a Memoir of his Life. By a Lady. Second edition.

NOVELS

The Wept of Wish-Ton-Wish; a Tale. By the Author of "The Pioneers," &c. In two volumes.

Sketches of American Character. By Mrs. Sarah J. Hale.

Ramon, the Rover of Cuba. The Personal Narrative of that celebrated Pirate. Translated from the original Spanish.

POETRY

A Poem delivered before the Porter Rhetorical Society in the Theological Seminary, Andover. By Richard H. Dana.

The Drowsiad. By a Dozer.

Quebec, The Harp, and other Poems. By W. F. Hawley.

POLITICAL ECONOMY

Lectures on the Restrictive System, delivered to the Senior Political Class of William and Mary College. By Thomas R. Dew.

SPEECHES AND ADDRESSES

Speeches on the Jew Bill, in the House of Delegates of Maryland, by H. M. Brackenridge, Col. W. G. D. Worthington, and John S. Tysen, Esq.

An Address pronounced on the Anniversary of the Concord Lyceum, November 4, 1829. By Cornelius C. Felton.

The Speech of Henry Clay, delivered at the Public Dinner at Fowler's Garden, near Lexington, Kentucky, on the 16th of May, 1829. By a Citizen of Virginia.

A Discourse delivered before the Trustees, Faculty, and Students of Rutgers College, at New Brunswick, New Jersey, on the 14th of July. By John Sergeant, LL. D.

THEOLOGY

American Christian Observer; a Religious and Literary Review and Magazine. No. 1.

A Sermon preached in Boston before the Pastoral Association of Massachusetts. By John H. Church.

A Sermon delivered at the Dedication of the Second Congregational Church, in Worcester, August 20, 1829. By Aaron Bancroft, D. D.

A Discourse delivered at Plymouth, Dec. 20, 1828, on the Two Hundred and Eighth Anniversary of the Landing of the Pilgrim Fathers. By Samuel Green.

A Sermon on Paul at Athens. By the Rev. Andrew Bigelow.

A Selection of the most Celebrated Sermons of M. Luther and J. Calvin. To which is prefixed a Biographical History of their Lives.

A Sermon preached in St. Paul's Church, Boston, June 17, 1829. By Joseph Muenscher.

Sermons. By the late Rev. Cornelius R. Duffie, A. M.

Eight Sermons addressed to Children, on the Duty of Obedience to Parents, and on the Lord's Prayer. By the late Rev. Cornelius R. Duffie, A. M.

The Essential Doctrines of the Gospel; a Sermon. By J. H. Fairchild.

An Essay on the Invalidity of Presbyterian Ordination. By John Ester Cooke, M. D.

A Treatise upon Theological Subjects. By William S. Andrews.

Consolation in Death, a Sermon, preached on Monday, September 7th, at the Funeral of the Rev. M. Bruen, A. M. By Samuel Cox, D. D.

A Sermon occasioned by the Death of the Rev. M. Bruen, preached in the Bleecker St. Church, New York. By Thomas H. Skinner.

A Discourse on the Sins of the Tongue. By Alexander Young. Second Edition.

The Monotessaron; or The Gospel History according the Four Evangelists. By the Rev. John S. Thompson.

Advice to a Young Christian on the Importance of Aiming

at an elevated Standard of Piety. By a Village Pastor.

Essays and Dissertations in Biblical Literature. By a Society of Clergymen. Vol. 1.

Review of Mr Beckwith's Dissuasive; from the American Baptist Magazine for October, 1829.

Charges, and Extracts of Charges, on Moral and Religious Subjects. By the Hon. Jacob Rush.

A Sermon delivered before the Society for Propagating the Gospel among the Indians and Others in North America. November 5th, 1829. By B. B. Wisner.

Principles of Congregationalism. By Charles Wentworth Upham, Jun.

An Inquiry into the Nature of Sin as exhibited in Dr Dwight's Theology, a Letter to a Friend. By Clericus.

Remarks on Prayer Meetings. Republished from the Episcopal Register.

VOYAGES AND TRAVELS

Lafayette in America, in 1824 and 1825. By A. Levasseur, Secretary to General Lafayette during his Journey.

AMERICAN EDITIONS OF FOREIGN WORKS

Aids to Reflection. By S. T. Coleridge. First American, from the first London Edition.

Lectures on the Sacred Poetry of the Hebrews. By Robert Lowth, D. D.

An Introduction to the Practice of Midwifery. By the late Thomas Denman, M. D. From the sixth London edition. By John W. Francis, M. D.

An Exposition of the Old and New Testaments. By Mathew Henry. Edited by the Rev. George Burder, and the Rev. Josoph Huges, A. M.

A Selection from the Public and Private Correspondence of Vice-Admiral Lord Collingwood. By G. L. N. Collingwood, Esq. F. R. S.

Peace Campaigns of a Cornet.

The New Forest. A Novel.

Waldegrave. A Novel.

Some Account of the Life of Reginald Heber, D. D., Bishop of Calcutta.

The Adventures of a King's Page.

Rybrent de Cruce. A Novel.

Prayers and Religious Meditations. By David Hartley, M. D. Second American edition.

The Veracity of the Gospels and Acts of the Apostles. By the Rev. J. J. Blunt.

Sketches of Irish Character. A Novel. By Mrs. S. C. Hall.

The Book of the Boudoir. By Lady Morgan.

A Memoir of Barbara Ewing. By her Husband, Greville Ewing.

A Course of Lectures for Sunday Evenings; containing Religious Advice to Young Persons.

DOCUMENT 29

English Theories of Taste and Imagination

Among English writers on literary and aesthetic theory during these years, perhaps the most influential in America were Lord Kames, Archibald Alison, and Samuel Taylor Coleridge. Lord Kames, the friend of Franklin, was spokesman for the eighteenth-century theory of a fixed and universal standard of taste which shaped so much of the neo-classical writing of the time; Archibald Alison spoke most clearly and eloquently for the Associationist theory of Hartley, which brought literature and art into more immediate relationship with experience and provided much of the rationale for the literary nationalism of the *North American Review*; Coleridge's theory of the imagination broke with the Associationist formula by distinguishing it from fancy, or taste, provided much of the idiom of American Transcendentalism, and helped to bring American literature to its own organic fulfilment.

(a) Henry Home, Lord Kames

STANDARD OF TASTE

Nature in her scale of pleasures has been sparing of divisions: she hath wisely and benevolently filled every division with many pleasures, in order that individuals may be contented with their own lot without envying that of others. Many hands must be employed to procure us the conveniences of life; and it is necessary that the different branches of business, whether more or less agree-

TEXT: *Elements of Criticism*, by Henry Home, Lord Kames, 1762, from the Second American Edition from the eighth London edition: Philadelphia, 1816, II, 362–67.

able, be filled with hands: a taste too refined would obstruct that plan for it would crowd some employments, leaving others no less useful, totally neglected. In our present condition, lucky it is that the plurality are not delicate in their choice but fall in readily with the occupations, pleasures, food and company that fortune throws in their way; and if at first there be any displeasing circumstance, custom soon makes it easy.

The proverb will hold true as to the particulars now explained; but when applied in general to every subject of taste, the difficulties to be encountered are insuperable. We need only to mention the difficulty that arises from human nature itself; do we not talk of a good and a bad taste? of a right and a wrong taste? and upon that supposition, do we not, with great confidence, censure writers, painters, architects and every one who deals in the fine arts? Are such criticisms absurd and void of common sense? have the foregoing expressions, familiar in all languages and among all people, no sort of meaning? This can hardly be; for what is universal must have a foundation in nature. If we can reach that foundation, the standard of taste will no longer be a secret.

We have a sense or conviction of a common nature not only in our own species, but in every species of animals: and our conviction is verified by experience, for there appears a remarkable uniformity among creatures of the same kind and a deformity no less remarkable among creatures of different kinds. This common nature is conceived to be a model or standard for each individual that belongs to the kind. Hence it is a wonder to find an individual deviating from the common nature of the species, whether in its internal or external construction: a child born with aversion to its mother's milk is a wonder, no less than if born without a mouth or with more than one.[1] This conviction of a common nature in every species, paves the way finely for distributing things into *genera* and *species*; to which we are extremely prone, not only

[1] See Essays on Morality and Natural Religion, Part I. Essay ii. ch. 1.

with regard to animals and vegetables where nature has led the way, but also with regard to many other things where there is no ground for such distribution but fancy merely.

With respect to the common nature of man in particular, we have a conviction that it is invariable not less than universal; that it will be the same hereafter as at present and as it was in time past; the same among all nations and in all corners of the earth. Nor are we deceived because, giving allowance for the difference of culture and gradual refinement of manners, the fact corresponds to our conviction.

We are so constituted as to conceive this common nature to be not only invariable, but also *perfect* or *right*; and consequently that individuals *ought* to be made conformable to it. Every remarkable deviation from the standard makes accordingly an impression upon us of imperfection, irregularity, or disorder: it is disagreeable, raises in us a painful emotion: monstrous births, exciting the curiosity of a philosopher, fail not at the same time to excite a sort of horror.

This conviction of a common nature or standard and of its perfection accounts clearly for that remarkable conception we have of a right and a wrong sense or taste in morals. It accounts not less clearly for the conception we have of a right and a wrong sense or taste in the fine arts. A man who, avoiding objects generally agreeable, delights in objects generally disagreeable is condemned as a monster: we disapprove his taste as bad or wrong because we have a clear conception that he deviates from the common standard. If man were so framed as not to have any notion of a common standard, the proverb mentioned in the beginning would hold universally, not only in the fine arts but in morals: upon that supposition, the taste of every man, with respect to both, would to himself be an ultimate standard. But as the conviction of a common standard is universal and a branch of our nature, we intuitively conceive a taste to be right or good if conformable to the common standard and wrong or bad if disconformable.

No particular in human nature is more universal than

the uneasiness a man feels when in matters of importance his opinions are rejected by others: why should difference in opinion create uneasiness, more than difference in stature, in countenance, or in dress? The conviction of a common standard explains the mystery: every man, generally speaking, taking it for granted that his opinions agree with the common sense of mankind, is therefore disgusted with those who think differently, not as differing from him, but as differing from the common standard: hence in all disputes, we find the parties, each of them equally appealing constantly to the common sense of mankind as the ultimate rule or standard. With respect to points arbitrary or indifferent which are not supposed to be regulated by any standard, individuals are permitted to think for themselves with impunity: the same liberty is not indulged with respect to points that are reckoned of moment: for what reason other than that the standard by which these are regulated ought, as we judge, to produce an uniformity of opinion in all men? In a word, to this conviction of a common standard must be wholly attributed the pleasure we take in those who espouse the same principles and opinions with ourselves, as well as the aversion we have at those who differ from us. In matters left indifferent by the standard we find nothing of the same pleasure or pain: a bookish man, unless swayed by convenience, relisheth not the contemplative man more than the active; his friends and companions are chosen indifferently out of either class: a painter consorts with a poet or musician as readily as with those of his own art; and one is not the more agreeable to me for loving beef, as I do, nor the less agreeable for preferring mutton.

I have ventured to say, that my disgust is raised, not by differing from me, but by differing from what I judge to be the common standard. This point being of importance ought to be firmly established. Men, it is true, are prone to flatter themselves by taking it for granted that their opinions and their taste are in all respects conformable to the common standard, but there may be exceptions, and experience shews there are some: there are instances without number of persons who are addicted to the grosser amusements of gaming, eating, drinking, without having any relish for more elegant pleasures, such, for example, as are afforded by the fine arts; yet these very persons, talking the same language with the rest of mankind, pronounce in favour of the more elegant pleasures, and they invariably approve those who have a more refined taste, being ashamed of their own as low and sensual. It is in vain to think of giving a reason for this singular impartiality other than the authority of the common standard with respect to the dignity of human nature: and from the instances now given, we discover that the authority of that standard, even upon the most grovelling souls, is so vigorous as to prevail over self-partiality and to make them despise their own taste compared with the more elevated taste of others.

Uniformity of taste and sentiment resulting from our conviction of a common standard leads to two important final causes; the one respecting our duty, the other our pastime. Barely to mention the first shall be sufficient because it does not properly belong to the present undertaking. Unhappy it would be for us did not uniformity prevail in morals: that our actions should uniformly be directed to what is good and against what is ill is the greatest blessing in society; and in order to uniformity of action, uniformity of opinion and sentiment is indispensable.

With respect to pastime in general and the fine arts in particular, the final cause of uniformity is illustrious. Uniformity of taste gives opportunity for sumptuous and elegant buildings, for fine gardens and extensive embellishments which please universally; and the reason is that without uniformity of taste, there could not be any suitable reward, either of profit or honour, to encourage men of genius to labour in such works and to advance them toward perfection. The same uniformity of taste is equally necessary to perfect the art of music, sculpture, and painting and to support the expense they require after they are brought to perfection. Nature is in every particular consistent with herself: we are framed by Nature to have a high relish for the fine arts, which are a great source of happiness and friendly in a high degree to virtue: we are, at the same time, framed with uniformity of taste to furnish proper objects for that high relish; and if uniformity did not prevail, the fine arts could never have made any figure.

And this suggests another final cause no less illustrious. The separation of men into different classes by birth, office, or occupation, however necessary, tends to relax the connexion that ought to be among members of the same state; which bad effect is in some measure prevented by the access all ranks of people have to public spectacles and to amusements that are best enjoyed in company. Such meetings, where every one partakes of the same pleasures in common, are no slight support to the social affections.

Thus, upon a conviction common to the species is erected a standard of taste, which without hesitation is applied to the taste of every individual. That standard, ascertaining what actions are right, what wrong, what proper, what improper, hath enabled moralists to establish rules for our conduct, from which no person is permitted to swerve. We have the same standard for ascertaining in all the fine arts what is beautiful or ugly, high or low, proper or improper, proportioned or disproportioned: and here, as in morals, we justly condemn every taste that deviates from what is thus ascertained by the common standard.

(b) *Archibald Alison*

ESSAY I

ON THE NATURE OF THE EMOTIONS OF SUBLIMITY AND BEAUTY

CHAPTER I

OF THE EFFECT PRODUCED UPON THE IMAGINATION BY OBJECTS OF SUBLIMITY AND BEAUTY

SECTION I

The emotions of sublimity and beauty are uniformly ascribed, both in popular and philosophical language, to the imagination. The fine arts are considered as the arts which are addressed to the imagination, and the pleasures which they afford are described, by way of distinction, as the pleasures of the imagination. The nature of any person's taste is, in common life, generally determined from the nature or character of his imagination, and the expression of any deficiency in this power of mind, is considered as synonymous with the expression of a similar deficiency in point of taste.

Although, however, this connexion is so generally acknowledged, it is not perhaps as generally understood in what it consists or what is the nature of that effect which is produced upon the imagination and by objects of sublimity and beauty. I shall endeavor therefore, in the first place, to state what seems to me the nature of this effect or in what that exercise of imagination consists which is so generally supposed to take place when these emotions are felt.

When any object either of sublimity or beauty is presented to the mind, I believe every man is conscious of a train of thought being immediately awakened in his imagination analogous to the character or expression of the original object. The simple perception of the object we frequently find is insufficient to excite these emotions unless it is accompanied with this operation of mind, unless, according to common expression, our imagination is seized and our fancy busied in the pursuit of all those trains of thought which are allied to this character of expression.

Thus when we feel either the beauty or sublimity of natural scenery—the gay lustre of a morning in spring, or the mild radiance of a summer evening, the savage majesty of a wintry storm, or the wild magnificence of a tempestu-

TEXT: *The Nature and Principles of Taste*, by Archibald Alison, 1790, from the American Edition of New York, 1830, pp. 17–28, 33–35.

ous ocean—we are conscious of a variety of images in our minds very different from those which the objects themselves can present to the eye. Trains of pleasing or of solemn thought arise spontaneously within our minds; our hearts swell with emotions of which the objects before us seem to afford no adequate cause; and we are never so much satiated with delight as when, in recalling our attention, we are unable to trace either the progress or the connexion of those thoughts which have passed with so much rapidity through our imagination.

The effect of the different arts of taste is similar. The landscapes of Claude Lorrain, the music of Handel, the poetry of Milton excite feeble emotions in our minds when our attention is confined to the qualities they present to our senses, or when it is to such qualities of their composition that we turn our regard. It is then only that we feel the sublimity or beauty of their productions, when our imaginations are kindled by their power, when we lose ourselves amid the number of images that pass before our minds, and when we waken at last from this play of fancy as from the charm of a romantic dream. The beautiful apostrophe of the Abbé de Lille, upon the subject of gardening

> N'avez-vous pas souvent, au lieux infrequentés,
> Rencontré tout-à-coup, ces aspects enchantés,
> Qui suspendent vos pas, dont l'image chérie
> Vous jette en une douce et longue rêverie?

is equally applicable to every other composition of taste; and in the production of such trains of thought seems to consist the effect which objects of sublimity and beauty have upon the imagination.

For the truth of this observation itself, I must finally appeal to the consciousness of the reader; but there are some very familiar considerations which it may be useful to suggest that seem very strongly to shew the connexion between this exercise of imagination and the existence of the emotions of sublimity or beauty.

SECTION II

That the emotions of beauty or sublimity are unfelt, unless this exercise of imagination is excited, seems capable of illustration from many instances of a very familiar kind.

I. If the mind is in such a state as to prevent this freedom of imagination, the emotion, whether of sublimity or beauty, is unperceived. As far as the beauties of art or nature affect the external senses, their effect is the same upon every man who is in possession of these senses. But to a man in pain or in grief whose mind, by these means, is attentive only to one object or consideration, the same scene or the same form will produce no feeling of admiration, which at other times, when his imagination was at liberty, would have produced it in its fullest perfection. Whatever is great or beautiful in the scenery of external nature is almost constantly before us; and not a day passes without presenting us with appearances, fitted both to charm and to elevate our minds; yet it is in general with a heedless eye that we regard them and only in particular moments that we are sensible of their power. There is no man, for instance, who has not felt the beauties of sunset; yet every one can remember many instances when this most striking scene had no effect at all upon his imagination; and when he has beheld all the magnificence with which nature generally distinguishes the close of day, without one sentiment of admiration or delight. There are times, in the same manner, when we can read the Georgics, or the Seasons, with perfect indifference, and with no more emotion than what we feel from the most uninteresting composition in prose; while in other moments, the first lines we meet with take possession of our imagination and awaken in it such innumerable trains of imagery as almost leave behind the fancy of the poet. In these, and of similar cases of difference in our feelings from the same objects, it will always be found that the difference arises from the state of our imaginations: from our disposition to follow out the train of thought which such objects naturally produce, or our incapacity to do it, from some other idea, which has at that time taken possession of our minds and renders us unable to attend to any thing else. That state of mind, every man must have felt, is most favorable to the emotions of taste in which the imagination is free and unembarrassed or in which the attention is so little occupied by any private or particular object of thought as to leave us open to all the impressions which the objects that are before us can create. It is upon the vacant and the unemployed, accordingly, that objects of taste make the strongest impression. It is in such hours alone that we turn to the compositions of music, or of poetry, for amusement. The seasons of care, of grief, or of business have other occupations and destroy for the time, at least, our sensibility to the beautiful or the sublime in the same proportion that they produce a state of mind unfavorable to the indulgence of imagination. . . .

In the effect which is produced upon our minds by the different appearances of natural scenery, it is easy to trace this progress of resembling thought, and to observe how faithfully the conceptions which arise in our imaginations, correspond with the impressions which the character of these seasons produce. What, for instance, is the impression which we feel from spring? The soft and gentle green with which the earth is spread, the feeble texture of the plants and flowers, the young of animals just entering into life, and the remains of winter yet lingering among the woods and hills—all conspire to infuse into our minds somewhat of that fearful tenderness with which infancy is usually beheld. With such a sentiment, how innumerable are the ideas which present themselves to our imagination! ideas, it is apparent, by no means confined to the scene before our eyes, or to the possible desolation which may yet await its infant beauty, but which almost involuntarily extend themselves to analogies with the life of man and bring before us all those images of hope or fear which, according to our peculiar situations, have the dominion of our hearts!—The beauty of autumn is accompanied with a similar exercise of thought: The leaves begin then to drop from the trees; the flowers and shrubs with which the fields were adorned in the summer months decay: the woods and groves are silent; the sun himself seems gradually to withdraw his light or to become enfeebled in his power. Who is there who, at this season, does not feel his mind impressed with a sentiment of melancholy? or who is able to resist that current of thought, which, from such appearances of decay, so naturally leads him to the solemn imagination of that inevitable fate, which is to bring on, alike, the decay of life, of empire, and of nature itself? In such cases of emotion, every man must have felt, that the character of the scene is no sooner impressed upon his mind than various trains of correspondent imagery rise before his imagination; that whatever may be the nature of the impression, the general tone of his thoughts partakes of this nature or character and that his delight is proportioned to the degree in which this uniformity of character prevails.

The same effect, however, is not produced upon all men. There are many whom the prospect of such appearances in nature excites to no exercise of fancy whatever; who by their original constitution are more disposed to the employment of attention than of imagination, and who, in the objects that are presented to them, are more apt to observe their individual and distinguishing qualities than those by which they are related to other objects of their knowledge. Upon the minds of such men, the relation of resemblance has little power; the efforts of their imagination, accordingly, are either feeble or slow, and the general character of their understandings is that of steady and precise rather than that of enlarged and extensive thought. It is, I believe, consistent with general experience, that men of this description are little sensible to the emotions of sublimity or beauty; and they who have attended to the language of such men, when objects of this kind have been presented to them, must have perceived, that the emotion which they felt, was no greater than what they themselves have experienced in those cases where they have exerted a similar degree of attention or when any other cause has restrained the usual exercise of their imagination. To the qualities which are productive of simple emotion, to the useful, the agreeable, the fitting, or the convenient in objects, they have the same sensibility that other men have; but of the superior and more complex emotion of beauty, they seem to be either altogether unconscious or to share in it only in the proportion to the degree in which they can relax this severity of attention, and yield to the relation of resembling thought. . . .

In these familiar instances, it is obvious how much the emotions of taste are connected with this state or character of imagination and how much those habits or employments of mind which demand attention, or which limit it to the consideration of single objects, tend to diminish the sensibility of mankind to the emotions of sublimity or beauty.

SECTION III

There are many other instances, equally familiar, which are sufficient to shew that whatever increases this exercise or employment of imagination, increases also the emotion of beauty or sublimity.

I. This is very obviously the effect of all associations. There is no man who has not some interesting associations with particular scenes, or airs, or books, and who does not feel their beauty or sublimity enhanced to him by such connexions. The view of the house where one was born, of the school where one was educated, and where the gay years of infancy were passed is indifferent to no man. They recall so many images of past happiness and past affections, they are connected with so many strong or valued emotions, and lead altogether to so long a train of feelings and recollections that there is hardly any scene which one ever beholds with so much rapture. There are songs also that we have heard in our infancy which, when brought to our remembrance in after years, raise emotions for which we cannot well account and which, though perhaps very indifferent in themselves, still continue, from this association and from the variety of conceptions which they kindle in our minds, to be our favorites through life. The scenes which have been distinguished by the residence of any person whose memory we admire produce a similar effect. "Movemur enim, nescio quo pacto, locis ipsis, in quibus eorum, quos diligimus, aut admiramur adsunt vestigia."[1] The scenes themselves may not be particularly beautiful, but the delight with which we recollect the traces of their lives blends itself insensibly with the emotions which the scenery excites, and the admiration which these recollections afford seems to give a kind of sanctity to the place where they dwelt and converts every thing into beauty which appears to have been connected with them. There are scenes undoubtedly more beautiful than Runnymede, yet to those who recollect the great event which passed there, there is no scene perhaps which so strongly seizes upon the imagination; and although the emotions this recollection produces are of a very different kind from those which the mere natural scenery can excite, yet they unite themselves so well with these inferior emotions and spread so venerable a charm over the whole that one can hardly persuade himself, that the scene itself is not entitled to this admiration. . . .

The sublime is increased, in the same manner, by whatever tends to increase this exercise of imagination. The field of any celebrated battle becomes sublime from this association. . . .

National associations have a similar effect, in increasing the emotions of sublimity and beauty as they very obviously increase the number of images presented to the mind. The fine lines which Virgil has dedicated in his Georgics to the praises of his native country, however beautiful to us, were undoubtedly read with a far superior emotion by an ancient Roman. The prodigies which the same poet has described, as preceding the death of Cæsar, and the still more minute description which Lucan, in the first book of his Pharsalia, has given of such events, on the approach of the civil war, must probably have given

[1] For we are somehow affected by those very places in which we behold the footsteps of those whom we love and admire.

to a Roman who was under the dominion of such national superstitions the strongest emotions of sublimity and terror. But we read them now without any other emotion, than that which arises from the beauty of the composition.

The influence of such associations in increasing either the beauty or the sublimity of musical composition, can hardly have escaped any person's observation. The tune called Belleisle March is said by a very eminent writer to have owed its popularity among the people of England to the supposition that it was the tune which was played when the English army marched into Belleisle and to its consequent association with images of fame and conquest and military glory. There are other tunes of the same character which, without any peculiar merit, always serve to please the people whenever they are performed. The natives of any country that possesses a national or characteristic music need not be reminded how strongly the performance of such airs brings back to them the imagery of their native land; and must often have had occasion to remark how inferior an emotion they excite in those who are strangers to such associations. The effect of the celebrated national song which is said to have overpowered the Swiss soldier in a foreign land with melancholy and despair, and which it is therefore found necessary to forbid in the armies in which they serve, cannot surely be attributed to its composition alone but to the recollections that it brings and to those images that it kindles in his mind of peace, and freedom, and domestic pleasure, from which he is torn and to which he may never return. Whatever may be the sublimity of Handel's music, the singular effect of it on some late occasions is doubtless not to be ascribed to that sublimity alone, but in a peculiar manner to the place where it was performed; not only from the sacredness of that place which is, of itself, so well fitted to excite many awful emotions; but in a considerable degree also, from its being the repository of so many "illustrious dead," and the scene, perhaps of all others most sacred to those who have any sensibility to the glories of their country.

There are associations also which arise from particular

professions or habits of thought which serve very well to illustrate the same observation. No man, in general, is sensible to beauty in those subjects with regard to which he has not previous ideas. The beauty of a theory or of a relic of antiquity is unintelligible to a peasant. The charms of the country are altogether lost upon a citizen who has passed his life in town. In the same manner, the more our ideas are increased or our conceptions extended upon any subject, the greater is the number of associations we connect with it and the stronger is the emotion of sublimity or beauty we receive from it.

(c) Samuel Taylor Coleridge

FANCY AND IMAGINATION

It remains, then, for me, first, to state wherein Hartley differs from Aristotle; then to exhibit the grounds of my conviction that he differed only to err; and next, as the result, to show, by what influences of the choice and judgment the associative power becomes either memory or fancy; and, in conclusion, to appropriate the remaining offices of the mind to the reason and the imagination. . . .

The IMAGINATION, then, I consider either as primary or secondary. The primary IMAGINATION I hold to be the living Power and prime Agent of all human Perception, and as a repetition in the finite mind of the eternal act of creation in the infinite I AM. The secondary I consider as an echo of the former, co-existing with the conscious will, yet still as identical with the primary in the *kind* of its agency, and differing only in *degree* and in the *mode* of its operation. It dissolves, diffuses, dissipates, in order to re-create; or, where this process is rendered impossible, yet still, at all events, it struggles to idealize and to unify. It is essentially *vital*, even as all objects, (*as* objects,) are essentially fixed and dead.

TEXT: *Biographia Literaria; or Biographical Sketches of my Literary Life and Opinions*, by Samuel Taylor Coleridge, 1817, from the first American Edition, New York: 1817, I, 68, 182–83.

FANCY, on the contrary, has no other counters to play with, but fixities and definites. The Fancy is indeed no other than a mode of Memory emancipated from the order of time and space, and blended with and modified by that empirical phenomenon of the will which we express by the word CHOICE. But, equally with the ordinary memory, it must receive all its materials ready made from the law of association.

Whatever, more than this, I shall think it fit to declare, concerning the powers and privileges of the imagination, in the present work, will be found in the critical essay on the uses of the supernatural in poetry, and the principles that regulate its introduction; which the reader will find prefixed to the poem of *The Ancient Mariner*.

Suggested Reading

The most comprehensive study of American literary nationalism is *The Quest for Nationality; An American Literary Campaign*, by Benjamin T. Spencer, (Syracuse, New York: Syracuse University Press, 1957) which tells the story from the Colonial beginnings to 1892. The broader cultural aspects of the story, but within our specific period, are discussed in *The Cultural Life of the New Nation, 1776–1830*, by Russel B. Nye (New York: Harper & Brothers, 1960) and *The Awakening of American Nationalism, 1815–1828*, by George Dangerfield (New York: Harper & Row, 1965). Many of the essential documents in this collection were first republished in one volume under the caption "The Awakening of Literary Consciousness" in *The Roots of National Culture*, by Robert E. Spiller and Harold Blodgett (New York: The Macmillan Company, 1949), and the pioneer study of them all was "On the Development of American Literature from 1815 to 1833," by W. B. Cairns (*Bulletin of the University of Wisconsin*, I, Madison, 1901). *The Origins of American Critical Thought, 1810–1835*, by William Charvat (Philadelphia: University of Pennsylvania Press, 1936) is still standard for its subject. Among the more useful articles relating to literary nationalism are "Concerning the Study of Nationalism in American Literature," by Robert Bolwell (*American Literature*, X, 1939), "Literary Criticism in the *North American Review*, 1815–1835*," by Harry Hayden Clark (*Transactions of the Wisconsin Academy of Sciences, Arts, and Letters*, XXXII, 1940), and "Association Psychology and Literary Nationalism in the *North American Review*," by Robert E. Streeter (*American Literature*, XVII, 1945). Two volumes in this

25 I

series are designed to provide visual and written documentation for American cultural development during this period: *Quest For America, 1810–1824*, edited by Charles L. Sanford (1964) and *The American Revolution*, to be edited by Theodore Hornberger.

Among the more substantial essays and orations on the subject of literary nationalism, not included in this volume, are those by Samuel Jarvis (1806), Daniel Webster (1809), John Knapp (1818), William J. Spooner (1822), John Neal (1824–25), George Bancroft (1827), Samuel Knapp (1829), Timothy Flint (1829), and Peter S. Du Ponceau (1834). For bibliography, see Spencer, Benjamin T., *op. cit.*, pp. 341–72, and Orians, G. Harrison, *A Short History of American Literature* (New York, 1940), pp. 27–127.

ANCHOR BOOKS

ANCHOR BOOKS

LITERARY ESSAYS AND CRITICISM